National Security and Core Values in American History

There is no book quite like *National Security and Core Values in American History*. Drawing on themes from the whole of the nation's past, William O. Walker III presents a new interpretation of the history of American exceptionalism; that is, of the basic values and liberties that have given the United States its very identity. He argues that a political economy of expansion and the quest for security led American leaders after 1890 to equate prosperity and safety with global engagement. In so doing, they developed and clung to what Walker calls the "security ethos."

Expressed in successive grand strategies – Wilsonian internationalism, global containment, and strategic globalism – the security ethos ultimately damaged the values citizens cherish most and impaired popular participation in public affairs. Most important, it led to the abuse of executive authority after September 11, 2001, by the administration of President George W. Bush.

William O. Walker III has taught at California State University, Sacramento; Ohio Wesleyan University; Florida International University; and the University of Toronto. He lives in Houston, Texas. Walker is the author of *Drug Control in the Americas* (1981, revised edition 1989) and *Opium and Foreign Policy: The Anglo-American Search for Order in Asia, 1912–1954* (1991). He has also edited or co-edited several books, including *Drugs in the Western Hemisphere: An Odyssey of Cultures in Conflict* (1996), and his articles have appeared in *Pacific Historical Review*, the *Journal of American History*, *Diplomatic History*, and *NACLA Report on the Americas*.

National Security and Core Values in American History

WILLIAM O. WALKER III

CAMBRIDGE
UNIVERSITY PRESS

CAMBRIDGE UNIVERSITY PRESS
Cambridge, New York, Melbourne, Madrid, Cape Town, Singapore, São Paulo, Delhi

Cambridge University Press
32 Avenue of the Americas, New York, NY 10013-2473, USA

www.cambridge.org
Information on this title: www.cambridge.org/9780521740104

First published 2009

Printed in the United States of America

A catalog record for this publication is available from the British Library

Library of Congress Cataloging in Publication data
Walker, William O., 1946–
National security and core values in American history / William O. Walker III.
p.   cm.
Includes bibliographical references and index.
ISBN 978-0-521-51859-8 (hardback) – ISBN 978-0-521-74010-4 (pbk.)
1. United States – Foreign relations.   2. National security – United States.
3. United States – History.   I. Title.
JZ1480.W.34   2009
355′.033073–dc22   2008042306

ISBN 978-0-521-51859-8 hardback
ISBN 978-0-521-74010-4 paperback

To the memory of
Charles A. Beard
and
William Appleman Williams
and for
Joan Hoff
Students of history, practitioners of civic virtue

The leaders of the New World Order would seem to be married to Fear...As a result they become unfamiliar with reality, whilst continuing to dream about, and of course to exercise, power.

John Berger, *Hold Everything Dear*

Contents

Preface and Acknowledgments

I unknowingly began this book many years ago as an undergraduate at Ohio State University after reading *The Tragedy of American Diplomacy* (1962) by William Appleman Williams; I continued it as a graduate student when the United States was still deeply involved in Vietnam and I read *Twelve against Empire: The Anti-Imperialists of 1898–1900* (1968) by Robert L. Beisner. Williams's book, whatever its shortcomings, and they are few, remains the seminal study of the foreign policy of the United States as a world power. *Tragedy* emphasizes the existence of a coherent worldview among policymakers and demonstrates that such a perspective fundamentally derives from an economic base. The conduct of American diplomacy has therefore served to protect and advance a market-based political economy. Beisner's book, by recreating the fears and anxieties of the anti-imperialists of the late nineteenth century, helped me understand that a republic, let alone a democracy, was only as strong as those who would defend its basic values against what Walter Millis, in his classic 1931 account of the war with Spain, called "the martial spirit."[1] Both the Williams and Beisner studies broached what then became for me the crucial, troubling question: Could the American republic truly exist as an imperial power?[2]

In search of an answer, this book asks whether the demands of national security undermine the integrity of liberty and weaken, perhaps irreparably, the values associated with it. The dependence of liberty on security policy became a matter of intense public debate in the late 1890s as the

---

[1] Walter Millis, *The Martial Spirit: A Study of Our War with Spain* (Boston: Houghton Mifflin, 1931).

[2] William Appleman Williams, *The Tragedy of American Diplomacy*, 2d rev. and enlarged ed. (New York: W. W. Norton & Company, 1972); Robert L. Beisner, *Twelve against Empire: The Anti-Imperialists, 1898–1900* (New York: McGraw-Hill, 1968). My introduction to Williams came with the 1962 edition of his book, first published in 1959.

United States engaged in its first imperial exploits outside the boundaries of North America. Symbolically arrayed on the opposite sides of the issue were two of the more formidable personalities of the day: the arch-expansionist Theodore Roosevelt and the avowed anti-imperialist Mark Twain. At the center of that heated struggle over empire was the question of how, or perhaps whether, traditional American values fit into a modernizing society that was increasingly global in its material ambitions. The emergence at that time of a novel, ultimately ingrained way of thinking about security – herein termed an ethos – among authorities and, increasingly, a public attuned to international affairs gave the question its vitality. Within two generations, this security ethos was taking precedence over individual rights and liberties whenever real or perceived threats to the nation appeared.[3] The extent to which American distinctiveness – cast throughout the nation's history as "American exceptionalism" – did or did not survive these various crises into the twenty-first century is an underlying concern of my study.

From the outset of my career, I realized that it was impossible for the United States to revert to a time when it was not yet a world power. Could it retain its distinctiveness if it continued acting as an imperial state as it was then doing in Southeast Asia and Latin America? For some years thereafter, other subjects of inquiry held my immediate interest, even though I viewed them as windows on larger matters of U.S. foreign relations and American history more generally. Finally, after reading Michael J. Hogan's *A Cross of Iron: Harry S. Truman and the Origins of the National Security State, 1945–1954* (1998) and reviewing for publication the second edition of Hogan and Thomas G. Paterson, eds., *Explaining the History of American Foreign Relations* (2005), I knew it was time to grapple with the questions I had earlier pondered.[4] In addition to Williams's *Tragedy*, another book examining the roots of modern American foreign policy that has influenced my thinking is Michael H. Hunt's *Ideology and U.S. Foreign Policy* (1987).[5] Hunt presents a typology identifying a national mission to promote liberty, the conundrum of race as a factor in the making of foreign policy, and a profound aversion to revolution as the most crucial determinants of policy. He has recently explored America's swift rise to global dominance, hegemony rather than empire in his telling, finding that a "union of wealth, confidence, and leadership provides the basis for sustained international

---

[3] Influential for framing the idea of a security ethos was Richard J. Barnet, *Roots of War: The Men and Institutions behind U.S. Foreign Policy* (New York: Atheneum, 1972); Barnet's concern was the mindset of U.S. policymakers in the early Cold War.

[4] Michael J. Hogan, *A Cross of Iron: Harry S. Truman and the Origins of the National Security State, 1945–1954* (New York: Cambridge University Press, 1998); Michael J. Hogan and Thomas G. Paterson, eds., *Explaining the History of American Foreign Relations*, 2d. ed. (New York: Cambridge University Press, 2005).

[5] Michael H. Hunt, *Ideology and U.S. Foreign Policy* (New Haven: Yale University Press, 1987).

success."[6] The present study is meant to be something of a complement to those of Hunt and Williams.

It is my contention that too many books concerning the early Cold War and U.S. foreign relations suffer from a debilitating liability: They are surprisingly ahistorical in both concept and exposition.[7] According to these books, the world and thus history, too, essentially began anew after World War II. As a result, an emphasis on state-to-state relations trumps other plausible ways of conceptualizing and writing history. That is, I submit, like calling oneself a geologist without examining anything more revealing than topographical maps; one has a general idea about what the earth looks like, but knows scarcely anything about its complex subsoil composition. The past therefore nearly becomes anathema to the present, in this case to informed scrutiny of the roots of American foreign policy.

A number of questions lie at the heart of my critique of Cold War scholarship and its uneasy relationship with the past. Could modern history be understood only through a so-called realist lens focused on a presumptive Soviet challenge to American national interests? What precisely were those interests? Had they sprung from nothing? Or did U.S. policy reflect the contours of American history, to borrow a phrase from Williams?[8] Melvyn P. Leffler, some of whose work I have criticized, has written that the Truman administration formulated national security policy with an eye to protecting America's core values.[9] How could it be otherwise if the study of history is to have any utility for an informed citizenry? Yet, what were those values or principles? In his superb book about Soviet-American relations, *For the Soul of Mankind* (2007), Leffler with little elaboration identifies them as "liberty, individual opportunity, and free enterprise."[10] How had they influenced the shaping of the national interest throughout history? And in that process, did American core values remain intact? About those questions, Leffler, Hogan to an extent, and other leading American scholars of the period commonly referred to as the Cold War, including John Lewis Gaddis

---

[6] Michael. H. Hunt, *The American Ascendancy: How the United States Gained and Wielded Global Dominance* (Chapel Hill: University of North Carolina Press, 2007). For a postmodern perspective on America's global presence, see Walter Hixson, *The Myth of American Diplomacy: National Identity and U.S. Foreign Policy* (New Haven: Yale University Press, 2008).

[7] My thoughts about this issue are similar to those of Michael H. Hunt, "Ideology," in Hogan and Paterson, eds., *Explaining the History of American Foreign Relations*, 221–40.

[8] William Appleman Williams, *The Contours of American History*, paper ed. (Chicago: Quadrangle Books, 1966).

[9] Melvyn P. Leffler, *A Preponderance of Power: National Security, the Truman Administration, and the Cold War* (Stanford: Stanford University Press, 1992); William O. Walker III, "Melvyn P. Leffler, Ideology, and American Foreign Policy," *Diplomatic History* 20 (Fall 1996): 663–73.

[10] Melvyn P. Leffler, *For the Soul of Mankind: The United States, the Soviet Union, and the Cold War* (New York: Hill and Wang, 2007), 39.

Preface and Acknowledgments

(with partial exception in *The Cold War: A New History* [2005]), Bruce Cumings, Carolyn Eisenberg, and Walter LaFeber, remain essentially silent.[11] A curious example of this genre is Wilson D. Miscamble's *From Roosevelt to Truman: Potsdam, Hiroshima, and the Cold War* (2006). Miscamble, a native of Australia, mentions core values in passing while contending that Harry Truman was hamstrung by both the untrustworthy Soviets and his predecessor's naïveté.[12]

One cogent exception to this general pattern, written by a non-American, is Odd Arne Westad's prize-winning volume, *The Global Cold War* (2005).[13] Westad's notable contribution to historiography of the Cold War is his locating in Soviet-American rivalry an unbridgeable divide about what it means to be modern. That is, should modernity for the Third World – a lamentably inelegant and demeaning appellation – in the post-1945 period emanate from America's Jeffersonian empire of liberty or what he calls the Soviet empire of justice? Values nourished in American history and spawned by the Bolshevik experiment are reflected in the antithetical imperial pretensions at play in the global struggle Westad describes. Whereas Westad implicitly addresses the problem that ethical behavior and values pose for the making of foreign policy, Joan Hoff places the matter at the center of her analysis in *A Faustian Foreign Policy from Woodrow Wilson to George W. Bush: Dreams of Perfectibility* (2008).[14] Hoff writes that "the United States was born in a fit of self-determination." That did not necessarily make for a responsible foreign policy. She briefly surveys American diplomacy since independence, noting that the fact of "[s]elf-determined, but not necessarily democratic, self-government . . . lay at the heart of its . . . drive to become the example for how the rest of the world should operate."[15] Woodrow Wilson transformed the ideal of self-determination into a universal guiding principle in foreign policy. Whether it actually fostered democracy was another matter.[16]

[11] John Lewis Gaddis, *We Now Know: Rethinking Cold War History* (New York: Oxford University Press, 1997); idem, *The Cold War: A New History* (New York: Penguin Press, 2005); Walter LaFeber, *America, Russia, and the Cold War, 1945–2006*, 10th ed. (Boston: McGraw-Hill, 2007); Bruce Cumings, *Origins of the Korean War*, vol. 1: *Liberation and the Emergence of Separate Regimes, 1945–1947* (Princeton: Princeton University Press, 1981); Carolyn Eisenberg, *Drawing the Line: The American Decision to Divide Germany* (New York: Cambridge University Press, 1996).

[12] Wilson D. Miscamble, *From Roosevelt to Truman: Potsdam, Hiroshima, and the Cold War* (New York: Cambridge University Press, 2006).

[13] Odd Arne Westad, *The Global Cold War: Third World Interventions and the Making of Our Times* (Cambridge: Cambridge University Press, 2005).

[14] Joan Hoff, *A Faustian Foreign Policy from Woodrow Wilson to George W. Bush: Dreams of Perfectibility* (New York: Cambridge University Press, 2008).

[15] Ibid., 22.

[16] Erez Manela, *The Wilsonian Moment: Self-Determination and the International Origins of Anticolonial Nationalism* (New York: Oxford University Press, 2007).

My rather disappointing encounter with Cold War scholarship has led me to pose the questions asked previously and raise others about values, interests, and American history that inform this study: What, for instance, has been the relationship between American core values and U.S. security policy? Did the republic, in becoming an imperial power in the 1890s, retain a capacity to protect the principles that made it distinctive commencing in the colonial era? Did the many individuals who presided over the growth of America's global power incorporate core values into their understanding of the nation's security? Can basic values, rights, and liberties, having been compromised in the name of security throughout modern American history, endure in the twenty-first century? Finding answers for these questions traces back to the colonial era.

A project of this scope, particularly one so long in the making, owes a lot to many people – some for their inspiration, others for the assistance they gave in a variety of ways. At Cambridge University Press, Lew Bateman, with whom I have worked for years, and especially Eric Crahan and Emily Spangler, who saw the book to publication, were marvelous editors. I thank, too, the readers for the Press; their splendid efforts helped make the book what it now is.

There are many others to thank. Father Robert Luchi showed me in high school at St. Charles in Columbus, Ohio, how passionate the study of history could be. At Ohio State University, no one was more helpful than John C. Rule; with a few kind words, he rescued me from law school. I would never have studied American foreign relations were it not for David Green and Marvin Zahniser. To this day, I recall with fondness the long conversations about history and the state of the world with Mark Rose and Mel Leffler. And thanks to Marvin, I did my doctoral work with Alexander DeConde at the University of California, Santa Barbara. Alex always supported the breadth of my interests, and I deeply thank him for that.

I was fortunate to have a somewhat peripatetic career. At California State University, Sacramento, one of the first persons I met was the now-eminent historian of the American West, Al Hurtado, then an MA student. At Rancho Ben Ali, in Rio Linda, or on camping trips high in the Sierra mountains, we talked endlessly about history. Those conversations continue to this day. Working as one of two American historians for sixteen years at Ohio Wesleyan University allowed me to continue to read and teach broadly as my research became more specialized. Two of my students there, Bob Buzzanco and Peter Hahn, were a joy to work with; they have my admiration for the ways in which they took on the study of history as their life's work. In my time at Florida International University in Miami, we had a marvelous, young department. The hours spent talking history and politics with Alex Lichtenstein and Clarence Taylor influenced portions of this book. At the University of Toronto, I would not have had the rewarding teaching experiences I did without the efforts of Bob Bothwell, Carol Chin, and Ron Pruessen. To thank them is not sufficient, though it will have to do. Also, *abrazos* for my "brothers," Rick Halpern and Ken Mills; what a time we had. Thanks to Bill Colgate and Joan Bendon, Cam and Lana MacInnes, Stephen Bright, Joe Gaitanis, Bruce Moffet, and Shiraz Tayyeb. What great sounds: the paradise of Saturday afternoons at the Dominion. You kept me sane and were nice enough to ask about the book. And a special thanks to Khris Harrold, for enduring friendship and a place to visit near the Rockies.

In writing this book, I have drawn on the work of many scholars. I thank Carol C. Chin and Jonathan Rosenberg, who provided help with several sources. For the example of their own work or the encouragement they gave this project, I thank Bruce M. Bagley, John M. Belohlavek, Robert Bothwell, Robert Buzzanco, Carol C. Chin, Frank Costigliola, Paul Gootenberg, Cheryl Lynn Greenberg, Rick Halpern, Walter Hixson, Joan Hoff, Michael J. Hogan, Michael H. Hunt, Albert L. Hurtado, Susan Kellogg, Stephanie Kelly, Walter LaFeber, Melvyn P. Leffler, Robert McMahon, Dennis Merrill, Thomas F. O'Brien, Stephen G. Rabe, Donald M. Rodgers, and Emily S. Rosenberg.

Two other groups deserve special mention. Years of reading U.S. History Advanced Placement exams were made memorable by the good times and discussions with, among others, John Belohlavek, Carol Berkin, Betty Dessants, Jim Giglio, Cheryl Greenberg, Nat Jobe, Tammie McDaniel, Mary McDuffie, Ted Morse, Linda Murdock, Berky Nelson, Lynn Rainard, Eric Rothschild, and Tom Zoumaras. Woody, Michael Woodward, knows how much our friendship and hours on hours of conversation mean to me. At the University of Toronto, a number of students in HIS 344 and TRN 410 improved the book with their love of learning, their questions, and their ideas, including Ohad Abrahami, Wendell Adjetey, Rahul Bhat, Sean Fear, Maria Felix Fernandez, Alison Jenkins, Mike Lawrence, Wynne Lawrence, Victor MacDiarmid, Steven Masson, Igor Puzevich, Stephanie J. Silverman, and Vinka Woldarsky. They were remarkable.

The dedication needs some elaboration. A fellow MA student at Ohio State introduced me to Charles Beard's work. The more I read, the more I understood that truly being a student of history is a lifelong endeavor, in which not everyone succeeds. I met Bill Williams once, some years after he moved to Oregon. The legendary fire for teaching and public engagement still burned bright. Fortuitously, as it turned out, my first job was as a temporary replacement for Joan Hoff. Her kindness then and our friendship over the years are a gift I hold dear.

Introduction

"A City upon a Hill"

We now have just cause to destroy [the Indians] by all means possible.
John Smith, 1622

The West has been a constructive force of the highest significance in our life.
Frederick Jackson Turner, 1896

"We shall be as a city upon a hill," Puritan leader John Winthrop told his fellow voyagers aboard the *Arbella* in 1630 as they were preparing to land on the Massachusetts shore. Winthrop and the other Puritan saints believed that the civilized, or European, world was holding its collective breath to see whether their godly venture would succeed. What is noteworthy is that Winthrop did not concoct his prediction out of nothing. Europeans had for years persuaded themselves that the Americas truly might be a special, if not utopian, place.[1] Although experience altered that exotic perception of the New World, the conviction that the land across the Atlantic Ocean was a promising locale for exploration and development never really disappeared.

Winthrop's words would later come to be seen, particularly during the twentieth century, as a declaration of exceptionalism that set England's American colonies apart from the old European world. As historian Jack P. Greene observes, "The concept of American exceptionalism with its positive connotations was present at the very creation of America."[2] In America, there would be freedom from the culture of corruption and from tyranny endemic to the English political system and religious establishment. Were their efforts at achieving reform through flight to be successful, the Puritans of Massachusetts Bay imagined themselves as offering hope to like-minded people.

[1] Jack P. Greene, *The Intellectual Construction of America: Exceptionalism and Identity from 1492 to 1800* (Chapel Hill: University of North Carolina Press, 1993), 8–33.
[2] Ibid., 6.

Power in Massachusetts Bay was exercised in the pursuit of specific political and religious objectives. Within a decade of the arrival of the colonists, expansion south and west became common practice under the supervision of the General Court. The ruling bodies of new towns, some of which would soon form the colony of Connecticut, strictly controlled public affairs. Government in New England was oligarchic, yet democratic – but only for those freemen who embraced Puritanism in its different forms. To sustain the commonwealth in its mission, a local and oceanic commerce rapidly developed. In a theme that serves as a prelude to the heart of this study, landed expansion and commercial growth became crucial guardians of the basic values for which the Puritans stood, thereby anticipating to an extent one aspect of the frontier thesis of the influential historian, Frederick Jackson Turner. "The West has been a constructive force of the highest significance in our life," Turner wrote for the *Atlantic Monthly* in his 1896 essay, "The Problem of the West." The fundamental task for people living on the frontier, he asserted, had been that of "conserving and developing what was original and valuable in this new country."[3]

Colonization outside of New England failed to create settlements that were as emblematic of future assumptions about American identity and character as those emerging from the Massachusetts Bay experience. If citizens and scholars have mainly dwelled on the endeavors of the Puritans, it is because religious overtones contained in the cultural fabric of the nation reflect a sense of providential chosenness that many Americans embrace.[4] The Dutch colony of New Amsterdam, which became New York in 1664 after being seized by English forces, and the Quaker colony of Pennsylvania, for all their potential as hubs of commerce and western expansion, never found a place in the public memory as progenitors of national character or a divinely inspired mission. And however central Jamestown and the growth of Virginia were to American history, the advent of slavery in 1619 limited the role Virginia would play in producing the belief that America should serve as a model for people seeking freedom from oppression. The irony is that freedom in considerable measure owes the promise it has long extended to many others to the nation's wrenching experience with enslaved labor.[5]

Although it is tempting to read the future into the past, doing so has the potential to rob history of its contingency. The uniqueness of the Puritan experiment argues against the inevitability of Massachusetts Bay making common cause with England's other North American colonies. Separatists

---

[3] Frederick Jackson Turner, "The Problem of the West," *The Atlantic Monthly*, September, 1896, pp. 289–97; quoted words, 289, 292.

[4] On the central place of providential chosenness in American history, see Anders Stephanson, *Manifest Destiny: American Expansion and the Empire of Right* (New York: Hill and Wang, 1995).

[5] Edmund S. Morgan, *American Slavery, American Freedom: The Ordeal of Colonial Virginia* (New York: W. W. Norton & Company, 1975).

were unflinchingly expelled from the Bay colony. And the Navigation Acts of the 1650s and 1660s – contemporaneous with England's civil wars and the Stuart Restoration – could not drive the colonies together, even though those acts curtailed the commercial freedom of action of colonies in the Chesapeake region and the West Indies, a lesson not lost on other, less affected colonies. Nevertheless, the rise of English mercantilism was a manifest success for homeland and colonies alike, with the result that the bonds of empire were greatly, if briefly, enhanced – at least in economic terms.[6] And yet, this development did not lead settlers soon to identify more closely with each other, let alone strengthen the real and sentimental ties with their home country.[7]

It took the imposition of what colonists denounced as arbitrary imperial rule, carried out under the authority given by James II to Edmund Andros and the Dominion of New England in 1685, to initiate the process by which some of them perceived important commonalities in their individual experiences. Americans also believed that their country did beckon others, as evidenced by the numbers of Europeans who reached America's shores throughout the eighteenth century, and especially after the French and Indian War.[8] A shared sense of history became all the more apparent in the decade immediately before the Revolution when Parliament used its power – as seen, for example in the Proclamation of 1763, the Sugar Act of 1764, the Stamp Act of 1765, the Townshend Act of 1767, and the Tea Act of 1773 – to limit colonial expansion and reassert London's economic supremacy. These developments led many Americans to rethink their identity as British subjects and increasingly to defend existing patterns of self-government, which in turn strengthened the rationale for independence.

The growth of a common identity occurred in another, less edifying and indirect way, one that foreshadowed the limits of American distinctiveness. Well into the seventeenth century, colonies protected the privileges of the founders and those who exercised political and economic power. By and large, oligarchy remained the political order of the day, yet there was usually room in the political process for those who acquired large tracts of land. The privileged also constructed legal walls to safeguard their status against challenges from disaffected, less advantaged colonists.

In the first fifty years or so after settlement, the prospects for democratic politics were at best nominal in English North America. Puritan Massachusetts and its New England offspring were only the most visible in how they sought to remain true to their original mission. The Half-Way

[6] Alan Taylor, *American Colonies* (New York: Viking, 2001), 257–9.

[7] Charles M. Andrews, *The Colonial Background of the American Revolution*, rev. ed. (New Haven: Yale University Press, 1931), 5–9.

[8] Bernard Bailyn with the assistance of Barbara DeWolfe, *Voyagers to the West: A Passage in the Peopling of America on the Eve of the Revolution* (New York: Alfred A. Knopf, 1986).

Covenant, begun in the 1660s, was the first indication that the Puritans could not hold back the tides of religious and, ultimately, political change.[9] Settlers in the Roman Catholic proprietary colony of Maryland, for their part, had to turn a profit not for the King of England, as was the case in royal colonies, but for the Calvert family. The efforts of the Calverts to reproduce a semi-feudal, manorial system in their vast realms failed. The growing attractiveness of Maryland to largely Protestant settlers, especially from Virginia, helped bring into being a colony in which political and legal structures were heavily biased in favor of the Calverts and their wealthy friends. The volatility of politics in Maryland by the mid-1600s, however, showed the reach of privilege to be long, though not absolute.[10]

The colonists of Virginia, originally a charter colony, owed their fealty to the English Crown after a disastrous encounter with native people in the early 1620s. Thereafter a royal colony, Virginia remained a contentious place dominated by the governor, his council, and the county courts. Abundant land seemed there for the taking, thereby enhancing the status of the privileged classes. At the same time, labor remained in short supply – an unhappy fact with two momentous consequences. Black slavery developed, albeit gradually, almost as a matter of course in Virginia and then spread throughout the Chesapeake and southern colonies. In addition, fierce disputes over land led to conflicts within Virginia, the most famous being Bacon's Rebellion, which in 1676 degenerated into a bloody civil war. Poor aspiring landowners on the colony's frontier, a number of whom had formerly been indentured servants, rejected Governor Sir William Berkeley's conservative land policies and domination of the Indian trade. Around the same time, well-connected tobacco planters claimed tracts of fertile land, leaving small or poor farmers with the prospect of becoming tenants. Nathaniel Bacon, himself a wealthy planter who coveted Indian land on the colony's frontier, promised freedom and arable land to those who fought with him against the governor and his allies. After a brief success, including Bacon's seizure of power and Berkeley's exile, England crushed the rebellion. Modest reductions in tax rates and increased access to land ensued. Virginia politics nevertheless remained foremost in service to the interests of the colony's aristocrats.[11]

In justifying their hold on power and privileged status before the Glorious Revolution of 1688, colonial elites anticipated how subsequent leaders would act to protect their understanding of American identity. They isolated suspected dissenters and branded them as radicals unworthy of the benefits of citizenship; they also restricted access to political power by extending patronage to their friends. And, importantly, elites depended on

---

[9] Taylor, *American Colonies*, 180–1.
[10] Ibid., 136–7, 140.
[11] Ibid., 125–31, 139–40, 149–51.

free or low-paid laborers – at least 150,000 indentured servants reached England's mainland colonies in the course of the seventeenth century – to build the very society that excluded them or lessened their opportunity for mobility.[12] Regeneration of privilege by social custom or political marginalization became common. If that tactic did not succeed, the powerful could fall back on the use of force against those who challenged their elevated status.

Paradoxically, the self-referential belief that America could serve as a beacon for oppressed peoples – "a shining city" as President Ronald Reagan put it – strengthened over time. It became a fundamental part of national identity in the twentieth century when, contrary to its tradition of disengagement from foreign political affairs, the United States became the world's greatest power. The relative absence of formal involvement in world politics until December 1941, excepting President Woodrow Wilson's quixotic diplomacy at the Versailles Peace Conference of 1919, did not prevent the United States from becoming supreme in global finance and dominant in international trade during the Great War. That era's incipient internationalism would be transformed into a thoroughgoing globalism on the eve of American entry into World War II.

How had so great a transformation come about? What effect did it have on that greatest of American traditions, freedom? By the twentieth century, freedom, which had been commonly referred to as liberty early in American history, symbolized what American citizens revered most. Core values, which were first given explicit expression in the Declaration of Independence and subsequently the Constitution and Bill of Rights, were more than abstract ideas. They were tangible principles about republican governance that, protected by the rule of law, offered the prospect of a common identity to all citizens, even if that identity was not truly democratic. These principles, as they emerged and evolved over time, encompassed what individual Americans deemed to be their inherent rights, including, and essential for present purposes, freedom of speech and assembly; freedom of the press; right to trial by a jury of one's peers; protection from unreasonable search and seizure, which essentially became synonymous with a right to privacy; and freedom from self-incrimination. Moreover, many citizens who were not among the ruling elite understood core values as guiding precepts that bolstered their abiding faith in democracy, however limited it actually was. It was in this sense that the popular classes shared with the privileged a preference for limited government; that is, one held in check by distinct separation of powers among three branches of government. The presumption of a common heritage turned the beacon of liberty into a powerful symbol, confirming for Americans the exceptional nature of their national

---

[12] Bernard Bailyn, *The Peopling of British North America: An Introduction* (New York: Alfred A. Knopf, 1985), 60–1.

experience. With some trepidation, the founding generation left to its successors the daunting task of sustaining the nation's devotion to republican principles. If the very idea of America suggested the existence of a distinctive character, that quality needed constant care and nurturing to safeguard it in an arguably hostile world. By the late nineteenth century, Americans who imagined their country in a prominent position on the world stage thought about the protection of liberty in tandem with the pursuit of security. The United States therefore selectively promoted abroad as part of its foreign policy these core values: the right of some to self-determination, the universal appeal of democracy, and the ideal of human rights. Did efforts to export core values enhance the nation's security? Critics thought not, charging especially after 1945 that values lost their salience when put in the service of grand strategy.

Providing for security had long entailed risks. John Winthrop's initial plans for the establishment of an exemplary colony never envisioned Massachusetts Bay as the harbinger of an idyllic utopia. His fabled city would metaphorically rest on a hill for good reason; it was from the vantage point of height that the Puritan community would be kept safe from its adversaries. To build a strong city upon a hill was therefore sound defensive strategy in that era of European colonization, which settlers in New England doubtless knew.[13] Winthrop's words embodied hopes and fears found throughout early America, even though how security would be achieved differed from colony to colony.

A common understanding of what constituted danger made freedom seem all the more uncertain almost from the first years of settlement. English colonists responded to the non-Europeans in their environs as a matter necessitating self-defense against those whom they were displacing. In viewing Indians as enemies, colonists developed a sense of entitlement about deciding whether others should live or perhaps perish because their mere presence threatened the work of the new settlers. Employing preemptive action, they also began to justify their treatment of native people as a means of forestalling the dire consequences that might accompany delay in acting decisively. Preemption, whether by legal means when possible or by military means when deemed necessary, assisted the development of colonial identity and contributed to the quest for security.[14]

Indians did not conceive of land as private property, nor did the exchange of goods make them proto-capitalists. Colonists abhorred these and other

---

[13] See, for example, John Childs, "The Military Revolution, I: The Transition to Modern Warfare," in Charles Townshend, ed., *The Oxford History of Modern Warfare* (Oxford: Oxford University Press, 2000), 20–39.

[14] The French also had the occasion to employ force when, for example, relations with the Natchez Indians in the lower Mississippi region turned violent; Robert Bothwell, *The Penguin History of Canada* (Toronto: Penguin Canada, 2006), 72–3.

presumed cultural deficiencies and distrusted the people whose lands they were seizing. The case of Powhatan, the most powerful chief in the Virginia region, and its aftermath is instructive. Powhatan tried to establish and maintain cordial trading relations with the English people. Pushed to the limit almost from the moment of Jamestown's founding, Powhatan's allies pushed back. The rapaciousness for arable land of a people in thrall to the tobacco plant meant trouble. With no middle ground separating the two sides, bloody conflict ensued in Virginia. Provocation followed on provocation until March 1622 when almost one-third of the colonists perished in an attack. John Smith, then in England, welcomed the slaughter: "We now have just cause to destroy [the Indians] by all means possible." Warfare continued intermittently and, with the help of diseases against which Indians were not immune, gradually reduced their numbers in Virginia from 24,000 in 1607 to about 2,000 sixty years later. Survivors who remained in the environs of the colony were regarded as threats to security. Colonial law in fact allowed landholders to shoot Indians who were found trespassing on their lands, an action that might be characterized as a kind of preemptive self-defense.[15]

Early white-Indian interactions were scarcely better in New England. William Bradford, soon to become governor of Plymouth Colony, imagined the new land to be "a hideous and desolate wilderness full of wild beasts and wild men." After settlement, he found confirmation for his views: Indians killed the livestock of settlers because their pigs and cattle ranged widely, thus destroying Indian customs of land usage. To limited effect, colonists endeavored to use legal instruments, deeds, to turn Indian land into private property. By the 1630s, the killing of livestock led to attempts to bring Indians to justice in Massachusetts for violating the property rights of white settlers. Justice remained elusive because fines levied for the offenses financed further expansion into native lands.

Tensions rose in southeastern Connecticut between settlers and the Pequot, who refused to pay tribute or submit to the white legal system. Aided by rivals of the Pequot, the English launched an attack in May 1637, killing some four hundred natives. Military and settlement leaders alike praised their God for blessing this effort. Four decades later in 1675, the Puritans provoked a confrontation with the Wampanoag Metacom, or King Philip as he was known, that lasted into the spring of 1676 when Indian resistance began to collapse. Survivors, especially chiefs, were executed and others were sold into slavery. An explanation for this brutality should focus, first, on fears the colonists had long held about the nonwhite people in the colonies and, second, on the unforeseen appeal of Indian culture in the structured Puritan world. In the words of Reverend Increase Mather, "Christians in this Land have become too like unto the Indians." Were that condition to

[15] Taylor, *American Colonies*, 125, 131–6; quoted words, 135.

spread, the political, religious, and economic rationales behind settlement and expansion would be jeopardized.[16]

Fear therefore became closely linked to the quest for freedom in early American history. To a considerable extent, the fears that European settlers experienced in their new environment were self-generated, the result of restrictive ideas about governance, the law, economic pursuits, and the Indians so close at hand. Despite its original contingency, this legacy of fear accompanying freedom in the colonial era would recur – particularly when Americans debated the need for a dynamic security policy after 1890. In the process, it became hard to distinguish between fear and nonclinical paranoia. Furthermore, a kind of apprehension has influenced the writing of history about national security. Historians are hardly immune from adopting as their own the assumptions and biases held by the individuals about whom they write. However purposeful or inadvertent that development, it is difficult to resist when thinking about the defense of cherished core values. It does not necessarily make for good history.

Three factors provide a framework for explaining the problematic nexus between basic rights and values and security policy: political economy, military power, and fear. The readiness to use preemptive force in the name of safety, whether perceived threats are imminent or not, from the earliest years of settlement and the role of fear in initiating the resort to armed force have already been addressed. Yet, there is much more to the matter of fear than its relationship to force. Fear often mobilizes people to give their support to policies of dubious provenance, such as global containment as we see later in the book, and can prevent the dispassionate assessment of presumed threats to the nation's security. The issue of political economy, particularly in regard to the structural demands of an expansive, marketplace capitalism and a reflexive attachment to foreign trade by elites and the general public, is addressed more fully in due course. Suffice it to note here that Americans typically have intimately linked commerce and freedom.

This introduction has presented a brief look not only at the origins of American exceptionalism but also at the disconcerting ways in which that distinctiveness was nurtured during the seventeenth century. Four parts comprise the remainder of the book. The first traces the origins of the security ethos, as set forth in the preface. Chapter 1, beginning after the Glorious Revolution, surveys the emergence of core values and examines how patterns of trade and continental expansion sustained those values and the Founders' commitment to republican virtue during the first century of nationhood. Regenerating the republican ideal was never an easy task. Republicanism had exclusionary aspects that the popular classes challenged with limited success throughout the 1800s. Chapter 2 revisits debates over expansion and empire in the 1890s, which lasted until about 1920, by which time a

---

[16] Ibid., 188–203; quoted words,188, 202.

proto-national security state had taken shape. By the end of World War I, the meaning of liberty had become unclear because the boundaries of individual rights, such as freedom of speech and assembly, had perceptibly narrowed from what they had been when those debates began. And, Woodrow Wilson's promise of self-determination as a consequence of war unwittingly invited discussions within America about who benefited most from the values extolled in a republic. That is, why did not basic freedoms and the right to self-determination apply equally to African Americans, to offer only the most obvious example?

Next, Part II surveys Wilsonian internationalism and its transformation into global containment. Chapter 3 considers whether Republican foreign policy during the 1920s and early years of the Great Depression protected core values from what numerous Americans believed was the contagion of internationalism. Chapter 4, which covers the 1930s and 1940s, assesses Franklin D. Roosevelt's persistent struggle to maintain his internationalist impulse amid waves of economic nationalism, the allure of isolationism, and a revival of militarism abroad. He linked America's future to global engagement without asking how that course of action might affect the nation's values. For Roosevelt, this humanistic globalism was the only viable option for the United States. The onset of the Cold War, followed by the establishment of a formal national security state during the Truman presidency, brought the integrity of founding principles into question. Chapter 5 scrutinizes the period from 1950 through 1973 – the era of Richard Nixon – and reveals an increasing incompatibility between U.S. security policy and core values like freedom of speech and assembly and also the longing for self-determination by postcolonial and oppressed peoples around the world.

Part III analyzes the age of strategic globalism, the years from 1973 to 2001, in which limits on the deployment of American power stand out as a defining characteristic. Chapter 6 examines the years encompassing Nixonian détente and the Reagan presidency and portrays them as a time in which the pursuit of presumed national interests markedly circumscribed the role of core values in deliberations over security policy. Of special importance in that respect is the intrusion of human rights considerations into the policy process. Chapters 7 and 8 then contend that American exceptionalism and the principles on which it had historically been based declined appreciably by the end of the Cold War and during the presidencies of George H. W. Bush and Bill Clinton. What emerged along with globalization after the Soviet Union faded from the scene were a new militarism and a pronounced unilateralism in the conduct of foreign policy.

Finally, Part IV examines the adverse influence of the Bush Doctrine on core values. Chapter 9 assesses the damage done to values in the name of security by George W. Bush. It also evaluates how the war on terror in the Persian Gulf region and beyond begat not only a remarkable accretion of presidential powers but also a palpable rejection of the rule of law by the executive branch. The conclusion engages the debate over the relationship between values and national security as carried on by prominent intellectuals. At length, after considering whether the government at the highest levels had fallen into the hands of right-wing authoritarians – a position put forward by John W. Dean, a White House counsel in the Nixon administration – it is no surprise to find that the war on terror in the first decade of the twenty-first century was waged by a government antithetical to individual rights and liberties. Whether there is a way out of this dilemma so as to restore some of the vitality of core values is then considered briefly.

At this juncture, several words are in order about the Second Amendment to the Constitution. The freedom that numerous Americans cherish most, the right to bear arms, looms large in the background of this study. Unlike federal courts, which have traditionally held the Second Amendment to mean a collective right to bear arms, many citizens have argued for the amendment's application as an individual right. By mid-2007, liberal lawyers and constitutional scholars were helping make the case for this broader interpretation, which the Supreme Court essentially accepted in a landmark ruling in June 2008.[17] To a remarkable degree, this development reflects changes in the ways Americans have thought about national security since the end of the Cold War. The paradoxical militarization of security discourse after the demise of the Soviet Union in 1991, and even more so since 2001, insinuates that advocacy of almost any guise of gun control equates with tyranny and oppression and, hence, must be resisted.

Ultimately, this book is concerned with security and foreign policy. Of necessity, it also constitutes an extended essay about the course of American history. Based on the work of many other scholars and on my own research, it reflects the considerations and reconsiderations of more than three decades of thinking, teaching, and writing about the United States, especially about why and how the nation has engaged the outside world. The costs of that engagement for America's place in the world, and for the rights and liberties of its citizens, have historically been great and will remain so far into the future, as the imbroglio that is the occupation of Iraq unfortunately demonstrates. It is my intent in writing this book to provide an explanation why.

[17] *New York Times*, May 7, 2007 and June 27, 2008. The case is *District of Columbia v. Heller*.

PART ONE

THE ORIGINS OF THE SECURITY ETHOS, 1688–1919

I

Commerce, Expansion, and Republican Virtue

Those who would give up essential Liberty, to purchase a little temporary Safety, deserve neither Liberty nor Safety.
                    Benjamin Franklin, 1755

I am persuaded that no constitution was ever before so well calculated as ours for extensive empire and self government. . . . Nothing should ever be accepted which would require a navy to defend it.
                    Thomas Jefferson, 1809

Armed shipping must follow the peaceful vessels of commerce.
                    Alfred Thayer Mahan, 1890

For more than a century following the Glorious Revolution, England and France vied for mastery of European affairs and until 1763 engaged in a struggle for imperial dominance across the Atlantic. The latter contest, fought mainly in Canada and the Great Lakes region of British America, produced a level of indebtedness that London could ill afford. Believing the American colonies to be the prime beneficiaries of France's defeat in the French and Indian War in 1763, Parliament enacted several laws intended to ease Britain's financial burden. Raising revenue through either direct or indirect taxation was a crucial way of paying for the security that would be required when France was ready to do battle again, as it doubtless would be.

Unfortunately for Great Britain, the wages of empire became burdensome at a time when the idea of a common past was taking hold in its colonies south of Canada. Broad cultural similarities existed across the colonies, despite their lack of political cohesion. The Protestant ethic, a belief in hard work in service to the Almighty, became deeply rooted because opportunities for individual enrichment seemed abundant. Class differences did not vanish, although enterprising free men found ways to transcend them by dint of their "activity and industry," as the *Columbian Magazine* put it in

13

1787.[1] The prospect of a prosperous life appealed to those thousands of people who emigrated from Europe to America after about 1725. The political developments that followed from migration would help ingrain what Americans considered their distinctive identity.

A growing sense of separation and autonomy set in as colonies coped with their own need for revenue and with the demands for order and protection brought on by expansion into territory previously unsettled by whites. In *A Mighty Empire*, Marc Egnal explains the sweeping effect of self-reliance: "[I]n each colony the revolutionary movement was led by an upper-class faction whose fervent commitment to fostering America's rise to greatness was evident well before 1763."[2] Expansion reflected not simply physical movement but also the conceptual underpinning for an American empire. Alone or with their families, men poured into backcountry lands, protecting themselves with guns, and thereby continuing the practice of preemptive self-defense begun in the first years of settlement. Historian Edmund S. Morgan puts the matter concisely: "The westerner in our history has always been a man with a gun."[3]

By the 1770s, the impact of recent immigration, patterns of economic growth and territorial expansion, and the exercise of power by popularly elected officials, together with the growing imposition of British authority, combined to spark a revolution while also shaping a common identity that encompassed all classes of free men and free women. Opposition to the right of Parliament to rule did more to finalize the break between the colonies and the Crown than to cause it. For present purposes, the most telling outcome of the American Revolution, after the fact of independence, was a determination to perpetuate America's distinctiveness. The people who fought against the British and participated in the making of a federal government in 1787 at Philadelphia believed they were a chosen, indeed a virtuous, people. Their example, wrote physician David Ramsay of South Carolina, had "enlightened mankind in the art of government."[4] One dilemma confronting the founding generation, however, like that of the Puritans before them, was how best to preserve for future generations the nation's faith in America's own unique attribute – its republican virtue.

---

[1] Quoted in Jack P. Greene, *The Intellectual Construction of America: Exceptionalism and Identity from 1492 to 1800* (Chapel Hill: University of North Carolina Press, 1993), 176.

[2] Marc Egnal, *A Mighty Empire: The Origins of the American Revolution* (Ithaca: Cornell University Press, 1988), 1.

[3] Edmund S. Morgan, "Conflict and Consensus in the American Revolution," in Stephen G. Kurtz and James H. Hutson, eds., *Essays on the American Revolution* (Chapel Hill: University of North Carolina Press, 1973), 305; John Shy, *A People Numerous and Armed: Reflections on the Military Struggle for Independence*, rev. ed. (Ann Arbor: University of Michigan Press, 1990), 4.

[4] Quoted in Greene, *The Intellectual Construction of America*, 194.

Federalist No. 10, written by James Madison in support of the Constitution and its checks and balances on the arbitrary use of power, conveyed the doubts of the Founders that this virtue could be sustained over time.

A major obstacle to the furtherance of republican virtue, sectional differences over slavery, formally arose with the Missouri Compromise of 1820 and proved to be insurmountable short of civil war. The moral and economic implications of pro-slavery and anti-slavery stances were not wholly antithetical, though; after all, what was produced in the South was a vital part of the nation's economy. Nevertheless, the paradox of slavery in a land espousing freedom at the heart of its identity could not be sustained.[5] The Civil War left basic values relatively unscathed in the abstract, fixing even more firmly in American lore the ideals of freedom and liberty.

Expansion also raised questions about the prospect of sustaining virtue over time and in new places. The West was not necessarily a congenial place in which to implant values that depended on the rule of law. From Texas to the Great Plains to California, conflict often accompanied the expansion of white America into lands possessed by others. If the ultimate outcome of conflict – statehood – was in some sense a victory for republican ideals, how it came about was hardly exemplary. In addition, the forays of adventurers, known as filibusterers, beyond the continental confines of the United States into Central America in the 1840s and 1850s can hardly be portrayed as attempts, however misguided, to extend the blessings of representative governance.

Moreover, Reconstruction and its aftermath ushered in decades of uncertainty for many working poor, newly arrived immigrants, and nonwhite people. During the Gilded Age, a term coined by Mark Twain, the powerful controlled the means by which the government responded to the basic needs of citizens and new immigrants. Prospects for economic opportunity, central to how Americans thought about their past, diminished in the face of labor strife, the visible chaos of urban life, and cyclical recession. Indeed, the statement in the 1890 federal census that the frontier had closed brought into question the future of American exceptionalism. How and where would new opportunities arise? Had the idea of republican virtue become obsolete? And how would the nation's core values fare in the nascent corporate age? This chapter surveys the intersection of ideas about liberty, the values attendant to it, and the meaning of security over two centuries to provide context for understanding the tensions between liberty and security that have existed since the end of the nineteenth century.

[5] On the tensions between slavery and freedom, see Eric Foner, *Free Soil, Free Labor, Free Men: The Ideology of the Republican Party before the Civil War* (New York: Oxford University Press, 1970).

Political Economy, Security, and Identity in Eighteenth-Century America

Britain and France fought seven wars between 1690 and 1815, during which time an American identity became fully formed. However loyal the colonists nominally were to the Crown after William of Orange overthrew James II, they were not averse to turning England's tribulations to their own advantage. King William's War, known in Europe as the War of the League of Augsburg, revitalized the authority of Parliament at home and emphasized the importance of empire abroad. Neither development could have occurred without the founding of the Bank of England in 1694.[6] Access to capital made success in conflict more likely because the Bank enabled the Crown to provide for the security of the realm. Funds would become available for building a fleet to protect the British Isles, which also could be dispatched to safeguard vital imperial interests in the West Indies or along the Atlantic seaboard.[7]

While British attention was understandably focused more on European than on colonial affairs in the decades following William's seizure of power, dramatic signs of economic growth appeared in America. Colonists linked this vibrant political economy of trade and development with their security. Around 1700, more than 250,000 white people lived in the colonies; that number increased to more than 630,000 by 1730 and exceeded 2 million by 1776. Only a thriving economy could sustain such an expanding population, all the more so because of the surge in immigration after 1760. At the turn of the eighteenth century, ships brought 20 percent of Britain's total imports from the transatlantic colonies, including the West Indies. By 1773, that figure had climbed to nearly 40 percent of all imports; the percentages for British exports were comparable.[8]

The colonies had become an economic safety valve for the mother country. In that mercantilist age, law made colonies dependent on markets in the homeland by generally precluding trade outside the British orbit. Almost imperceptibly, however, Britain was also becoming economically reliant on its colonies. The Iron Act of 1750 illustrated the economic challenge that the colonies might pose to the suzerainty of Britain. It allowed the smelting of iron ore into pig iron, but reserved further processing for British mills. Were Americans to find that restriction too onerous, a clash between

---

[6] Paul Kennedy, *The Rise and Fall of the Great Powers: Economic Change and Military Conflict from 1500 to 2000* (New York: Random House, 1987), 80.

[7] Andrew Jackson O'Shaughnessy, *An Empire Divided: The American Revolution and the British Caribbean* (Philadelphia: University of Pennsylvania Press, 2000), *passim*.

[8] Bernard Bailyn with the assistance of Barbara DeWolf, *Voyages to the West: A Passage in the Peopling of America on the Eve of the Revolution* (New York: Alfred A. Knopf, 1986), 24–6; Jack P. Greene, "An Uneasy Connection: An Analysis of the Preconditions of the American Revolution," in Kurtz and Hutson, eds., *Essays on the American Revolution*, 43–4.

mercantile philosophy and American assumptions about security would be inevitable.[9]

Numbers tell only part of the story of economic growth in the eighteenth century. Qualitative data suggest a link between diversification and development of an American identity. To be sure, agriculture remained the mainstay of the economy. Just the same, mercantilism guaranteed the shipping of a greater volume of British goods to the colonies as population increased. The results of a dependable commerce were several. Port cities grew at a fast rate. The presence of immigrants from Ireland and Scotland and more than 100,000 Germans from the Rhine valley created a burgeoning demand for a variety of goods. Artisans and common laborers were drawn to American cities in search of a prosperous and better life; demand for their goods gave rise to a competitive, expanding market. America's export trade enabled the New England shipping industry to thrive so much that it comprised as much as one-third of the empire's commercial fleet. By mid-century, therefore, the quality of life of free colonists may have been unsurpassed in Europe or the Atlantic world, which colonists attributed to the copious opportunities they judged to be unique to America.

During the ministry of Robert Walpole in the 1720s and 1730s, colonists got a taste of political autonomy as Parliament enacted few laws that directly affected their interests. Out of this experience there arose a belief that the rights of colonists as English subjects were quite secure, that they could govern themselves through the lower houses of assembly in their individual colonies. The Stamp Act imbroglio of the mid-1760s brought the problematic nature of the transatlantic relationship to light, although the foundation for that confrontation over authority had been laid years earlier. The Glorious Revolution had not settled precisely who was represented in Parliament.[10] In 1748, as the War of the Austrian Succession ended, Parliament displayed renewed resolve to assert imperial prerogatives. This change quickly resulted in an increase of administrative authority for the Board of Trade.[11] That development reflected a mounting concern that colonies might go their own way economically, if not politically, as they matured.

The proximate cause of this change in policy was a series of disturbances within several colonies that erupted in the late 1740s and early 1750s, coinciding with the resumption of war in Europe. This turmoil led governors throughout North America to complain about their inability to govern and

---

[9] On the tensions inherent in a mercantile economy, see Charles M. Andrews, *The Colonial Background of the American Revolution*, rev. ed. (New Haven: Yale University Press, 1931), 69–118. On the Iron Act, see T. O. Lloyd, *The British Empire, 1558–1983* (New York: Oxford University Press, 1984), 68.

[10] On the intellectual and governing dilemmas occasioned by the idea of representation, see J. R. Pole, *Political Representation in England and the Origins of the American Republic* (Berkeley: University of California Press, 1971), 3–26.

[11] Greene, "An Uneasy Connection," 68–71.

to criticize what they deemed the excessive power of the lower houses. The Glorious Revolution had served as a catalyst for the activities of elite factions in several colonies, including Massachusetts, New York, Pennsylvania, Virginia, and South Carolina, who imagined that a policy of expansion, broadly conceived, would further their own interests.[12] These elites shared an organic worldview, derived in part from their understanding of the history of colonial growth and their plans for future expansion. They believed that the intoxicating process of expansion, once underway, would inevitably take on a life of its own. Their sense of entitlement to subdue the environment with people and institutions resembled the motives underlying nineteenth-century continentalism in the form of "manifest destiny," as we see later.

In 1754, Benjamin Franklin envisioned the founding of two large colonies beyond the Appalachian Mountains, then the western frontier. The natural advantages accruing to the West, where "all can have full employ, and there is Room and Business for Millions yet unborn," would attract a population whose objective would be to extend the glory of America.[13] The wily Pennsylvanian had also advocated a policy of expansion three years earlier in his "Observations concerning the Increase of Mankind."[14] He understood that his vision of American grandeur guaranteed trouble with the French and Indians; it would also elicit grave concern in London. The French had a sparse presence in North America, numbering around 70,000, stretching from the lower Mississippi River region to the Mississippi and Ohio valleys and across the Great Lakes into Canada. They ruled this vast expanse of territory more by guile and diplomacy than by any visible and forceful administrative presence.

Colonial relations with native people had been relatively tranquil since the early 1700s compared to the seemingly incessant bloody clashes of the previous century. The likelihood of conflict remained a distinct possibility, however, as the French and Indians found it convenient to rely on one another to curb American incursions into their lands. In fact, Indians held the balance of power between France and Britain in North America because of their strategic location between the two empires and their military prowess. Alarmed by the aggressive patterns of British settlement, many Indians preferred to deal with the French, whose lesser numbers arguably made them more manageable and more inclined to deal with tribes on a reciprocal basis through diplomacy instead of deadly force. Should a conflict arise, time, numbers, and resources would favor the British, however.[15]

---

[12] This discussion is based on Egnal, *A Mighty Empire*.

[13] Bailyn, *Voyages to the West*, 356–7; Leonard W. Labaree et al., eds., *Papers of Benjamin Franklin*, vol. III: *January 1, 1745 through June 30, 1750* (New Haven: Yale University Press, 1961), 441.

[14] *Benjamin Franklin's Autobiography*, introduction by Dixon Wecter, and Larzer Ziff, ed., *Selected Writings* (New York: Holt, Rinehart and Winston, 1959), 216–25.

[15] Alan Taylor, *American Colonies* (New York: Viking, 2001), 423–8.

The French and Indian War, known in Europe as the Seven Years' War (1756–63), broke out in 1754 when military forces under the leadership of a young George Washington, acting at the behest of a coterie of land speculators with whom he was associated, tried to compel the French to leave the Ohio Valley. This attempt failed. During the next two years, the war went badly for the British and Americans, with combined French and Indian forces seizing forts in northern New York and Indians expelling white settlers from their outposts in western Pennsylvania. Prewar tensions had moved Governor George Clinton of New York to convene a conference on Indian relations in 1751. When this venture did not succeed, in 1754 Franklin drafted the Albany Plan of Union, which proposed the creation of a governing body with the power to levy taxes, address Indian problems, and provide for the common defense.[16]

The Albany Plan failed more because it was premature – representatives of only seven colonies met at Albany – than because of inherent flaws in its underlying logic about autonomy, liberty, and empire. Americans were not then ready to make a united stand politically; economic interests, far more than politics, constituted their common identity. Franklin was certain that war would lead to vigorous attempts to impose the Crown's authority, with negative consequences for American rights and ambitions. His prescience was on display in a 1755 letter to the governor of Pennsylvania, in which he wrote, "Those who would give up essential Liberty, to purchase a little temporary Safety, deserve neither Liberty nor Safety."[17] If Franklin was then no more than a shrewd purveyor of British imperialism, as Gordon S. Wood would have it,[18] his uncommon insight into the personal and collective travail that empire might bring helped set the stage for his own subsequent Americanization and the growth of patriotism throughout the colonies south of Canada.

Ultimately, the French and their Indian allies could not withstand the power of the combined British and colonial armed and naval forces. By 1760, virtually all of known Canada was in British hands; French forces surrendered to British troops in September of that year.[19] The Peace of Paris in 1763 formally removed French influence from land east of the Mississippi River; Louisiana and territory west of the river became part of Spain's empire. Britain's great expenditure on the war in North America,

---

[16] The most accessible survey of the war is Fred Anderson, *Crucible of War: The Seven Years' War and the Fate of Empire in British North America, 1754–1766* (New York: Vintage Books, 2001).

[17] Labaree et al., eds., *Papers of Benjamin Franklin*, vol. VI: *April 1, 1755 through September 30, 1756* (New Haven: Yale University Press, 1963), 242.

[18] Gordon S. Wood, *The Americanization of Benjamin Franklin* (New York: Penguin Press, 2004).

[19] Robert Bothwell, *The Penguin History of Canada* (Toronto: Penguin Canada, 2006), 81–8.

some £4 million, raised the ominous prospect of an irresolvable dispute over the authority of Parliament to impose a share of that burden on the colonies without their express approval.[20]

The impending defeat of France also created a crisis for Indians living at the edges of white settlement. South Carolinians residing in the back-country provoked a conflict with the Cherokees in 1759 and forced them to make peace within two years. Fearing they would experience a similar fate, northern Indians in the Ohio Valley and Great Lakes regions attempted to make common cause against the British and land-hungry Americans. War, known as Pontiac's Rebellion, broke out in May 1763 and lasted until December. Indian successes came quickly in parts of Pennsylvania, Maryland, and Virginia, but the loose coalition of forces could not take Fort Pitt or fortifications at Detroit and Niagara.[21]

To the extent that a *modus vivendi* had actually existed between native people and white Americans prior to the war with France, any reservoir of good will, as manifested in accommodationist practices, soon disappeared in a sea of racial hatred. British pressure brought Pontiac's Rebellion to a halt, leaving the remaining imperial forces already stationed in the West as the last line of defense against American depredations. Authorities in London issued the Proclamation of 1763 in an effort to retard further encroachment against Indian lands, the result of which was to anger settlers and land speculators alike. One leading member of the Six Nation Iroquois was also not appeased, commenting that the British presence in fortifications on what were then Indian lands "gives our warriors and women the greatest uneasiness, and makes us apt to believe every bad report we hear of your intentions toward us."[22] This assessment was not far off the mark. Washington derided the Proclamation of 1763, deeming it a "temporary expedient to quiet the minds of the Indians... [which] must fall, of course, in a few years." Other Americans would also see the detachments of British soldiers on the frontier in negative terms, depicting their presence as a harbinger of tyranny.[23]

Keeping the colonies secure after the French and Indian War resulted in the further dispossession of Indians from their lands. War nearly eliminated diplomacy as an option, yet armed conflict was not the only means of removal. Disease assisted the cause of the British. One man wrote from Fort Pitt during Pontiac's Rebellion, "We gave them two Blankets and an

[20] Taylor, *American Colonies*, 428–33.

[21] Richard White, *The Middle Ground: Indians, Empires, and Republics in the Great Lakes Region, 1650–1815* (New York: Cambridge University Press, 1991), 269–314.

[22] Quoted in Daniel K. Richter, *Facing East from Indian Country: A Native History of Early America* (Cambridge: Harvard University Press, 2001), 193.

[23] Jared Sparks, ed., *The Writings of George Washington* (Boston: Little, Brown, 1855), vol. II, p. 347.

Handkerchief out of the Smallpox Hospital."[24] And alcohol, long a staple of trade between whites and Indians, ably served American objectives as new settlements placed added pressure on Indian lands. An economic downturn in the 1760s, precipitated by the scarcity of credit from London because of the expenses of war, also worked to the disadvantage of native people. Tobacco planters in Virginia, who watched their level of indebtedness rise as a result of weak demand for their crop, moved inland in search of new opportunities. Farmers and lumbermen in South Carolina fared better than many people elsewhere; they brought additional backcountry land into production and thus avoided financial ruin. The treaties of Hard Labor and Fort Stanwix, signed in 1768, were efforts in the midst of recession to rebuild frontier diplomacy, respect the spirit of the Proclamation of 1763, and open to settlement land in present-day West Virginia and Kentucky. These attempts to construct separate spheres failed to appease the insatiable interests of squatters and land speculators. Parliament's imposition of the Townshend duties in 1767, an attempt to pay for the rising costs of security, worsened the situation for Indians when British troops were sent eastward to quell opposition to the duties. Too few troops on the frontier meant instability there, and the presence of redcoats, especially in New York and Massachusetts, further undermined British authority.[25]

When the American Revolution finally began in April 1775, the implications for native people were as clear as they were devastating. Combat for them in what was their own war for independence was already under way; the Revolution in British America produced a new nation in which there would be no secure space for Indians east of the Mississippi.[26] An expansionist ethos had taken hold and would not be denied. In 1780, minister to Spain John Jay instructed a legation secretary to inform Spanish officials about the people of "Virginia and the Western Country near the Mississippi. Recount their achievements against the Savages, their growing numbers, [and] extensive settlements. Let it appear from your Representations that ages will be necessary to settle those extensive Regions."[27] Indeed, excluding Indians was not achieved as quickly as removing the British; it would take until the mid-1790s for the conflict between native people and

---

[24] Quoted in Colin G. Calloway, *The American Revolution in Indian Country: Crisis and Diversity in Native American Communities* (New York: Cambridge University Press, 1995), 4.

[25] Robert Middlekauff, *The Glorious Cause: The American Revolution, 1763–1789* (New York: Oxford University Press, 1982), 143–73, 192–201.

[26] Calloway, *The American Revolution in Indian Country*, 24.

[27] John Jay's Instructions to William Carmichael, January 27, 1780, in Mary A. Guinta, ed., *The Emerging Nation: A Documentary History of the Foreign Relations of the United States under the Articles of Confederation, 1780–1789*, 3 vols., vol. 1: *Recognition of Independence, 1780–1784* (Washington, DC: National Historical Publications and Records Commission, 1996), 18.

the United States to reach a hiatus.[28] Although Americans perceived Indians as a threat to their security after the treaties of 1768, assumptions of racial superiority made them confident that they could contain the threat. That conviction was borne out in 1794 at the Battle of Fallen Timbers and in 1795 with the signing of the Treaty of Greenville. After that, Indians no longer posed a serious obstacle to the growing white presence in the vast Ohio territory.[29]

Ironically, American security also depended, or so many colonists believed, on the enslavement of Africans. Slavery was the terrible engine of prosperity for France and Great Britain in the New World. It is hard to conceive of the British Empire without the trade in sugar from the Indies or, to a lesser extent, tobacco from the American South. By 1770, some 450,000 Africans and their descendants were living in British North America. Their labor gave much arable land its value in the Chesapeake region and the Carolinas. The desire to acquire property created a culture of expansion, emphasizing how closely free Americans associated property with liberty. To own property and to trade its bounty therefore meant freedom. Unfree laborers hastened the exploitation of that bounty and thus preserved liberty for those who put their economic fate at risk in the marketplace. Accordingly, it was the public duty of free men to govern responsibly to maintain the link between property and liberty.[30]

Free Americans increasingly believed that the Crown and Parliament could not guarantee that connection. A revolution may not have been inevitable, but discord within the empire would be impossible to avert after the Seven Years' War.[31] Displays of parliamentary power, which commenced in the mid-1760s, exacerbated suspicions on both sides of the Atlantic. The Sugar, Revenue, and Currency Acts asserted the power of Parliament to regulate trade and finance, though not all in the colonies were adversely affected. For its part, the Stamp Act of 1765 was seen as an affront to all Americans, sparking demands for a broadly based response, which furthered the public's thinking both about who they were and what they believed in common beyond tangible economic interests. Colonists' understanding of themselves as Americans thereafter arose out of what many considered their unique political situation.[32] Notwithstanding their status as subjects of the Crown, they claimed that only their own elected representatives could levy taxes on them – a position that was diametrically at odds

---

[28] Calloway, *American Revolution in Indian Country*, 272–91.

[29] Alan Taylor, *The Divided Ground: Indians, Settlers, and the Northern Borderland of the American Revolution* (New York: Alfred A. Knopf, 2006), 111–41; Patrick Griffin, *American Leviathan: Empire, Nation, and Revolutionary Frontier* (New York: Hill and Wang, 2007), 248–50.

[30] Greene, *The Intellectual Construction of America*, 182; Edmund S. Morgan, *American Slavery, American Freedom* (New York: W. W. Norton & Company, 1975), 363–87.

[31] Greene, "An Uneasy Connection," 74.

[32] Greene, *The Intellectual Construction of America*, 162 ff.

with the Declaratory Act of 1766. The colonial bonds had been stretched almost to the breaking point as a common American identity crystallized.

Independence and Republican Virtue

In the widely read pamphlet *Common Sense*, published January 1776, and other writings, Thomas Paine gave voice to America's distinctiveness by emphasizing its virtues and the New World's superiority over the Old World. In the political realm, he passionately argued against property qualifications for voting; free men had a right and an obligation to vote. At the same time, Paine did not accept the proposition, then current in Britain and France, that government should regulate economic activity in pursuit of general welfare, even in times of economic crisis. This position did not mean that Paine opposed justice; quite the contrary. Regulation through the device of price controls precluded free trade, which he accepted as fundamental to independence and liberty itself. For Americans, free trade in that era meant trade not constrained by the bounds of a mercantilist philosophy. Adam Smith's *The Wealth of Nations* was published in Britain shortly after *Common Sense* in 1776; the two treatises converged on the principle of unfettered trade as a crucial attribute of free people. Paine would later write, "In all my publications...I have been an advocate for commerce." For Smith and Paine, commercial society would create economic bounty for all its members, thereby enhancing the chances for the success of republican governance.[33]

The independence of America would be "a continued good to all posterity," Paine wrote in his *Letter to Abbé Raynal*.[34] Defeating Britain allowed Americans to proclaim and celebrate their distinctive political economy. Success produced the firm belief that independence had long been part of the nation's history. Historian Bernard Bailyn notes, "There was no calm before the storm. The storm was continuous, if intermittent, throughout the [eighteenth] century."[35] That storm, oppositional politics, was not the same thing as independence. This convenient fiction nevertheless enabled Americans to create the social basis for presumptive equality among propertied men, thus giving life to Thomas Jefferson's pronouncement in the Declaration of Independence.

Responsible revolution was therefore not an impulsive undertaking. The cause of America, wrote one revolutionary, "is the cause of *self-defense*, of *public faith*, and of the *liberties of mankind*."[36] By seeing themselves as

---

[33] Eric Foner, *Tom Paine and Revolutionary America* (New York: Oxford University Press, 1976), 143–56; quoted words, 160.

[34] Quoted in Greene, *The Intellectual Construction of America*, 166.

[35] Ibid., 174; Bernard Bailyn, *The Origins of American Politics* (New York: Alfred A. Knopf, 1968), 159.

[36] Quoted in Bernard Bailyn, *The Ideological Origins of the American Revolution* (Cambridge: Harvard University Press, 1967), 139–40 (emphasis in original).

the last line of defense for liberty, whose existence was tenuous, Americans were not only making an argument based upon classical Whig principles; their brief was also millennial in intent and carried an apocalyptic warning: should liberty fail in America, the end of history (at least Whig history) was nigh. Such was the underside, as it were, of the belief in exceptionalism.

Democracy therefore had to be tempered because it likely portended popular irresponsibility. In the Revolutionary era, Bailyn wrote, it "denoted the lowest order of society ... [and] was generally associated with the threat of civil disorder and the early assumption of power by a dictator."[37] The realistic antidote for excessive democracy, many contemporary leaders affirmed, was a republic. Yet, if the people were sovereign, and American radicals clung to that belief, then the question had to be asked whether a republic – the essence of centralized authority – would not invite corruption on the part of the state. The Revolution did not end this dispute. The nature of the new government would remain unsettled not just until ratification of the Constitution, but in actuality until the end of the Civil War.

Meanwhile, the Articles of Confederation went into effect in 1781, reflecting the will of the people to safeguard their liberty by placing sovereign power in the hands of the thirteen states. The issue of western lands almost derailed this initial effort at national governance in the United States even before it got underway. Only after states including Virginia, the Carolinas, and Connecticut, whose charters granted them nearly unlimited tracts of land, had ceded their claims on the West to the government were the Articles ratified. The ongoing British presence in frontier posts until the controversial Jay Treaty of 1795 threatened American security, if not independence.[38] A similar compromise was not possible on the matter of trade. Radicals distrusted the more conservative merchant class. Accordingly, Congress was empowered to enter into treaties with foreign nations, yet no treaty of commerce could violate the right of states to impose duties or prohibit trade as they individually saw fit.[39]

The conviction that sovereignty ultimately rested in the people resonated also with Americans who favored the centralization of power that would epitomize republican government. For them, the weaknesses of the Articles where regulation of commerce and fiscal and monetary policy were concerned raised the specter of class conflict. Excesses of public liberty, as exemplified by mass democratic protests, like Shays' Rebellion of 1786–7

[37] Ibid., 282.
[38] Todd Estes, *The Jay Treaty Debate, Public Opinion, and the Evolution of Early American Political Culture* (Amherst: University of Massachusetts Press, 2006).
[39] Merrill Jensen, *The Articles of Confederation: An Interpretation of the Social-Constitutional History of the American Revolution, 1774 – 1781* (Madison: University of Wisconsin Press, 1940), 167–9, 177–8.

against debts and state taxes, had the potential to threaten private liberty or property rights – the basis of economic freedom. Massachusetts officials perceived a direct challenge to the rule of law in the rebellion by farmers, who, in contrast, imagined themselves as liberty's defenders against arbitrary authority. The chaotic license of the disgruntled, nationalists like James Madison and Alexander Hamilton believed, should not be mistaken for individual rights. If, as prominent Americans such as these had long assumed, virtue emanated from a society that was guided by the rule of law, then a sober republic held the key to virtue and, thus, to the perpetuation of freedom.[40]

If public virtue was going to hold back the tide of anarchy, there "must be," John Adams wrote in 1776, "a Decency, and Respect, and Veneration introduced for Persons in Authority, of every Rank, or We are undone." Public virtue flowed from private commitments to good will in matters of governance, with the greatest manifestation of virtue being an orderly republic. Conservative Americans therefore saw virtue as the very lifeblood, "the only Foundation" as Adams put it, of a republic, which was the sole form of government capable of averting descent into tyranny.[41] Belief in the primacy of order faced a serious challenge in the early years of the nation when the derisively named Whiskey Rebellion of 1794 against taxes on distilled spirits, whose perpetrators took a stand for liberty, in this case popular regulation of government, in the manner of Shays and his followers, failed only after President George Washington dispatched more than 10,000 troops to western Pennsylvania to disperse the unfortunate democrats.[42]

Determining which patriots – radical democrats or proponents of republicanism – were better able to cultivate public virtue leads to further consideration of the centrality of the market in the economic life of Americans as they distanced themselves from the strictures of mercantilism. Just as Thomas Paine extolled the benefits of international commerce, as we have seen, the Model Treaty or Plan of 1776, crafted in large part by John Adams, articulated the principle that "free ships make free goods."[43] In practice, neutral rights were anathema to the warring states of Europe. What was worse, they were claimed by a people in revolution against legitimate authority.

[40] Bailyn, *Ideological Origins*, 77, 83–4.
[41] Gordon S. Wood, *The Creation of the American Republic, 1776–1787* (Chapel Hill: University of North Carolina Press, 1969), 18–28, 65–9 (quote, p. 67); Drew R. McCoy, *The Elusive Republic: Political Economy in Jeffersonian America* (Chapel Hill: University of North Carolina Press, 1980), 69.
[42] James Roger Sharp, *American Politics in the Early Republic: The New Nation in Crisis* (New Haven: Yale University Press, 1993), 92–100; see also Terry Bouton, *"Taming Democracy" "The People," the Founders, and the Troubled Ending of the American Revolution* (New York: Oxford University Press, 2007), 7–8, 216–43.
[43] For more on the following discussion generally see Samuel Flagg Bemis, *The Diplomacy of the American Revolution* (Bloomington: Indiana University Press, 1957), 45–66.

The Plan was a bold, even foolhardy conceit about the allure of American commerce, especially because the young nation could not protect its ships and goods. Though seemingly a paradox, the closer the United States drew to France, the greater became the prospect of freedom. France could not abide the implications of enhanced British power were the Americans to lose their struggle for independence. Yet, few Americans were so naïve as to credit the French with the ability to withstand British military might in the long run. Hence, an association with France was to be a limited one, made possible by the lure of free goods. It turned out to be much more, however. The political and military provisions of the Franco–American Alliance of 1778 threatened to embroil the Americans in European conflicts.[44]

Guiding the United States through this diplomatic thicket would be men like Ben Franklin, cautious, scheming nationalists whose greatest desire was to construct a free republican political economy. The Plan of 1776 was intended to advance commercial ventures, yet it would have failed without a tradition of westward expansion. When the Plan appeared, America's imperial ambitions were revealed for European powers to see. Adherence to neutral rights for a growing foreign trade and economic development that would have otherwise been impossible without expansion signified that imperial intent.[45] From the vantage point of the twenty-first century, the Plan of 1776 remains one of the seminal documents of American foreign policy.

Given the importance of political economy to American identity and security, a few additional words are in order about Adam Smith and the merchant class. In Gary Wills's rendering, Smith would have rejected being cast as a defender of nineteenth-century liberalism. A Scottish moral and economic philosopher, Smith did not hold competition and cooperation to be polar opposites. Wills forcefully argues that Smith based his economic ideas on cooperation, not the market competition that lay at the base of British mercantilism. The "invisible hand" concerned "*harmonies* within society." Smith praised merchant competition, yet as "as a form of *cooperation* with producers and buyers." Whatever ideological purposes his writings later served, Adam Smith "began as a good communitarian of the Scots school," Wills concludes. Another scholar observes that in "an age of *political* economy," Smith welcomed government's involvement "in the operation of a country's society and economy."[46] The crucial issue for Smith was not how

44 Alexander DeConde, "The French Alliance in Historical Speculation," in Ronald Hoffman and Peter J. Albert, eds., *Diplomacy and Revolution: The Franco–American Alliance of 1778* (Charlottesville: University Press of Virginia, 1981), 4–9, 13.

45 Richard W. Van Alstyne, *The Rising American Empire* (New York: Oxford University Press, 1960), 29.

46 Garry Wills, *Inventing America: Jefferson's Declaration of Independence* (Garden City: Doubleday, 1978), 232 (emphasis in original); McCoy, *Elusive Republic*, 41 (emphasis in original).

to maintain the unfettered working of the market, but rather how to ensure that a government stood for liberty against tyranny.

Understanding Smith as other than a progenitor of laissez-faire economics is important because it helps explain, first, why radical and republican Americans alike venerated the Declaration of Independence. In so doing, differences over the extent of governmental involvement in public affairs became matters of degree, not kind, and did not violate Whig tradition. Also, Smith as communitarian spoke to conciliatory impulses in the American body politic. Having just freed themselves from an oppressive imperial power, few Americans were eager to engage in a divisive civil conflict. Accordingly, a belief in economic freedom in the form of property rights overcame the perturbations of the 1780s and 1790s. In the late eighteenth century, Smith's influence was considerable on a nation largely unified in its receptivity to all manner of commercial activity.[47]

Nevertheless, acrimonious debate over the ratification of the Constitution reveals the contingency of national identity in the early republic. From the outset, the most crucial issue was the extent of federal power – that is, the power of ruling elites – even more than the protection of individual liberties, although the Bill of Rights is usually thought to be more concerned with the latter. Americans found sufficient common meaning in their past, however, to forge an identity across classes replete with shared basic values, which they deemed integral to the rights of all free people. Incorporation of these values into the Bill of Rights therefore accorded political legitimacy to the federal Constitution, the very embodiment of republican virtue.

James Madison, who had previously judged a bill of rights redundant because he thought the Constitution itself could guard against abuses of authority, led the effort, which appeared as *The Federalist*, to amend that document. He told Jefferson, who had earlier opined that the Constitution "stagger[s] all my dispositions to subscribe to what ... [is] proposed," that amendments would soon become "the fundamental maxims of free government, and as they become incorporated with the national sentiment, counteract the impulses of interest and passion."[48] John Adams found much that was modern, much to admire in the Constitution: "But as all the great Principles necessary to order, Liberty and Safety are respected in it,... the United States now stand in an elevated Situation, and they must and will be respected ... while they keep themselves neutral."[49]

---

[47] Generally, see McCoy, *Elusive Republic*, 35–47.

[48] Thomas Jefferson to John Adams, November 13, 1787, in Guinta, ed., *The Emerging Nation*, vol. III: *Toward Federal Diplomacy, 1780–1789*, 651; Stanley Elkins and Eric McKitrick, *The Age of Federalism: The Early American Republic, 1788–1800* (New York: Oxford University Press, 1993), 58–62.

[49] John Adams to John Jay, 16 December 1787, in Guinta, ed., *Toward Federal Diplomacy*, 677–78.

This understanding of identity – a conservative order, based on the rule of law, that was widely perceived as exceptional – drew on a trajectory from past to present in the nation's history. After the ratification of the Constitution, what being American entailed became for men of property who exercised political power a conceit about the political economy of republicanism.[50] They recognized that republican principles needed to be revitalized over time to preserve their unique character and thus ward off opposing persons and ideas, whatever their provenance.

Empire and the Preservation of Virtue

It fell to that exemplar of contradiction, Thomas Jefferson, and his successor James Madison, more than to their predecessors George Washington and John Adams, to sustain the cause of republican virtue and thereby protect the nation's core values. To Jefferson, all men were created equal, yet he owned slaves; he characterized his election to the presidency as the "Revolution of 1800," yet his inaugural address was conciliatory in tone; and he espoused limited government, yet he wielded exceptional executive power with the purchase of Louisiana. His inconsistencies indicated how difficult it was to set the republic on a steady course in its early years. In another example, when general war resumed in Europe, Washington issued controversial neutrality proclamations in 1793 and 1794. The former ignored the 1778 alliance with France and asserted executive primacy in the making of foreign policy, whereas the latter promised prosecution of anyone putting pressure on Spanish lands in the West. That potential threat to further economic growth was removed by Pinckney's Treaty with Spain of 1795, which obtained the right of navigation on the Mississippi River, now recognized as the boundary of the nation, and limited privilege of deposit at New Orleans. The treaty ended a decade of intrigue about the fate of the West and Southwest, thereby preparing the way for further expansion of the new republic.[51]

The Jay Treaty, which included a commercial pact with the British, was ratified by the Senate in 1795, purchasing a decade or more of peace perhaps because of Britain's refusal to recognize America's assertion of neutral rights. The treaty exposed a profound factional chasm in American politics; it seemed overly deferential to the British, violated the spirit of the French alliance, and helped bring about the quasi-war with France. Like Britain,

---

[50] The classic treatment examining the origins of a republican political economy is Charles A. Beard, *An Economic Interpretation of the Constitution of the United States* (New York: Macmillan, 1913).

[51] Arthur Preston Whitaker, *The Spanish-American Frontier, 1783–1795: The Westward Movement and the Spanish Retreat in the Mississippi Valley*, Bison Book ed. (Lincoln: University of Nebraska Press, 1969), 185–222.

France treated the neutrality of American shipping with contempt, which became evident in an attempt to humiliate the United States in the failed "XYZ" affair.[52] Even a country so in thrall to commercial activity as the United States could not in short order overcome existing sectional jealousies. In 1798, President John Adams, having approved the enhancement of a small navy, openly supported the Alien and Sedition Acts, which were intended to silence an opposition press. More important for present purposes, these acts returned fear of arbitrary power to the heart of American politics.[53] During the Adams presidency, such maladroit governance by the Federalists left the impression that civil liberties in the Bill of Rights were little more than ornaments on the Constitution. The "violence of faction" that Madison cautioned against in *Federalist* No. 10 less than a decade earlier seemingly remained unchecked.

What could Jefferson do, as the first non-Federalist president, to assure a healthy future for republican government? It was not enough, as he had done in the Kentucky Resolution of 1798, to assert the rights of states in opposition to the federal government. He had to make a case for transcending classical republicanism and the limits it imposed on the pursuit of virtue. The question was one of vision and political economy. Just as Adam Smith and other Scottish Enlightenment thinkers on political economy influenced the writing of the Declaration of Independence,[54] they also informed Jefferson's plans to transform republicanism. The harmonies Smith had found in the operation of the market went beyond mere economics to what Jefferson, who had avidly supported the inclusion of a bill of rights into the Constitution, saw as the entwined issues of progress, often understood in economic terms, and human freedom.[55] His main purpose was to make republicanism anew; in that sense, the Revolution of 1800, with its intimation of political inclusion for free men, signified a return to the foundational principles of 1776.

Jefferson attached virtue and liberty to land and the political acumen of "the common people." He had written Madison at the end of 1787, "I think our governments will remain virtuous for many centuries; as long as they are chiefly agricultural; and this will be as long as there shall be vacant lands in any part of America."[56] Madison, more the Calvinist than Jefferson,

---

[52] Van Alstyne, *The Rising American Empire*, 75–6, 83–4; Arthur Burr Darling, *Our Rising Empire, 1763–1803* (New Haven: Yale University Press, 1940), 282–92.

[53] Alexander DeConde, *Entangling Alliance: Politics and Diplomacy under George Washington* (Durham: Duke University Press, 1958), 101–40, 226–31, 248–51; idem, *The Quasi-War: The Politics and Diplomacy of the Undeclared War with France, 1797–1801* (New York: Charles Scribner's Sons, 1966), 94–103, 194–6.

[54] Wills, *Inventing America*, 168–80, 229–39.

[55] Joyce Appleby, "Republicanism in Old and New Contexts," *William and Mary Quarterly*, 3rd. Ser., 43 (January 1986): 20–34.

[56] Thomas Jefferson to James Madison, 20 December 1787, in Guinta, ed., *Toward Federal Diplomacy*, 682.

reflected these confident sentiments when he observed in *Federalist* No. 10, "Extend the sphere and you take in a greater variety of parties and interests; you make it less probable that a majority of the whole will have a common motive to invade the rights of other citizens."[57] Taming the West, where increased land ownership was the goal, would spread the ideals of republicanism across the continent. As commercial interests and political ideals converged in Jefferson's "empire of liberty," the ostensible inconsistencies between his Revolution of 1800 and the purchase of Louisiana disappeared. To a considerable extent, those developments were the building blocks of Jeffersonian democracy.

Jefferson believed deeply in the resiliency of the American system of government. "I am persuaded," he wrote Madison in 1809, "no constitution was ever before so well calculated as ours for extensive empire and self government." Despite this ebullience, his experience moved him to add a cautionary note, "Nothing should ever be accepted which would require a navy to defend it."[58] To engage in foreign affairs in the European style as a matter of national policy might therefore rob the United States of its greatest assets.

The continuing European conflict tested the resiliency of the republic under Jefferson and Madison. Their foreign policy was born not of caution, like that of the Federalists, but reflected calculated risk taking. The fundamental differences with the Federalists were over association with Great Britain and the primary role of commerce and manufactures as revealed in Alexander Hamilton's thinking. The problem was that European rivalries imperiled U.S. sovereignty from the late 1790s through 1815 because of the nature of America's political economy. The allure of trade free from mercantile restraints and an unshakable faith in westward movement portended trouble for the nation, whose bold ambition in these two spheres would ultimately challenge Europe's dominance over international affairs. True independence for the United States was not possible, however, until European powers managed to vanquish Napoleon Bonaparte's revolutionary schemes. The emergence after the Congress of Vienna in 1815 of a system that inclined toward balance and restraint in Europe well served America's own vital interests.[59]

Radical Richard Price, whose devotion to civil liberty through universal suffrage raised the specter of mob action among those who opposed

---

[57] *The Federalist Papers*, with an introduction by Clinton Rossiter (New York: Mentor Books, 1961), 77–84.
[58] Jefferson to Madison, 27 April 1809, in Andrew A. Lipscomb, ed., *Writings of Thomas Jefferson* (Washington, D.C.: The Thomas Jefferson Memorial Association, 1903), XII: 274, 277.
[59] On European politics see Paul W. Schroeder, *Systems, Stability, and Statecraft: Essays on the International History of Modern Europe*, ed. David Wetzel, Robert Jervis, and Jack S. Levy (New York: Palgrave Macmillan, 2004), 23–34, 270–8.

parliamentary reform,[60] had offered a way out of the dilemma that power politics posed to a weak, young nation. He envisioned a self-sufficient America without the potentially deleterious effects of foreign commerce. With identity tied to foreign trade as the servant of agriculture, accepting Price's suggestion that "the American States...make a world within themselves" would have meant reversing far more than the course of republicanism in the new nation; it would have turned on its head more than 150 years of American history.[61] Yet, neither history nor the government had an answer for the inequalities of power when Algiers, at Great Britain's behest, declared war on the United States in 1785, the same year that Price published his *Observations on the Importance of the American Revolution*.[62] The United States soon accommodated Algiers, and other Barbary powers, without suffering great humiliation. In the long run, American officials would inexorably turn to naval power to protect the country's commerce. Price's intriguing idea, which acknowledged the distinctiveness of the American experiment, never had a chance of being considered seriously. A world power since its birth in 1776, America would become a great power after the Civil War and would do so on its own terms. For outward-looking Americans whose aspirations were at stake, the aversion to conflict that characterized European politics after 1815 gave them time to work out the details.[63]

Republican foreign policy reflected a sense of desperation, which led to a second war for independence, the War of 1812. The anarchy visited on the world by the imperial pretensions of Napoleon reminded Americans that the rule of law depended on the powerful for its very existence, something they already knew from their preemptive moves against Indian lands. Neither Jefferson nor Madison could make a credible defense of American interests in a dangerous world. Free ships did not make free goods in the minds of the British or the French, as we have seen. The remarkable growth of the American merchant fleet between 1802 and 1810 threatened the two major European powers; both feared the other might gain an advantage from greater trade with the United States. In the years before the war, Jefferson and Madison each considered aligning the nation with Great Britain, yet did not do so because of what they perceived as London's lack of respect for American independence. Napoleon's continental system, which arguably rejected the concept of neutrality, was no more respectful of American sovereignty. The United States became hostage to events beyond its control. Macon's Bill

[60] Pole, *Political Representation in England*, 462–8.
[61] Richard Price, *Observations on the Importance of the American Revolution, and the Means of Making It a Benefit to the World* (London: Haswell and Russell, 1785), 58.
[62] Robert J. Allison, *The Crescent Observed: The United States and the Muslim World, 1776–1815* (Chicago: University of Chicago Press, 1995), 3–5.
[63] On the nomenclature of the nation's status see Thomas A. Bailey, "America's Emergence as a World Power: The Myth and the Verity," *Pacific Historical Review* 30 (February 1961): 1–16.

No. 2 of 1810, by asserting the trading rights of neutral powers from a position of weakness, reversed Jefferson's controversial embargo of 1807 that had closed ports and made exports illegal, and thus surrendered American sovereignty to the power of the British navy.[64]

Ultimately, Madison could not overlook British depredations, particularly the impressment of sailors, and chose war. Ironically, a severe recession, accompanied by public protests, compelled the government to repeal the offensive Orders in Council on June 23, 1812, six days after Madison had obtained a declaration of war from Congress. To an extent, the embargo, which made a mockery of republican economic principles, had worked. This development bothered the aging Federalist John Adams, who wrote Jefferson, "Whether you or I were right Posterity must judge. I have never approved of Non Importations, Non Intercourses, or Embargoes for more than Six Weeks. [And] I have never approved and can never approve of . . . the neglect of the Navy."[65] Only many decades later would American leaders link the defense of principle to military preparedness.

Restraints on trade directly threatened the distinctiveness of American identity, which no citizen could accept with equanimity. Popular confidence in the exceptionalism of the United States remained strong, in part as a result of the Treaty of Ghent, which was signed on December 24, 1814, and ended the war. Moreover, Andrew Jackson's victory over British forces at New Orleans weeks later awakened in Americans a profound martial pride, a quality that many citizens thereafter would find central to the nation's identity. The 1816 election of James Monroe then ushered in a widespread, superficial spirit of unity – the misnamed "era of good feelings." Fleeting though it was, it also seemed to testify to the truth of exceptionalism.[66]

The incongruities in America's political economy would shortly be on display, though, over banking and the tariff, boundary questions, and slavery in Missouri. The War of 1812 nearly bankrupted the federal government; by 1817, a currency crisis was in the offing as a result of the circulation of depreciated state monies. Although the creation of the Second Bank of the United States in 1816 helped stabilize the currency, the outflow of silver to China to promote trade with Canton alarmed Americans in the West and South, who began to resent the primacy of the Northeast in financial and commercial affairs. The passage of tariff legislation in 1816, though not controversial at the time because many in the South anticipated the rise of

---

[64] Generally, see Bradford Perkins, *The First Rapprochement: England and the United States, 1795–1805* (Berkeley: University of California Press, 1955); idem, *Prologue to War: England and the United States, 1805–1812* (Berkeley: University of California Press, 1963).

[65] Adams to Jefferson, 1 May 1812, in Lester J. Cappon, ed., *The Adams-Jefferson Letters: The Complete Correspondence Between Thomas Jefferson and Abigail and John Adams* (Chapel Hill: University of North Carolina Press, 1959), 301.

[66] The classic study is George Dangerfield, *The Era of Good Feelings* (New York: Harcourt, Brace, 1952), which can still be read with profit for the tenor of the times.

manufacturing there, was also a harbinger of serious regional differences and discontent.

The Rush–Bagot Agreement of 1817 demilitarized the Great Lakes and set the stage for the subsequent peaceful resolution of boundary disputes between Canada and the United States. The disposition of Florida and the trans-Mississippi West was a matter of potential controversy, however. War against the Seminole Indians and the killing of two British subjects in Florida returned Jackson to public attention. Secretary of State John Quincy Adams defended the general's unwarranted actions as showing "the purest patriotism."[67] He convinced President James Monroe that both American credibility and presidential authority were at stake in Florida and justified broad presidential powers: "There is no doubt that *defensive* acts of hostility may be authorized by the Executive."[68] Asserting the right to self-defense through expansion by force of arms proved widely popular and assisted the signing of the Transcontinental Treaty in 1819, whereby the United States obtained Florida and claimed western lands all the way to the Pacific Ocean.[69]

In contrast to financial matters or expansion, however, it was hard to infuse slavery with any degree of common nationalism. A palpable oxymoron, sectional nationalism, became the order of the day, with the North and South each claiming to represent the true republican tradition. Which section would prevail could not be foretold, though foreign policy and continental expansion were soon enmeshed in the contest. After 1815, a burgeoning factory demand in Great Britain for raw cotton meant that the issue of slavery would not soon go away; cotton was rapidly becoming the nation's leading export commodity. The Missouri Compromise of 1820 vividly exposed the tragic limits of republican political economy.[70] Because American prosperity, growth, and cotton were inextricably joined, American freedom would continue to rest uncomfortably on, as it had for more than a century, the enslavement of black people – the inhabitants of what one scholar has termed an "internal African colony."[71] In foreboding tones,

---

[67] John Quincy Adams to George W. Erving, 28 November 1818, *American State Papers 04, Foreign Relations*, vol. 4, 15th Cong., 2d sess., Publication No. 311, p. 541.

[68] Charles Francis Adams, ed., *Memoirs of John Quincy Adams Comprising Portions of His Diary from 1795 to 1848* (Philadelphia: J. B. Lippincott & Company, 1875), vol. IV: 108 (emphasis in original).

[69] Adams's hubris and bravado impressed neo-conservative intellectual Robert Kagan, an avid proponent of going to war against Iraq after September 11, 2001, who approvingly writes of Adams's "certainly aggressive behavior on the part of the very young nation." Robert Kagan, *Dangerous Nation: America's Place in the World from its Earliest Days to the Dawn of the Twentieth Century* (New York: Alfred A. Knopf, 2006), 137.

[70] Ibid., 181–223 for a provocative discussion of slavery, foreign policy, expansion, and republican values.

[71] Odd Arne Westad, *The Global Cold War: Third World Interventions and the Making of Our Times* (Cambridge: Cambridge University Press, 2005), 10.

John Adams observed to Jefferson, "Slavery in this Country I have seen hanging over it like a black cloud."[72]

By 1820, some Americans were asking what had happened to political virtue since the heady days of 1787.[73] Had they surrendered so completely to the intoxicating lure of manufactured commodities, and thus to dreaded luxuries, that their nation was losing its moral distinctiveness? (It now seems quaint that the founding generations feared that excessive materialism might impair the health of the republic.) Would a culture of individual responsibility continue to have a purpose in the public realm? Or had the "harmonies" of Adam Smith lost their relevance to the United States? It appeared so. Unadulterated veneration of martial men like Andrew Jackson, the emergence of a manufacturing economy, and fears about the durability of the republican ideal indicated that the future of America might no longer emphasize the pursuit of virtue. Instead, it would become a celebration of market capitalism as expressed in devotion to individual liberties and couched in the rhetoric of the democratic potential of the nation.

The decline of virtue as a defining attribute of American political life passed almost unnoticed at the time. Continued expansion and the market revolution were both integral to the furtherance of what came to be called Manifest Destiny, the providential favoring of the United States and its endeavors as a growing power.[74] Over the next several decades, the welter of events obscured what was happening to republican virtue. In retrospect, it is clear that Manifest Destiny had a prominent role in its travail.

Indeed, the quest for commercial opportunities seemed quintessentially American. Revolution in Latin America was a godsend in that regard. William Duane, editor of the Philadelphia newspaper *Aurora*, put it clearly in 1819. The American people, he wrote, "*will after all* have to look to the regions of the south on the same continent as the source of their *future prosperity, commerce, and security.*"[75] In practice, this meant limiting European trade with Latin America if there was going to be an empire of liberty. Peace in 1815 had revitalized American commerce and shipping, most especially with Britain and France. Merchants wanted more, however, so they welcomed revolution in Latin America against Spain, seeing profit in the economic dislocation that was sure to ensue. Although the comparative dollar value and volume of trade were relatively small then, the prospect of a reliable market without formal ties of empire was compelling. In that realization reside important roots of the Monroe Doctrine of 1823. What was

---

[72] Adams to Jefferson, 3 February 1821, in *The Adams-Jefferson Letters,* 571.

[73] See Steven Watts, *The Republic Reborn: War and the Making of Liberal America, 1790–1820* (Baltimore: Johns Hopkins University Press, 1987), 64–86, 218–24.

[74] This understanding of Manifest Destiny is adapted from Anders Stephanson, *Manifest Destiny: American Expansion and the Empire of Right* (New York: Hill and Wang, 1995).

[75] Quoted in Arthur P. Whitaker, *The United States and the Independence of Latin America, 1800–1830* (Baltimore: Johns Hopkins University Press, 1941), 110 (emphasis in original).

most revealing about American intentions, though, was the focus on Cuba, still a Spanish colony, for both its commercial and strategic value.[76] How this sense of entitlement – to insert American interests into the affairs of others – would affect core values would not be apparent for decades.

But for the omnipresent challenge of slavery and the use of the "gag rule" to prevent discussion of abolition in the House of Representatives, foundational principles went largely untested. Moreover, John Quincy Adams's address of July 4, 1821, seemed like a bridge between past and future. Virtue might be preserved if America remained "the ruler of her own spirit" and did not "[go] abroad in search of monsters to destroy."[77] To Adams, commerce and a thriving merchant marine would protect the nation, not put it at risk. Indeed, as president, Adams's support for a program of internal improvements followed Madison's lead; better communications and education would serve to enrich and safeguard the republic. Yet, more than responsible governance was at work. In his first annual message, Adams wrote, "[L]et us not be unmindful that liberty is power, that the nation blessed with the largest portion of liberty must in proportion to its numbers be the most powerful nation upon earth."[78]

How would power be exercised in liberty's name? Jefferson had dreamed since at least 1808 of an expansive empire of liberty stretching throughout the Americas: "What a Colossus shall we be when the Southern continent comes up to our mark."[79] Adams as president counseled caution in foreign affairs, whereas as secretary of state in relations with Spain and in framing the Monroe Doctrine, he helped President Monroe prepare the way for subsequent foreign entanglements. Adams understood power as a given in human affairs, believing that America would use its power responsibly.

Andrew Jackson and his successors found themselves having to determine how that task might be accomplished. The tariff of 1828, or "Tariff of Abominations," and the resultant nullification crisis in South Carolina, the ruthless, arbitrary process of Indian removal, the use of the gag rule, and controversy over the annexation of Texas in 1845 showed that core values were potentially at risk in the Jacksonian era. Ironically, Jackson, who came to the presidency as an ardent defender of states' rights, became a passionate supporter of the union and federal authority. The import of the issues confronting presidents Jackson, John Tyler, and James K. Polk challenges the idea of beneficence in an empire of liberty and belief in a manifest destiny. It also undermines Madison's conviction in *Federalist* No. 10 that

---

[76] Ibid., 127.

[77] Walter LaFeber, ed., *John Quincy Adams and American Continental Empire: Letters, Papers, and Speeches* (Chicago, Quadrangle Books, 1965), 42–6.

[78] James Richardson, ed., *A Compilation of the Messages and Papers of the Presidents, 1789–1897* (Washington, D.C.: Government Printing Office, 1899), II: 316.

[79] Jefferson to Adams, 1 August 1816, in *The Adams–Jefferson Letters*, 484; Whitaker, *The United States and the Independence of Latin America*, 43.

westward movement would curtail the violence of faction. As if to amplify the forgotten counsel of Richard Price while explaining its irrelevance to the subsequent American experience, historian Drew McCoy notes, "The United States could isolate itself from foreign affairs and the potential for conflict only if it was willing to resign its tenacious commitment to westward expansion and free trade."[80] By the late 1830s, the likelihood of conflict at home was rapidly increasing.

John Quincy Adams railed against the use of the gag rule to prevent debate over slavery in Congress. In a sharp break with his hope as secretary of state to bring Texas into the union, he fiercely condemned the movement for annexation from his place in the House of Representatives: "I regard it as the apoplexy of the Constitution."[81] An aging Albert Gallatin, Jefferson's secretary of the treasury, published an antiwar pamphlet, *Peace with Mexico*, which envisioned war with Mexico over Texas as likely to erode the foundations of freedom and destroy the integrity of the republic.

Opposition to annexation and war was more related to the issue of slavery than it was a philosophical or ideological position against empire. Adams, for instance, would have neither understood nor shared Price's concerns about the threat of expansion and empire to republican governance. He long desired the annexation of Cuba, regarding it as "indispensable to the continuance and integrity of the Union."[82] His most sympathetic biographer, Samuel Flagg Bemis, appreciated the island's strategic location. "Cuba," he wrote, "was of vital interest to the United States."[83] This premise – equating expansion with security and, accordingly, the preservation of republican exceptionalism – also led Adams to support acquisition of the Oregon Territory from Great Britain, just as Polk relied on it to force a confrontation with Mexico.[84] The Mexican War brought a vast swath of land, including California and the present-day Southwest, into the possession of the United States.

At a remove of almost fifty years from the Louisiana Purchase in 1803, at which time Congress countenanced the expansion of presidential power in the name of western security, the rule of law in newly acquired territories was not the foremost consideration. It never had been, whether in the Old Northwest, the Floridas, or Louisiana prior to its acquisition. Scoundrels

[80] McCoy, *The Elusive Republic*, 204.
[81] Allan Nevins, ed., *The Diary of John Quincy Adams, 1794–1845: American Diplomacy, and Political, Social, and Intellectual Life, from Washington to Polk*, reprint ed. (New York: Frederick Ungar Publishing, 1969), 574.
[82] Worthington Chauncey Ford, ed., *Writings of John Quincy Adams*, vol. VII: *1820–1823* (New York: Macmillan, 1917), 373.
[83] Samuel Flagg Bemis, *John Quincy Adams and the Foundations of American Foreign Policy* (New York: Alfred A. Knopf, 1949), 372.
[84] Thomas R. Hietala, *Manifest Design: Anxious Aggrandizement in Late Jacksonian America* (Ithaca: Cornell University Press, 1985), 173ff.

like James Wilkinson, whose loyalties were not to be trusted by either Spain or the United States as he sought fame if not fortune on the southwestern frontier in the late eighteenth century, nevertheless served a useful purpose.[85] They were catalysts for expansion because their own dreams of glory, as personified by the exploits of Stephen F. Austin, intrepid son of the early Anglo settler Moses Austin, in Texas and the Swiss-born, Mexican national John Sutter in California, could never be completely realized. What they excelled at was attracting ambitious settlers into their fiefdoms. The Republic of Texas, which was founded in 1836, was coveted by Great Britain as well as the United States. And Sutter's proposal, whether genuine or not, to fashion a republic on the Pacific drew the attention of France, the United States, and obviously Mexico.[86] The process of settlement and the diversity of economic activity in the Southwest and West turned Mexican authority into fiction, thereby creating a vacuum only the United States could fill.

The American experience in Texas had been a violent one since its inception, which one historian characterizes as a brutal "ethnic cleansing" by vigilantes and local authorities of native Mexicans and tribes like the Comanches.[87] Moreover, by the time war with Mexico actually began, traders from Texas to California, whose loyalties were monuments to expedience and self-interest, had established patterns of supplying Indians with arms that were then used to destabilize the Mexico's northern frontier.[88] Their entrepreneurial spirit meshed well with the interests of colonists and adventurers like the Austins and Sutter. In northern California as the Mexican War was beginning, U.S. forces employed volunteer Indians to help rebellious Bear Flag Anglos subdue the local population, or *californios*.[89] Not surprisingly, respect for either the rule of law – in this case Mexican law – or Mexico's sovereignty was absent in the process of acquiring and securing land that stretched to the Pacific Ocean. Using preemptive military force to achieve security was an American tradition, as we have seen, one typically couched in the language of self-defense and premised on racial superiority.

Most Americans perceived domination of the continent south of Canada as the fulfillment of history's promise; to many, it was divinely ordained. If

---

[85] Whitaker, *The Spanish-American Frontier, 1783–1795*; John A. Logan, Jr., *No Transfer: An American Security Principle* (New Haven: Yale University Press, 1961), 36, 108–11.

[86] David J. Weber, *The Mexican Frontier, 1827–1846: The American Southwest Under Mexico* (Albuquerque: University of New Mexico Press, 1982), 158–78; Albert L. Hurtado, *John Sutter: A Life on the North American Frontier* (Norman: University of Oklahoma Press, 2006).

[87] Gary Clayton Anderson, *The Conquest of Texas: Ethnic Cleansing in the Promised Land, 1820–1875* (Norman: University of Oklahoma Press, 2005).

[88] Weber, *The Mexican Frontier*, 95–103.

[89] Albert L. Hurtado, *Indian Survival on the California Frontier* (New Haven: Yale University Press, 1988), 77–85.

common language and obviously similar cultural traits made Canada appeal-ing to expansionists, and that allure persisted even after Canada achieved dominion status in 1867, they also made its union with the United States more unlikely. That exception to the pattern of expansion suggests that respect for the sovereignty of other nations depended rather more on cir-cumstance than any fixed principle.[90] As for the expansionists who desired to bring all of Oregon under America's wing, they were swimming against the tide. Had Polk followed their lead, he might have been faced with the possibility of a two-front war, which would have rent the nation. Accepting the limits of power, not an easy thing to do then, enabled him to focus on what he judged to be the greater prizes of Texas and California.[91]

Eagerly embraced by much of the American public in the mid-1840s, this sense of providential destiny that coveted the trans-Mississippi West had been at the heart of John Quincy Adams's thinking about the nation's future for decades. It would have pained him greatly, however, to see expan-sion, for which he held as much responsibility as anyone of his generation, destroy the republic he had helped build. His death in 1848 spared him that sorrow.

Industrial America

The Compromise of 1850 constituted an admission that the empire of liberty had lost its way. The Wilmot Proviso of 1846, excluding slavery from all land acquired from Mexico, never became law, yet it revealed the unbridgeable divisions stemming from war with Mexico as they related to the extension of slavery. The harm done to the ideal of a virtuous republic became evident as the Democrat Party splintered over the slavery issue and the short-lived Free Soil Party arose. Both of these developments raised the question of states' rights versus federal authority. In his final address to the U.S. Senate, which illness prevented him from giving, John C. Calhoun of South Carolina saw a troubled nation dominated by the political and economic power of the North: "The character of the Government has changed in consequence from a federal Republic, as it originally came from the hands of its founders, into a great national consolidated Democracy."[92]

Not all Americans shared Calhoun's lament. Free Soilers viewed them-selves as uniquely preserving the legacy of an earlier republicanism that largely equated American identity with land ownership and economic oppor-tunity. The latter was important because the economic depression begin-ning in 1837 and the protectionist tariff of 1842 reminded Americans just

[90] Generally see Bothwell, *The Penguin History of Canada*.
[91] Kagan, *Dangerous Nation*, 224–34, 246–52.
[92] Clyde N. Wilson and Shirley Bright Cook, eds., *The Papers of John C. Calhoun*, vol. XXVII: *1849–1850 with Supplement* (Charleston: University of South Carolina Press, 2003), 195.

how dependent they were on events beyond their control. Responses to the depression had three major effects. They transformed the economic axis of the United States from one pointing South-to-North to West-to-Northeast, ushered in a period of extensive industrial growth, and gave laissez-faire economic policies an exalted status. These changes not only turned Adam Smith into an icon for the exponents of economic individualism but also cast doubt on the centrality of Jefferson's agrarian vision as the lifeblood of the republic's identity. Americans, some of whom now possessed immense tracts of land to exploit with the newest technologies, increasingly believed that a people characterized by manufacturing would lead "the most powerful nation upon earth" to a more profitable future than would a primarily agrarian polity.[93]

Yet, expansionist schemes, which mainly served regional interests, ultimately threatened to transform the identity of the republic. The "All Mexico" movement of the late 1840s, renewed interest in Cuba, as symbolized by several ill-fated expeditions to seize the island from Spain by Narcisco López around 1850 and the 1854 Ostend Manifesto – a transparent pro-slavery document the Pierce administration rejected, and a series of forays into Central America by filibusterers, especially the notorious William Walker: Each represented a competing imperial identity within the American populace. Although these adventurers and the U.S. government found themselves at odds, it was more because of potential diplomatic embarrassment and the possible spread of slavery accompanying the quixotic efforts of the former than the result of any reconsideration of the propriety of expansion. Manifest Destiny, as it turned out, was not easy to dismiss because it never was a unitary movement.

Some Americans, including Walt Whitman, deluded themselves into believing that Mexicans might want to join the Union. Even James K. Polk's cabinet considered the absorption of part or all of Mexico. Whigs and opposition Democrats would not hear of it. Although pro-expansionist northerners saw the All Mexico crusade as a humanitarian effort, other advocates viewed it as a way of containing British ambition while simultaneously acknowledging the expansive character of America's political economy. For that, a transoceanic canal would someday be a necessity, and the Isthmus of Tehuantepec seemed a possible route. What was not certain in the late 1840s was how a Mexico incorporated into the Union would affect debates over slavery. On ratification of the Treaty of Guadalupe Hidalgo in 1848, however, the force behind All Mexico soon dissipated. The effort failed because neither its proponents nor foes could countenance large numbers of Spanish-speaking Mexicans, many of whom were not white, as citizens in a republic. The conceit that America beckoned all reasonable people gave way

---

[93] Michael Adas, *Dominance by Design: Technological Imperatives and America's Civilizing Mission* (Cambridge: Belknap Press of Harvard University Press, 2006), 67–105.

to the fear that such immigrants as Mexico would provide could somehow sully the nation's distinctiveness.[94]

Filibustering, whether in the cause of independence for Cuba or empire in Central America, has often been misconstrued as the southern dream of a Caribbean empire and, thus, a defense of slavery.[95] Although true to an extent, it was never so simple. Venezuelan-born Narcisco López desired to transport republicanism to his home island. Among his supporters were members of the Havana Club, a group of wealthy entrepreneurs and professionals in Cuba, and exiles living in New York City who desired annexation by the United States for their country.[96] Occurring in the political maelstrom surrounding the Compromise of 1850, the initial attempt to vanquish Spanish rule in Cuba was nationalist in character. Freedom for Cubans, not including the island's 435,000 enslaved blacks, would redound to the material and strategic advantage of the United States. Urging on López was none other than John L. O'Sulllivan, the New York City journalist who had coined the term "manifest destiny," just as he supported the idea of All Mexico and would give his backing to William Walker. López's hopes were a chimera. The Taylor and Fillmore administrations, though willing to buy Cuba from Spain, nevertheless distanced themselves from López, judging his activities a violation of the Neutrality Act of 1818.

If López ultimately served as an unwitting tool of pro-slavery interests, Walker's more familiar Nicaraguan odyssey became consciously so in short order. The nominal difference is that López met his end with a garroting after an unsuccessful second attempt to liberate Cuba in August 1851, whereas Walker was to die by hanging in Honduras in September 1860. By that time, whatever nationalist intentions or backing he once enjoyed had all but vanished. Anxious to gain aid for his failing regime in Nicaragua, he legalized slavery there in September 1856, the results of which were the formation of a regional alliance against him and the withdrawal of significant portions of support in the North, especially among anti-slavery Democrats and Republicans.[97]

The birth of the Republican Party made clear the fundamental divide separating the American people. The leaders of this sectional party believed that northern industrial production and financial independence would determine

---

[94] This paragraph draws upon Frederick Merk, with the collaboration of Lois Bannister Merk, *Manifest Destiny and Mission in American History: A Reinterpretation* (New York: Alfred A. Knopf, 1963), 107–43, 180–201.

[95] That characterization comes from Robert E. May's book, *The Southern Dream of A Caribbean Empire, 1854–1861* (Baton Rouge: Louisiana State University Press, 1973).

[96] The most thorough study of López's exploits is Tom Chaffin, *Fatal Glory: Narcisco López and the First Clandestine U.S. War against Cuba* (Charlottesville: University Press of Virginia, 1996).

[97] Robert E. May, *Manifest Destiny's Underworld: Filibustering in Antebellum America* (Chapel Hill: University of North Carolina Press, 2002), 251–72.

the economic future of the country. Further expansion into the West would serve to buttress the Republican vision of a powerful state.[98] Emerging in the mid-1850s, fueled by immigrant labor and bolstered by protective tariffs, this new state would be reflective more of Hamiltonian than Jeffersonian or Jacksonian ideals. As agrarian Democrats became stigmatized as supporters of slavery, which was true for many living in the South, prospects for collective civic virtue declined in America.

The outcome of the Civil War did not soon restore the integrity and vitality of the republic. Sectional divisions, indicative of opposing economic and political philosophies, were neither overcome by the hated presence in the South of military Reconstruction nor by the passage of time. While the West became profitably joined to the Northeast, the South chafed in semi-colonial status. The rise of the Ku Klux Klan soon after surrender by General Robert E. Lee at Appomattox in 1865 showed the capacity of violent factions to plague the land. The same might be said about the conflicts with Native Americans that broke out as miners and ranchers poured into the Great Plains and the West in hopes of realizing the promises of prosperity they associated with the Homestead Act of 1862. For many, the trek west became a fool's errand, the unhappy result of a political economy that owed more to avarice protected by law than to civic virtue or responsibility.

Civil liberties fared poorly under the duress of the Civil War. Setting a precedent for future chief executives, President Abraham Lincoln used the power of his office in the name of security. Freedom of speech, freedom of the press, and freedom of association were curtailed in pursuit of Union victory. Twice, Lincoln suspended the writ of habeas corpus in attempting to check what were deemed disloyal activities. The courts typically sided with the president, only curbing presidential power – in *Ex parte Milligan*, for instance – after the war had ended.[99] Basic liberties, the heart of the Bill of Rights, no longer seemed inviolable, raising the possibility of abuse of power at the highest level of government. That Lincoln was not a tyrant made his use of executive power appear exceptional at the time.

The first two decades after the Civil War were a time of remarkable transition in American politics and society. The cherished myth of yeomen farmers in a democratic land persisted even as industrial barons refashioned the nation's laws and economy to serve their expanding corporate interests. By the late 1880s, the priorities of Jeffersonian America had been reversed. Social Darwinism, the idea that some organizations or people were best suited for the rigors of modern life, provided a rationale for pushing aside the poor and the weak in the name of enterprise. Agriculture, along with mining

---

[98] For a somewhat different emphasis see Foner, *Free Soil, Free Labor, Free Men*, 13–18, 163–85.

[99] J. G. Randall and David Donald, *The Civil War and Reconstruction*, 2d rev. ed. (Lexington: D.C. Heath, 1969), 295–309.

and ranching, existed to advance the commercial needs of manufacturers and the investment priorities of financiers. Thus, the Panic of 1873 and the recession of the mid-1880s, the rise of organized labor and the frequency of strikes, and migration to rapidly growing cities and immigration from abroad necessitated a kind of societal organization that an agrarian nation could not provide.

The deference of public policy to the interests of the powerful during the Gilded Age is a familiar story. The enactment of three laws in 1887 typified this development and hinted at the how the past would find a place when the nation showed an interest in world affairs. More than any other industry, railroads represented progress in the United States in the second half of the nineteenth century. The Interstate Commerce Act brought a modicum of regulation to the railroad business, essentially leaving the industry in the hands of its managers to rationalize operations and assure an uninterrupted flow of commerce.[100] The Dawes Severalty Act, promoted as an attempt to make Indians citizens and landowners, broke apart tribes as autonomous units and opened millions of acres of Indian lands to thousands of white settlers.[101] And the Hatch Act, a highly valuable tool in the development of corporate farming, accelerated the establishment of agricultural experiment stations. Taken as a whole, these three pieces of legislation symbolized the emergence of a modern, industrial nation, one in which land usage retained a crucial, though diminishing status.[102]

Conclusion

What was underway at the time of the Gilded Age was the initial construction of a proto-national security state. However unlikely that contention may seem, it places in context the use of federal law, police, and private armies against labor unions, the disenfranchisement of African Americans, the lethal efficiency of the U.S. Army at the Battle of Wounded Knee on December 29, 1890, which resulted in the death of perhaps 200 Sioux Indians (many of whom were women and children), and the passage of protective tariffs like the 1890 McKinley Tariff against foreign industrial competition. Throughout American history, and especially since the mid-eighteenth century, threats to the welfare of the general populace emanated from both domestic and foreign sources. Jefferson and his successors had hoped to

---

[100] Alfred D. Chandler, Jr., *The Visible Hand: The Managerial Revolution in American Business* (Cambridge: Harvard University Press, 1977), 130, 143–4, 171–2.

[101] One historian concludes that the grim process of Indian assimilation "stemmed from white economic self-interest." See Morton Keller, *Affairs of State: Public Life in Late Nineteenth Century America* (Cambridge: Harvard University Press, 1977), 457–60; quoted words, 457.

[102] John A. Garraty, *The New Commonwealth, 1877–1890* (New York: Harper & Row, 1968), 64–5.

provide security through a political economy of expansion and commerce. Their empire of liberty had vanished for a while, reappearing in far different guise after the Civil War and Reconstruction. Liberty and freedom thus gradually became equated with the modernization of industry and finance and with the enterprises of the powerful at home and abroad.

Absent from this tableau was a serious discussion of the relationship between this Second Industrial Revolution and republican virtue. The promise of democracy remained the hope of the many, while the advantages of wealth and power became the reality of the few. Walter Quentin Gresham of Indiana, a Union general, federal judge, and secretary of state, decried the lack of attention to the ideals of the early republic. The country needed leaders, he said in 1891, "with strong and resolute character, unspoiled by luxury,... able to see men and things as they really are, undeceived by outward show and conventionality."[103] Gresham feared the excesses of the laboring class and, in response, evoked the forgotten harmonies of Adam Smith by calling for "a more equitable division of the joint product of capital and labor."[104] About the imperial urge of his day, to which he contributed as Grover Cleveland's secretary of state from 1893 until his death in May 1895, he evidently never contemplated the similarities between this assertive impulse and Jefferson's invocation of an empire of liberty.

Gresham revered the sense of responsibility in America's founding generations and lamented the absence of comparable virtue in his own day. He would have been mistaken, though, had he celebrated the past as a better, simpler time. Despite widespread regard for an agrarian republic, which explains the strong appeal to many Americans in the late nineteenth century of populism and Henry George's idea of a single tax on real estate, the Jeffersonian Republicans and the Jacksonian Democrats who came after them were worldly and complex men. They lived for a future in which the United States would show the rest of humankind the power that resided in American liberty.

Conditions in 1890 were not promising for the realization of that ideal. The U.S. census had declared the frontier closed; Frederick Jackson Turner would shortly sound the alarm about the dire implications of that development for democracy's future. Labor discord was in the air as cities struggled under the weight of waves of immigration. Black Americans wondered, as did women, about their place in the industrial republic. The Farmers Alliance in the South and West challenged the verities of an industrial political economy and the arrogance of its barons, bankers, and corporate

---

[103] Quoted in Charles W. Calhoun, *Gilded Age Cato: The Life of Walter Q. Gresham* (Lexington: University Press of Kentucky, 1988), 4.

[104] Ibid., 5; on Gresham's concern about the excesses of democracy see Walter LaFeber, *The New Empire: An Interpretation of American Expansion, 1860–1898* (Ithaca: Cornell University Press, 1963), 14.

managers. Yet, few Americans were then prepared to address the effect of such turbulence on the nation.

In intellectual circles outside the observable rhythms of daily life, a response was nevertheless taking shape. Congregational minister Josiah Strong had published a book in 1885, *Our Country: Its Possible Future and Its Present Crisis*, in which he forecast a commanding position for the United States on the world stage. As did some other intellectuals at the time, especially John Quincy Adams's grandson Brooks Adams, Strong had a fascination with the so-called laws of history. He therefore contended that civilization – in his rendering, the center of empire – had arrived at "our mighty West, there to remain, for there is no further West." Beyond, he wrote with disdain, was "the Orient."[105] Naval captain Alfred Thayer Mahan was similarly resolute in his assessment of America's future. The historical importance of commerce to American identity made it imperative to build a modern navy, even if that activity led European powers to attribute it to the flowering of imperial ambitions. "Armed shipping," Mahan would declare in his 1890 classic, *The Influence of Seapower upon History*, "must follow the peaceful vessels of commerce."[106] In penning those words, he expressed no reservations about naval power similar to those Jefferson had held in 1808. Some years later, Charles A. Beard found a preview of Mahan's thesis as he considered the meaning of the Constitution. "The army and navy," he wrote, " . . . may be used also in forcing open foreign markets."[107]

With individual liberties diminished by a federal court system in thrall to Social Darwinism and corporate rights and a ruling elite devoted to laissez-faire economics, it remained to be seen what a turn toward empire meant for America's core values. Walter Quentin Gresham, whose independent spirit and defense of republican traditions made him a possible presidential candidate of the Populist Party in 1892, removed his name from consideration, but only after telling his supporters that the United States might not "escape a bloody revolution before this plutocracy of wealth surrenders its hold."[108] As secretary of state, he did much to found a proto–national security state, best symbolized by the ongoing construction of a modern navy. Indeed, Gresham's interventionist policies in the Americas and across the Pacific logically derived from the sense of mission that proponents of republican virtue had long accepted.[109]

---

[105] Josiah Strong, *Our Country: Its Possible Future and Its Present Crisis* (New York: Becker and Taylor, 1885), 29.

[106] A. T. Mahan, *The Influence of Seapower upon History, 1660–1783*, American Century Series ed. (New York: Hill and Wang, 1957), 71.

[107] Beard, *An Economic Interpretation of the Constitution*, 173.

[108] Quoted in Calhoun, *Gilded Age Cato*, 116.

[109] LaFeber, *The New Empire*, 197–241.

2

The First National Security State

Today the United States is practically sovereign on this continent, and its fiat
is law upon the subjects to which it confines its interposition.
Richard Olney, 1895

[Roosevelt is] clearly insane... and insanest upon war and its supreme glories.
Mark Twain

American institutions are on trial before a court of American citizens.
Eugene V. Debs, 1918

From the vantage point of the twenty-first century, it is evident that there
was more certainty than contingency in the emergence of the United States
as a great power in the 1890s. Advocates of an international presence for
the United States were hopeful of building their imperial dreams on the
dynamic growth of capital and industry at home.[1] For those living through
that tumultuous time, however, the growth of American power did not seem
inevitable. For many, the 1890s were fundamentally a time of passionate
conflict about what it meant to be an American and the critical importance
of basic values to the conduct of public affairs.

Three Americans who were born within a two-year span – Theodore Roosevelt in 1858 and William Jennings Bryan and Charlotte Perkins (Gilman)
in 1860 – had markedly contrasting ideas about identity and values. Add
to the list the slightly older Eugene V. Debs (1855), and the spectrum of
views reflects contemporary thinking about modernity and industry in a
global imperial age.[2] Questions about what constituted modernity and what

---

[1] On the context in which the "large policy" of imperial expansion occurred, see Walter
LaFeber, *The American Search for Opportunity, 1865–1913* (New York: Cambridge University Press, 1993), 1–128.
[2] Also born in 1860, Jane Addams would have much to say about the meaning of democracy
for core values in industrial America. And, she opposed American entry into World War I;
see Louise W. Knight, *Citizen: Jane Addams and the Struggle for Democracy* (Chicago:
University of Chicago Press, 2006).

direction modernization should take were fiercely debated around 1900 in a nation that was decidedly liberal in the nineteenth-century sense, yet replete with the prospect of democratic inclusion except for most nonwhite Americans. Many women were pressing for a greater presence in the public realm. Modernity here therefore refers to the vibrant condition of America as seen in the political economy and changing social relations of the time.

Progress had brought prosperity to the nation and would continue to do so. The success of a capitalist political economy imbued late-nineteenth-century America with an unprecedented accumulation of wealth and luxury. Faith in material progress was all but the national norm. For many Americans, the fears held by the Puritans and the founding generation that moral decay necessarily followed economic success were laid to rest. For others, the rapid growth of corporate power and the recent emergence of a professional managerial class brought into question the continued vitality of the republican ethos. The passions and emotions of the time delayed a reckoning between values and progress. There nevertheless existed considerable potential for widespread alienation from the modern industrial era and, thus, for the rise of a love-hate relationship with America itself among the masses – particularly those with little power or privilege. They questioned whether democratic values could exist in a heavily class-based political economy. The internationalist turn in foreign policy ultimately provided an answer, one buttressing the new expansionism. How that pressing issue got addressed in the short term is reflected in the ideas and lives of the four contemporaries.

As moralist and reformer, Theodore Roosevelt concealed profound anxieties about the nation's future (and his place in it) in a whirlwind of energy.[3] His political connections and accomplishments in New York landed him the post of assistant secretary of the navy in President William McKinley's first administration. In that capacity and as a volunteer in the war with Spain, his self-righteousness and belief in a providential destiny for his country made Roosevelt the embodiment of prevailing myths about modern America. Just as the nation had recovered from the travail of the Civil War, the once physically frail Roosevelt had made his body strong. Just as the nation was shedding its rural, agrarian past, the educated Easterner moved confidently into an industrial world still in its infancy. And just as the nation opened its arms to millions of newcomers, Roosevelt the politician – not beholden to the rapacious "robber barons" of a somewhat earlier day – pronounced

[3] Several occasionally contradictory sources have influenced my thinking about Roosevelt. See John Morton Blum, *The Republican Roosevelt* (Cambridge: Harvard University Press, 1965); Edmund Morris, *The Rise of Theodore Roosevelt* (New York: Coward, McCann and Geoghegan, 1979); John Milton Cooper Jr., *The Warrior and the Priest: Woodrow Wilson and Theodore Roosevelt* (Cambridge: Harvard University Press, 1983); Sarah Watts, *Rough Rider in the White House: Theodore Roosevelt and the Politics of Desire* (Chicago: University of Chicago Press, 2003).

himself the friend of America's workers. He was at once the voice of reason in the making of public policy and, in historian Sarah Watts's telling, an advocate of "violence as an unfortunate but necessary, and even edifying, element in the grand themes that drove history."[4] Like Brooks Adams, who tendered a sobering view of history in *The Law of Civilization and Decay* (1896), Roosevelt proclaimed it America's mission to preserve civilization. Yet, he also deeply feared the inevitability of personal and, thus, national decay. It would require, he averred, "the warlike power of a civilized people" to stem the tide of history.[5]

William Jennings Bryan positioned himself as champion of the nation's farmers and those dispossessed in an impersonal, industrial age. Running for president in 1896 as the candidate of the Democrat Party and the People's Party, Bryan hoped to reinvigorate the democratic legacy of Jefferson and Jackson. He eloquently denounced the gold standard, the bankers who supported it, and the world they were making. Despite his rhetorical fire, Bryan's was a cautious radicalism favoring the monetary inflation that "free silver" would bring. Yet, he remained strangely out of touch with the cooperative philosophy characteristic of much of the Populist movement throughout the South and the Great Plains. The Omaha Platform of 1892, the manifesto of the National Farmers Alliance, had not advocated rejecting the power of corporate industry; rather, it sought to harness its manifest excesses and temper them with direct democracy. The movement culture of the Alliance envisioned a vital nation whose most important frontier – economic and political reform – was still open.[6]

Like many of their agrarian predecessors and contemporaries, neither Bryan nor members of the Northwestern Farmers Alliance and other bimetallists questioned the propriety of the search for markets for American products.[7] By 1896, the cooperative spirit of the Alliance movement had been subsumed into a much less radical version of political economy, one more congenial to American traditions. This fusion of Alliance objectives with local or regional politics has led to Populism being equated with antimodernism. Yet, in the hands of the National Farmers Alliance, Populism was an attempt, however flawed, to ask whether modernity could be faithful to America's basic values. Historian Jackson Lears observes that modern culture was marked by "the craving for comfort and the triumph of clock

---

[4] Watts, *Rough Rider in the White House*, 4.

[5] Quoted in ibid., 23.

[6] Lawrence Goodwyn, *Democratic Promise: The Populist Moment in America* (New York: Oxford University Press, 1976); on Bryan and Alliance politics in the early 1890s see Michael Kazin, *A Godly Hero: The Life of William Jennings Bryan* (New York: Alfred A. Knopf, 2006), 21, 24, 26, 36.

[7] William Appleman Williams, *The Roots of the Modern American Empire: A Study of the Growth and Shaping of Social Consciousness in a Marketplace Society* (New York: Random House, 1969), 299, 387, 391–2.

time." Moreover, nervous American bankers and industrialists had appropriated the ideas of Adam Smith, viewing them as the building blocks of modernity and, thus, as servant to their own misguided celebration of liberal individualism.[8] The Alliance question about modernity got lost in the 1896 presidential campaign and in the continuing quest for an expanding marketplace, an objective that met with great favor throughout the agrarian South and the ranching and mining West.

The diverse experiences of Charlotte Perkins Gilman and Eugene V. Debs had predisposed them to favor a political economy that was far more communitarian in nature than that supported by most politicians and industrial capitalists. Gilman's reformist convictions reflected the activist history of her famous relatives, the Beechers, including Lyman Beecher and Harriet Beecher Stowe. A child of privilege, Gilman, unlike Roosevelt, rejected the traditional role a person of her status was expected to play. Despite grave self-doubts that were every bit as debilitating as those of her male contemporary, Gilman turned her own anxieties into a feminist critique of industrial society. By 1890, she was railing against the concentration of wealth in America and found herself in sympathy with the radical message of Social Gospel advocates, the National Farmers Alliance, and the labor movement.

The little-remembered Nationalist Clubs, inspired by the writings of Edward Bellamy, especially his acclaimed *Looking Backward* (1888), provided an outlet for her reform politics. The Nationalists, who condemned the excesses of the Gilded Age, called for a return to ethical behavior and the pursuit of equality in public life. There existed, however, a serious contradiction in Nationalist sentiment; it was inherently paternalistic and, as such, possessed authoritarian tendencies, which Gilman shared.[9] By the mid-1890s, she had immersed herself in women's politics in California and honed a critique of male power and authority that found expression in perhaps her best-known work, *Women and Economics* (1898). In it, she criticized patterns of material consumption by women as "unnatural greed," arguing that they derived from "the brutal ferocity of excessive male energy struggling in the market-place as in a battlefield." Given the onset of war with Spain, the military comparison was surely intentional. Gilman believed that unchecked economic power produced alienation and could only be comprehended if the role of men in its creation was convincingly demonstrated.[10] Such was one purpose of *Women and Economics*.

---

[8] T. J. Jackson Lears, *No Place of Grace: Antimodernism and the Transformation of American Culture, 1880–1920* (New York: Pantheon Books, 1981), 11; quoted words, 18–19.

[9] Mary A. Hill, *Charlotte Perkins Gilman: The Making of a Radical Feminist, 1860–1896* (Philadelphia: Temple University Press, 1980), 167–82.

[10] Charlotte Perkins Gilman, *Women and Economics: A Study of the Economic Relation between Men and Women as a Factor in Social Evolution*, ed. with an introduction by Carl N. Degler (New York: Harper & Row, 1966), 117–21; quoted words, 119.

Debs, who was skeptical of the good intentions of the middle-class Nationalists and for a time suspicious of the Populist Party, saw the salvation of an industrial nation "in a dignified wage [that] was the *sine qua non* of a participatory citizenship," as one of his biographers writes. Industrial America could only act humanely and be true to American traditions if a self-reliant working class dominated political life. A cooperative commonwealth would give meaning to those traditions. Anything less would constitute an abandonment of the nation's core values, as Debs understood them.

Like other radicals and reformers, indeed like all prominent public figures of the late nineteenth century, Debs had his contradictions. His emphasis on individual responsibility and his veneration of home-grown democracy resulted in great antipathy toward immigrant labor, an animus he only partly suppressed after 1893 when he began to focus on the oppression of all labor by corporate power.[11] By the election of 1896, which would bring the friend of industrialists and tariff advocate William McKinley to the presidency, Debs was not yet fully committed to socialism. What he did support, as did the Populists, was an equitable distribution of wealth, something that silver coinage, to which Bryan was deeply committed, could not produce.[12] When Debs finally embraced socialism, he located it within an American Christian and democratic tradition that was not beholden to any foreign ideology.

In Theodore Roosevelt's parlance, the warlike power of a civilized people would be called on to take on a bevy of new, unfamiliar responsibilities commencing in 1898. From Lincoln's secretary of state, William Henry Seward, through Mahan and Roosevelt, men who did not doubt the nation's destiny answered the call of empire. Dissent from the amoral norms of industrial America as voiced in the 1890s, whether by Debs, Bryan, or Gilman, was rendered largely irrelevant. Within a generation, those new responsibilities would lead the United States into a global conflict. When that occurred, Americans – as they confronted a modern, dangerous world not really of their making – would discern the unhappy fate awaiting their cherished core values.

Creating a Security State

Time was a fearful thing for those opposed to industrial culture or uncertain about what it meant for the American republic. Material progress increased the amount of leisure time of the propertied classes and ruling elites, and leisure arguably prefigured moral lassitude and, therefore, national decay.

---

[11] Nick Salvatore, *Eugene V. Debs: Citizen and Socialist* (Urbana: University of Illinois Press, 1982), 99–108; quoted words, 100.
[12] Ibid., 156.

Economist and social critic Thorstein Veblen observed that it was "not sufficient merely to possess wealth or power. The wealth or power must be put in evidence." Conspicuous leisure, he maintained, was the inevitable result of the acquisition of property. Veblen's critique of wealth and class, *The Theory of the Leisure Class* (1899), questioned one of the enduring verities of the American experience: the felicitous connection between ownership, typically of land, or accumulation of wealth and progress.[13]

A basic question of the age was whether progress could be reconciled with tradition. Bryan's answer was to try to slow the onset of industrial modernity in order to compel an accommodation between business corporations and the agricultural heartland. The Great Commoner got more than he bargained for with the rapid emergence of modern agriculture through technological innovation and mechanization,[14] a development that helped keep him at the margins of public life despite his several attempts to win the presidency. (He would serve Woodrow Wilson as secretary of state until resigning as a result of the *Lusitania* crisis.) The more thoroughgoing critiques of corporate growth and modern culture by Gilman and Debs, complementary in their analyses of the divisive power of the market, resonated with significant but limited numbers of Americans.[15]

War in the Caribbean and the Pacific in 1898 and the acquisition of colonies as one of its outcomes ended the contest over who would define modernity. From that time onward, the proponents of an active global role for the United States put aside their residual anxieties about engagement abroad and endeavored to preserve traditions, as they understood them, through the exercise of power. In short, the long-held belief in American exceptionalism had entered a new phase: The United States was compelled, and hence entitled, to play a leading role in the international arena. How had that happened and, more to the point, how did this belief come to be exemplified by a national security state?

The answer to these questions involves a consideration of political economy, the growth of military power, and the projection of a renascent national identity. The severe depression of the 1890s shook the public's faith in the laissez-faire basis of the American economy, in the ability of the market to provide growth and security. The cacophony of voices offering alternatives to unfettered capitalism challenged that aspect of national identity even as the closing of the frontier apparently foretold the end of providentially blessed expansion. Like Brooks Adams and others, Roosevelt feared for the future of capitalism in America; worried that a depression was at hand, he

---

[13] Thorstein Veblen, *The Theory of the Leisure Class: An Economic Study of Institutions,* Modern Library ed. (New York: Random House, 1961), 28–31; quoted words, 29.

[14] Olivier Zunz, *Making America Corporate, 1870–1920* (Chicago: University of Chicago Press, 1990), 150–73.

[15] Gilman, *Women and Economics,* 68.

thus characterized the social and economic chaos of the day as a dire threat to class, nation, and civilization itself.[16] Although he was scarcely more at ease with bankers than the querulous Adams, Roosevelt placed no faith in silver as a primary currency.

Freedom as he conceived of it was at stake for Roosevelt in matters of money, banking, and commerce. Too much silver in circulation and low tariffs that failed to protect agriculture and manufacturing, for example, were not good for America and could impair its civilizing mission. Roosevelt and like-minded contemporaries did not consider the possibility that their fear of economic catastrophe, whether genuine or not, was the result of an unbroken history of expansion without serious consequence or accountability. Nor did they acknowledge that their understanding of freedom, a conjuncture of laissez-faire thought and a belief in Social Darwinism, was exclusionary in that it was becoming indistinguishable from individual economic rights. As the outlook for boundless opportunity appeared to dim and chaos loom, commercial, financial, and governing elites devoted themselves to asserting America's uniqueness. In the process, they transformed their nation into an international power, albeit one that by virtue of its core values clung to exceptionalist assumptions.

Threats to the rule of law and fissures in the prevailing social order seemed to pervade the United States in the aftermath of the Civil War. Opposition to Radical Reconstruction, the emergence of the first Ku Klux Klan, labor strife, conflict with the Plains Indians, the rise of the Farmers Alliance, and advocacy of the rights of women challenged the legal and societal status quo. The response of governing and business elites put the power of the state on display in ways that led directly to a global presence for the United States. What transpired in the three decades after 1865 might fairly be called internal colonialism. Where practicable, as in the South, this result was achieved by the infusion of technology and capital. In effect, southern political autonomy, as manifested in the return to power by Democrats, became the quid pro quo for rejoining the Union and the acceptance of a subordinate economic role. Colonialism in the West was of a rather different order. The West as an internal colony, which provided food, minerals, an outlet for investment, and markets for eastern interests, existed partly as a result of the wanton destruction of the nonmarket culture of the Plains Indians. The tools of destruction were biocide – that is, the near extinction of the buffalo – and technology, whereby the gun was used to quell what remained of Indian resistance to the advance of American civilization.[17]

At the time of the battle between U.S. Army forces and the Sioux at Wounded Knee in late 1890, officials believed that many Indians stood in

[16] Watts, *Rough Rider in the White House*, 32–3.
[17] Michael Adas, *Dominance by Design: Technological Imperatives and America's Civilizing Mission* (Cambridge: Belknap Press of Harvard University Press, 2006), 96–108.

the way of civilization.[18] Their defeat accelerated incipient efforts by the political class to get laboring citizens and recent immigrants invested in the future of a corporate, industrial nation. These attempts to civilize, or Americanize, society's lower orders were problematic, though, because they raised questions about the scope of democracy and, ultimately, core values. The "business unionism" of the American Federation of Labor accepted an economic division of labor in the United States, thereby lessening the likelihood of serious clashes between capital and at least the skilled sectors of the working class.

America's civilizing mission was becoming synonymous with the preservation and projection of core values. To the extent that civilization was more or less secure at home by the mid-1890s, the expansionist legacy of the colonial era determined that its fate thereafter would depend on acceptance abroad. That development was welcome to men like Roosevelt who longed for a new frontier to conquer. The most appealing, yet not the only, object of their attention was East Asia, where entrepreneurs, diplomats, and missionaries could draw on their individual and collective expertise to revitalize what they believed to be backward or premodern societies.[19]

With the issuance of the Open Door notes of 1899 and 1900 and the dispatch of troops to China, the occupation of Cuba, and the military response to Emilio Aguinaldo's rebellion in the Philippines, the first national security state came into existence. Some years earlier, President Benjamin Harrison's secretary of state, James G. Blaine of Maine, a leader in the Republican Party, had begun its construction. Blaine believed in American exceptionalism, embodied the political culture's search for regional security by resorting to the Monroe Doctrine (thus prefiguring the Roosevelt Corollary), and agreed with prevailing racialist notions about the superiority of Anglo-Saxon values and institutions.[20] As a result, he was predisposed to think about American identity in terms familiar to post-1945 national security officials.

This statement merits further consideration. One prominent scholar has asserted, "The concept of a national security policy emerged in the United States only after World War II."[21] This understanding of security policy ignores similarities between the 1890s and the later era. To be sure, the language of security policy and, as the debates over empire in the 1890s revealed, the extent of consensus supporting a national security state differed in the two periods. Nevertheless, the development of unprecedented

---

[18] Jeffrey Ostler, *The Plains Sioux and U.S. Colonialism from Lewis and Clark to Wounded Knee* (New York: Cambridge University Press, 2004), 289–337.

[19] Michael H. Hunt, *The Making of a Special Relationship: The United States and China to 1914* (New Haven: Yale University Press, 1983); Adas, *Dominance by Design*, 105–9.

[20] David Healy, *James G. Blaine and Latin America* (Columbia: University of Missouri Press, 2001), 1–16.

[21] Richard D. Challener, *Admirals, Generals, and American Foreign Policy, 1898–1914* (Princeton: Princeton University Press, 1973), 11.

firepower, the perception of hostile states threatening America's vital interests and therefore its values, and the use of local forces and covert activities
for internal security purposes resonated across time.

Blaine did not shrink from selective engagement abroad. His policy
toward Latin America was intended to protect U.S. interests in the Western
Hemisphere. He had hoped to convene an inter-American conference in
1881 during his first term as secretary of state. In the interim, pressures
increased in Congress to expand commerce with Latin America even to
the point of forming a hemispheric trading bloc. Under Blaine's aegis, an
inter-American meeting opened in Washington in October 1889. From Latin
America came diplomats who were met by businessmen and financiers, few
of whom spoke any Spanish or Portuguese. Argentina and Chile expressed
reservations about U.S. maneuvers aimed at dominating the proceedings,
which lasted until April 1890. An idea to form a regional customs union,
which Republicans in Congress would not have tolerated, gave way to blan-
dishments about freer trade; proposals for the arbitration of disputes ran
aground on the shoals of nationalism and sovereignty. An expressed willingness to create an inter-American bank, to be headquartered in Washington,
went untested.[22]

What to make of Blaine's efforts? In short, they represented the new
thinking about political economy and foreign policy that was gaining favor
with some intellectuals and among the business and political classes. Blaine
focused his efforts on Latin America, yet shared the conviction of his age that
American power would manifest itself around the world, notably in China,
through entry into generally untapped markets. That Blaine was an avowed
sinophobe does not vitiate his determination in that regard. Reciprocity
provisions in the 1890 McKinley Tariff afforded an opportunity to advance
American power. Brazil provided the laboratory with the signing of a trade
pact in 1891, which also resulted in ties with the Brazilian military.[23] This
relationship heralded the emergence of a security ethos; that is, a way of
thinking about security that thereafter assumed military prowess to be the
most reliable guarantor of prosperity.

Among economic and political elites, what it meant to be American –
forward looking and self-reliant – had long been tied to commercial opportunity. Alfred Thayer Mahan, in an 1890 essay entitled "The United States
Looking Outward," quoted Blaine as saying, "It is not an ambitious destiny
for a country so great as ours to manufacture only what we can consume, or
produce only what we can eat."[24] More than a century after British radical
Richard Price had counseled America about political economy and security,

[22] Healy, *James G. Blaine*, 147–59.
[23] Steven C. Topik, *Trade and Gunboats: The United States and Brazil in the Age of Empire* (Stanford: Stanford University Press, 1996), 2.
[24] A. T. Mahan, "The United States Looking Outward," *The Atlantic*, December 1890, p. 817.

his advice was again disregarded. In a world increasingly viewed as dangerous, the identity or "destiny" that Blaine envisioned needed protection. On that premise was America's first national security state constructed.

Some of its constituent parts were already in place. Gaining currency was the belief that war was a viable instrument of national policy. The wars against the Plains Indians had demonstrated the technological and doctrinal readiness of the U.S. Army to play a greater role in national affairs. Also, Mahan was hardly the only officer calling for the modernization of the navy; Benjamin Harrison's Secretary of the Navy Benjamin F. Tracy supported a battleship fleet and a change of mission. The expense of a battleship navy would be a small price to pay for security and the safety of American commerce. In 1889, Tracy observed that "war, though defensive in principle, may be conducted most effectively by being offensive in its operations." Echoing Mahan two years later, he predicted, "The sea will be the future seat of empire. And we shall rule it as certainly as the sun doth rise." In fact, public support for a powerful navy and a security policy that might place American interests at risk grew when one of the first ships of the new navy was christened the USS *Iowa*.[25] Linking the nation's agricultural heartland with industry, commerce, and security helped circumvent opposition to the unprecedented changes taking place in the public expression of American identity.

The historian Richard Hofstadter concluded that "the civic frustrations of the era created also a restless aggressiveness, a desire to be assured that the power and vitality of the nation were not waning."[26] He believed that America's power and vitality resided in its basic values and democratic institutions. Hofstadter erred, though, in suggesting that the aggressiveness of the 1890s sprang solely from the unsettling events of that turbulent decade. In fact, they were only symptomatic of something more troubling.

Force had long held a central place in American political culture, as seen in the long history of slavery and inhumane treatment of Indians. It also found expression in Roosevelt and his closest associates, who identified American core values as the last bastion of civilization. A bold statement reflecting the transformation of American foreign policy, one designed to protect basic values, came in 1895 during the Venezuelan boundary crisis. Secretary of State Richard Olney, in effect, renounced John Winthrop's image of America as a model for others. Henceforth, the United States would articulate its identity more widely and assertively. "Today the United States is practically sovereign on this continent," intoned Olney in a heated diplomatic note to Great Britain, "and its fiat is law upon the subjects to which it confines its

---

[25] Walter LaFeber, *The New Empire: An Interpretation of American Expansion, 1860–1898* (Ithaca: Cornell University Press, 1963), 121–7; quoted words, 123, 127.
[26] Richard Hofstadter, *The Paranoid Style in American Politics and Other Essays* (New York: Vintage Books, 1967), 158.

interposition."[27] Remaining uncertain after Olney's declaration and also on the eve of the war with Spain in 1898 was the effect on the nation's core values of a foreign policy backed by force of arms.

Virtue, Values, and Security

For Theodore Roosevelt, self-interest and a presumption of selflessness coalesced in the pursuit of empire. "We made the promise to give Cuba independence," he wrote in his autobiography with a righteous conviction echoed by Ronald Reagan's support in the 1980s of anti-Sandinista forces in Nicaragua, "and we kept that promise."[28] Roosevelt's ostensible solicitude for Cuban independence belies the intensity of the domestic debate over involvement in a war for empire.[29] He and other turn-of-the-century national security officials never saw war with dispassionate eyes. War was a political and personal testing ground. During the crisis with the British over Venezuela, Roosevelt declared, "[T]his country needs a war."[30] All they held dear as public and private men was at stake in the contest for empire on the global frontier; the logic of their actions since 1890 had left them with no choice but to enter the fray in Latin America and Asia.

To the relief of men like Secretary of State John Hay and Republican senators Henry Cabot Lodge of Massachusetts and Albert J. Beveridge of Indiana, among others, both the European powers and the United States supported the cause of reform in China at the time of the Boxer Uprising of 1898–1900. Broadly based military action against the Boxers let the Americans know that they were not to be the sole guardians of civilization against what Roosevelt fearfully termed "savagery and barbarism."[31] As clearly as any official at the time, Beveridge understood the vital connection between political economy and security, a linkage that prefigured economic planning at the end of World War II. In one version of his famous September 1898 campaign speech, "The March of the Flag," Beveridge intoned,

Today, we are raising more than we can consume. Today, we are making more than we can use. Today, our industrial society is congested; there are more workers than there is work; there is more capital than there is investment. We do not need more money – we need more circulation, more employment. Therefore we must find

[27] U.S. Department of State, *Papers Relating to the Foreign Relations of the United States, 1895* (Washington, DC: Government Printing Office, 1896), I: 551.

[28] Theodore Roosevelt, *An Autobiography* (New York: Macmillan, 1913), 504.

[29] Louis A. Pérez, Jr., *The War of 1898: The United States and Cuba in History and Historiography* (Chapel Hill: University of North Carolina Press, 1998), 34–44.

[30] Elting E. Morison et al., eds., *The Letters of Theodore Roosevelt*, vol. I: *The Years of Preparation, 1868–1898* (Cambridge: Harvard University Press, 1951), 504.

[31] Quoted in Hunt, *Making of a Special Relationship*, 206.

new markets for our produce, new occupation for our capital, new work for our labor.[32]

To do other than defend nascent security interests with force would not only undermine the basis of American prosperity, it perhaps also would put civilization itself at risk. The advocates of empire worried that the task they had set for themselves was too difficult. "This nation [must] keep undimmed," Roosevelt implored, "the honorable traditions inherited from the men who with the sword founded it and by the sword preserved it."[33] Engaging in military conflict would thus ensure national unity, joining Americans in common cause not evident since long before the Civil War.

This desire for combat as essential to national identity helps explain the hatred of Roosevelt and his compatriots for pacifists and anti-imperialists. Roosevelt condemned pacifists as "active agents of the devil" whose aversion to conflict would lead to the decline of America.[34] Anti-imperialists, he wrote to General Leonard Wood in 1901, were "unhung (*sic*) traitors."[35] Only heroic action stood between civilization and chaos. Anti-imperialists like Mark Twain could not abide the reflexive glorification of war. Roosevelt is "clearly insane," Twain would subsequently comment, "and insanest upon war and its supreme glories."[36] In the political contest over empire in 1898, it seemed as if the final battle over American identity was being waged. As a group, the anti-imperialists opposed the annexation of the Philippines, yet not all opposed war with Spain, let alone annexation of Hawaii. The acquisition of Puerto Rico scarcely caught their attention. What to do about Cuba confounded Americans on all sides of the imperial question.[37]

In fact, there was less to the debates over empire than met the eye. Expansionists had framed the debate years earlier, arguing that a strong international posture would protect old and new commercial markets – the substance of America's dynamic corporate economy. For leading anti-imperialists, the question became not whether to go abroad in search of markets to exploit, but how best to exploit them.

Some individuals who might have offered a persuasive case against empire were hamstrung by their own contradictions. William Jennings Bryan, for one, damaged his credibility because of his unflagging support for silver in a gold-standard world and because he urged senators to vote to ratify the

---

[32] Located in Chauncey M. Depew, ed., *The Library of Oratory, Ancient and Modern* (London: Globe Publishing Co., 1902), 439; my thanks to Carol C. Chin for this source.

[33] Theodore Roosevelt, *The Strenuous Life: Essays and Addresses* (London: Thomas Nelson & Sons, n.d. [1902?]), 266 for the words quoted.

[34] Quoted in Watts, *Rough Rider in the White House*, 215.

[35] Morison et al., eds., *The Letters of Theodore Roosevelt*, vol. III: *The Square Deal, 1901–1903* (Cambridge: Harvard University Press, 1951), 60.

[36] Quoted in Morris, *The Rise of Theodore Roosevelt*, 12.

[37] This story is still best followed in Robert L. Beisner, *Twelve against Empire: The Anti-Imperialists, 1898–1900* (New York: McGraw-Hill, 1968).

treaty with Spain and, thus, acquire the Philippines. To vote to ratify the treaty while opposing annexation put Bryan in an untenable position. He had contributed to making the American empire a reality, notwithstanding the fire of his subsequent anticolonial rhetoric.[38] Ultimately, Bryan's politics were at base exclusionary, as manifested at home and abroad. In the aftermath of *Plessy v. Ferguson*, 163 U.S. 537 (1896), he no more judged Cubans or Filipinos to be capable of self-government than he was prepared on principle to oppose the Supreme Court's ruling that curtailed the rights of African Americans. Bryan's view of the role of blacks in American society was not at odds with that of William Graham Sumner, who in 1899 declared, "[T]he negro's (*sic*) day is over. He is out of fashion."[39] The rights and benefits accompanying the tradition of republican governance were not to be indiscriminately extended. Even for the Great Commoner, democracy was not then meant to be universally enjoyed.

After Eugene Debs turned to socialism in 1897, he sought to craft a type that fit within the American political tradition, one in which electoral politics might mitigate the oppression of labor by industry. Debs was less straightforward about empire. Like many other public figures, he harbored considerable animosity toward racial minorities, which he rationalized by arguing that the Socialist Party was color-blind. Biographer Nick Salvatore writes that Debs "opposed the American annexation of the Philippines, Cuba, and Puerto Rico – while welcoming the absorption of Hawaii – on essentially racial grounds."[40] That Debs judged Hawaii to be an exception to his general rule, even more so because of its white entrepreneurial elite, seems incongruous.

Like her contemporaries, Charlotte Perkins Gilman did not escape the prejudices of her age, with all that meant for perpetuating an exclusionary politics. Yet, as much as Debs and rather more than Bryan, she wrestled with the contradictions in the American economy. Focusing on the place of women in society, Gilman observed how an industrial economy "denied free productive expression" to women (and to the majority of the laboring class). Encouraged, instead, was the development of an inveterate consuming ethos – the "habit and desire of taking." She wrote that "the world is full of the desire to get as much as possible and to give as little as possible." This struggle to prevail over others existed in the marketplace and on the battlefield.[41] Theodore Roosevelt, for one, would not have disagreed.

What few Americans understood was that exclusionary politics and an economy premised on unfettered growth had serious consequences for their

---

[38] Kazin, *A Godly Hero*, 89–93.

[39] Albert Galloway Keller and Maurice R. Davie, eds., *Essays of William Graham Sumner*, 2 vols. (Hamden: Archon Books, 1969), II: 297.

[40] Salvatore, *Eugene V. Debs*, 174–7, 185–7, 194; quoted words, 226.

[41] Gilman, *Women and Economics*, 117–9.

hallowed traditions. War with Spain and acquisition of the Philippine Islands did not bode well for the future of virtue in the American republic. Populist Tom Watson was one who did comprehend the costs of infusing identity with a martial spirit: "The Spanish War finished us. The blare of the bugle drowned the voice of the Reformer."[42] The first crucial test of the effect of empire on values arose with the question of self-governance for Cuba and the Philippines. Matters of race and ethnicity at once became signposts of deep prejudices that were inseparable from the course of empire.

After the onset of the initial rebellion against Spain in 1868, efforts to base Cuban identity on the relative absence of race as a critical component of society, which would have lessened the power of class structures, met with increasing resistance. By the time of U.S. intervention in 1898, white Cuban leaders were striving to present the movement for independence as an attempt to construct a civilization that would resonate with prevailing attitudes about modernity in the United States. Ironically, this endeavor amounted to a quest for the island's own form of republican virtue. The problem was that American leaders were ill disposed to see most Cubans as comparably civilized.[43] An independent, nationalist Cuba therefore constituted a threat to America's imperial identity. According to historian Louis A. Pérez Jr., in 1898 "the United States confronted the anathema of all American policymakers since Jefferson – the spectre of Cuban independence." The timing of intervention was intended to forestall its realization.[44] Cuban leaders knew well the bind they were in. Máximo Gómez exclaimed, "We are before a Tribunal, and the Tribunal is formed by the Americans."[45] Cuba Libre, or independence, was too uncertain to leave to Cubans who, in the damning words of General S. B. M. Young, "are no more capable of self-government than the savages of Africa."[46]

Before 1890, America's core values were held up to others as qualities worthy of emulation. Thereafter, the United States actively engaged the world to protect its economic interests and enhance its security. The question quickly became how best to preserve order abroad so that others would have an opportunity to make American values their own. The case of Cuba, to which values like self-determination evidently did not then apply, would prove highly instructive to future policymakers while also showing the implicit contradictions in an imperial foreign policy. Drawing on its newly

[42] Quoted in Charles Bergquist, *Labor and the Course of American Democracy: US History in Latin American Perspective* (London: Verso, 1996), 53.

[43] Ada Ferrer, *Insurgent Cuba: Race, Nation, and Revolution, 1868–1898* (Chapel Hill: University of North Carolina Press, 1999).

[44] Louis A. Pérez, Jr., *Cuba between Two Empires, 1878–1902* (Pittsburgh: University of Pittsburgh Press, 1983), 170–8; quoted words, 170.

[45] Quoted in Ferrer, *Insurgent Cuba*, 188.

[46] Quoted in Walter Millis, *The Martial Spirit: A Study of Our War with Spain* (New York: Houghton Mifflin, 1931), 362.

burnished identity as an arriviste great power, the United States intervened in Cuba in opposition to Cuban freedom.[47] The United States occupied the island from 1899 until May 1902; Secretary of War Elihu Root, who understandably feared a violent insurrection against the American presence, coordinated occupation policies.

Endeavoring to bring order to Cuba, Washington acted on two fronts. First, it created the preconditions for a protectorate under which self-rule and economic growth might occur. The 1901 Platt Amendment gave the United States unprecedented power to influence Cuban affairs. Included among its provisions was a prohibition on treaty making without U.S. approval. In addition, the United States would receive rights to a naval base at Guantánamo Bay, and the U.S. government reserved the right to intervene as it deemed necessary to preserve independence by preempting the onset of disorder. Should Cuba not accept the Platt Amendment, free trade in sugar – the lifeblood of the island's economy – would end. With no plausible alternative, Cuba acceded to the onerous terms of the amendment. Not even the most ardent anti-imperialist, such as Republican Senator George F. Hoar of Massachusetts, strongly opposed it. The Platt Amendment would set the contours of U.S.-Cuban relations until its repeal in 1934 and long remain a rallying cry against Washington's meddling in Cuban politics.[48]

Establishing a protectorate, however, did not provide Washington with the security it desired in the Florida straits and the Caribbean, particularly after the independence of Panama in 1903 made possible the construction of a canal across the isthmus of that country. The vicissitudes of Cuba's domestic politics raised fears of revolution in Washington, leading to intervention under the terms of the Platt Amendment. The second occupation of Cuba lasted from September 1906 until January 1909. Along with the Marines, U.S.-trained local forces became vital security assets, as had been the case in conflicts with Indians after the Civil War.[49] This same tactic would also be adopted in the Dominican Republic in 1915 when the United States formed a *Guardia Nacional Dominicana* to assume police functions.[50] In Haiti, Marine General Smedley D. Butler also moved in 1915 to create a *Gendarmerie d'Haiti* to provide for stability and order.[51] About the work of the Army of Cuban Pacification and the Rural Guard, Theodore Roosevelt

---

[47] David Healy, *Drive to Hegemony: The United States in the Caribbean 1898–1917* (Madison: University of Wisconsin Press, 1988), 47.

[48] Louis A. Pérez, Jr., *Cuba under the Platt Amendment, 1902–1934* (Pittsburgh: University of Pittsburgh Press, 1986).

[49] Allan Reed Millett, *The Politics of Intervention: The Military Occupation of Cuba, 1906–1909* (Columbus: Ohio State University Press, 1968), 122–33, 222–7.

[50] Bruce J. Calder, *The Impact of Intervention: The Dominican Republic during the U.S. Occupation of 1916–1924* (Austin: University of Texas Press, 1984), 54–62.

[51] Mary A. Renda, *Taking Haiti: Military Occupation and the Culture of U.S. Imperialism, 1915–1940* (Chapel Hill: University of North Carolina Press, 2001), 31–2.

would counsel Secretary of War William Howard Taft, "If any bloodshed occurs it should be between Cubans and Cubans."[52] Cuba had thus become integrated into the American political and military system and was an essential part of its defense perimeter, which Root had earlier called "our line of exterior defense."[53]

Subduing an anti-American uprising in the Philippines created a site for pursuing strategic interests across the Pacific. The situation in the Philippines was more fraught than conditions in Cuba for two reasons. The Monroe Doctrine, which in the guise of the Roosevelt Corollary arguably served as a rationale for efforts to impose stability in Cuba, had nothing to do with extra-hemispheric affairs. Indeed, the difficulty of defending the islands was evident at a time when Japanese power was markedly on the rise. Japan's dramatic victory in war with Russia suggested that a U.S. policy of deterrence would have little effect. Furthermore, the physical reality of a formal empire greatly unsettled many Americans, even if they were not active anti-imperialists, leading them to ponder the fate of their republic.

Those concerns were not unfounded. Could the Filipinos be prepared for self-government any more than African Americans? The implication at home and abroad of the ruling in *Plessy* in favor of separate but equal legal spheres suggested that not all people were entitled to share the bounty of republican governance. A similar conclusion characterized American immigration policy; excluding as many Chinese, Japanese, Filipinos, Hawaiians, and Cubans as possible from entry into the United States lay at the heart of the policy after 1900.[54] Roosevelt, who in 1896 had denounced Bryan and the Populists as purveyors of terror, found in democratic politics the roots of national and personal weakness. He inveighed against ineffectual men "who cant about 'liberty' and the 'consent of the governed.'"[55] As Sarah Watts aptly observes, "Roosevelt valued the idea of democracy more than its reality."[56]

The opponents of annexation of the Philippines, including some members of the Fourth Estate who had briefly engaged in self-censorship while reporting on the war, had their patriotism questioned, were threatened with legal action for possible sedition, and were denounced as weaklings unable to shoulder the rigors of modern life. No one hectored the foes of empire better than Albert Beveridge. He embraced the very idea of empire not just as the salvation of civilization but also as fulfillment of the will of God, who "has marked us as his chosen people, henceforth to lead in the regeneration

[52] Roosevelt to Taft, 2 October 1906, quoted in Millett, *The Politics of Intervention*, 123.
[53] Quoted in Healy, *Drive to Hegemony*, 133.
[54] Robert E. Hannigan, *The New World Power: American Foreign Policy, 1898–1917* (Philadelphia: University of Pennsylvania Press, 2002), 110.
[55] Quoted in Watts, *Rough Rider in the White House*, 64.
[56] Ibid., 63.

of the world."[57] As on the plains of the American West and in the mountains of Cuba, native forces would do the bidding of the U.S. government in the unfriendly terrain of the Philippines.[58] Crucial to the success of the counterinsurgency effort were the Native Scouts who employed propaganda, bribery, assassination, and the bioterror of crop destruction to weaken opposition to the United States.[59] Resistance subsided after Emilio Aguinaldo's capture in 1901.

Despite Roosevelt's conviction that national character was forged in combat and, thus, empire, he understood that a modern political economy was necessary to sustain an international presence. Yet, whatever the dramatic advances in technology and management meant for America's productive capacity around 1900, there were not commensurate gains in economic knowledge or policy planning. Roosevelt fled from his responsibility to engage the tariff question; in a letter to Henry Cabot Lodge in 1895, he denounced free trade, which he had supported as a young man, as a "pernicious indulgence," claiming that it produced "fatty degeneration of the moral fiber."[60] As president, Roosevelt feared the harm that rate adjustment would do to the political fortunes of the Republican Party. Similarly, investment banking in the early 1900s depended more on the faith of finance capitalists in one another than on the regulation of banking practices by law. The Panic of 1907, which threatened local stock exchanges and led to runs by depositors on several major banks, revealed the poverty of economic thought that characterized American banking; only timely intervention by J. Pierpont Morgan to bolster federal efforts kept the system intact.[61] The salient point is that, if the fate of civilization depended on U.S. leadership in the global economy, then the health of what Roosevelt, Lodge, and others called the civilized world was indeed precarious. Not until the passage of the Underwood Tariff and the Federal Reserve Act of 1913 during the presidency of Woodrow Wilson would Congress and the executive branch seriously address these vital matters of global political economy.[62]

---

[57] Quoted in Stuart Creighton Miller, *"Benevolent Assimilation": The American Conquest of the Philippines, 1899–1903* (New Haven: Yale University Press, 1982), 131.

[58] Walter L. Williams, "United States Indian Policy and the Debate over Philippine Annexation: Implications for the Origins of American Imperialism," *Journal of American History* 66 (March 1980): 810–31.

[59] Brian McAllister Linn, *The U.S. Army and Counterinsurgency in the Philippine War, 1899–1902* (Chapel Hill: University of North Carolina Press, 1989).

[60] *The Letters of Theodore Roosevelt*, I, 504.

[61] For an instructive example of how bankers like Morgan put U.S. strategic objectives second to their own interests in the early 1900s, see LaFeber, *The American Search for Opportunity*, 206.

[62] Martin J. Sklar, *The United States as a Developing Country: Studies in U.S. History in the Progressive Era and the 1920s* (New York: Cambridge University Press, 1992), 119–23, 129–32.

America's determination to exert influence in those parts of the globe where its material and newfound strategic interests lay inevitably made demands on the nation's economy. Concern among officers over German expansion into the Caribbean, especially at the time of the Venezuelan crisis of 1902–3, kept the U.S. Navy in the forefront of strategic planning. In 1897, Kaiser Wilhelm II had inaugurated his new foreign policy, *Weltpolitik*, signaling a greater role for the German navy in world affairs. Subsequent German and American war plans envisioned the possibility of conflict; the U.S. Navy created its Caribbean squadron in October 1902. The crisis over outstanding debts owed by Venezuela to European powers proved useful to American policymakers. Conditions seemed to validate the emphasis on security that was increasingly central to U.S. foreign policy, which compelled Congress to revise budgetary priorities. These developments provide a useful context for understanding the origins of the 1904 Roosevelt Corollary to the Monroe Doctrine, whereby the United States declared itself willing to employ force in the name of stability to preempt foreign intervention in the Western Hemisphere.[63]

By mid-decade, the U.S. Navy was identifying its mission as defense of the Monroe Doctrine, the Open Door, and the Panama Canal that was then under construction. At about the same time as the 1907 Panic, the General Board of the Navy was calling for Congress to authorize a fleet of forty-eight battleships, the result of which would be a two-ocean navy.[64] Systematic budgeting was not yet an integral part of the political process in Washington, yet the military, especially the navy, was staking a claim to a prominent place in fiscal planning in the name of national security. In 1906, the United States began working on what soon became War Plan Orange, a scenario for war that envisioned Japan as the likely enemy in an Asian conflict. The next year, as Japan was extending its influence to Korea and part of Manchuria, Roosevelt sent the fleet around the world, including a stopover in Japan. The idea for the voyage may have started with a presumption about the deterrent effect the fleet might have on Japan; in short order, it became an expression of Roosevelt's respect for the legitimacy of U.S. and Japanese interests in Asia. Then, in November 1908, the Root-Takahira Agreement more formally recognized Tokyo's vital interests in Manchuria.[65]

By the time Roosevelt left office, core values were tied as never before to external events. The emergence of a national security state, whose creators argued that it would safeguard what was exceptional about America, had already put that exceptionalism at some risk. War in Cuba and the

[63] Nancy Mitchell, *The Danger of Dreams: German and American Imperialism in Latin America* (Chapel Hill: University of North Carolina Press, 1999), 21–7.

[64] Challener, *Admirals, Generals, and American Foreign Policy*, 17–36.

[65] Hannigan, *The New World Power*, 115–17.

Philippines showed how easily basic rights could be compromised in the name of security as dissent came under attack from the proponents of empire. At the time, the basic right of citizenship, voting, was not mandated by federal law for women. Women in Roosevelt's America, both the sexually free New Woman and women seeking a public voice, threatened the chauvinistic, martial worldview of the former Rough Rider, though he did value women as active participants in a marketplace economy. Voting rights for African Americans were withheld, even though black troops fought bravely in Cuba and the Philippines.[66] Yet, other than when it was politically expedient to do so, Roosevelt showed little more leadership on the race question than he did on tariffs.

Moreover, the growth of presidential authority inevitably had a chilling effect on freedom of the press as stories critical of foreign policy were seen in a negative light. As never before, the identity of the nation was linked to events that the American people had neither made nor were substantially able to affect. The anti-imperialists of 1898 wondered whether a republic could be true to its principles if it became an imperial power. That issue had nearly vanished from political discourse a decade later when, as a major power, the United States was pursuing greater global strategic and commercial interests.

In the Time of Taft and Wilson

Before the outbreak of the Great War in 1914, the role of the state in an industrial political economy was central to public discourse in the Progressive era.[67] William Howard Taft, Roosevelt's successor, is known for his devotion to the rule of law, as seen in his administration's prosecution of antitrust cases, and for the foreign policy of "dollar diplomacy." To Taft, the preeminence of the law was the only way to safeguard the values that he most closely identified with freedom and with individual and property rights. Taft and Secretary of State Philander C. Knox understood dollar diplomacy as more than the single-minded pursuit of profit or imperial rapacity. Although agreeing that "modern diplomacy is commercial," Taft found in it not only "idealistic humanitarian sentiments" but also "the dictates of sound policy and strategy."[68] The president and other proponents of dollar diplomacy,

---

[66] Willard B. Gatewood, *"Smoked Yankees" and the Struggle for Empire: Letters from Negro Soldiers, 1898–1902* (Urbana: University of Illinois Press, 1971); Miller, *"Benevolent Assimilation,"* 192–3.

[67] See Sklar, *The United States as A Developing Country*, 78–142; idem, *The Corporate Reconstruction of American Capitalism, 1890–1916: The Market, the Law, and Politics* (New York: Cambridge University Press, 1988), 359–430.

[68] U.S. Department of State, *Papers Relating to the Foreign Relations of the United States, 1912* (Washington, DC: Government Printing Office, 1919), x.

progressives like Willard Straight who moved comfortably between government service and positions of importance in the private sector (in his case
the House of Morgan and National City Bank), were not simple-minded
profit seekers. Taft as secretary of war had observed in 1907, "American
dollars are made to perform a high moral duty." Likewise, Straight placed
businessmen in "the rank and file of the army of peace."[69]

The outcome of the election of 1912 ultimately settled the question of
the role of the state in modern America. Roosevelt espoused the growth
of federal power through the means of administrative reform. Defeating
Taft, Roosevelt, and Socialist candidate Debs, Democrat Woodrow Wilson
offered the voting public the New Freedom, his vision of the minimal state
in a country populated by millions of recent European immigrants and
dominated by an industrial economy. As it happened, within two years
Wilson's position on state power was remarkably similar to what Roosevelt
had been proposing. Thus, the administrative state, as symbolized by the
Federal Trade Commission and the Federal Reserve Board, became a reality.
The former was designed to regulate markets; they would not be government
directed. The latter was meant to bring order to the banking system, holding
out the enticing prospect of foreign banking joining capital investment as a
critical aspect of America's global presence.

Journalist Herbert Croly's 1909 book, *The Promise of American Life*,
advanced the idea of enhanced federal power as the surest guarantor of core
values in an industrial democracy. Croly advocated a proactive security policy in defense of national interests. "The Christian warrior must accompany
the evangelist," he declared, sounding much like Roosevelt.[70] Taft ideally
wanted to confine America's mission to the realm of commerce and finance
and also to avoid potentially unmanageable foreign entanglements, yet that
detachment seemed impossible, if not dangerous. Revolutions in Mexico
and China necessitated a more engaged response.

In Asia, Taft's belief in the importance of historic Sino-American ties
and the China market reversed Roosevelt's efforts to work harmoniously
with Tokyo. Even if one disagreed with them, pro-China arguments at the
time sounded strikingly familiar to advocates of an international presence
for America. "[T]he fate of China and the course of events in the Far East
are of fundamental importance to our Nation and to the future course
of civilization," journalist Thomas F. Millard wrote to Knox.[71] The vital
interests of Japan and other powers in Manchuria made it impossible for the

---

[69] Taft and Straight quoted in Sklar, *United States as a Developing Country*, 99; see also Eric
Rauchway, "Willard Straight and the Paradox of Liberal Imperialism," *Pacific Historical
Review* 66 (August 1997): 363–97.

[70] Herbert Croly, *The Promise of American Life* (New York: Dutton, 1909), 305, 210.

[71] Thomas F. Millard to Philander C. Knox, 12 August 1909, Philander C. Knox Papers,
Manuscript Division, Library of Congress, Washington, DC, Box. 27. My thanks to Carol
C. Chin for providing this document.

Taft administration to ignore possible intrigue by foreign powers when the Qing Dynasty fell in 1911. An international banking consortium, which the Qing had welcomed, was a proximate cause of the revolution. In its aftermath, the United States favored the stability that military strongman Yuan Shikai promised over the republican aspirations of the Nationalists of Sun Yat-sen. It would be left to Woodrow Wilson to sort out American interests in East Asia; that process would include an unsuccessful effort by Minister Paul Reinsch and others to educate Chinese leaders about the virtues of republican governance.[72] By mid-decade, warlord rule was on the rise in much of China.

If dollar diplomacy had difficulty making friends in Asia, as Willard Straight acknowledged,[73] it still had the potential to serve U.S. interests in Latin America where investment bankers saw an opportunity to displace European lenders. Yet, revolution in Mexico and the prospect of disorder in the Caribbean threatened to undermine hopes for a hemispheric political economy in which dollars would provide the basis for progress and stability. The downfall of Porfirio Díaz in 1910 was applauded by those bankers and businessmen who were close to his successor, Francisco Madero. Yet, when Mexico's revolution turned radical late in 1911, Taft sent troops to the border. On September 15, 1912, Ambassador Henry Lane Wilson demanded that Madero protect foreign property. Madero could not do so and was soon overthrown and murdered in February 1913 by forces backing General Victoriano Huerta. Unlike in China, there was no façade of republican governance in Mexico.

The promise of dollar diplomacy was in retreat, and again, Wilson would have to sort things out. His decision to occupy Veracruz in April 1914 demonstrated how security considerations, whether real or not, were influencing the conduct of U.S. foreign policy. Wilson struggled to find a policy that would affirm the right of self-determination and produce an acceptable form of government south of the Rio Grande. Events beyond his control – Germany's sinking of the British liner *Lusitania* and China's acquiescence to many of Japan's infamous Twenty-One Demands – contributed in the summer of 1915 to Wilson's de facto recognition of the conservative constitutionalist forces of Venustiano Carranza.

Wilson acted more forcefully in the Caribbean region to promote order if not self-determination. He maintained a small legation force in Nicaragua and sent troops into Haiti and the Dominican Republic in 1915 and 1916, respectively, to ensure public order and guarantee financial stability to foreign creditors. As in the Philippines, intervention provoked local resistance

[72] Noel H. Pugach, *Paul S. Reinsch: Open Door-Diplomat in Action* (Millwood, NY: KTO Press, 1979).

[73] Scott Nearing and Joseph Freeman, *Dollar Diplomacy: A Study in American Imperialism* (New York: B. W. Huebsch, 1925), 50.

and U.S. reprisals. Wilson did not believe that U.S. actions in Haiti, "the dusky little republic," would concern other Latin Americans because, "being negroes (*sic*), [Haitians] are not regarded as of the fraternity!" Moreover, as Wilson's foremost biographer Arthur S. Link wrote, the president "did not believe that the peoples of northern Latin America were much beyond the stage of political infancy."[74]

Wilson assumed it to be his country's duty to help those peoples mature because the United States espoused "the development of constitutional liberty in the world."[75] A mentoring relationship would bond the hemisphere together under U.S. leadership. Why did Wilson link the nation's identity to those peoples for whom he had such disdain? In late 1914, he had proposed the idea of a Pan-American pact, which historian Arthur P. Whitaker called "a true regional security system."[76] Tutoring the nations of Latin America in the ways of good government and economic responsibility, while tending to presumed common security needs, had become for Wilson the modern equivalent of pursuing republican virtue at home more than a century earlier.

The Great War and Core Values

The effort to protect core values by spreading them abroad had one obvious consequence in the Philippines and the Caribbean – the potential loss of life for those insurgents who resisted the U.S. military. In China, allegiance to the principles of constitutional governance was ephemeral at best.[77] At home, the impact of the Great War brought into high relief the tension between individual rights and restraint on arbitrary power, on the one side, and on the war policy of the Wilson administration on the other.

This latter clash took place in the context of a growing atmosphere of freedom, except for African Americans. Vast numbers of immigrants arrived seeking economic opportunity; a modern consumer economy was beginning to take shape, fulfilling one promise of the industrial age; and more and more women were demanding the freedom to work in a marketplace economy. Progressives took advantage of this general quest for personal economic freedom to fashion a more orderly society through the working of the regulatory

---

[74] Arthur S. Link et al., eds., *The Papers of Woodrow Wilson*, vol. 34: *July 21–September 30, 1915* (Princeton: Princeton University Press, 1980), 208, 209 for the words quoted; Arthur S. Link, *Wilson: The Struggle for Neutrality, 1914–1915* (Princeton: Princeton University Press, 1960), 479.

[75] Link et al., eds., *Papers of Woodrow Wilson*, vol. 28: *1913* (Princeton: Princeton University Press, 1978), 451.

[76] Arthur P. Whitaker, *The Western Hemisphere Idea: Its Rise and Decline* (Ithaca: Cornell University Press, 1954), 123.

[77] Noel Pugach, "Embarrassed Monarchist: Frank J. Goodnow and Constitutional Development in China, 1913–1915," *Pacific Historical Review* 42 (November 1973): 499–517.

state. What was not clear was how dissent from orthodoxy would fare in times of crisis.

The years 1917 and 1918 showed, as had the debate over empire in 1898, the great difference in power and resources between those who would uphold individual rights as the crux of national identity and those who would compromise them in the name of security. Passage of the Espionage and Sedition Acts; federal control of the mail under Postmaster General Albert S. Burleson, which resulted in excluding leftist publications like *The Masses* from the mails; and activities of the Committee on Public Information represented the government's power to alter, perhaps irreparably, the rights of citizens, and, thus, the inviolability of core values.[78] Concerning freedom of speech, the Supreme Court began treating it as a fundamental value after the dissent of Justice Oliver Wendell Holmes Jr., in the famous Sedition Act case, *Abrams v. United States,* 250 US 616 (1919).[79] Furthermore, the Selective Service Act of 1917 required almost 25 million men to register with the draft, compelling participation in a war for democracy, as Wilson put it. For those who equated corporate rights with individual rights, the authority of the War Industries Board under Wall Street financier Bernard Baruch to oversee all facets of production came as a surprise, even though the regulatory state had been a decade in the making.

Standing up for individual rights, or civil liberties, was fraught with risk after Wilson's war message to Congress in April 1917. The National Civil Liberties Bureau, created after passage of the Espionage Act, had trouble convincing the public that defense of the Bill of Rights was not the same thing as opposition to the war, which many in the United States denounced as unpatriotic.[80] Leading intellectuals such as Thorstein Veblen and John Dewey found pacifism objectionable. "Dewey was largely prepared to jettison liberty as a value worth serious concern during the war period," historian Paul L. Murphy concluded. *The New Republic* magazine – imagining the war as an extension of the struggle at home for democracy – supported entry, as did Veblen and the noted historian Charles A. Beard, who thought it was critical to vanquish German military power.[81] Yet, ever the individualist, Beard resigned his tenured position at Columbia University when the school's trustees endeavored to fire those professors who opposed conscription and when Columbia's president, Nicholas Murray

---

[78] Generally see Paul L. Murphy, *World War I and the Origins of Civil Liberties in the United States* (New York: W. W. Norton & Company, 1979); Stephen L. Vaughn, *Hold Fast the Inner Lines: Democracy, Nationalism, and the Committee on Public Information* (Chapel Hill: University of North Carolina Press, 1980).

[79] Anthony Lewis, "Privilege and the Press," *The New York Review of Books,* July 14, 2005, p. 4.

[80] William Preston, Jr., *Aliens and Dissenters: Federal Suppression of Radicals, 1903–1933* (Cambridge: Harvard University Press, 1963), 142 ff.

[81] Murphy, *World War I and the Origins of Civil Liberties,* 146–56; quoted words, 148.

Butler, sought to squelch antiwar dissent among the faculty.[82] Hoping that entering the war would preserve American ideals, Beard cared little about the mission to spread democracy abroad.[83]

To advocate peace and to reject entry into the war or participation once war was declared ran afoul of the prevailing public mood, although support for going to war was not unanimous. Pacifist Jeanette Rankin of Montana, elected to Congress in 1916, voted against the war and was defeated in her try for reelection. She would return to the House of Representatives in 1940 and again decry America's participation in war, this time after the Japanese attack on Pearl Harbor in December 1941. Jane Addams and radical Crystal Eastman opposed the war, as did the National Women's Party. Charlotte Perkins Gilman, however, broke with the Women's Peace Party and supported Wilson's decision.[84]

In one of the more unlikely efforts to keep the United States out of war, a small group of strong-willed Oklahoma draft resisters – some of whom were Socialists, others Democrats, and some who had ties to the Industrial Workers of the World (IWW) or Wobblies – fomented the Green Corn Rebellion in August 1917. Their intent was to march to Washington, fueling their anger with a diet of beef and ripe corn. They wanted to prevent "Big Slick," as they called Wilson, from sending young men off to war. The affair was a fiasco, all the more so because it led to the repression of radicals and poor farmers. The Green Corn rebels opposed the war, one historian of the rebellion wrote, but "their action was linked to a long chain of confrontations" between the rural poor and propertied people of cotton country.[85] As such, it was not unlike embattled insurgents abroad who fought to prevent the spread of U.S. influence into their homelands. The difference, of course, was that the lives of the Oklahoma rebels were not immediately at stake in their rejection of federal authority to send them to war.

Pressure to fall in line with prowar sentiment proved hard to resist. At stake on some basic level for Wilson was the composition of national identity. Like Roosevelt, Wilson did not recoil from the horrors of war; he accepted war as a means of achieving order and stability. *The New Republic* used the debates over preparedness in 1915 to call attention to "the instinctive fighting spirit of the early Americans" and to advocate a foreign

---

[82] Richard Hofstadter, *The Progressive Historians: Turner, Beard, Parrington* (New York: Alfred A. Knopf, 1968), 285–7.

[83] Warren I. Cohen, *The American Revisionists: The Lessons of Intervention in World War I* (Chicago: University of Chicago Press, 1967), 18.

[84] Rosalind Rosenberg *Divided Lives: American Women in the Twentieth Century* (New York: Hill and Wang, 1992), 71–2.

[85] James R. Green, *Grass-Roots Socialism: Radical Movements in the Southwest, 1895–1943* (Baton Rouge: Louisiana State University Press, 1978), 357–68.

policy "fac[ing] the realities of international politics."[86] Randolph Bourne captured well the dramatic transformation of American identity that had taken place in the era of industrial and corporate capitalism. "War is the health of the State," he wrote in an unpublished essay.[87] The acerbic Bourne directed the majority of his wrath at fellow intellectuals whose support for "war-liberalism" tied them to the ruling classes, "the least democratic forces in American life."[88] The issue was joined: Who best represented America's traditional values? Was it the economic and political elites for whom security demanded preparedness or the popular class, which traditionally had found security in the exceptionalism of political isolation?

Wilson's idea of advancing "constitutional liberty" through self-determination was only superficially similar to the devotion of Bourne and others on the Left to the ideal of democracy. Wilson's goal was comparable to that of America's founding generation in that all peoples should aspire to republican governance, whereas the reality was that it would come sooner for some than for others, such as non-Anglo-Saxons, people of color, and avowed radicals. As a wartime expedient, women in America, which in practice meant white women, had received the right to vote. How best to perpetuate republican virtue as a national trait worthy of emulation seemed destined to remain in the hands of elites, who equated virtue with a healthy economy and political orthodoxy.

This controlling power over the nation's political economy did not bode well for many Socialists or radical labor, as personified by the IWW. Debs went to jail in 1918 under the Espionage Act for giving a speech against the war; while in prison in 1920, he received 900,000 votes as a presidential candidate. The IWW, which was strong among miners and dockworkers in the West, was subjected to state harassment, and federal agents raided its offices around the country in August 1917 under a broad construction of the Espionage Act. The Socialist Party was collapsing under government pressure and from its internal contradictions about the war effort. Civil liberties had never seemed so precarious. To leftist critics, the crisis of progressivism in wartime revealed the limits of Wilson's liberal capitalist politics. As Louis Hartz observed in his classic 1955 study, *The Liberal Tradition in America*, liberalism's "compulsive power has been so great that it has posed a threat to liberty itself."[89]

---

[86] "'Preparedness' for What?," *The New Republic,* 26 June 1915, p. 188.

[87] Randolph S. Bourne, *War and the Intellectuals: Collected Essays, 1915–1919*, ed. with an introduction by Carl Resek (New York: Harper & Row, 1964), 71. Influenced by Beard at Columbia, Bourne wrote for *The New Republic*; he died at age thirty-two in the influenza epidemic of 1918.

[88] Ibid., 5.

[89] Louis Hartz, *The Liberal Tradition in America* (New York: Harcourt, Brace & World, 1955), 11.

Conclusion

American participation in the Allied intervention in Russia in 1918–20, which occurred soon after the Bolshevik Revolution, remained limited in scope compared to the exertions of Great Britain and France. Yet, in conjunction with the Red Scare at home in 1919–20, which was overseen by Attorney General A. Mitchell Palmer, this intervention showed how interrelated the efforts to make the nation safe and to protect core values had become over three decades. Many were those who believed that Russia was destined to become a democracy like the United States. The Bolshevik seizure of power was therefore nothing less than a terrible betrayal; it could not stand.[90] The mentality that moved Americans to confront their foes reflected the security ethos. Whether the United States actually faced a serious threat from foreign or domestic radicals was beside the point. The founders of America's first national security state had transformed antiradicalism and anticommunism into an important aspect of American identity. In that way, fear became affixed to modernity.[91] "The world was on fire," Wilson exclaimed in March 1919. "Every minute lost assists the forces of unrest."[92] Such sentiments were not a novel development. The specter of enemies desirous of harming America had roiled the nation's political culture since the earliest years of colonial settlement. By about 1920, that trepidation had become inseparable from the thinking of many Americans about their rights and responsibilities as citizens. Debs endeavored in 1918 without success to warn his jurors about the inescapable pitfalls of fear, telling them, "American institutions are on trial before a court of American citizens."[93]

Over time, the nation's core values would be diminished by fear and the security ethos that helped sustain it. Paradoxically, the ideal of republican virtue was not lost as the Great War came to a close and a new era dawned. Pursuit of the lofty promises of republican governance was being democratized. Women could vote; African Americans were demanding recognition of their basic rights. These developments ran counter to the history of selective political inclusion by the wealthy and politically powerful. What was unclear around 1920 was how this novel civic virtue would fare when rights were again imperiled in the name of security. The unhappy likelihood was

---

[90] David S. Foglesong, *The American Mission and the "Evil Empire": The Crusade for a "Free Russia" since 1881* (New York: Cambridge University Press, 2007), 34–59.

[91] Alan Dawley, *Changing the World: American Progressives in War and Revolution* (Princeton: Princeton University Press, 2003), 270.

[92] Link et al., eds., *Papers of Woodrow* Wilson, vol. 56: *March 17–April 4, 1919* (Princeton: Princeton University Press, 1987), 247.

[93] Quoted in Salvatore, *Eugene V. Debs*, 295.

that the more the United States entered the global arena, the more liberty might be at risk. The post-1890 sense of mission in foreign policy – that is, the movement toward internationalism – and the belief in market entitlement by financial and commercial interests suggested a future fraught with uncertainty and contention.

Woodrow Wilson's aspirations for the world, encapsulated in the term "liberal capitalist internationalism," were nothing new.[94] Although decidedly secular in their import, his words conveyed the strong millennial assumptions that coursed throughout American history. To Wilson and others who envisioned a grander role for the United States, the millennial dream was abiding proof of the exceptional qualities that America possessed. It had long been so. Wilson was hardly the only prominent American who believed his country was destined to make the world anew.[95] Thomas Paine had written, "We have no occasion to roam for information into the obscure field of antiquity.... We are ... as if we had lived in the beginning of time."[96] In Paine's rendering, history was irrelevant to experience. More than a century later, those who did not embrace the security ethos could take no comfort in the end-of-history, or perfectionist, assumptions that Wilson and those he subsequently influenced brought to the conduct of American foreign policy.

[94] N. Gordon Levin, *Woodrow Wilson and World Politics: America's Response to War and Revolution* (New York: Oxford University Press, 1968).

[95] Anders Stephanson, *Manifest Destiny: American Expansionism and the Empire of Right* (New York: Hill and Wang, 1995).

[96] Quoted in William Pfaff, "Manifest Destiny: A New Direction for America," *New York Review of Books*, February 15, 2007, p. 54.

PART TWO

INTERNATIONALISM AND CONTAINMENT, 1919–1973

3

The Postwar Era and American Values

Tradition will not work in the complexities of modern life.
Walter Lippmann, 1914

American capital will be the controlling factor in public and private finance.
William S. Culbertson, 1930

By the end of the Great War, the military prowess and technological capability of U.S. armed forces had reached unprecedented heights. Showing the geographic sweep of the security ethos, U.S.-trained constabularies were trying to maintain order from the Caribbean and Central America to the Philippines. In addition, intervention in Mexico in futile pursuit of Pancho Villa in 1916–17 and subsequently against the Bolsheviks in Russia showed a willingness to deploy troops to far-flung regions of the globe in defense of national interests. Making the immediate postwar years different from the late nineteenth century was America's status as the world's foremost power, replacing Great Britain. Also evident was the weariness brought on by the human and material costs of the war. Mark Twain's *cri de coeur* denouncing war and empire, *The War Prayer*, which first appeared in 1916, evinced a greater understanding of the travail of war than did Roosevelt's fears about civilization and manhood absent the presumed glories of combat.

The treaty written at Versailles by Woodrow Wilson and the Allies did not necessarily hold the key to a better world; rather, it provided a hiatus of unspecified length during which the powers might try to build a foundation for a durable peace. In addition, the League of Nations did constitute a novel forum for addressing crucial international issues. The postwar years were therefore not devoid of expectations that diplomacy and the rule of law might prevent the outbreak of another general war. In fact, the global economy, although badly torn apart, was not irreparably damaged. To be sure, the command of gold had been altered; substantial quantities of gold were under American control by the war's end, making the United States the world's foremost creditor nation.[1] This is not to argue that American economic leadership was inherently superior to that of Great Britain, the former hegemon. Rather, given the dominant reality of a capitalist world order, growth and development would be more likely to occur in the postwar world if the United States, which suffered little from the war, shouldered the responsibility of financial and commercial primacy. As Wilson observed in 1916, "[T]hose who finance the world must understand it and rule it with their spirits and with their minds."[2] It appears in retrospect, however, that American businessmen and bankers were not prepared to repair a devastated global economy.[3]

Even as the United States returned to a kind of political isolationism, it did not abandon the precepts that had taken it into the world since 1890. After entering the war in 1917, Americans could not think about foreign policy without reference to security considerations affecting their own safety and that of others. In this way, the legacy of the first national security state was fixed. Core values could not be protected as they had historically been through a call to republican virtue in domestic politics; values were now inextricably linked to developments abroad. The protection of values therefore required a healthy political economy and the promise of self-determination in a peaceful world. The combination of political skill and good fortune necessary to create and sustain such a set of conditions would prove to be remarkably elusive in the 1920s and tragically absent from the 1930s.

However the United States engaged the world after the signing of the Versailles Treaty, the controlling discourse would reflect the prevalence of strategic concerns and national security in thinking about foreign policy. In that respect, the historian William Appleman Williams understated the persistence of an illusion in his classic essay, "The Legend of Isolationism in the 1920s."[4] Only if isolationism is understood as a political phenomenon, and particularly one related to a formal association with foreign powers, is it accurate to draw something of a clear line between isolationism and internationalism. The American economy in the first three decades of the twentieth century was integral to the global economy, as it long had been. The idea that economic engagement abroad was indicative of isolation from world affairs could not easily be dispelled, however, despite the reality of worldwide strategic interests. Americans and their government would not

[1] John Milton Cooper, Jr., "The Command of Gold Reversed: American Loans to Britain, 1915–1917," *Pacific Historical Review* 45 (May 1976): 209–30.
[2] Quoted in Scott Nearing and Joseph Freeman, *Dollar Diplomacy: A Study in American Imperialism* (New York: B. W. Huebsch, 1925), 273.
[3] Generally, see Dan P. Silverman, *Reconstructing Europe after the Great War* (Cambridge: Harvard University Press, 1982).
[4] William Appleman Williams, "The Legend of Isolationism in the 1920s," *Science and Society* 18 (Winter 1954): 1–20.

truly abandon the fiction of isolationism until the Japanese attack on Pearl Harbor in December 1941.

In a book about Republican foreign policy in the 1920s, Joan Hoff coined the term "independent internationalism," which might also be rendered as "selective internationalism."[5] Hoff's insight captures well the intent of Mahan, Lodge, Roosevelt, and others as they linked security concerns to political economy and actively pursued what they saw as the nation's strategic interests in the war with Spain and beyond. It applies, too, to the dollar diplomacy of Taft and Knox who never conceived of their foreign policy in the narrow terms usually ascribed to it. And it also helps illuminate Wilson's efforts to convince a world embroiled in a devastating war of the desirability of emulating the American experience through a liberal economic system.

Self-Determination, Disarmament, and Core Values

Two issues demonstrate the crucial link and tensions between American-style internationalism and core values in the aftermath of global war: self-determination and disarmament. The fifth of Wilson's Fourteen Points gave attention to self-determination, an imprecise reflection of republican governance at home. (Other points addressed the right to security of specific nationalities or groups living in conditions that were not conducive to autonomy or full sovereignty.) The issue promised to be a prickly one because the histories of European imperialism and colonialism in Africa, Asia, and Latin America could just as easily have been stories of the denial of self-determination. The same held true about the growth of Japanese power in East Asia.

If the United States was going to succeed in replacing the older, European order with a new anti-imperial, liberal one, then self-determination would have to become a cornerstone of that order. Yet, having offered its institutions and values to the world as being worthy of emulation, the limits of self-determination at home and in its spheres of interest were rather problematic. For instance, the Nineteenth Amendment to the U.S. Constitution, giving women the right to vote in federal elections, was not ratified until August 1920. Women's rights on a global scale, especially suffrage, did receive passing consideration with professions of support at Versailles from Wilson and other leaders, but did not become an important part of the deliberations. Italy saw the issue as a domestic matter, and so it remained.[6]

---

[5] Joan Hoff Wilson, *American Business and Foreign Policy, 1920–1933* (Lexington: University Press of Kentucky, 1971); see also her elaboration of this concept in Joan Hoff, *A Faustian Foreign Policy from Woodrow Wilson to George W. Bush: Dreams of Perfectibility* (New York: Cambridge University Press, 2008).

[6] Margaret MacMillan, *Paris 1919: Six Months That Changed the World* (New York: Random House, 2002), 59.

Wilson did not challenge that position, commenting that the conference had convened to consider international issues.[7]

Like the promise of democracy, the allure of self-determination was strong. In the United States, where ruling elites had traditionally sought to contain through republican governance presumed excesses of democracy, self-determination raised the specter of equality among races and ethnic minorities. Black veterans returned from the war to find their freedoms curtailed at home. Their situation was less promising for better treatment than was that of foreigners. For Latin Americans, Wilson had said that the United States would teach them to elect good men. For the Japanese, if the Lansing-Ishii Agreement of 1917, which acknowledged Tokyo's special interests in part of China, did not imply equality with white people, it did recognize that Japan could not easily be ignored in international affairs.

Sadly, during and after the war, African Americans could not expect either comparable tutelage or respect on their road to democracy. Indeed, Wilson had segregated the federal government and permitted D. W. Griffith's classic racist film, *Birth of a Nation*, to have its premiere in the White House in 1915. This paradoxically self-righteous president made no pretense of resolving America's vexing racial problem. In this environment, evocative of the heyday of Social Darwinism and *Plessy v. Ferguson*, the racial disturbances of 1917 in East St. Louis, Illinois, and the violence against blacks in Chicago, Washington, D.C., Omaha, and elsewhere in the Red Summer (and autumn) of 1919 were not surprising.

At Versailles, considerable pressure was placed on leaders of the victorious nations to make self-determination a reality. Several examples indicate how that issue relates to the larger question of values and security.

The case of China was not precisely a matter of self-determination. It was one of sovereignty, as it had been since the 1890s, if not since the first opium war of the late 1830s. The Twenty-One Demands, which threatened to turn China into a protectorate of Japan, and the unchecked power of regional warlords brought into question China's ability to determine its own fate. Japan's presence in Shantung, which China had accepted by treaty, became the acid test of self-determination at Versailles so far as a divided China was concerned. Wilson, breaking with Britain and France, essentially agreed; he termed the Twenty-One Demands "an invasion of Chinese political and administrative independence."[8] Japan, which had failed to get a racial equality clause included in the treaty, was in no mood to compromise and threatened not to support the creation of the League of Nations if it did not get its

---

[7] Leila J. Rupp, *Worlds of Women: The Making of an International Women's Movement* (Princeton: Princeton University Press, 1997), 211.

[8] Arthur S. Link et al., eds., *The Papers of Woodrow Wilson*, vol. 58: *April 23–May 9, 1919* (Princeton: Princeton University Press, 1988), 221.

way in China. Wilson gave way, angering the Chinese and casting doubt on the authenticity of his new global order. The May Fourth movement, which revitalized anti-Western nationalism among Chinese intellectuals, began one week later.[9]

Less likely than China to succeed in promoting the cause of self-determination at Versailles was a pan-African movement. Africa and late nineteenth-century imperialism were ingloriously linked,[10] and the American W. E. B. Du Bois and a black French deputy from Senegal, Blaise Diagne, resolved to hold a Pan-African Congress at the same time as the victors were meeting. The U.S. delegation was not enthusiastic about the congress and was more concerned about its meaning for racial politics at home. Wilson's adviser Colonel Edward M. House met with Du Bois, yet made no commitment to support pan-African goals.[11] Du Bois's efforts in Paris and his poorly calculated, if strategic support for the war, as seen in "Close Ranks," an editorial in the July 1918 issue of *The Crisis*, reflected his own considerable *noblesse oblige* toward other African Americans.[12]

Du Bois, a leader of the National Association for the Advancement of Colored People (NAACP), was no radical democrat or socialist when he left for Europe in December 1918. His own thinking about governance more resembled that of Herbert Croly and the writers at *The New Republic* than the socialism of Debs. Biographer David Levering Lewis writes, "Du Bois and the NAACP were civil rights militants, not social revolutionaries – defenders of the Constitution, not exponents of class war."[13] The calamitous events of the Red Scare of 1919–20 and his outrage about race relations inexorably impelled Du Bois not into revolutionary politics but toward the militancy of racial democracy. In an effort to atone for the glaring myopia of "Close Ranks," Du Bois prepared "Returning Soldiers" for the July 1919 issue of *The Crisis*. In ringing prose he wrote, "Make way for Democracy! We saved it in France, and by the Great Jehovah we will save it in the United States of America, or know the reason why."[14]

Du Bois advocated fair treatment for blacks in a white-dominated society quaking with fear, so much so that *The Crisis* seemed seditious to some officials in A. Mitchell Palmer's Justice Department. In 1918 and 1919, when more than 130 deaths turned lynching into something of a national pastime

[9] MacMillan, *Paris 1919*, 322–41.

[10] Adam Hochschild, *King Leopold's Ghost: A Story of Greed, Terror, and Heroism in Colonial Africa* (Boston: Houghton Mifflin, 1998), is one of the best recent examples of this sordid history.

[11] MacMillan, *Paris 1919*, 104–6; David Levering Lewis, *W. E. B. Du Bois: Biography of a Race, 1868–1919* (New York: Henry Holt, 1993), 561–78.

[12] W. E. B. Du Bois, "Close Ranks," *The Crisis* 16 (July 1918): 111.

[13] David Levering Lewis, *W. E. B. Du Bois: The Fight for Equality and the American Century, 1919–1963* (New York: Henry Holt, 2000), 4.

[14] W. E. B. Du Bois, "Returning Soldiers," *The Crisis* 18 (July 1919): 14.

and 250 more African Americans died in the Red Summer, Du Bois's angry call for resistance to racism had the ring of revolution to those like J. Edgar Hoover, head of the new General Intelligence Division in the Department of Justice. It was not easy to silence *The Crisis*, whose circulation was larger than either *The New Republic* or its rival, *The Nation*. Even the possibility that *The Crisis* might be suppressed (especially the "Returning Soldiers" issue) or seized for sedition emboldened Du Bois to speak out in defense of freedom of speech and assembly for radical voices on his left in American politics.[15]

In retrospect, advocacy of racial militancy arguably gave Du Bois an association, one that he would have disdained at the time, with revolutionary activities on a global scale. The Pan-African Congress cemented for him the linkage between democracy and self-determination and, by implication, the burgeoning anticolonial movement. And it was in Point Five of the Fourteen Points, where democracy and anticolonialism met on the terrain of self-determination, that Du Bois came together with Ho Chi Minh (then known as Nguyen Tat Thanh, or "he who will succeed"), the other great nonwhite figure on the periphery at Versailles.

Ho's journey from Vietnamese patriot to anticolonial revolutionary took him abroad in the 1910s. A brief stopover in the United States has become legendary, if not wholly verifiable. Ho surely witnessed the plight of African Americans while living in Boston and New York. By 1918, he was part of a growing Vietnamese enclave in Paris that was conscripted to do factory work while young Frenchmen served in the military. That community increasingly turned to politics, ultimately forming the Association of Annamite Patriots in 1919. Ho, who had begun to use the name Nguyen Ai Quoc, or "Nguyen the Patriot," wrote a petition demanding political autonomy and democratic freedoms for Vietnam and an end to taxes on salt, opium, and alcohol. Colonel House probably gave a copy of the petition to President Wilson. Ho received no response from either the National Assembly in Paris or the delegates at Versailles, leading him to observe that he had been deceived by Wilson's "song of freedom."[16]

Autonomy and democracy evidently raised the prospect of renewed instability for the architects of the postwar order. This was no idle concern because of Bolshevism's discomfiting appeal in part of war-torn Europe. What that development portended elsewhere could not realistically be envisioned, especially because it was a fear – this "spuriously inflated bogy of Bolshevism" in historian Arno J. Mayer's words – fit for exaggeration then

---

[15] Lewis, *The Fight for Equality*, 4–8. On *The New Republic*, see Christopher Lasch, *The New Radicalism in America, 1889–1963: The Intellectual as a Social Type* (New York: Vintage Books, 1965), 220–1.

[16] William J. Duiker, *Ho Chi Minh* (New York: Hyperion, 2000), 22–3, 42–62; quoted words, 61.

and for seven decades thereafter.[17] Wilson had tried in the months after his Fourteen Points address of January 1918 to find a way to include Bolshevism under the umbrella of liberal internationalism. Lenin refused to be so co-opted and rejected liberalism, its basic values, and its institutions.[18] The lesson U.S. officials learned and passed down to their successors was that self-determination and sovereignty itself could become a threat to order, especially when practiced by radical nationalists, let alone communists.

Freedom's song, such as it was, also met its match in the mandate system, which had a direct relationship in 1919 to the issue of self-determination. Turning Germany's former colonies in Africa and the Pacific into mandates encouraged the victorious powers to assume that they could contain the aspirations of people who could not secure their own freedom. Yet, the mandate system became scarcely more than annexation by another name.[19] Indeed, British officials saw it as a way to perpetuate London's hold on the Middle East following the break-up of the Ottoman Empire; new states would remain part of Britain's imperial system even after gaining independence. The French had similar intentions.[20] Furthermore, mandates resembled the U.S. Supreme Court's indecorous creation in *Plessy v. Ferguson* – an indefinitely separate but in time putatively equal status for the millions of men, women, and children who were not truly free.

Self-determination largely remained unrealized in the years after the war. Unmet expectations became the source of disappointment in China, among those favoring a pan-African movement, for opponents of colonialism, and for the many who equated the old order's *realpolitik* with the mandate system. In addition, making self-determination a key aspect of U.S. foreign policy actually lessened the chances for greater democracy at home. If freedoms won in America led to nonwhite or colonial peoples trying to control their own fate, then chaos might ensue, creating a political vacuum that only radicalism could fill.

Such a concern arose during the Red Scare. Wilson feared that returning black soldiers, seeking to use the war experience to their advantage, would be expert at "conveying Bolshevism to America."[21] The climate in which

[17] Arno J. Mayer, *Politics and Diplomacy of Peacemaking: Containment and Counterrevolution at Versailles, 1918–1919* (New York: Alfred A. Knopf, 1967), *passim*; quoted words, 10.

[18] N. Gordon Levin, *Woodrow Wilson and World Politics: America's Response to War and Revolution* (New York: Oxford University Press, 1968), 61–4.

[19] MacMillan, *Paris 1919*, 98–106.

[20] David Fromkin, *A Peace to End All Peace: The Fall of the Ottoman Empire and the Creation of the Modern Middle East* (New York: Henry Holt, 1989), 283, 410–1. Not until the signing of the Treaty of Sèvres in August 1920 did the Allied war with the Ottoman Empire formally come to an end.

[21] Link et al., eds., *Papers of Woodrow Wilson*, vol. 55: *February 8–March 16, 1919* (Princeton: Princeton University Press, 1986), 471.

the president could entertain such thoughts made limiting freedom at home seem prudent. In reality, it reflected growing paranoia in government about revolution and explains the seriousness with which military intelligence at the Army War College drew up War Plans White to counter presumed disloyalty, especially among African Americans and ethnic Americans. Strikes at the steel plants in Gary, Indiana, in the fall of 1919 evoked concern that Bolshevism was making inroads among America's working class. Coinciding with the Palmer raids against labor and radical organizations, which resulted in the arrest and deportation of hundreds of immigrant radicals, War Plans White constituted a desperate attempt to protect the Constitution from America's political Left.[22] By casting doubt on the loyalty of groups of citizens and recent arrivals, the government was showing disdain for values such as freedom of speech and assembly.

Far less of a challenge to postwar order was the appearance of a movement for disarmament. Among its principal proponents, other than the U.S. government, were peace societies, women's organizations, and internationalists who were skeptical of the League of Nations.[23] Hence, the convening of the Washington Naval Conference of 1921–2 by the administration of Warren G. Harding heartened committed pacifists and peace advocates, isolationists in Congress and among the general public, and self-styled foreign policy realists like Walter Lippmann. Each was hoping to influence the nation's debates about security after what each saw as the debacle at Versailles.

Jane Addams and the Women's International League for Peace and Freedom (WILPF), a radical, pacifist organization that was founded in 1915, did not believe in the Wilsonian mission to make the world safe for democracy. What was needed, Addams argued, was "a new internationalism" based on "a more reasonable world order" than that which had plunged the world into war in 1914.[24] The Washington Naval Conference had the potential to be a step in that direction. Addams and her compatriots from the many national sections of the WILPF linked the causes of peace and women's rights. The prescience of its analysis about the need for an engaged citizenry notwithstanding,[25] the women's movement remained on the periphery of male-dominated international affairs into the 1920s.

Additional calls for disarmament arose in response to the Borah Resolution of December 1920, with which William E. Borah, a Republican

---

[22] Alan Dawley, *Changing the World: American Progressives in War and Revolution* (Princeton: Princeton University Press, 2003), 258, 271–6.

[23] Selig Adler, *The Isolationist Impulse: Its Twentieth-Century Reaction* (New York: Collier Books, 1961), 126–8.

[24] Rupp, *Worlds of Women*, 26–30; Jane Addams, *Peace and Bread in Time of War* (New York: Macmillan, 1922), 84.

[25] On Addams and the imperative of democracy from below, see Jonathan M. Hansen, *The Lost Promise of Patriotism: Debating American Identity, 1890–1920* (Chicago: University of Chicago Press, 2003), 137–8.

senator from Idaho, sought to reduce naval expenditures by 50 percent over a five-year period. Borah believed that naval competition among the British, Japanese, and Americans would soon prove to be ruinous economically and thus threaten security. The outgoing Wilson administration worried that any unilateral movement toward disarmament would be dangerous because Borah's resolution did not directly address the issue of the Anglo-Japanese Alliance. That alliance had worried U.S. authorities since its inception in 1902 because it appeared to legitimate the supremacy of Japanese power in East Asia. Meanwhile, six million Americans, spurred on by Protestant peace action, petitioned Washington in support of disarmament in 1921. In September of that year, the National Council for the Limitation of Armaments was established to mobilize additional support for disarmament.[26]

Lippmann and the editors of *The New Republic* opposed the Versailles treaty, contending it would lead to another European war. In their view, the existence of the League of Nations could not redeem so great a diplomatic failure and abdication of progressive democratic goals.[27] Lippmann believed that naval limitation would curb the growth of military power that led to war. He therefore worked behind the scenes with the maverick Borah on that and other issues during the 1920s.[28] Did arms limitation reflect the freedom of action that Lippmann and others were drawn to, or was it consistent with Wilsonian principles? Norman H. Davis, a banker, adviser to Wilson at Versailles, and member of the newly formed Council on Foreign Relations, thought that Wilsonian principles were at odds with proposals on arms control.[29] Whether true or not, it should not obscure a larger point: The appeal of disarmament indicated the influence of the security ethos on discussions by informed citizens about the United States and foreign affairs.

President Harding and Secretary of State Charles Evans Hughes outmaneuvered the pacifists and feminists who suspected that neither security nor protection of core values was possible under a Wilsonian order or an engaged foreign policy, no matter how independent. America's place in the world was much less debatable in 1921 than it had been in 1890. Lippmann had written in 1914 in his classic work, *Drift and Mastery*, "[T]radition will not work in the complexities of modern life.... The only possible cohesion

---

[26] John Chalmers Vinson, *The Parchment Peace: The United States Senate and the Washington Conference, 1921–1922* (Athens: University of Georgia Press, 1955), 51–7; Charles DeBenedetti, *Origins of the Modern American Peace Movement, 1915–1929* (Millwood: KTO Press, 1978), 84–8.

[27] Ronald Steel, *Walter Lippmann and the American Century* (Boston: Atlantic–Little, Brown, 1980), 155–62.

[28] Ibid., 252–6.

[29] Vinson, *The Parchment Peace*, 190; Robert D. Schulzinger, *The Wise Men of Foreign Affairs: The History of the Council on Foreign Relations* (New York: Columbia University Press, 1984), 9–10, 21–4.

now is a loyalty that looks forward."[30] The assault on civil liberties between 1917 and 1920, historian William E. Leuchtenburg concluded, amounted to "a wholesale violation" of basic rights.[31] It remained to be seen whether the harm done to values by "modern complexities" could be undone.

The odds were not good. War planning exercises before 1914 merged with the reality of world war to generate expectations about the importance of preparedness. Thus, naval officers and officials like Wilson's Secretary of the Navy Josephus Daniels used the 1916 Naval Act to maintain a program of naval building. They embraced the security ethos, averring that capital ships would be decisive should the United States enter the war.[32] Nevertheless, even after Wilson asked Congress in April 1917 for a declaration of war, the idea of safety through the construction of capital ships seemed disingenuous to Americans who favored isolation from foreign entanglements. As such, advocates of a modern security policy had to put tradition on the defensive, a feat they accomplished at the Washington Naval Conference.

U.S. efforts to bring about arms limitation had their counterpart in London and Tokyo. The British, sensitive to the high cost of ongoing naval preparedness, wanted to find a way out of the alliance with Japan while preserving a seaworthy presence in Asia. The Japanese, fearful of the union of British and American strategic interests in East Asia, saw disarmament as the best way to achieve an enhanced international standing and credibility in the postwar era. Also providing an impetus for arms control was a downturn in the global economy; a naval race would have further imperiled postwar recovery, or so it was widely believed.

Establishing a 10-10-6 ratio for the tonnage of capital ships did not constitute a victory for isolationists. To be sure, the three Washington agreements did not commit the United States to deeper involvement in Asia in defense of its own interests – the Open Door – or those of China, a nation still deeply divided. Should troubles arise, the powers agreed to confer, which was more a gesture of goodwill than evidence of entanglement. The most contentious accord in this regard, the Four-Power Treaty, ended the Anglo-Japanese Alliance.[33] Not clear at the time was the containment of isolationism as a factor in American politics; it briefly regained strength in the 1930s with the Nye Committee hearings and the passage of neutrality legislation. Isolationists in the U.S. Senate and several peace communities had failed to lessen the influence of the security ethos on the thinking of informed citizens and

[30] Walter Lippmann, *Drift and Mastery: An Attempt to Diagnose the Current Unrest*, reprint ed. (Englewood Cliffs: Prentice Hall, 1961), 146–7.

[31] William E. Leuchtenburg, *The Perils of Prosperity, 1914–1932*, 2d ed. (Chicago: University of Chicago Press, 1993), 78.

[32] The following discussion is based on Roger Dingman, *Power in the Pacific: The Origins of Naval Arms Limitation, 1914–1922* (Chicago: University of Chicago Press, 1978), 3–63.

[33] For a synopsis of the Five-Power, Nine-Power, and Four-Power treaties, see Vinson, *The Parchment Peace*, 175–6, 218.

federal officials about what constituted the national interest. This development did not necessarily bode well for civil liberties. In the early postwar era, security became synonymous with a new national purpose that was at heart Wilsonian in nature, the result of which would be problematic for core values.

Ingraining the Security Ethos

As war enveloped Europe, concerned Americans formed groups like the National Security League and joined with the Navy League and the Army League to educate the general population about security. The *Lusitania* crisis in the summer of 1915 pushed Wilson in the direction of preparedness.[34] After the Washington Conference, the government became increasingly proactive about security; in the private sector, the Foreign Policy Association and the Council on Foreign Relations promoted greater awareness of world affairs. Americans continued to assume that national well-being and a healthy political economy were mutually reinforcing. As Walter Lippmann told members of the Council on Foreign Relations in 1923, there no longer existed a significant difference between economic interests and political matters in world affairs. During the 1920s and into the early 1930s, it fell to the Republican Party to make even stronger the links between the commercial and financial activity abroad and security.[35]

The security ethos was more than merely a set of ideas about how to defend America's vital interests. The structural dimension of a security mentality, exemplified by developments in technology and communications, hastened its acceptance as a normal part of public discourse about foreign affairs. The growth and mobility of a battleship fleet and the rise of military aviation helped determine the outcome of the Great War and created a belief that a nation prepared to defend itself with the latest technology would be a secure nation. Just as conducive to trust in technology and the connection between it and security was the opening of the Panama Canal in 1914. The canal made the likelihood of a two-ocean navy an alluring prospect, which Japanese naval officers could not help but notice.[36] In addition, it served to confirm Mahan's dictum about the importance of naval power in protecting oceangoing commerce.

Also furthering the security ethos, along with the canal and naval and air power, which was then in its infancy, were advances in the means of modern communication, including cables and radio. Wilson was so concerned

---

[34] Arthur S. Link, *Woodrow Wilson and the Progressive Era, 1910–1917* (New York: Harper & Row, 1954), 174–80.

[35] Schulzinger, *The Wise Men of Foreign Affairs*, 16.

[36] Michael Adas, *Dominance by Design: Technological Imperatives and America's Civilizing Mission* (Cambridge: Belknap Press of Harvard University Press, 2006), 185–203.

about a secure communications system that he considered government action to create it, should private enterprise be inadequate. At the outset of the war, Great Britain dominated the global cable system. Slightly more than a decade later, All-American Cables controlled almost 32,000 miles of cable in the Western Hemisphere in an effort to displace the British. As for radio, in 1914 the U.S. Navy operated wireless stations in Virginia and California, the Canal Zone, and Hawaii, Guam, and the Philippines. By the early 1920s, the Radio Corporation of America (RCA) was building an American-dominated radio system in the Western Hemisphere. RCA took more of a cooperative approach in Asia, reflecting a sensitivity to Japanese interests and the untested belief about foreign policy, as historian Emily S. Rosenberg puts it, that "multilateralism [could serve] as a co-optive device."[37]

Efforts to infuse the U.S. military and diplomatic corps with a greater sense of professionalism paralleled the marriage of technology and security. The numbers and the mission of attachés and the services intelligence branches tell that part of the story.[38] Attachés were essential to the gathering of intelligence, and thus to security planning, by the army and navy. In 1920, 149 naval attachés were serving in twenty-three countries; subsequent consolidation did not alter their mission. By 1938, there were 57 attachés and related personnel stationed abroad; in December 1941, the figure was more than 330. The Office of Naval Intelligence (ONI), founded in 1882, employed 16 officers and civilians in 1916, a figure that grew to 306 by 1918 and stabilized at 18 officers and 22 civilians by the mid-1920s, only to increase again in the late 1930s. As was the case with ONI, the Military Intelligence Division (MID), which began in 1885 as the Division of Military Information, shrank in numbers after World War I from 1,440 in 1918 to 90 in 1922 and to 66 in 1936, about the same as in Europe. The number of attachés fluctuated from a high of 111 in December 1918 to 30 plus assistants in 1922. In the mid-1930s, Congress capped the number of military attachés at 32, the third largest in the world behind France and Great Britain.

Indicative of the greater attention being paid to security was a major effort to collect and evaluate information about military planning in Japan, Germany, Great Britain, and elsewhere. For its part, ONI prepared monographs with political, economic, and military information about countries of interest. Beginning in 1919, a *Monthly Information Bulletin* provided classified data and analysis of the country to which a naval attaché was accredited. MID did much the same for personnel at the Army War College. Military

---

[37] Emily S. Rosenberg, *Spreading the American Dream: American Economic and Cultural Expansion, 1890–1945* (New York: Hill and Wang, 1982), 87–97; quoted words, 96.
[38] The following information is taken from Thomas G. Mahnken, *Uncovering Ways of War: U.S. Intelligence and Foreign Military Innovation, 1918–1941* (Ithaca: Cornell University Press, 2002).

attachés counted among their number John J. Pershing; Sherman Miles, assistant chief of staff in 1941; and Joseph W. Stillwell. Although it seems redundant to state that the U.S. military was concerned with the nation's security, what developed after 1919 was a commitment by the military services to make intelligence collection and assessment more professional and thus more useful to foreign policy deliberations.

Cultivation of the security ethos also occurred in the Department of State. From its inception, the diplomatic corps had been the preserve of educated and wealthy men.[39] By 1931, a foreign service, staffed by men interested in foreign policy, was turning a diplomatic career into professional work; this activity was similar to developments in military intelligence and the focus on security at the Council on Foreign Relations and like-minded groups. The Rogers Act of 1924 created the modern Foreign Service; the chaos that was affecting the chance for stability in Germany and Eastern Europe in 1919 moved Congress to action, along with the backing of the U.S. Chamber of Commerce. The Rogers Act created a Foreign Service School to train new recruits; instruction was too important to be left to university professors, some of whom one scholar found "underestimated the competitive nature of world politics. . . . The purpose of the entire course of study was to encourage young diplomats to develop a 'realistic' and professional outlook on world politics."[40] In this way, the modernization of the Foreign Service further implanted the idea of a security ethos into the American approach to world affairs.

It hardly needs to be pointed out that defining the world as potentially dangerous and thereafter charting a course to ensure security remained a task for white men. In the early years of the Foreign Service, few African Americans and women took the difficult qualifying examinations and fewer still became officers. Whoever populated the Foreign Service, they accepted American exceptionalism as a given. The universalistic form it took after World War I was one of Wilson's legacies; the modern Foreign Service existed as an instrument of that legacy.

Security and the Political Economy of Growth

Even before reform of the diplomatic corps was complete, the United States faced two troublesome situations it could not ignore because they were magnified by the postwar recession. The Versailles treaty had not settled the questions of reparations, war debts, or the place of Germany in a reconstructed Europe. There was a conspicuous unreality to Allied demands for

---

[39] This discussion is based on Robert D. Schulzinger, *The Making of the Diplomatic Mind: The Training, Outlook, and Style of United States Foreign Service Officers, 1908–1913* (Middletown, CT: Wesleyan University Press, 1975).

[40] Ibid., 81–2.

reparations; to meet its obligations, Germany would have to tax itself into oblivion. The British were nearly as alarmed about what they judged to be the extreme nature of French security demands as they were insistent that Germany begin making payments.[41] The failure of the Genoa Conference in 1922, a British effort to restore European order on London's terms, meant that the continent would remain in turmoil until outstanding economic and security issues were addressed. The United States refused to attend that meeting, let alone make any commitments to the financial and commercial rehabilitation of Europe.[42]

Washington, wary of becoming embroiled in situations it could not control, which seemed all the more true after France occupied the Ruhr in 1923, did not develop a coherent position on reparations and related economic issues until it informally supported the 1924 Dawes Plan. Named for Charles G. Dawes, a Chicago banker and Francophile, the plan restructured the German monetary system, recommended international loans to stem capital flight, and stipulated a schedule for payment of reparations that had more to do with budgetary credibility than with actual disbursements. The expectation was that international investments, including substantial capital from American banks such as J. P. Morgan and Company, would help cover Germany's financial obligations. The political counterpart to the Dawes Plan, the 1925 Locarno pact, addressed some French security concerns by settling the issue of Germany's western border, to which Foreign Minister Gustav Stresemann proved receptive. Resolving the matter of eastern borders, including the one separating Germany and Poland, did not seem impossible at mid-decade.[43] The United States, though not a participant at Locarno, approved of the accord.

The other matter of concern for Washington arose in East Asia. The persistence of instability in China, together with the regional aspirations of Japan, meant disquiet for the United States and also Great Britain, whose extensive economic interests there were potentially in jeopardy. The Soviets, chafing at the postwar limits of their influence in Europe, had signed the Treaty of Rapallo with Germany in April 1922, whereby these former enemies recognized one another, renounced existing financial claims, and reached an agreement for trade on a most-favored-nation basis.[44] The Soviets, building on this diplomatic success, were also hoping to regain influence

[41] Bruce Kent, *The Spoils of War: The Politics, Economics, and Diplomacy of Reparations, 1919–1932* (Oxford: Clarendon Press, 1989), 103–208.

[42] See Carole Fink, *The Genoa Conference: European Diplomacy, 1921–1922*, 2d ed. (Syracuse: Syracuse University Press, 1993), especially 262–6 on Soviet difficulties at the conference; Zara Steiner, *The Lights That Failed: European International History, 1919–1933* (Oxford: Oxford University Press, 2005), 164–8, 206–13.

[43] Steiner, *The Lights That Failed*, 240–8, 387–410; Patrick O. Cohrs, *The Unfinished Peace after World War I: America, Britain and the Stabilisation of Europe, 1919–1932* (Cambridge: Cambridge University Press, 2006), Parts I and II.

[44] Steiner, *The Lights That Failed*, 166–7.

in North China and Manchuria and establish constructive relations with Sun Yat-sen's Nationalists in Canton.

The United States viewed these aspirations as a clear threat to the foundation of strategic stability erected at the Washington Naval Conference. The establishment of diplomatic relations between the Soviets and Sun's Guomindang (GMD), as a prelude to furthering Russia's interests in the Chinese Eastern Railway and Outer Mongolia, was met with alarm in Washington. The fear was that the activities of the Comintern would radicalize the Chinese people and their government against the Washington powers. An accord reached in January 1923 between the GMD and the Soviets brought the two closer together; it put additional pressure on the powers to provide Sun with financial assistance that would enable him to defeat the northern regime in Beijing. When they balked at a request, the GMD and the Chinese communists allied to reject preexisting obligations while asserting the sovereignty of Chinese people over China. This revitalization of nationalism bore a radical stamp that the Washington powers could not ignore.[45]

Whatever goals the powers set for themselves in China, they also had to consider the growth, marketing, and consumption of opium – a serious threat to their objectives.[46] Indicative of the many nettlesome complications that opium brought to the conduct of foreign policy was this proposal of the warlords in Fujian province: "Salvation from Poverty through Opium-growing."[47] Limited progress against opium in the early 1920s meant that foreigners would continue to associate opium usage with an inherent weakness among the Chinese people. Japanese disdain for those who could not cast off the opium habit further convinced Tokyo of the rectitude of Japan's primacy in East Asia. Not until the Northern Expedition unified China in 1928 did opium suppression have any chance of success. Yet, even then effective control proved illusory as the GMD under Jiang Jieshi (Chiang Kai-shek) could not break its lengthy dependence on opium revenues. Although Sun Yat-sen had also relied on revenues from opium to bolster his regime's shaky finances, he knew the risks in doing so. Sun once proclaimed, "The problem of Opium Suppression in China is synonymous with the problem of good government."[48] During much of China's history under the Nationalists, it would so remain.

Because the Washington Conference had reduced the likelihood of conflict between the major powers for the time being, the United States could turn to economic foreign policy in its quest for global stability. Since the late 1890s,

---

[45] Akira Iriye, *After Imperialism: The Search for a New Order in the Far East, 1921–1931* (New York: Atheneum, 1969), 37–45.

[46] William O. Walker III, *Opium and Foreign Policy: The Anglo-American Search for Order in Asia, 1912–1954* (Chapel Hill: University of North Carolina Press, 1991), 26–53.

[47] Board of Missions of the Methodist Episcopal Church, *Annual Report... for the Year 1920* (New York: Board of Foreign Missions, 1921), 57.

[48] Quoted in Dr. R. Y. Lo, "A Review of the People's Anti-Opium Movement in China," *Opium: A World Problem* 2 (January 1929), 25.

the threat of instability had persisted in areas of strategic and economic importance to the United States; namely, China and certain parts of Latin America. Although several major Wall Street banks played a major role in international financial activities, no American is more identified with this effort than Herbert Hoover, who served as secretary of commerce from 1921 until becoming president in 1929. He anguished about the fate of political virtue in a dynamic industrial-cum-technological society because modernization inevitably affected basic values. For Hoover, the security focus in U.S. foreign policy, when viewed through an economic lens, reflected the limits of modernity. That is, the tension between his belief in a global division of labor favoring the developed world and the desire for equitable treatment by peoples in colonial or dependent lands meant that the road to modernity did not have universal access.[49] Put differently, the appeal of self-determination was not merely political or economic; it posed a challenge to the security priorities in the 1920s of the major powers, perhaps especially to those of the United States. In what ways, Hoover wondered, could available resources best be used in the pursuit of peace?

Renowned for his celebration of the individual, Hoover was most interested in how the individual acted to sustain the common good. This interest was not an idle intellectual exercise on his part; violations of civil liberties during the Red Scare had greatly alarmed him. He feared, too, that an inordinate inequality of wealth would lead to irresistible calls for socialism. Cooperative capitalism should be both meliorative and the hallmark of true progressivism for the United States. In that sense, Hoover was more in line with the original communitarian philosophy of Adam Smith than with those who appropriated Smith's ideas for their own enrichment to the detriment of others.[50] Hoover, though a selective internationalist like many other public and private leaders, doubted that a close connection with Europe was the *sine qua non* of American prosperity. He favored a protean capitalism that would incorporate all others, including Europeans, into a new economic regime on American terms. Hoover did not believe that China, because of its inefficiency and lack of productivity, would soon contribute to the peace of the world.[51] "China," he once commented, "is not going to be made occidental."[52]

[49] See, for example, Frank Ninkovich, *Modernity and Power: A History of the Domino Theory in the Twentieth Century* (Chicago: University of Chicago Press, 1995), xi–xii, 71.

[50] Joan Hoff Wilson, *Herbert Hoover: Forgotten Progressive* (Boston: Little, Brown, 1975), 38–43 and *passim*.

[51] Patrick Hearden, "Herbert Hoover and the Dream of Capitalism in One Country," in Lloyd C. Gardner, ed., *Redefining the Past: Essays in Diplomatic History in Honor of William Appleman Williams* (Corvallis: Oregon State University Press, 1986), 143–5; Wilson, *Herbert Hoover*, 202–4.

[52] Herbert Hoover, *The Memoirs of Herbert Hoover*, vol. I: *Years of Adventure, 1874–1920* (New York: Macmillan, 1951), 72.

Hoover's faith in the efficacy of reform, mainly through managerial expertise, was emblematic of his worldliness. It also kept him at odds with the isolationists and motivated him to identify Latin America as a likely laboratory for U.S. foreign policy.[53] Hoover shared Wilson's assessment of hemispheric unity as "the only available offset to the follies of Europe."[54] Conducting this experiment seemed critical because, should it succeed, the process of economic growth would construct barriers to conflict just as imposing as arms limitation. Out of increased productivity a new order would emerge that, with the help of preventive diplomacy, could make obsolete the reflexive resort to war by major powers in times of crisis.

Hoover and others were betting, in effect, that a global system predicated on economic growth would compel European leaders to fashion a lasting peace, however fruitless those efforts had been into the early 1920s. What Hoover could not do was revert to a time when the security ethos did not exist. Indeed, his roles in the Great War as food administrator and as the head of several relief operations were consistent with the union of security concerns and economic foreign policy. As such, Hoover's worldview did not greatly diverge from that of Lippmann or the Council on Foreign Relations, for example. What differences there were reflected the commerce secretary's conviction that economic matters must precede political accords to keep the latter from being ephemeral. On taking office in 1921, he commented, "In the upbuilding of our relations [with Latin America] there is nothing more important than our common interest in trade.... This ... interchange of goods ... [will] contribute to our joint advance in civilization."[55] The pursuit of economic growth in the 1920s would be the counterpart for Hoover to the promotion of democracy by the supporters of preparedness in 1915.

The specifics of his efforts are of some interest.[56] If modernization was the primary objective, the question must be asked: Modernization for whom? A variety of historical, political, and conceptual problems confronted American officials. U.S.-Mexican relations, over which Hoover had little influence, had served as a barometer of the health of hemispheric affairs. In the early 1920s, the issue of oil was at the center of a turbulent bilateral relationship. U.S. investors insisted on access to Mexican oil fields, which Article 27 of the 1917 Constitution had brought into question. Without guaranteed access to

---

[53] This idea and some of the subsequent discussion build on William Appleman Williams, "Latin America: Laboratory of American Foreign Policy in the Nineteen-Twenties," *Inter-American Economic Affairs* 11 (Autumn 1957): 3–30.

[54] Link et al., eds., *Papers of Woodrow Wilson*, vol. 66: *August 2–December 23, 1920* (Princeton: Princeton University Press, 1992), 183.

[55] Press Statement: For South American Papers, 9 March 1921, Herbert Hoover Presidential Library (HHPL), West Branch, Iowa, File: Public Statements.

[56] See William O. Walker III, "Crucible for Peace: Herbert Hoover, Modernization, and Economic Growth in Latin America," *Diplomatic History* 30 (January 2006): 83–117.

petroleum deposits in the Middle East, American companies looked to Mexico (along with Venezuela and Colombia) to meet their growing needs.[57] The Bucareli Accords of 1923 briefly reduced tensions over the exploitation of subsoil resources. The issue remained unsettled for several years,[58] recurring in 1938 when the government of Lázaro Cárdenas seized the holdings of foreign companies. The point here is that petroleum had become an indispensable lubricant for growth and symbol of the linkage between the security ethos and a dynamic political economy.

During the 1920s, Washington had to respond to bitter memories of interventions old and new, notably in Central America and the Caribbean. Even the withdrawal of U.S. forces, as in the case of the Dominican Republic and Nicaragua until their return in 1927, was insufficient to quell the anger.[59] Departing troops left behind repressive U.S.-trained *Guardia Nacional* units. Latin Americans therefore began to insist that the United States renounce the presumed right to intervene, a major legacy of the Blaine-Olney-Roosevelt era. They opposed intervention as a violation of sovereignty and a clear denial of self-determination, as seen in the ongoing presence of U.S. Marines in Haiti and unresolved tensions between Washington and Mexico City, for example.[60]

This issue produced what has been termed a "diplomatic defeat" for the United States at Havana in 1928 at the Sixth International Conference of American States, as latent antagonism to the practice of intervention spilled over into outright hostility.[61] Department of State officials knew that a confrontation might ensue.[62] Latin Americans denounced the presumptive right of the United States to intervene in their affairs, even though Washington did block a formal resolution to that effect. As we presently see, the context in which events unfolded at Havana emphasized sovereignty in the face of pervasive U.S. dominance of the region. Hoover's subsequent goodwill trip to South America, occurring shortly before he became president, implicitly acknowledged the validity of Latin American grievances, though it did not

---

[57] Stephen J. Randall, *United States Foreign Oil Policy since World War I: For Profits and Security*, 2d ed. (Montreal and Kingston: McGill–Queen's University Press, 2005), 13–58.

[58] Linda B. Hall, *Oil, Banks, and Politics: The United States and Postrevolutionary Mexico, 1917–1924* (Austin: University of Texas Press, 1995).

[59] Bruce J. Calder, *The Impact of Intervention: The Dominican Republic during the U.S. Occupation of 1916–1924* (Austin: University of Texas Press, 1984), 250–2.

[60] See the section, "The Commodification of Haiti," in Mary Renda, *Taking Haiti: Military Occupation and the Culture of U.S. Imperialism, 1915–1940* (Chapel Hill: University of North Carolina Press, 2001), 212–23; Robert Freeman Smith, *The United States and Revolutionary Nationalism in Mexico, 1916–1932* (Chicago: University of Chicago Press, 1972), 229–65.

[61] Laurence Duggan, *The Americas: The Search for Hemisphere Security* (New York: Holt, 1949), 52.

[62] U.S. Department of State, *Papers Relating to the Foreign Relations of the United States, 1928*, 3 vols. (Washington, D.C.: Government Printing Office, 1942), I: 573.

alter the U.S. government's sense of entitlement about intervention. Louis Hartz would observe in 1955 that political thought in the United States, liberalism in his telling, "does not understand sovereign power, ... [thus] the sense of the past is altered, and there is about it all ... a vast and almost charming innocence of mind." Had they been asked, Latin Americans surely would not have agreed that intervention was either innocent or charming.[63]

The most serious political problem retarding the emergence of an American-led world order in the 1920s was an economic one. No U.S. official could explain away the contradictions in tariff and loan policies, which ultimately precluded a "joint advance in civilization" and cast doubt on the universality of American-style modernization. Like other Republicans including Theodore Roosevelt, Hoover disdained a tariff policy that might harm the nation's agricultural sector. Protective tariffs exemplified Hoover's belief in an economic division of labor and furthered the dependent status of much of Latin America on the United States. William S. Culbertson of the U.S. Tariff Commission (later ambassador to Chile) contended that "economic disarmament" should precede disarmament agreements beyond the Washington accords, but failed to include tariffs among the "aggressive measures" (such as monopolies) he decried.[64]

Loan policy potentially offered the best hope for attaining peace and prosperity. "It is essential in the interest of security, as well as in the promotion of trade and in maintaining world stability, that [our] loans should be used for productive purposes," Hoover told a gathering of bankers in 1923.[65] For capital to succeed as a diplomatic tool, some form of loan supervision was essential. The Department of State would not accept more than nominal supervision despite the cavalier way in which Wall Street banks lent money to countries like Bolivia and Colombia, to name only two. This practice cast doubt on the business acumen and professional expertise of leading American bankers.

Careless lending exposed a profound conceptual flaw among finance capitalists and government officials about the working of a modern economy. Hoover's belief in an associational relationship for economic sectors, in this case banking, did not hark back to an era of laissez-faire economics nor did it go far enough in the direction of government supervision or regulation. It promised, instead, to leave the American economy and, thus, the world economy rudderless in time of crisis. That crisis, the Great Depression, was at hand as Hoover assumed the presidency in 1929. Herbert Feis, long a State

---

[63] Louis Hartz, *The Liberal Tradition in America* (New York: Harcourt, Brace & World, 1955), 7.

[64] Transcript: "Open Conference on International Finance in the Commercial Policies of Nations," held at Institute of Politics, Williamstown, Massachusetts, 4–26 August 1924, pp. 333–4, William S. Culbertson Papers, Manuscript Division, Library of Congress, Washington, D.C., Box 117.

[65] Investment Bankers Association Address, 30 October 1923, HHPL, File: Public Statements.

Department economic adviser, later wrote, "The investment and banking houses ... were untrained – it must be said – unfit for the task of guiding the flow of American capital abroad."[66] Assistant Secretary of State Francis White concurred, seeing in the avarice of many in the banking community evidence of the conviction in Latin America that "Pan Americanism is purely for the benefit of the United States."[67]

The limits of economic wisdom in the 1920s had other negative consequences that soon became apparent. With the security ethos influencing the policymaking process, the principle of the open door became a fiction, at least in the Americas where a closed door defined business reality.[68] As a result, questionable loans turned Bolivia, for example, into a debt-ridden vassal of the Equitable Trust Company of New York. "Bolivia," one scholar wrote, "had to surrender exceptional sovereignty to foreign financial houses and inspectors."[69] In Peru, Augusto B. Leguía, who ruled for eleven years as the first modern president of his country, accepted extensive dependence on American bankers and businessmen in the name of progress.[70]

The forced surrender of sovereignty afflicted Central America as well. Bonded indebtedness and rampant administrative corruption worked together to inhibit economic diversification beyond the staple crops of coffee and bananas. Such a situation impaired the creation of democratic civil society as foreigners colluded with local elites in matters of politics and economics.[71] Strong resistance to North American hegemony nevertheless emerged in the region, nowhere more surprisingly or, for some time, successfully than among Nicaragua's Americanized elites. By the late 1920s, they were rejecting the very values that they once thought would make them modern and prosperous. The imposition of American-style democracy in rural Nicaragua hastened the appearance of revolution, led by Augusto Sandino, and its opposite, authoritarian rule. Profiting from the disorder brought on by Americanization, Anastasio Somoza and his family dominated Nicaragua from 1936 until 1979.[72]

[66] Herbert Feis, *The Diplomacy of the Dollar, 1919–1932* (Baltimore: Johns Hopkins University Press, 1950), 3.

[67] Francis White to Secretary of State Henry L. Stimson, 14 February 1932, Francis White Papers, Record Group 59, National Archives, Suitland, MD, File: Latin America: General, 1927–1933, Box 3.

[68] Wilson, *American Business and Foreign Policy,* 157–83.

[69] Paul W. Drake, *The Money Doctor in the Andes: The Kemmerer Missions, 1923–1933* (Durham: Duke University Press, 1989), 174.

[70] Walker, "Crucible for Peace," 92.

[71] Victor Bulmer-Thomas, *The Political Economy of Central America since 1920* (New York: Cambridge University Press, 1987), 1–47.

[72] Michel Gobat, *Confronting the American Dream: Nicaragua under U.S. Imperial Rule* (Durham: Duke University Press, 2005), especially chapters 8 and 9. I thank one of my former students at the University of Toronto, Maria Felix Fernandez, whose insights into Gobat's superb book influenced my own understanding of it.

Reflecting the inherent weaknesses of economic knowledge at the time, the Commerce Department under Herbert Hoover also contributed to the diminution of sovereignty. It provided data on financial conditions to bankers desirous of making profitable loans to states whose ability to meet their obligations was doubtful. The department's Bureau of Foreign and Domestic Commerce, through its commodity divisions, promoted the export of American industrial goods, thereby perpetuating an economic division of labor.[73] Implicit in this activity was the assumption that American values could not truly be exported. If values were not readily transferable, what, then, should be made of the universality in the Wilsonian grand strategy? No public official dared raise that troubling question.

The political economy of growth therefore retarded the chances for wide-ranging development and democracy in colonial and dependent areas. Growth, if events in Latin America were typical, resulted from the workings of exclusionary banking and market forces. Development, in contrast, portended a political economy of dynamic competition, which in turn could be conducive to economic democracy, however alien that concept actually was in the 1920s. As we saw in the political realm, democracy, if understood as evidence of self-determination, and security were frequently at odds after the gathering at Versailles. The centers of commercial and financial power in the industrial world, most notably in the United States, were loath to relinquish their elevated status. Agents of economic democracy they were not.

The manifest contradictions of economic policy elicited defensiveness from U.S. officials; Hoover placed a heavy onus for the Great Depression on the major European powers. There was much self-delusion in his position. Historian Zara Steiner writes, "By the time the decade [of the 1920s] drew to a close the building-blocks to form a reconstructed Europe had been put in place."[74] Patrick O. Cohrs echoes this assessment, while dating much earlier an opportunity lost. The Dawes Plan and subsequent London reparations settlement of 1924, together with the Locarno Pact, offered the prospect of integrated European reconstruction, what Cohrs calls the Anglo-American stabilization of Europe and the *Pax Anglo-Americana*.[75] Washington's disinclination to build on these achievements imperiled the London-Locarno system.

U.S. denial of responsibility became pugnacious at times. William S. Culbertson declared in 1930, "Economic forces make inevitable our dominant position in South America.... American business will more than take care of itself.... American capital will be the controlling factor in public and private finance... If anti-American critics wish to describe this as our

---

[73] Walker, "Crucible for Peace," 102.
[74] Steiner, *The Lights That Failed*, 602.
[75] Cohrs, *The Unfinished Peace*.

'imperialism' let them make the most of it."[76] Although he confined his remarks to the Americas, Culbertson was not alone in failing to comprehend how inappropriate policies and the arrogance underlying them had set the stage for global economic disaster. Hoover's encomium to trade at the 1927 Pan-American Financial Conference ignored the limits of U.S. policy. Commerce and capital, he told the delegates, have "a far higher purpose than the making of money by merchants;... [they are] vital to the maintenance of our modern civilization."[77] If trade and investment capital were so important, then America's mission as Hoover defined it was in imminent danger.

Security, Values, and Radicalism from the New Era to the New Deal

The guarded, if unwarranted, optimism of Republicans like Hoover about the benefits of a new economic order concealed the strong antidemocratic biases of the era, notably through welfare capitalism. This domestic division of labor had the capacity to erode civil liberties, particularly after relations in the workplace were couched in the security ethos. Alleging that the Boston police strike of 1919 constituted a "crime against civilization," Woodrow Wilson linked his administration's crusade against radical labor, with its suspected ties to Bolshevism, to Theodore Roosevelt's turn-of-the-century rhetoric about America's sacred duty to safeguard Western civilization. Wilson could have said the same thing about the Seattle general strike. In a climate constructed on fear, bias against workplace democracy knew few bounds, much like the contemporaneous bias against racial democracy.[78] And, much like African Americans, industrial workers attempted to translate their wartime patriotism into postwar improvement of their social and economic status. The mindset that had given rise to the security ethos and the public policies it engendered stood in their way.

An effort in autumn 1919 to unionize steelworkers in towns around Pittsburgh became a test case. Steel magnates Red-baited their workers and brought in blacks from the South as strikebreakers. There was little labor solidarity at the time; the craft-based American Federation of Labor (AFL) declined to extend more than token support to the trade unionists. One historian concludes, "First Amendment rights did not exist in these small [steel towns.]"[79]

---

[76] Culbertson to Hoover, 21 November 1930, Herbert Hoover Presidential Papers, HHPL, File: Foreign Affairs, Diplomats, Culbertson.

[77] Address to the Third Pan-American Commercial Conference, 2 May 1927, HHPL, File: Public Statements.

[78] Quoted in David J. Goldberg, *Discontented America: The United States in the 1920s* (Baltimore: Johns Hopkins University Press, 1999), 67.

[79] Ibid.

The bloody violence of strikebreaking then gave way to the tactic of co-optation, with welfare capitalism as the chosen instrument. To keep unions on the defensive, big business offered stock plans, profit sharing, pensions, and group insurance to workers. Management also pushed the idea of the open shop, calling it the American Plan to cement its identification with industrial capitalism's brand of patriotism. The goal was both to destroy radical trade unions and also to emasculate the craft-based AFL which lost 30 percent of its members by mid-decade. Ironically, Samuel Gompers, head of the AFL, had supported American entry into the war in 1917 as an effort to align labor with the security ethos. With few exceptions, welfare capitalism defeated efforts to unionize labor in America. There would not be, as the Industrial Workers of the World (IWW) had desired, "one big union." By associating labor with foreign ideologies and in the process denying freedom of speech and assembly to their workers, corporate America struck a blow against civil liberties in the workplace.

The struggle between capital and labor at home in the 1920s occurred in a context that contributed to near paranoia about security. Using the word "paranoia" in a political, not clinical, context is an adaptation of the concept as employed by Richard Hofstadter.[80] The conjured fear that a constellation of forces could endanger the nation's safety was a prevalent emotion among those who identified themselves as the last line of defense of American exceptionalism and civilization itself.[81] Except for some like Hoover who acknowledged that workers and managers had important overlapping interests, many authorities looked askance at labor activism among foreign workers, despite their wartime nationalism.

The idea of labor as an active global phenomenon, and the Marxism it possibly presaged, proved unsettling in the postwar political economy, not just in the United States but in Europe as well, where the ideas of Henry Ford about worker productivity and reduced costs greatly impressed anti-union employers.[82] Fear of labor derived from the specter of Bolshevism and its appeal in the first years after the war; these fears led to a backlash against the working class. Before the Depression, union membership had declined throughout Europe. In Britain, bourgeois values competed with socialism for the loyalty of the working class, whereas in France, preindustrial attitudes and an influx of immigrants negatively affected living standards. In Germany, relatively strong trade unions endeavored to work within the

[80] See Richard Hofstadter, *The Paranoid Style in American Politics and Other Essays* (New York: Vintage Books, 1967), 4.

[81] See, for example, Theodore Roosevelt to Henry Cabot Lodge, 27 December 1895, in Elting E. Morison et al., eds., *The Letters of Theodore Roosevelt*, vol. I: *The Years of Preparation, 1868–1898* (Cambridge: Harvard University Press, 1951–54), 503.

[82] Frank Costigliola, *Awkward Dominion: American Political, Economic, and Cultural Relations with Europe, 1919–1933* (Ithaca: Cornell University Press, 1984), 156–7.

capitalist system.[83] By 1930, labor was in retreat as the self-interest of job security tended to trump the democratic ideal of solidarity in the workplace.

An upsurge of labor radicalism in Latin America was retarded in ways that reflected the paranoia elsewhere about the real or imaginary power of the working class. It is worth noting that numerous Mexican laborers during the 1910s found the IWW a congenial organization, which raised fears of social revolution in states along the open border with Mexico. The Inter-American High Commission, created at a Pan-American financial conference in 1915, was one vehicle used to keep labor in check. Bankers and businessmen throughout the hemisphere devoted themselves to exchanging data about trade and investment, although an apparent lack of coordination and cooperation between country committees and the United States Section impaired the effectiveness of the Commission. One thing its members did agree on, however, was the necessity of currency reform, meaning stricter control over the money supply. This diagnosis paved the way for financial expert Edwin W. Kemmerer of Princeton University to undertake a series of missions to South America, the purpose of which, beyond banking reform, was to demonstrate the virtues of managerial expertise to the business class.[84] His efforts, combined with those of the High Commission, met with only mixed results, yet that is beside the point. They sustained the prevailing economic division of labor on which U.S. officials based their understanding of order and security.

Banking reforms and the introduction of professional management techniques became important to America's civilizing mission.[85] This corporate culture not only promoted the Americanization of business but it also begat extraordinary changes in the daily habits of industrial and agricultural workers in many regions of Latin America. When that process, at times similar to welfare capitalism, met with resistance, American companies and compliant local managers dismissed the discontent as evidence of the inherent racial or behavioral inferiority of the workforce.[86] The unstated goal of Americanization, acerbically characterized by one scholar as "the triumph of scientific civilization over nature and primitive superstition," on numerous occasions encountered angry workers and less acquiescent managers.[87] Whether in the Andes, Central America, Cuba, or Mexico, this dichotomy persisted throughout the 1920s and into the Depression years as an inclusive

---

[83] John A. Garraty, *The Great Depression* (San Diego: Harcourt, Brace, Jovanovich, 1986), 86–95.

[84] Generally, see Drake, *The Money Doctor in the Andes*.

[85] Emily S. Rosenberg, *Financial Missionaries to the World: The Politics and Culture of Dollar Diplomacy, 1900–1939* (Cambridge: Harvard University Press, 1999), 95.

[86] Thomas F. O'Brien, *The Revolutionary Mission: American Enterprise in Latin America, 1900–1945* (New York: Cambridge University Press, 1996), *passim*.

[87] Fredrick W. Pike, *The United States and Latin America: Myths and Stereotypes of Civilization and Nature* (Austin: University of Texas Press, 1992), 226.

populist nationalism took its stand against American efforts to impose corporate values and exclusionary forms of modernization. Nicaraguan Liberal and revolutionary Augusto Sandino assessed the impact of North American corporate culture in blunt terms: "The working class of all Latin America today suffers a double exploitation, that of imperialism, mainly that of the Yankee, and that of the nationalist capitalists and exploiters."[88] Even if the actual dichotomy was not quite what Sandino charged, his lament did not exaggerate the general conditions against which he rebelled.

By the late 1920s, working-class radicalism seemed less of a threat than it had a decade earlier. Organized labor traditionally had scarcely a better chance than African Americans to find a niche in the democratic process. In that respect, the severity of the Great Depression offered industrial labor an unexpected opportunity to recoup the rights that business and the state had taken away. The struggle to achieve the right to organize and bargain collectively was a reminder that republican governance must apply to all citizens if core principles were to resonate over time. Some years later, in 1935, federal mediator Lloyd Garrison told a Senate committee hearing, "I regard organized labor in this country as our chief bulwark against Communism and revolutionary movements."[89] United Mine Workers (UMW) head John L. Lewis strongly concurred, averring that labor stood on guard against those "who would lay waste to our traditions and institutions."[90]

The Wagner Act of 1935, which recognized the rights of labor to engage in the political process in order to pursue market stability, was hardly perfect. The supervisory function of the National Labor Relations Board (NLRB) approximated a mandate system, like that created at Versailles, in which mediators in essence served as trustees. Yet, despite strife within the labor movement – as seen in the founding in 1935 of the Congress of Industrial Organizations resulting from philosophical differences with the AFL and the desperate, violent resistance to labor's gains in the automobile and steel industries – the momentum toward workplace democracy was irresistible.[91] Achieving their goal would ultimately bring most trade unions into conformity with the security ethos; in the mid-1930s that development could not have been easily foreseen.

Another reaction to the impact of the Depression showed that, although radicalism had been contained in the New Era of the 1920s, it had not been vanquished. The plight of the Bonus Army emphasized the power of the

[88] Quoted in Thomas O'Brien, *The Century of U.S. Capitalism in Latin America* (Albuquerque: University of New Mexico Press, 1999), 93.

[89] Quoted in Irving Bernstein, *Turbulent Years: A History of the American Worker, 1933–1941* (Boston: Houghton Mifflin, 1970), 332.

[90] Quoted in Melvyn Dubofsky and Warren Van Tine, *John L. Lewis* (New York: Quadrangle/New York Times, 1977), 183.

[91] Colin Gordon, *New Deals: Business, Labor, and Politics in America, 1920–1935* (New York: Cambridge University Press, 1994), 204–39.

security ethos over public discourse, by then not something unusual, while offering the tantalizing possibility that it had run its course. The subdued response of the Hoover administration to Japan's seizure of Manchuria in 1932 suggested that a rethinking of foreign policy was then underway. The misery of the times, however, impaired the capacity of isolationists, beguiled by the false promise of the Kellogg-Briand Treaty of 1928 and the meager results of the London Naval Conference of 1932, to implement a less internationalist direction in policy. Known as the Stimson Doctrine after Secretary of State Henry L. Stimson, the principle of "nonrecognition of the fruits of aggression" constituted an example of selective internationalism from which Hoover did not dissent. In fact, both men took credit for the idea.[92] Charles A. Beard would later describe Stimson as "an imperialist of the Theodore Roosevelt-Lodge-Mahan-Beveridge School." Beard based his harsh assessment on the secretary's opposition to granting full independence to the Philippines.[93] Stimson's defense of a strategic presence in Asia would help preclude a reassessment of U.S. interests there, both after the start of the Sino-Japanese War in 1937 and at the end of World War II.

Conclusion

In the summer of 1932, the great harm the security ethos could do to civil liberties was on display for Americans to see. The U.S. Army's brutal assault on veterans of the Great War was arguably worse than the damage inflicted on core values during the Red Scare. Wartime enforcement of the Espionage and Sedition laws could perhaps be defended as an unavoidable necessity, like Lincoln's suspension of the writ of habeas corpus during the Civil War. Nevertheless, portraying citizens who had served honorably in the military as enemies of the state had no precedent in American history; yet, that is precisely what Chief of Staff Douglas MacArthur and his deputy Brigadier General George Van Horn Moseley proceeded to do. Moseley called for extraordinary measures in times of crisis – to the point of exiling "important public officials when circumstances required" and placing "carefully selected military governors ... in all our states and the District of Columbia." Whether Herbert Hoover learned about Moseley's remarkable and dangerous recommendations is not known.[94]

What is certain is that some Americans were more prepared than the president to defend core values, as railroad unions helped protect the veterans in

---

[92] Robert H. Ferrell, *American Diplomacy and the Great Depression: Hoover-Stimson Foreign Policy, 1929–1933* (New Haven: Yale University Press, 1957), 87–105, 150–69; Wilson, *American Business and Foreign Policy*, 221–30.

[93] Charles A. Beard, *American Foreign Policy in the Making, 1932–1940: A Study in Responsibilities* (New Haven: Yale University Press, 1946), 113.

[94] Quoted in David Burner, *Herbert Hoover: A Public Life* (New York: Alfred A. Knopf, 1979), 306–7.

their trek across the country. Hoover had opposed giving veterans a bonus prior to the scheduled date of 1945. To his credit, he initially tried to down-play the presence of 20,000 veterans in the nation's capital, but changed his mind when communists urged marchers to take direct and, if need be, violent action. MacArthur, ignoring Hoover's orders, moved on July 28 to quell the "revolution." The general ordered his forces to burn the veterans' camp, which Hoover did not disavow. Instead, he blamed what transpired on communists and criminals, a claim he minimized in his *Memoirs,* as if protesting citizens were not entitled to exercise their freedoms of speech and assembly.[95] Hoover's ambivalence about how to respond to radicalism was reflected in his decision not to reduce the size of the U.S. Army as a money-saving measure. To do so, he asserted, would "lessen our means of maintaining domestic peace and order."[96]

Franklin Roosevelt told his friend Felix Frankfurter that his election as president was a certainty. Amid widespread outrage over the routing of the veterans, even the American Legion denounced Hoover. In an inchoate way, the legitimacy of the security ethos came under critical scrutiny. It was the American people's rejection of the New Era that swept Roosevelt to victory in 1932. Was a revival of traditional isolationism at hand? Superficially, the record of New Deal foreign policy suggests that such developments were possible. A closer look indicates otherwise. The link between security policy and core values, and the latter's dependence on the former, would remain intact even as segments of the popular classes and some public officials and intellectuals endeavored to transform what remained of republican virtue into a more democratic, or civic, culture.

[95] Ibid., 309–12; Wilson, *Hoover,* 162.
[96] Quoted in Garraty, *The Great Depression,* 165.

4

The Construction of Global Containment

Liberty is not the exclusive right of any racial or other group.
Walter White, 1936

Give them a share. They think they are just as good as we are, and many of them are.
Franklin D. Roosevelt, 1940

[H]ow hard it is for a democracy to conduct a successful foreign policy.
George F. Kennan, 1948

Franklin D. Roosevelt had impeccable internationalist credentials. Secretary of State Henry L. Stimson instructed him about foreign policy matters after the 1932 election. A grateful Roosevelt opined that "we do pretty good teamwork."[1] This mutual appreciation is unsurprising. Stimson served as secretary of war from 1911 to 1913 and Roosevelt as assistant secretary of the navy from 1913 through 1920. If Stimson drank at the strategic fount of Mahan, so too did Roosevelt, who had read two of Mahan's books on sea power by the age of sixteen.[2] His lifelong love of the sea found expression in his embrace of "the big-navy views" of Mahan; he took the logic of preparedness, especially naval preparedness, as a given. In that sense, Roosevelt as president disdained what he saw as the parochial worldview of the isolationists. Yet, he did not have the luxury of ignoring them because of their political clout, even though they could not compel a fundamental reevaluation of U.S. foreign policy.[3] Despite being buffeted by calls to return to a simpler time when politics ostensibly did stop at the water's edge, the

---

[1] Quoted in Henry L. Stimson, with McGeorge Bundy, *On Active Service in Peace and War* (New York: Harper & Row, 1947), 293.

[2] Frank Friedel, *Franklin D. Roosevelt: The Apprenticeship* (Boston: Little, Brown, 1952), 46–7.

[3] Wayne S. Cole, *Roosevelt and the Isolationists, 1932–1945* (Lincoln: University of Nebraska Press, 1983), *passim*; quoted words, 4.

security ethos remained essentially unscathed during Roosevelt's first two terms as president.[4]

In the time between the outbreak of war in Europe in September 1939 and the Japanese attack on Pearl Harbor in December 1941, Roosevelt charted an irreversible course in foreign policy. Isolationism stood discredited as a relic of an antiquated past and as a danger to the welfare of the nation.[5] Advocates of noninvolvement were depicted as the anti-modernists of their day who would despoil the basic values for which America stood. Making the crucial point that the demands of security must transcend partisanship, Roosevelt brought the Republican Stimson at seventy-two years of age into his cabinet as secretary of war. The president told Stimson that he "would be a stabilizing factor in whom both the Army and the public would have confidence."[6] During occasionally testy confirmation hearings before the Senate Committee on Military Affairs, Stimson observed, "I do not believe that the United States can be safely protected by a purely passive or defensive defense."[7] An exemplar of the security ethos, Stimson was at ease with the direction of Roosevelt's foreign policy.

Although Stimson was not meant to be a stalking horse for a turn toward globalism in foreign policy, Roosevelt needed all the experienced help he could get in committing the nation to a new kind of internationalism, one that would welcome rather than abjure the responsibilities of leadership. Despite the efforts in the mid-1930s of some intellectuals, most notably Charles A. Beard, to find a middle way between isolationism and reflexive internationalism, the war and Roosevelt's own thinking about power and responsibility made such an endeavor impossible. "We shall bear our full responsibility," the president pledged in October 1944, "exercise our full influence, and bring our help and encouragement to all who aspire to peace and freedom."[8]

Nothing better represents Roosevelt's intent than the Atlantic Charter. One admiring scholar contends that he desired "the internationalization of the New Deal."[9] Whether a combination of internationalism and liberalism on a grand scale was possible without endangering American values could

---

[4] This conclusion differs from that of Robert Divine, *The Illusion of Neutrality: Franklin D. Roosevelt and the Struggle over the Arms Embargo* (Chicago: University of Chicago Press, 1962).

[5] The battle the isolationists lost is best related in Justus D. Doenecke, *Storm on the Horizon: The Challenge to American Intervention, 1939–1941* (Lanham: Rowman & Littlefield, 2003).

[6] Stimson, *On Active Service in Peace and War*, 323.

[7] Ibid., 325.

[8] Quoted in Odd Arne Westad, The *Global Cold War: Third World Interventions and the Making of Our Times* (Cambridge: Cambridge University Press, 2005), 20.

[9] Elizabeth Borgwardt, *A New Deal for the World: America's Vision for Human Rights* (Cambridge: Belknap Press of Harvard University Press, 2005), 3.

not be foreseen in August 1941 when Roosevelt met with British Prime Minister Winston S. Churchill off the coast of Newfoundland and gave voice to the Four Freedoms. The task was a formidable one, however. The president's aspirations got caught up in the conduct of the war, leading to compromises reminiscent of Wilson's after the Great War and to the curtailment of civil liberties, the internment of Japanese Americans being merely the best known. And despite Roosevelt's intentions and efforts, the Grand Alliance could not survive the war. Franklin Roosevelt died before Cold War with the Soviet Union destroyed his vision of power politics mixed with humanistic globalism.

Harry S. Truman bears some responsibility for what is called the "Cold War." Three events of February–March 1946 – Joseph Stalin's election speech, George F. Kennan's "Long Telegram," and Churchill's Iron Curtain address – previewed the coming estrangement. Yet, on the American side of the divide, Truman and his advisers implemented policies based on assumptions about security that reflected a history of suspicion, fear, and the preemptive use of forces. This way of seeing the world assured a future of flawed decision making.[10]

Truman's insecurity about ascending to the presidency, his lack of knowledge about foreign affairs, and his having to deal with leaders like Churchill and Stalin, whom he held in awe, left little room for him to ponder how security considerations might affect American institutions and values. His conduct in a meeting with Soviet Foreign Minister Vyacheslav Molotov in late April 1945, his actions at the Potsdam Conference, and his decisions about ending war with Japan do not show a disposition to self-reflection. Nor did the milieu in the White House encourage second-guessing; the president insisted on unswerving loyalty from those around him.[11] Truman, as an able machine politician and U.S. senator from Missouri, and James F. Byrnes, like the president a former senator and Roosevelt's director of war mobilization who became secretary of state in July 1945, were parochial and strongly nationalist in their approach to politics. One scholar concludes, "Byrnes was as ignorant of foreign affairs as the president."[12]

Furthermore, the insularity of the men who influenced Truman's thinking about foreign policy in his early years as president precluded flexibility in the tumultuous international setting. This insularity of businessmen, diplomats, and lawyers, including Averrell Harriman, George F. Kennan, Dean G. Acheson, Henry Stimson, and James Forrestal, among others, reflected their Atlanticist view of the world. Europe came first in their understanding

---

[10] For an interpretation that harks back to interpretive battles that were waged in the 1970s, see Wilson D. Miscamble, *From Roosevelt to Truman: Potsdam, Hiroshima, and the Cold War* (New York: Cambridge University Press, 2006), especially 43–86.

[11] Arnold A. Offner, *Another Such Victory: President Truman and the Cold War, 1946–1953* (Stanford: Stanford University Press, 2002), 22–3.

[12] Patricia Dawson Ward, *The Threat of Peace: James F. Byrnes and the Council of Foreign Ministers, 1945–1946* (Kent: Kent State University Press, 1979), 5.

of security, political economy, and culture, as it had for Roosevelt.[13] Call it hegemony or "empire by invitation," the global order that took shape after 1945, including the international monetary system devised at Bretton Woods in 1944, was Washington's creation.[14]

However natural that development must have seemed to Truman's advisers, it did not necessarily bode well for the future of U.S. foreign policy or American core values.[15] As containment of communism became the central objective of policymakers, the United States squandered an opportunity to assist nationalist and anticolonial movements. It is no small irony that Franklin Roosevelt's anticolonial pretensions, which lay at the heart of the Atlantic Charter, ultimately had no more substance than did Wilson's commitment to self-determination. These ideals fell victim to the security ethos whose power was never clearer than in debates over the modern national security state that formally took shape in 1947 with the passage of the National Security Act.

Roosevelt's thinking about global war assisted the creation of a security state. If the Four Freedoms of the Atlantic Charter were supposed to inspire others, they were also meant to serve as guidelines for security policy in a dangerous world. The United Sates would oppose all states, political systems, and ideologies threatening its freedom. Nazi Germany's attack on the Soviet Union in June 1941 forced a tactical reassessment of the universality of this conviction. It did not change it, however, and by 1946, the Truman administration, following the logic of Roosevelt's viewpoint, was ready to stand up to the challenge posed by the Soviet Union.[16]

Walter Lippmann, fearing that an internationalist foreign policy would slip into unchecked globalism, advocated the continuation of the Grand Alliance in his 1943 book, *U.S. Foreign Policy: Shield of the Republic.* Cordial relations among America, Britain, and Russia would protect the republic while the allies built a manageable world order in which each power had a stake. His hopes were dashed by the difficulties plaguing the alliance during the latter stages of the war, by Roosevelt's death, and by the Truman administration's lack of trust in the Soviets.[17] In a series of columns published in 1947 as *The Cold War,* a response to Kennan's famous

---

[13] See, for example, John Lamberton Harper, *American Visions of Europe: Franklin D. Roosevelt, George F. Kennan, and Dean G. Acheson* (New York: Cambridge University Press, 1994).

[14] Geir Lundestad, "Empire by Invitation?: The United States and Western Europe, 1945–1952," *Journal of Peace Research* 23 (September 1986): 263–77.

[15] For an insightful look at the common background of national security managers, see Richard Barnet, *Roots of War: The Men and Institutions behind U.S. Foreign Policy* (New York: Atheneum Publishers, 1972), 48–75.

[16] This paragraph draws on Anders Stephanson, "Fourteen Notes on the Very Concept of the Cold War," (especially notes 11 and 12) that appeared on the H-Diplo discussion network in May–June 1996. It can be accessed electronically at http://h-net.msu.edu.

[17] Ronald Steel, *Walter Lippmann and the American Century* (Boston: Little, Brown, 1980), 404–11.

"Mr. X" article – the public version of the Long Telegram – in *Foreign Affairs*, Lippmann feared that containment would have few limits; that is, it would be a blank check to be drawn on the account of the "American constitutional system." He deemed it equally threatening to the nation's economy.[18]

By early 1950, the Policy Planning Staff (PPS) of the Department of State under Paul H. Nitze's direction was preparing one of the seminal documents of postwar foreign policy, National Security Council (NSC) Document 68 (NSC-68), which Truman received on April 7. Nitze had a background as an investment banker; he admired authority and discipline, leading some critics to pronounce him pro-Nazi.[19] As an aide to Forrestal, he shared his mentor's views about the dangers of communism and the precarious state of American exceptionalism.[20] NSC-68, which can be seen as a statement about political economy as well as strategy, declared that "a new fanatic faith, antithetical to our own" animated the Soviet Union, which "seeks to impose its absolute authority over the rest of the world." Washington therefore had to respond; the republic would survive the uncertainties of globalism. "The integrity of our system," the authors contended, "will not be jeopardized by any measures, covert or overt, violent or non-violent, which serve the purposes of frustrating the Kremlin design."[21]

Having drawn on Kennan's emotional denunciation of the Soviet system in the Long Telegram as the basis for their alarmist prescriptions, Nitze and his colleagues, as self-styled realists, were arguing that the ends justified the means.[22] Moreover, they appropriated the work of thinkers like Reinhold Niebuhr and Hans Morgenthau, giving their ideas, which earlier had posited a universal human nature – with Morgenthau's the darker view – a spurious political instrumentalism.[23] Niebuhr, the Lutheran theologian and co-founder in 1947 of the liberal, anticommunist Americans for Democratic Action, vigorously criticized antiwar radicals in the late 1930s and leftist dissent against the Cold War a decade later. In his classic work, *Politics among Nations* (1948), Morgenthau argued that a foreign policy devoted to the pursuit of balance might temper the nationalist lust for power. By

---

[18] Walter Lippmann, *The Cold War: A Study in U.S. Foreign Policy*, introduction by Ronald Steel (New York: Harper Torchbooks, 1972), 9–10.

[19] Bruce Kuklick, *Blind Oracles: Intellectuals and War from Kennan to Kissinger* (Princeton: Princeton University Press, 2006), 43.

[20] Ibid., 44–7.

[21] U.S. Department of State, *Foreign Relations of the United States, 1950*, vol. I: *National Security Affairs; Foreign Economic Policy* (Washington, DC: Government Printing Office, 1977), 237, 244 (quoted words).

[22] Frank Costigliola, "'Unceasing Pressure for Penetration': Gender, Pathology, and Emotion in George Kennan's Formation of the Cold War," *Journal of American History 83* (March 1997): 1309–39.

[23] Campbell Craig, *Glimmer of a New Leviathan: Total War in the Realism of Niebuhr, Morgenthau, and Waltz* (New York: Columbia University Press, 2003), 78, 79.

1951 in his book, *In Defense of the National Interest*, the German expatriate was much less dispassionate, calling for the rearmament of Europe, a position consistent with the dicta of NSC-68 and a cudgel that could be used to silence domestic foes of globalism.[24] More than ever before, the fate of tradition and basic liberties was tied to how the governing elite acted to make the nation secure.

Franklin D. Roosevelt and the Emergence of American Globalism

All that lay in the future as the Great Depression worsened in the early 1930s. The London Economic Conference held in 1933 called Roosevelt's internationalism into question; he refused to consider a currency stabilization scheme because of the condition of the American economy. Why was the meeting in London objectionable to Roosevelt? To be sure, the domestic economy needed immediate attention, and concern about the possible power of the Left in American politics was growing in 1933. Not until two years later would the play *Waiting for Lefty* by Clifford Odets be performed, although business bankruptcies, bank closings, mortgage foreclosures, and long breadlines demonstrated why some Americans already had lost faith in the New Era's brand of capitalism.

The London Economic Conference was a political forum as well as an economic gathering. To have participated fully there and at the concurrent disarmament sessions at Geneva, where Democratic stalwart Norman H. Davis represented American interests, would have betokened a more thoroughgoing internationalism than was then possible. Although Roosevelt and other internationalists were concerned about Japan's regional ambitions and the rise to power in Germany of Adolf Hitler, they were not sufficiently alarmed to change course and commit the nation to a security pact in either Europe or East Asia. Thomas W. Lamont of J. P. Morgan and Company and like-minded bankers did not want to impair financial relations with Japan, which economic sanctions or a security pact would have done.[25] Davis, ever the Atlanticist, was not wrong, only premature when he recommended in January 1933 making overtures to Great Britain and France for "maintaining a similar policy for coping with the [current] situation which is of such vital importance to the three countries."[26]

On reflection, Roosevelt's vacillation over the direction of foreign policy was not unusual. Like Hoover and Wilson, he believed that a militarized

[24] Ibid., 54–83.

[25] Joan Hoff Wilson, *American Business and Foreign Policy, 1921–1933* (Lexington: University Press of Kentucky, 1971), 230–2.

[26] Norman H. Davis to Franklin D. Roosevelt, 10 January 1933, in Edgar B. Nixon, ed., *Franklin D. Roosevelt and Foreign Affairs*, 3 vols., Vol. I: *January 1933–February 1934* (Cambridge: Belknap Press of Harvard University Press, 1969), 3.

political economy would not produce lasting peace and prosperity. That approach to world affairs evoked the failure of the nineteenth-century world order. Even though Roosevelt agreed with Davis that European stability was crucial to America's future, he nevertheless shared the reservations of his two predecessors about too close an association with Britain and France.[27] Thus, there would be no discretionary arms embargo, no concerted movement toward disarmament, no war-debt relief, no tariff reduction, and no currency stabilization. After the failure in London, the French attitude toward the United States was "one of contempt," a sentiment echoed by some in the British government who were advocating improved relations with Japan to protect Britain's economic interests in China. William C. Bullitt, an adviser at Versailles who broke with Wilson over policy toward Russia, also informed Roosevelt, "The general opinion here is that war in Europe is inevitable."[28]

The foreign policy of Roosevelt and Secretary of State Cordell Hull was often one of caution. The administration endeavored to keep the isolationists at bay, both during the Nye Committee hearings in 1934 over bankers, munitions makers, and American entry into the Great War and on the volatile issue of neutrality legislation. At other times, an internationalist dimension was more evident. Policy toward Latin America, the Good Neighbor policy, stands out in that regard. Roosevelt promised to improve hemispheric relations, and on the surface he delivered admirably. Despite a rocky start with Cuba in 1933–4, when it considered invoking the Platt Amendment, the administration turned away from intervention as a foreign policy tool. Formal acceptance of nonintervention came at a conference in Buenos Aires in December 1936 with Roosevelt present. Hull also hoped to use the Reciprocal Trade Agreements Act of 1934 and the newly created Export-Import Bank to begin the reconstruction of foreign economic policy, particularly in the Western Hemisphere. The desire for better relations led to negotiation instead of confrontation after Bolivia and Mexico eliminated foreign oil concessions in 1937 and 1938, respectively. At the Lima Conference in 1938 and at Havana in 1940, the conferees moved toward a multilateral defense strategy in the event of attack. By the latter year, the State Department was envisioning the Export-Import Bank as a key source of funds for resource exploitation and development of light industry in Latin America.[29] The sense of regional comity was perhaps at its height in January 1940 when Roosevelt mused about the nations south of the Rio Grande, "Give

[27] This assessment is suggested in Davis to Roosevelt, 7 April, 1933, ibid., 44–8.

[28] William C. Bullitt to Roosevelt, 8 July 1933, ibid., 289–95; quoted words, 291.

[29] Frederick C. Adams, *Economic Diplomacy: The Export-Import Bank and American Foreign Policy, 1934–1939* (Columbia: University of Missouri Press, 1976), 68–97, 129–59, 188–225.

them a share. They think they are just as good as we are, and many of them are."[30]

The ostensible success of the Good Neighbor policy moved Sumner Welles, the leading Department of State official on hemispheric affairs and a close confidant of the president, and the Council on Foreign Relations to imagine Latin America as the model for U.S. foreign policy.[31] The turn toward some reciprocity in regional affairs was evocative of Wilson's post-presidential hope that "we might be given another opportunity to set the country right in the view of Latin America."[32] For more than three decades, U.S. officials had not actually determined where the vital interests of the nation were located: The Open Door policy suggested Asia, trade patterns and cultural heritage indicated Europe, and political and economic developments after the Great War pointed to Latin America. The point is that the security ethos, born of fear and a sense of exceptionalism, left scant room for objectives like self-determination or, as we see later, human rights in decision-making councils.

In fact, abrogation of the Platt Amendment in 1934 and Roosevelt's pledge not to intervene, removal of troops from Haiti, and forbearance in the face of property seizures concealed the limits of reciprocity in American policy. U.S. forces sailed away, leaving behind strongmen such as Fulgencio Batista in Cuba, Anastasio Somoza in Nicaragua, and Rafael Trujillo in the Dominican Republic. There were, it should be noted, other ways to maintain U.S. dominance in the region, including a willingness by businessmen and the State Department to curry favor with leaders irrespective of their political credentials, the role of the Export-Import Bank in creating an updated dollar diplomacy, and the advent of military missions.[33] Complementing a reliance on military and police forces as guardians of order in Latin America during the Depression, starting in mid-1940 the Federal Bureau of Investigation (FBI) was charged with preventing Nazi subversion in the hemisphere.[34] This mission further cemented a security nexus among the majority of the American republics.

---

[30] Quoted in David Green, *The Containment of Latin America: A History of the Myths and Realities of the Good Neighbor Policy* (Chicago: Quadrangle Books, 1971), 38.

[31] Irwin F. Gellman, *Secret Affairs: Franklin Roosevelt, Cordell Hull, and Sumner Welles* (Baltimore: Johns Hopkins University Press, 1995), 108–9; Robert D. Schulzinger, *The Wise Men of Foreign Affairs: The History of the Council on Foreign Relations* (New York: Columbia University Press, 1984), 47–53.

[32] Arthur S. Link et al., eds., *The Papers of Woodrow Wilson*, vol. 67: *December 24, 1920– April 7, 1922* (Princeton: Princeton University Press, 1992), 385.

[33] Adams, *Economic Diplomacy*, 224; Brian Loveman, *For la Patria: Politics and the Armed Forces in Latin America* (Wilmington: Scholarly Resources, 1999), 67–72.

[34] Max Paul Friedman, *Nazis and Good Neighbors: The United States Campaign against the Germans of Latin America in World War II* (New York: Cambridge University Press, 2003), 61–73.

Internationalist impulses also impelled policy toward East Asia. In a book about U.S. policymaking in the 1930s subtitled "A Study in Responsibilities," Charles Beard wrote that his reading of sources in 1934 led him "to the conclusion that the Roosevelt Administration would eventually involve the United States in a war with Japan."[35] Even if Beard, writing at the end of World War II, was engaged in ex post facto reasoning, he was asking whether an assertive policy in Asia had been in the nation's best interest. The seizure of Manchuria had sounded alarm bells previously set off by the Twenty-One Demands. Wilson biographer Ray Stannard Baker commented in 1919 as Tokyo pursued its interests at Versailles, "Left to the mercies of Japan . . . , the Orient would soon be arrayed in arms against the Occident."[36] The announcement in 1933 that Tokyo would leave the League of Nations and the enunciation of the Amau Doctrine of 1934, which set out what might be called Japan's Roosevelt Corollary for Asia, greatly concerned American authorities.[37] In addition, Tokyo's decision to abrogate the Washington naval treaty helped harden American and British antagonism. To Beard, the critical issue of responsibility for the deterioration in relations with Japan should have been at the heart of public debates about foreign policy.

In East Asia, the ambivalence of the State Department toward China's military strongman Jiang Jieshi also complicated the making of policy. Ambassador Nelson Trusler Johnson denounced Chinese authorities in March 1933 for "maintaining [their] own satrapy and extorting the maximum from the people" through taxes on salt and opium and customs duties.[38] Joseph Stilwell, U.S. military attaché, whose animus toward Jiang is well documented, felt similarly. As the intent of Japan's Kwantung Army to expand into North China became apparent, U.S. reservations about Jiang changed. No longer was his government "pathetically naïve" as Johnson had put it in 1932; by mid-1934, it had become "realistic" in dealing with its enemies. Although the ambassador was referring to Nanjing's opium policy, his assessment mirrored a shift in overall attitudes in Washington.[39] Stanley K. Hornbeck of the Division of Far Eastern Affairs argued, in defense of the Open Door policy

---

[35] Charles A. Beard, *American Foreign Policy in the Making, 1932–1940: A Study in Responsibilities* (New Haven: Yale University Press, 1946), 162 n. 13.

[36] Link et al., eds., *The Papers of Woodrow Wilson*, vol. 58: *April 23–May 9, 1919* (Princeton: Princeton University Press, 1988), 231.

[37] For several translations of the statement by Japanese Foreign Office spokesman Eiji Amau and comment on the matter, see Joseph C. Grew, *Ten Years in Japan* (New York: Simon & Schuster, 1944), 128–33.

[38] Nelson Trusler Johnson to the Department of State, March 29, 1933, Record Group (RG) 59, File 893.00 P.R./65, General Records of the Department of State, National Archives (NA), Suitland, MD.

[39] Johnson to the Department of State, July 6, 1932, RG 59 893.114 Narcotics/370, NA; Johnson to Stanley K. Hornbeck, May 31, 1934, Nelson T. Johnson Papers, Box 23, General Correspondence, Manuscript Division, Library of Congress, Washington, DC.

and the Washington naval agreement, that acquiescing in Japan's ambitions "would mean that either we *change our whole foreign policy* . . . or make a definite and specific exception as regards the Far East."[40]

Hornbeck's perspective showed how America's quest for security could impair determining to what extent U.S. interests were actually at stake in East Asia. Since the days of dollar diplomacy U.S.-Japanese relations had often been on the verge of crisis. The sense of entitlement to greater influence in Asian affairs, reflective of the security ethos, also moved Hornbeck to assert, "The Chinese have been and are easygoing and complacent, whereas the Japanese have been and are active, aggressive and inclined to be bellicose."[41] By mid-decade, Washington and London agreed that Japanese expansion posed a threat to Asian stability.

In retrospect, Roosevelt appears to have used events to begin developing his own style of internationalism, one that was less beholden either to Wilsonian strategy or Hull's economic diplomacy. An evolutionary line runs from Stimson's desire to attach sanctions to his nonrecognition policy, through Roosevelt's position in late 1934, to the president's Quarantine Speech of October 1937, and beyond. Disarmament had run its course as a viable means to contain Japan; the Greater East Asia Co-Prosperity Sphere was becoming a reality. And Tokyo's virtual autarky precluded using economic foreign policy to support moderates within the Japanese government. The basic goal for the Roosevelt administration as its strategic planning became more globalist was to deter Japan and thereby show support for the British war effort in Europe. Ironically, the inevitable freeze on Japanese assets in July 1941 and the consequent trade embargo limited Washington's options.[42] Avoiding war was then nearly impossible because of the chasm between Roosevelt's intentions and the actions of Japanese forces in China and their occupation by August 1941 of much of French Indochina.

A change in U.S. policy from selective internationalism to globalism would have been impossible without a close relationship with European democracies. As the threat posed by Germany increased, Roosevelt had to take into account neutrality laws in devising a response. Appeasement at Munich must therefore be viewed in the context of lingering Anglo-French mistrust of the United States. The time between Munich and his decision in late 1939 to aid Britain and France with repeal of the arms embargo and to provide war supplies on a "cash and carry" basis allowed Roosevelt to lobby American citizens for a more active global role and to forge a reliable basis for a transatlantic partnership. After Munich, he associated

---

[40] U.S. Department of State, *Foreign Relations of the United States, 1935*, vol. 3: *The Far East* (Washington, DC: Government Printing Office, 1953), 832 (emphasis added).

[41] *Roosevelt and Foreign Affairs*, I: 660.

[42] Michael A. Barnhart, *Japan Prepares for Total War: The Search for Economic Security, 1919–1941* (Ithaca: Cornell University Press, 1987), 218, 225–6.

the national interest with preventing German hegemony over Europe. The endeavor led the president toward rearmament, a peacetime draft, and a 500 percent increase in the defense budget.[43] About Roosevelt's slowness in telling the public how dire he thought the international situation truly was, Stimson wrote in late 1940 after Lend-Lease had been presented to the nation, "The President went as far as he could at the present time."[44]

Roosevelt was then fully committed to a foreign and strategic policy that was global in scope. In a real sense, he had turned Wilson's worldview on its head. Like Wilson, as historian David Reynolds observes, Roosevelt and his foreign policy team believed that "the United States had a unique duty as exemplar to the world." This time, however, America would lead, with the result that Britain, "the world's greatest empire," would soon be "dependent on American power."[45] Lend-Lease probably saved Britain from greater harm by Nazi Germany; it also symbolized the overweening economic might of the United States. Before long, the demands of the American political economy would threaten to put an end to imperial prerogatives.[46] Whether the globalism that Roosevelt envisioned was commensurate with the national interest was a question the president did not directly engage. Assuming the universality of American objectives came easily to the president and cabinet members like Stimson in 1941.

New Deal Liberalism, Its Limits, and Critics

New Deal liberalism had two main pillars. On taking office, Franklin Roosevelt set out to save marketplace capitalism within a context of general government activism; meliorative social reforms would come later, especially in 1935. Consistent with the president's wishes, Congress cut $400 million from payments to veterans and trimmed $100 million from the pay of federal employees. These actions followed an interregnum of unemployment, bank failures, business closings, chaos for America's farmers, and general despair. It was not apparent in March 1933 how the government would balance many competing demands for increased spending and the historical practice of economic contraction in bad times. The New Dealers, with a governing philosophy evocative of the ideas of Herbert Croly, John Dewey, and the young Walter Lippmann, among others, favored some combination of business-government cooperation and regulatory authority. Jettisoning the gold standard in April tilted the New Deal toward economic nationalism

---

[43] Mark A. Stoler, *Allies in War: Britain and America against the Axis Powers, 1940–1945* (London: Hodder Arnold, 2005), 5–17.

[44] Stimson, *On Active Service in Peace and War*, 366.

[45] David Reynolds, *The Creation of the Anglo-American Alliance, 1937–41: A Study in Competitive Co-operation* (Chapel Hill: University of North Carolina Press, 1981), 252; quoted words, 253.

[46] Ibid., 274–80.

and monetary inflation, without which the reconstruction of American capitalism would have been less likely.

These tactics were interim, confidence-building maneuvers that did not produce sustained recovery, and informal efforts to stabilize the dollar against British and French currencies with the Tripartite Money Agreement in September 1936 had limited effect. With the recession of 1937, Roosevelt turned to pump priming as an essential economic tool. In his classic 1984 essay, "From New Deal to Normalcy," Thomas Ferguson shows that the New Dealers were determined to forge a coalition to reorganize the American economy, comprising "capital-intensive industries, investment banks, and internationally oriented commercial banks."[47] Therein lay the roots of multinational liberalism, the second pillar.

These constituencies stood to prosper from freer international trade. The business sector, attempting to keep radical labor and tariff protectionists in check, worked with the government to transcend the economic nationalism of the early New Deal. The National Industrial Recovery Act of 1933, with its controversial Section 7a that recognized the rights of workers to form unions, failed. The subsequent 1935 National Labor Relations Act held considerable appeal for big business, in part because of the workplace stability that collective bargaining seemed to promise. Business leaders hoped, too, that the conservative American Federation of Labor would retard the spread of communism in the working class. In addition, capital-intensive industries supported the Social Security Act; despite its regressive payroll taxes, the act offered a dependable means of giving the workforce a stake in the health of the economy. The allure of reciprocal trade ruptured the anti-Roosevelt business alliance that was the Liberty League; protectionism had come to mean economic stagnation for many Republican industrialists. Disaffected Democrat and former Treasury Department official Dean Acheson and Texas cotton baron William L. Clayton swung to the president's side shortly before the 1936 election, indicating that the historic influence of protective tariffs over economic policy was at risk. Gradually, a multinational business bloc was forming; before long, it would provide the commercial and financial underpinnings for Roosevelt's globalist aspirations.

One promise of twentieth-century liberalism had encompassed the promotion and protection of group welfare in a capitalist democracy; consideration of individual rights, which was seen as a nineteenth-century conceit by reformers who equated individualism with laissez-faire ideas, was transformed into a concern about civil liberties in general. The structure of the American political economy and foreign policy goals in the era of the New Deal impaired the cause of self-determination – a useful indicator since 1919

---

[47] Thomas Ferguson, "From Normalcy to New Deal: Industrial Structure, Party Competition, and American Public Policy in the Great Depression," *International Organization* 38 (Winter 1984): 85–92; quoted words, 46.

of the durability of core values – at home and abroad. Whatever else may have characterized liberalism by the time of Japan's attack on Pearl Harbor, caution was surely a central feature. Historian Alan Brinkley makes the plausible argument that liberals endeavored to "reshape their convictions in response to the realities of the world they knew."[48]

Brinkley's assessment reduces the role of agency and, thus, responsibility for the deleterious consequences of public policy. In practice, New Deal liberalism facilitated America's turn to globalism in business and foreign affairs. In the process, critical voices that emerged in opposition to such dramatic change were relegated to the margins of political debate, leaving isolationists as the sole legitimate representatives of dissent. Congressional isolationists were living in the past; the legislation they enacted into law, in effect, was an effort to keep the United States out of the Great War. Stimson put it thusly: "Until America is willing with sympathy and intelligence to do her part in [preventing war], the life of our whole civilization may be at the mercy of the next war.... In our recent efforts to avoid war ... we have endangered our own peace."[49]

Among the body of critics were student radicals, African Americans, a portion of the labor movement, and intellectuals, including Charles A. Beard, who offered a forceful critique of New Deal politics. What transpired as each endeavored to bring an alternative voice into the public arena reveals the uneasy relationship between core values and New Deal liberalism. These new critics competed in various ways with the future globalists to define the national interest, albeit at times without precision. To the extent that they embraced isolationism or advocated selective involvement abroad, their efforts were a means to an end, harking back to the promotion of democracy and self-determination after the Great War. Freedom of speech became integral to extra-governmental efforts to define the national interest. It did not necessarily fare well.

Scarcely any New Deal critic imagined a situation in which foreign trade would not have a major role to play in restoring the nation's health. A political economy based on markets abroad was a political act of faith. As such, the campaign of Upton Sinclair for governor of California in 1934 is largely unremembered. Long a socialist, Sinclair could not stand by and accept what the Great Depression was doing to the country and its people. Ever the utopian, he elected to run as a Democrat for governor with a program called End Poverty in California, or EPIC. He planned to use idle land, factories, and labor and issue scrip to resuscitate the state's economy. Production for use, he believed, would be more compelling to the unemployed than production for profit.

---

[48] Alan Brinkley, *The End of Reform: New Deal Liberalism in Recession and War* (New York: Vintage Books, 1996), 4.

[49] Stimson, *On Active Service in Peace and War*, 309, 312.

Roosevelt and party officials at all levels were wary of Sinclair and his campaign; with more than a month to go before the election, they had distanced themselves from him so as to avoid any taint by association for the New Deal. California Republicans denounced Sinclair and EPIC, employing a brew of fact and fiction, abetted by the state's media. He lost by 250,000 votes. His hope that EPIC might become a national program lay in ruins. It is easy to ridicule Sinclair, as did Democrats, Republicans, Marxists, and communists alike. Less risible was his warning that America might lose its uniqueness were it to become too involved in world affairs. Sinclair touched a nerve. Arthur M. Schlesinger Jr. wrote, "The propertied classes saw in EPIC the threat of social revolution by a rabble of crazed bankrupts and paupers – a horrid upheaval from below."[50] Sinclair arguably did pose a grave danger to multinational liberalism. Other critics of that time proved not to be so threatening.

Student activism predated the New Deal by more than a year.[51] Young socialists, communists, and other leftists, appalled by the failure of capitalism as symbolized by the Depression, looked for an alternative. Richard Hofstadter, often and wrongly praised as the quintessential "consensus" historian, briefly joined the Communist Party, not with "enthusiasm but with a sense of obligation. . . . I don't like capitalism and want to get rid of it."[52] The analysis of the disaffected went beyond economic matters to include the consequences of internationalism in foreign policy. Historian Henry May, then a student, recalled, "Everything that was happening . . . was important and relevant. Each of us was a responsible student of the world."[53] In 1933, students in the United States adopted their own version of the Oxford Pledge, a manifesto denouncing war and the xenophobic nationalism it extolled. Pacifism had merged with isolationism, yet there was more going on than "disillusionment with the First World War," as Robert Cohen concludes.[54] Student activism was intent on promoting political democracy.[55]

The Oxford Pledge would become an albatross for the American Student Union (ASU), founded in December 1935 in Columbus, Ohio, at a meeting of the communist National Student League and the socialist Student League for Industrial Democracy. The ASU was alarmed about Italy's

---

[50] Arthur M. Schlesinger Jr., *The Age of Roosevelt: The Politics of Upheaval* (Boston: Houghton Mifflin, 1960), 109–23; quoted words, 117.

[51] Information on this topic is drawn from Robert Cohen, *When the Old Left Was Young: Student Radicals and America's First Mass Student Movement, 1929–1941* (New York: Oxford University Press, 1993).

[52] Quoted in Eric Foner, *Who Owns History?: Rethinking the Past in a Changing World* (New York: Hill and Wang, 2002), 27; the year was 1938.

[53] Henry May, *Coming to Terms: A Study in Memory and History* (Berkeley: University of California Press, 1987), 207.

[54] Cohen, *When the Old Left Was Young*, 81.

[55] Ibid., 83.

invasion of Ethiopia, asking in a sense whether Europe's apparent return to militarism threatened America's national interests. A national strike against war in spring 1936, in which perhaps half of the nation's students participated, showed the politicization of higher education in the Depression. It also exposed an unbridgeable gap in the ASU between the many noninterventionists and communists, particularly after the Spanish Civil War began that summer and following Roosevelt's Quarantine Speech in October 1937. Internecine squabbles concerned the politics of free speech as much as they highlighted the emotional issue of collective security versus isolationism. Universities tended to side with supporters of collective security, as seen in the suspension of a relationship some administrators had formed with the Federal Bureau of Investigation in which they turned over the names of potential "troublemakers." For a time, that category was simply too general to be considered useful. When the ASU gave its support to the Nazi-Soviet Non-Aggression Pact in 1939 and promoted the cause of nonintervention, the FBI renewed ties with universities in an effort to suppress the free speech of radical students.[56]

Lost in the uproar were student campaigns to build a more egalitarian America. At its best, the student movement was trying to break down barriers of class and race. Despite the shortcomings of the ASU and the fact that the struggles over politics among the student movement's leaders were hardly democratic, the majority of students who took a political stance in the Depression linked the spread of democracy, or self-determination, at home with the need to debate where and how the national interest of the United States was at stake abroad.

As much as any other issue, race illustrates the interrelationship between core values and the national interest in the New Deal. The capital-intensive emphasis of the New Deal hurt African Americans. Innumerable sharecroppers and tenant farmers, many of whom were black, were thrown off their land as a result of New Deal programs.[57] This development galvanized a citizenship movement among African Americans, even to the point of trying to form coalitions with poor whites who similarly were relegated to the margins of national life. That progress came slowly, most notably in the South, is beside the point.[58] As Walter White of the National Association for the Advancement of Colored People (NAACP) commented in a 1936 radio address, "Liberty is not the exclusive right of any racial or other group." White was discussing how Nazism was similar to racial prejudice in the United States, noting that black Americans had faced a kind of fascism

[56] Ibid., 134–40, 152–4, 170–1, 278–300, 323–36.
[57] William E. Leuchtenburg, *Franklin D. Roosevelt and the New Deal, 1932–1940* (New York: Harper & Row, 1963), 137–8.
[58] Patricia Sullivan, *Days of Hope: Race and Democracy in the New Deal Era* (Chapel Hill: University of North Carolina Press, 1996), 85–101.

since their arrival in America three centuries earlier.[59] The logic of White's argument, resembling that of Du Bois at Versailles in 1919, suggested that democracy and self-determination were inseparable and that it was in the national interest to cultivate race-based liberty.

To stand for equality at home was to support freedom abroad. The situation in Ethiopia after Italy invaded in the fall of 1935, which the NAACP equated with the grave threat fascism posed to liberty, became a litmus test about whether the national interest encompassed racial matters. Isolationists cheered the decision to invoke the Neutrality Act of 1935 and apply an arms embargo against both parties; oil was not part of the embargo, however.[60] By early 1938, Roosevelt was seeking to link condemnation of Italy with resistance to Japanese advances in Asia. British recognition of Italy's aggression and opposition from the State Department slowed the president's internationalist impulses.[61] Although pleased that Roosevelt refused to recognize Italy's conquest of Ethiopia, the NAACP urged black Americans to go beyond his limited response and do what they could privately to help the cause of the African nation. White, denouncing the "arrogance of white nations and their . . . exploitation of colored races," was suggesting that trying to avert the absorption of Ethiopia into an Italian empire by invoking neutrality law did not amount to including racial democracy or anticolonialism in public deliberations about America's national interest.[62]

By the end of the 1930s, sectors of organized labor were also criticizing the New Deal in ways that can be framed around issues of security and the national interest. The head of the Congress of Industrial Organizations (CIO), John L. Lewis, did not trust the Roosevelt administration to protect labor's traditional objective of workplace democracy against industry's growing international orientation.[63] Lewis's animus toward Roosevelt and the National Labor Relations Board obscures the fact that his isolationism derived not from reflexive opposition to America's role in the Great War but partly concerned the power that capital could wield over labor in a market economy. This situation could become problematic in two ways. First, trade expansion might lead the country to the verge of conflict, which was not out of the question given the economic autarky of the era and growing tensions with Japan. Second, the rank and file might break with its leadership

---

[59] I am grateful to Jonathan Rosenberg for providing me with White's quotation. See Rosenberg's *How Far the Promised Land?: World Affairs and the American Civil Rights Movement* (Princeton: Princeton University Press, 2006), 111.

[60] Cole, *Roosevelt and the Isolationists*, 117.

[61] Robert Dallek, *Franklin D. Roosevelt and American Foreign Policy, 1932–1945* (New York: Oxford University Press, 1979), 154–8.

[62] Quoted in Rosenberg, *How Far the Promised Land?*, 109.

[63] Irving Bernstein, *Turbulent Years: A History of the American Worker, 1933–1941* (Boston: Houghton Mifflin, 1971), 712–14, 717–20.

and take a militant stance on foreign policy issues, a possible development in the early months of World War II. Lewis detested the leftist tendencies of many union members while sharing their opposition to involvement in war. "Labor in America wants no part of any war," he intoned in September 1939, "Labor wants the right to work and live – not the privilege of dying...to sustain the...errors of current statesmen."[64]

The extent of radical unionism among seamen and longshoremen in the 1930s reveals the appeal of an enhanced decision-making role for rank-and-file union members. In that respect, the drive for efficiency in capital-intensive industries, a precondition for recovery from the ravages of the Depression, directly threatened workplace democracy. Yet, as New Deal economy policy evolved into wartime economic management, the interests of organized labor increasingly assumed a globalist hue. Walter Reuther of the United Auto Workers underlined that important change when he observed in 1942, "Labor's new status in America and its hopes for further progress could not survive an Axis triumph."[65] Job growth, increasing wages, and the lure of abundance portended the demise of labor militancy in the pursuit of industrial democracy. By the end of World War II, the majority of organized workers had tacitly accepted the security ethos, which was then essentially synonymous with globalism, as fundamental to their own understanding of the national interest.[66]

Unlike others who commented on aspects of New Deal foreign policy and in so doing raised questions about the status of values and the democratic process in the United States, the scholar Charles A. Beard had long been in the public eye.[67] From the outset of the New Deal, he scrutinized how the president defined the national interest. In the late 1920s, Beard was reassessing his support for America's entry into war in 1917. Were economic interests worth fighting for? By asking this question, Beard was moving toward an understanding of security at great odds with the imperative of strategic engagement articulated by Mahan and his disciples. For his part, he wanted to find a way to keep the nation's heritage safe from debilitating foreign influences.

Pursuing his argument in two books, *The Idea of National Interest* (1934) and *The Open Door at Home* (1935), Beard in effect charged Mahan with "creating a strategic situation [that] called for a huge naval

---

[64] On this latter point, see Nelson Lichtenstein, *Labor's War at Home: The CIO in World War II* (New York: Cambridge University Press, 1982), 27–31; quoted words, 31.

[65] Walter P. Reuther, "Labor's Place in the Wartime Pattern," *New York Times Magazine*, December 13, 1942.

[66] Aspects of this discussion are based on Brinkley, *The End of Reform*, 201–26.

[67] The following discussion draws on Warren I. Cohen, *The American Revisionists: The Lessons of Intervention in World War I* (Chicago: University of Chicago Press, 1967) and portions of Ronald Radosh, *Prophets On the Right: Profiles of Conservative Critics of American Globalism* (New York: Simon & Schuster, 1975).

establishment . . . with fateful significance for the course of American civiliza-tion." He emphasized the crucial link between "the promotion of economic interests abroad" and "developing the doctrine of national interest."[68] The commercial and dollar nexus he found in security policy since the 1890s bothered Beard, who doubted that any such association could successfully protect American institutions.

The assertion of economic nationalism at the 1933 London Conference buoyed Beard. He termed it "a resurrection of the basic relationship between nationalism and internationalism implied . . . in the *Federalist*."[69] Beard saw a chance for economic planning and the return to a foreign policy that would minimize the likelihood of war as a result of trade disputes, which were the inevitable byproduct of unfettered commercial expansion. In short, Beard proposed a different kind of capitalism, one that evoked the continentalism of an earlier era. It might lead to a just society without either reliance on excessive quantities of foreign goods or indebtedness to the special interests that profited from them.[70] "The American nation," he wrote, "[must be] the center of interest and affection . . . [in order to achieve] security of life for the American people."[71]

Neither a pacifist nor an isolationist, Beard believed that the less the coun-try was engaged abroad, the better.[72] This position was the very antithesis of the security ethos. The minimalism he advocated in *The Open Door at Home* was markedly out of step with America's traditional political econ-omy, which had long affirmed the sanctity of foreign trade. He also opposed piecemeal economic reforms at home, believing that they were paving the way for business internationalism and the administration's turn to global-ism. If, unlike doctrinaire revisionists like Charles Callan Tansill, Beard did not posit a conspiracy behind U.S. entry into World War II, he nevertheless averred that Roosevelt's diplomacy had made a clash with Japan a virtual certainty.[73]

The surprise attack on Pearl Harbor brought war to the United States. Easily lost in the enormity of that event is the connection between the security ethos and America's political economy.[74] Beard's ideas presented a strong dissent from the growth ideology of American capitalism. His fears

[68] Charles A. Beard, with the collaboration of G. H. E. Smith, *The Idea of National Interest: An Analytical Study in American Foreign Policy*, ed. by Alfred Vagts and William Beard (Chicago: Quadrangle Books, 1966), 87, 107, 112; on Mahan see ibid., 223–7.

[69] Ibid., 427.

[70] Radosh, *Prophets on the Right*, 23.

[71] Charles A. Beard, *The Open Door at Home: A Trial Philosophy of National Interest* (New York: Macmillan, 1935), 261.

[72] Cohen, *The American Revisionists*, 239–40.

[73] Radosh, *Prophets on the Right*, 40 ff.

[74] See the related discussion in Emily S. Rosenberg, *A Date Which Will Live: Pearl Harbor in American Memory* (Durham: Duke University Press, 2003), 17 ff.

for the future of American civilization echoed concerns expressed in the early republic about the permanence of civic, or public, virtue. Yet, he was fighting a losing battle by 1940; the bounds of civic virtue were limited. It was no longer axiomatic that public virtue was synonymous with debates over how best "to sacrifice private to public interests," as Edmund S. Morgan once put it.[75] America's national interest had become synonymous with whatever the administration said it was. Dean Acheson, as assistant secretary of state, in effect delivered the response of the globalists to Beard's dissent when, with words evocative of Albert J. Beveridge's "The March of the Flag" in 1898, he gave this testimony in 1944 to a special committee of Congress:

I take it the Soviet Union could use its entire production internally. If you wish to control the entire trade and income of the United States, ... you could probably fix it so that everything produced here would be consumed here, but that would completely change our constitution, our relations to property, human liberty, our very conceptions of law. And nobody contemplates that. Therefore, you find you must look to other markets and those markets are abroad.[76]

Liberty, Globalism, and the National Interest

In the early years of World War II, Americans associated civil liberties, particularly freedom of speech and association, with the very meaning of freedom. The Department of Justice had created a Civil Liberties Unit in 1939. Freedom was far from absolute, however. The House of Representatives established its Un-American Activities Committee in 1938 as a guard against disloyalty or subversion. As in the past, many in Congress feared threats from the political Left – from communists, labor leaders and union rank and file, and African Americans – rather than from the Right. Passage of the Smith Act in 1940, which made it illegal to "teach, advocate, or encourage" the overthrow of the government, further entwined the ideal of freedom with the changing winds of security.

After Pearl Harbor, as Americans fought to defend freedom and extend it as the Atlantic Charter promised, liberty almost seemed a bar to victory. The long-term hostility toward the Japanese and Japanese Americans was played out in the drama of internment of 110,000 people as a result of Executive Order 9066. Oddly, Hawaii was not covered by Roosevelt's order. Internment was no ad hoc decision; as early as 1936, the president had indicated that Japanese citizens or noncitizens in Hawaii who were suspected of acts of subversion or espionage "would be ... placed in a concentration camp in

[75] Edmund S. Morgan, "Inventing the 'Liberal Republican' Mind," *New York Review of Books*, November 16, 2006, p. 32.
[76] Quoted in William Appleman Williams, *The Tragedy of American Diplomacy*, 2d rev. and enlarged ed. (New York: W. W. Norton & Company, 1972). 236; on Beveridge see chapter 2, n. 32.

the event of trouble."[77] The emotion that accompanied the decision to intern all but eviscerated the "probable cause" clause of the Fourth Amendment in the name of security. In Congress, only Republican Senator Robert A. Taft of Ohio spoke against internment.[78] The U.S. Supreme Court, in the case, *Korematsu v. United States* 323 U.S. 214 (1944), refused to hear an appeal, thus upholding the restriction of basic rights.

One of the stranger developments related to the fate of liberties in wartime was the internment in the United States of some 6,600 Germans, Japanese, and Italians who were deported from Latin America as a result of fears, originating in the late 1930s, about a "fifth column" there that might be loyal to the Axis powers.[79] Bernard M. Baruch, the director of the War Industries Board during World War I and an economic adviser to Roosevelt, worried that "economic penetration could bring [Latin America] under [Germany's] control without firing a shot."[80] In truth, Germans were expelled as much for the economic competition they represented, which was seen as a security threat, as for the actual dangers they posed. Sometimes, Jews of German descent found themselves in concentration camps in the United States alongside self-professed Nazis. In addition, Latin Americans felt compelled to defer to Washington over how to interpret the rights of their German immigrants and residents. The spirit of reciprocity that had partly characterized the Good Neighbor policy gave way to a quest for absolute security; in that quixotic venture, the protection of core values was circumscribed, leaving problematic how well those values served as examples to peoples elsewhere.

The turn toward globalism in wartime precluded extensive discussion of what constituted the national interest. The "war guilt" clause in the Versailles Treaty had presumably been the wellspring of Nazi Germany's *revanchism*. Accordingly, demands for unconditional surrender by the Axis powers assumed that total victory was the only way to guarantee postwar safety for the United States and its allies. Similarly, officials saw globalism and security as complementary goals: Such was the essence of the official version of Henry Luce's American Century. No major advisers in either the Roosevelt or the early Truman administrations considered that the desire for the first goal, globalism, would render the second one, security, more elusive still.

How was the national interest understood as World War II gave way to a Cold War between the former allies? In the tumultuous political environment

---

[77] Quoted in Peter Irons, *Justice at War: The Story of the Japanese American Internment Cases* (New York: Oxford University Press, 1983), 20.

[78] Radosh, *Prophets on the Right*, 134–5; Irons, *Justice at War*, 68.

[79] This remarkable story is told in Friedman, *Nazis and Good Neighbors*.

[80] Bernard M. Baruch, *My Own Story: The Public Years* (New York: Holt, Rinehart, and Winston, 1960), 275.

of the late 1940s, various possibilities existed. Taken as a whole, they amounted to a debate about civic virtue as an essential component of public life before NSC-68 in effect announced the supremacy of globalism. The logic of NSC-68 made wide-ranging public debates about security and foreign policy less desirable.[81] In such an environment, core values would become further imperiled.

The years from 1945 through 1948 saw increasing suspicion of the Soviet Union by American and British officials. British scholar Geoffrey Roberts writes that Stalin "did not want a cold war with the west and hoped for continued negotiations with Britain and the United States about the postwar peace settlement." Instead, he was seeking secure European borders, effective containment of Germany, and détente with Britain and America.[82] Stalin's growing concern about the turn in 1947 toward confrontation led him to defend Soviet interests, and in that way he contributed to the breakdown of the Grand Alliance.[83] During the war, Stalin had been prepared to accommodate what he saw as progressive impulses in U.S. foreign policy, offering to exchange scarce raw materials for American goods.[84] There is no way of knowing what effect his tolerating Roosevelt-style globalism, if we may put it thus, would have had on world affairs. It seems reasonable to suggest, though, that Stalin's pragmatic understanding about the locus of political and economic power might have led to caution and compromise in his foreign policy. As he told Churchill during their October 1944 meeting in Moscow, the "Soviet Union [does] not intend to organize a Bolshevik Revolution in Europe."[85]

Could Franklin Roosevelt have averted the descent into the Cold War? In the final weeks before his death on April 12, 1945, Roosevelt wrote to Churchill that "we must not permit anybody to entertain a false impression that we are afraid" and that he "would minimize the general Soviet problem as much as possible.... We must be firm, however, and our course is thus far correct."[86] Historian Wilson Miscamble argues that Roosevelt saddled Truman with an "uncertain legacy," remaining "trapped by the same hopes

[81] This conclusion draws on Michael J. Hogan, *A Cross of Iron: Harry S. Truman and the Origins of the National Security State, 1945–1954* (New York: Cambridge University Press, 1998).

[82] Geoffrey Roberts, *Stalin's Wars: From World War to Cold War, 1939–1953* (New Haven: Yale University Press, 2007), 24.

[83] Ibid., 25–7.

[84] Ibid., 181; U.S. Department of State, *Foreign Relations of the United States: The Conferences at Cairo and Tehran, 1943* (Washington, D.C.: Government Printing Office, 1961), 483–4.

[85] Quoted in Roberts, *Stalin's Wars*, 222.

[86] Warren F. Kimball, ed., *Roosevelt and Churchill: Their Complete Correspondence*, 3 vols., Vol. III: *Alliance Declining* (Princeton: Princeton University Press, 1984), 602–31; quoted words, 617, 630.

and, sadly, it must be said, illusions regarding the possibility for genuine cooperation with Stalin that had guided his actions from 1941 onward."[87] Desirous of making the case for Truman as a prescient and highly able chief executive, Miscamble misses the greater importance: the conceptual continuity that globalism brought to the conduct of U.S. foreign policy.[88]

The dropping of two atomic bombs on Japan provided a window of opportunity for dissent from globalism by those who did not see the atom bomb, in the words of William Appleman Williams, as a "self-starting magic lamp . . . [that] would produce their long-sought City on the Hill" in the form of the American Century.[89] The bombs challenged the *raison d'être* of the national security state, formally created in July 1947 with the passage of the National Security Act. Among the questions raised after August 9, 1945, were those about the efficacy of world government, the dilemma of race in world affairs, and, remarkably, the identity of the republic under the shadow of containment. Ironically, the author of that fabled doctrine, George F. Kennan, developed strong doubts by 1950 about the domestic consequences of what he had set in motion.

If Walter Lippmann had discounted the capacity of tradition to cope with "the complexities of modern life,"[90] neither tradition nor modernity seemed up to the task of responding to the transformative effect of atomic power. Norman Cousins, editor of the *Saturday Review of Literature*, imagined that it would alter "every aspect of man's activities, from machines to morals, from physics to philosophy, from politics to poetry."[91] Prominent columnists Max Lerner and Dorothy Thompson were among the first to call for a world state.[92] For them and others, like the young Cord Meyer, who would head the United World Federalists on its founding in April 1947 before later working for the Central Intelligence Agency (CIA), the option was clear: world government or world doom.[93] Depending on how pollsters framed the question, between 33 and 50 percent of Americans then favored some form of world government. Cousins and Robert M. Hutchins, president of the University of Chicago, were among the best-known proponents

---

[87] Miscamble, *From Roosevelt to Truman*, 70, 79.

[88] Miscamble is unwittingly correct in asserting, "To avoid seeking to understand [the Cold War] more fully is to engage in a most curious scholarly denial." Ibid., xvi.

[89] William Appleman Williams, *The Contours of American History*, paper ed. (Chicago: Quadrangle Books, 1966), 17.

[90] See Chapter 3.

[91] "Modern Man Is Obsolete," *Saturday Review of Literature*, August 18, 1945, p. 5.

[92] This section is based on Paul Boyer, By *the Bomb's Early Light: American Thought and Culture at the Dawn of the Atomic Age* (New York: Pantheon Books, 1985), 33–45, and Lawrence S. Wittner, *One World or None: A History of the World Nuclear Disarmament Movement through 1953* (Stanford: Stanford University Press, 1993).

[93] Cord Meyer, *Facing Reality: From World Federalism to the CIA* (New York: Harper & Row, 1980).

of the idea. Even Lippmann had to admit the powerful attraction of world federalism.

Critics were not inactive, however. Former Department of State official Sumner Welles denounced the idea as impractical, all the more so because it played into the hands of the Kremlin. Secretary of State George C. Marshall in 1948 questioned the ability of world federalism to lessen international tensions. His successor, Dean Acheson, thought the movement incapable of assisting with "the practical difficulties in dealing with the Soviet Union." Acheson would later admit to misleading the American people in order to motivate them to respond with conviction to the Soviet threat.[94] Liberal theologian Reinhold Niebuhr condemned world government as being idealist and illusory.[95] To his dismay, Cord Meyer learned there was a considerable price to pay for departing from the anticommunist orthodoxy of the early Cold War. Right-wing critics of the United World Federalists denounced him as a Soviet dupe and traitor. Meyer subsequently reflected, "Any proposal for radical reform of society, no matter how well intentioned, brings down on the reformer's head a heavy weight of emotional hatred."[96]

Unlike other public officials, including Senators J. William Fulbright or Claude Pepper who found the idea of a world government movement congenial enough to back the drafting of a "Federal Constitution of the World," Secretary of Commerce Henry A. Wallace remained on the movement's periphery. Wallace had long supported the idea of one world, yet in the early years of the movement, he was committed to transforming U.S. foreign policy before a catastrophe occurred.[97] He advocated sharing nuclear technology with the Soviets in order to develop a new relationship that would forestall an arms race. After his break with the Truman administration in September 1946, which led to his departure from office, Wallace mounted a quixotic campaign for the presidency in 1948. It further split the already sectarian American Left and gave a boost to the proponents of globalism.[98] That Wallace had endeavored to open a discussion about the national interest of the United States in the postwar world got lost in the heated political controversy that his beliefs sparked. Eleanor Roosevelt compared him to

[94] Acheson quoted in Wittner, *One World or None*, 269; Madeleine Albright with Bill Woodward, *Madam Secretary: A Memoir* (New York: Miramax Books, 2003), 659.

[95] Sumner Welles, "The Atomic Bomb and World Government," *Atlantic Monthly*, January 1946, pp. 39–42; Reinhold Niebuhr, "The Illusion of World Government," *Foreign Affairs* 27 (April 1949), 379 ff.

[96] Meyer, *Facing Reality*, 51.

[97] John Morton Blum, ed., *The Price of Vision: The Diary of Henry A. Wallace, 1942–1946* (Boston. Houghton Mifflin, 1973), 617, 625, 630–1.

[98] See, generally, Graham White and John Maze, *Henry A. Wallace: His Search for a New World Order* (Chapel Hill: University of North Carolina Press, 1995), 217–81.

Neville Chamberlain and Arthur M. Schlesinger Jr. derided Wallace, saying that he "thinks of Russia as a sort of Brook Farm community."[99]

The Federal Bureau of Investigation had engaged in surveillance of Wallace during his tenure as vice president and secretary of commerce. Although never explicitly accused of being a communist, like many other progressives or radicals after 1945, he suffered through guilt by association with a wide spectrum of leftists. FBI reports raised questions about his patriotism and faith in capitalism. As if in league with Charles Beard, Charlotte Perkins Gilman, Eugene V. Debs, or even Robert Taft, Wallace asked whether America's political economy advanced the national interest or the avarice of special interests. In May 1948, he remarked, "American foreign policy today is based on serving private corporations and international big business, rather than on serving great masses of people."[100] As we have seen, the relationship that Wallace was criticizing was the very foundation of a globalist political economy, which Dean Acheson had ardently defended in his 1944 testimony before Congress.

The obstacles encountered by one of Wallace's causes, racial justice on a grand scale, also showed the limits of heterodoxy as African Americans attempted to sustain an internationalist outlook after the war. The creation of the United Nations (UN) and the deterioration of Soviet-American relations renewed expectations about exercising basic rights and addressing the question of social and economic justice. Many black Americans were wondering if their role in the struggle against fascism would translate into racial victory. Experiences in the Depression had not been positive for African Americans, and many of them equated international capital with colonialism and racial oppression. Thus, at the founding conference of the UN, African Americans not only were thinking about how to secure their constitutional liberties but also were planning to advance the cause of human rights for all people of color.[101]

Membership in the NAACP swelled in the early 1940s, growing from 50,000 in 1940 to more than 400,000 in 1945, which, along with the return of W. E. B. Du Bois after a ten-year absence, gave the organization more political capital than it had possessed in years. At San Francisco, Mary McLeod Bethune revealed the breadth of the NAACP's agenda: "Negro women like all other women must take part in building this world." In a similar vein, Walter White wrote of the "ferment of freedom" he sensed, burning "like a prairie fire among brown, yellow, and black peoples" around

[99] Arthur M. Schlesinger Jr., *A Life in the Twentieth Century: Innocent Beginnings, 1917–1950* (Boston: Houghton Mifflin, 2000), 456; 408 for the quoted words.

[100] Quoted in White and Maze, *Henry A. Wallace*, 269.

[101] Carol Anderson, *Eyes Off the Prize: The United Nations and the African American Struggle for Human Rights, 1944–1955* (New York: Cambridge University Press, 2003).

the world.[102] Over the next three years, Truman took several steps to attack racial discrimination in America, including the formation of a presidential committee on civil rights. He also addressed the NAACP convention in late June 1947, declaring that the elimination of racial oppression was in the national interest.[103]

Although there is no reason to doubt Truman's sincerity about confronting legal bars to freedom for African Americans, it is worth noting that his efforts occurred as the public was learning about the sweep of his containment policy. The Truman Doctrine had been enunciated in March and the Marshall Plan announced in June. The July issue of *Foreign Affairs*, the journal of the Council on Foreign Relations, published Kennan's article, "The Sources of Soviet Conduct," in which "Mr. X" alerted the American people to the need for vigilance against the dangers posed by the Soviet regime. By that time, the Atlanticists in Washington had reversed their opposition to the return of colonialism in French Indochina and were desirous of securing access to vital resources in the Dutch East Indies.[104] They were also preparing the Rio Pact for the defense of the Americas, which over time provided an impetus to the National Security Doctrine of the region's military and the "dirty wars" waged against many liberals, progressives, and advocates of human rights.[105]

The conjunction of liberty and containment alarmed the African American Left. Du Bois had chaired a Pan-African Congress that met in Manchester in Great Britain in October 1945; its final declaration urged "the emancipation of all African peoples and also other dependent peoples and laboring classes everywhere."[106] The effect of putting colonialism on notice was to assert that, unlike in the aftermath of the Great War, self-determination would not take a back seat to anything, including Washington's efforts to contain communism. Although moderate American blacks were wary of the Left, they also had reservations about containment. White chided the government's promotion of democracy abroad while failing adequately to do the same in the South. Referring to the European-centered Marshall Plan, he reminded the Senate Foreign Relations Committee that "hunger is as painful to brown, yellow, and black stomachs as it is to white ones."[107] Indicative

[102] Quoted in Rosenberg, *How Far the Promised Land?*, 162, 163.
[103] Ibid., 181–2. Truman in July 1948 issued an executive order to desegregate the armed forces.
[104] William J. Duiker, *U.S. Containment Policy and the Conflict in Indochina* (Stanford: Stanford University Press, 1994), 33–67; Robert J. McMahon, *Colonialism and Cold War: The United States and the Struggle for Indonesian Independence, 1945–49* (Ithaca: Cornell University Press, 1981).
[105] Loveman, *For la Patria, passim.*
[106] Quoted in Penny M. Von Eschen, *Race against Empire: Black Americans and Anticolonialism, 1937–1957* (Ithaca: Cornell University Press, 1997), 52.
[107] Quoted in Rosenberg, *How Far the Promised Land?*, 178.

of the unbridgeable conceptual and political gulf separating the anticolonial and anticommunist agendas, Eleanor Roosevelt submitted her resignation from the NAACP's board of directors at the end of 1947. White, in convincing her to change her mind, signaled that the leadership of the NAACP might soon acknowledge that winning the Cold War should take precedence over the global struggle for human rights.[108]

In a way, the utopian hopes of the world federalists, Henry Wallace's dissent from Cold War orthodoxy, and the postwar activism of African Americans amounted to a call for public discussion about the national interest; that is, for a return to the times when civic virtue could be practiced by an engaged citizenry. Robert Taft attempted to set the terms of discussion in an address to the American Bar Association in 1943. He said that, after a brief period of postwar reconstruction, the United States "must keep out of the internal affairs of other nations" and that "any effort to impose democracy on the entire world . . . would be impossible and far more likely to cause war than prevent it."[109] A corollary to Taft's concerns was the conviction that a peacetime economy, one dominated by the private sector, could not sustain a globalist foreign policy any more effectively than it had protected the independent internationalism of the 1920s.

The logic of the Bretton Woods system and containment demanded a security-based political economy.[110] The managers of Truman's national security state came more from large corporations, the banking community, and Wall Street law firms than they did from either the Department of State or the U.S. military. Like the experts Herbert Hoover trusted to administer a modern political economy two decades earlier, they may not have possessed the capacity to assess the nation's security requirements. Franklin Roosevelt's global intentions made it unlikely that they would ask fundamental questions about the implications of the security ethos for the nation's welfare. The national interest could not be disentangled from either their corporate interests or the reflexive anticommunism that also shaped their worldviews. Their control over U.S. foreign policy was nearly immune from substantive challenge; if anything, the Republican-dominated Congress that came to power with the 1946 election accelerated the creation of the national security state. In the main, what remained open to debate were only its particulars.

Nonetheless, the globalists and their opponents, Republican or Democrat alike, agreed that the United States must not become a garrison state. The tradition of civilian supremacy over the military was sacrosanct. Furthermore, those who feared the threat posed by a national security state to the

---

[108] David Levering Lewis, *W.E.B. Du Bois: The Fight for Equality and the American Century, 1919–1963* (New York: Henry Holt, 2000), 526–34.

[109] Quoted in Cole, *Roosevelt and the Isolationists*, 521.

[110] The following discussion derives in part from Hogan, *A Cross of Iron*.

nation's republican heritage defeated a proposal for universal military training. In their view it guaranteed a militarized society, something that NSC-68
would accomplish less directly. The security managers, appropriating the
language of fear that had accompanied the belief in exceptionalism since
colonial times, argued that only a formal security state could keep America
free. The threat confronting the nation was so extreme that only they – the
men who held the secrets and made foreign policy – had the wherewithal to
safeguard American values. Their conviction that "peace and freedom were
each indivisible" left the American people, concludes historian Michael J.
Hogan, "with little choice but to defend their own security and their own
liberty by defending peace and freedom everywhere."[111]

The drawbacks of the early national security state underlined the problem
with this kind of thinking. Almost from the start, the CIA was plagued by
grave structural weaknesses and a zeal that blocked dispassionate threat
assessment; this latter condition was also evident in Kennan's 1946 telegram
and his evaluation of the world situation for the State Department. The
turn to covert activities after the Czech coup of February 1948 made the
situation more fraught, in that success in preventing communist gains in
Italian elections in April did not mean that the CIA operated either effectively
or efficiently.[112] In fact, the communist vote in Italy would subsequently
decline less there than elsewhere in Western Europe.[113] As U.S. foreign
policy took on a militarized caste through what one scholar has termed the
"constitutionally dubious powers" of the CIA, nonconforming discourse
about strategy and values became even harder to hear.[114]

Conclusion

Globalizing the security ethos not only delayed the realization of aspirations
for racial justice in social, economic, and political terms but it also challenged
the scope of basic freedoms enjoyed under the Constitution and Bill of
Rights. Violations of civil rights and liberties under the pretext of making
Americans safe have long been chronicled.[115] The activities of the House

---

[111] Ibid., 14.

[112] Tim Weiner, *Legacy of Ashes: The History of the CIA* (New York: Doubleday, 2007),
25–38.

[113] Tony Judt, *Postwar: A History of Europe since 1945* (New York: Penguin Press, 2005),
225; Christopher Andrew and Vasili Mitrokhin, *The Sword and the Shield: The Mitrokhin
Archive and the Secret History of the KGB* (New York: Basic Books, 1999), 276–8.

[114] Michael S. Sherry, *In the Shadow of War: The United States since the 1930s* (New Haven:
Yale University Press, 1995), 130–31, 184–5; quoted words, 131.

[115] See, for example, Stanley I. Kutler, *The American Inquisition: Justice and Injustice in the
Cold War* (New York: Hill and Wang, 1982); Ellen Schrecker, *Many Are the Crimes:
McCarthyism in America* (Boston: Little, Brown, 1998), *passim*; and Richard Gid Powers,
Secrecy and Power: The Life of J. Edgar Hoover (New York: Free Press, 1987), 228–311.

Committee on Un-American Activities and Truman's loyalty program led to the excesses of McCarthyism; even more important, they legitimated the diminution of civil liberties in the name of national security. Lincoln's suspension of writs of habeas corpus during the Civil War and the attack on civil liberties in the late 1910s arguably pale by comparison. What transpired in the second half of the 1940s has had a disturbing shelf life of more than six decades.

Perhaps it had to be. The political economy constructed on pillars of corporate profit, military power, and fear left limited room for divergent perspectives. Like civil liberties, dissent also had its legitimacy circumscribed in the milieu of the Cold War. Of course, the once "reputable" voices who questioned orthodoxy were not so much silenced as ignored. Charles Beard admired Herbert Hoover for his understanding of the limits of power and presidential authority, just as Hoover appreciated how Robert Taft insisted that the Marshall Plan would inevitably lead to greater entanglement abroad. And Walter Lippmann, who did not oppose aligning the United States with European democracies, still feared the implications for American institutions that might result from open-ended commitments to freedom brought on by the heated rhetoric of anticommunism.

The problem was more deeply entrenched than Lippmann realized. As globalism metamorphosed into containment, Truman's national security officials, like many of their predecessors throughout the American experience, were evading history. They never did inquire about the tradition of believing in trade and access to foreign markets, the costs notwithstanding: a reflexive readiness to employ force against real or imagined enemies and the resort to fear to mobilize the public in defense of exceptionalist myths and realities.

Perhaps fittingly, it was George F. Kennan who would sound the tocsin about the deleterious impact of the national security state on American traditions.[116] By 1949 at the latest, he despaired that Western civilization could survive unbounded containment. He would soon break ranks with the Truman administration over the grand strategy, global containment, for which he was in some considerable measure responsible. In a letter to Lippmann, which Kennan never sent, the government's foremost expert on the Soviet Union mused, "[H]ow hard it is for a democracy to conduct a successful foreign policy."[117] Like Lippmann, he wanted an informed public to support stronger ties with Europe; for Kennan, however, it was as much for cultural as for strategic reasons. He was never comfortable with the pace of modern life. Demands for justice and equality were arcane abstractions

---

[116] See Joshua Botts, "'Nothing to Seek and . . . Nothing to Defend': George F. Kennan's Core Values and American Foreign Policy, 1938–1993," *Diplomatic History* 30 (November 2006): 839–66.

[117] Ibid., 858.

that detracted from the pursuit of order. Discipline, refinement, and order were his core values, and they were in grave danger of becoming ephemera in the world of containment. The tragedy of George Kennan is that the conservative civic virtue he espoused was every bit an evasion of history as the globalist foreign policy he had come to oppose.

5

Civic Virtue in Richard Nixon's America

Damn it, I happen to love this country.
J. Robert Oppenheimer, 1953

[I]f Richard Nixon is not sincere, he is the most dangerous man in America.
Rev. Martin Luther King Jr., 1957

Have our values been so twisted . . . that we are prepared to rationalize murder as an acceptable counter-insurgency weapon?
Viron P. Vaky, 1968

One cannot adhere to values of individual liberty and then remain silent while those values are destroyed.
Senator Edward M. Kennedy, 1973

If the U.S. Census of 1890 announced the closing of the old frontier, then NSC-68 proclaimed the "free world" as America's new frontier.[1] Yet, that world seemed a fearful place to many Americans by mid-1950. The flight to Taiwan by Jiang Jieshi in January 1949 and Guomindang officials in the wake of the victory of Mao Zedong and the Communist Party in China by October, the successful atomic test by the Soviet Union, the public emergence of Senator Joseph R. McCarthy, and the beginning of the Korean War – all combined to tear at the fabric of national memory about security. The resultant uncertainty about the present and the future affected how Americans thought about core values over the next quarter-century. When confronted with the consequences of the globalist turn in foreign policy, more than a few citizens saw in the world around them a betrayal of the past by their leaders. How did Americans respond, for instance, to the seemingly

---

[1] On NSC-68, see John Fousek, *To Lead the Free World: American Nationalism and the Cultural Roots of the Cold War* (Chapel Hill: University of North Carolina Press, 2000), 162–5.

131

endless state of tension with the Soviet Union, the civil rights movement, the disintegration of social order in the 1960s, and the president's abuse of power in the Watergate affair?

No American better exemplifies the vicissitudes of globalism and its impact on basic liberties than Richard Nixon. Exploiting fears of threats to national welfare on the road to his final crisis, Watergate, he accepted ideas about political economy and the utility of power that lay at the heart of a globalist foreign policy.[2] A word of explanation is in order about Nixon and political economy early in his public career. As a Californian, he possessed something of an instinctual distrust of Eastern bankers; furthermore, as the son of a small businessman, he looked with skepticism at the growing power of large corporations. Just the same, he was no throwback to the laissez-faire autarky of the late nineteenth century. Nixon evoked a Republican lineage that stretched from William McKinley to Herbert Hoover. Like McKinley, who addressed the National Association of Manufacturers at its founding convention in 1895, Nixon – more interested in geopolitics than economics – acknowledged the vital importance of foreign trade to the nation's well-being.[3] Thus, the self-styled champion of family-run businesses in effect embraced the associational spirit fostered in the Hoover era by the Bureau of Foreign and Domestic Commerce. As Dwight D. Eisenhower's vice president, Nixon would make an uneasy peace with America's corporate commonwealth.[4] Had he done otherwise, his self-imposed isolation from the economic mainstream would have relegated him to the periphery of postwar history.

Perhaps the only other individual who lived during Nixon's political prime to have as profound an effect on the nation was Rev. Martin Luther King Jr. King reminded black and white Americans that they were not powerless in the face of the past they inherited. Both of these men met a tragic fate, King all the more so because an assassin took his life. His brief presence in the public arena loudly echoed previous calls of other people who fought against the limits imposed by fear and desired to revive a national discussion about the importance of civic virtue. In stark contrast, Nixon parlayed his profound sense of entitlement as a member of the governing class to constrain open political debate. He lived his public life with a *noblesse oblige* similar to that of Franklin Roosevelt, believing with the unreflective arrogance of the powerful that he knew what was best for his country.

[2] Roger Morris, *Richard Milhous Nixon: The Rise of an American Politician* (New York: Henry Holt, 1990), *passim*.

[3] Walter LaFeber, *The New Empire: An Interpretation of American Expansion, 1860–1898* (Ithaca: Cornell University Press, 1963), 192–3.

[4] Robert Griffith, "Dwight D. Eisenhower and the Corporate Commonwealth," *American Historical Review* 87 (February 1982): 87–122.

Martin Luther King first encountered Richard Nixon in Ghana where both were attending the inauguration in March 1957 of Kwame Nkrumah as president of the new nation. Those in attendance from the United States, black and white, tended to see the event in ColdWar terms, hoping that Ghana might lead Africans toward Western-style modernization.[5] The drift away from black international solidarity, first apparent in the late 1940s, had become pronounced by 1957. Nevertheless, the Department of State refused to allow either W. E. B. Du Bois or the activist Paul Robeson to travel to Ghana. On returning to Washington, Nixon declared that Africa could be "the decisive factor in the conflict between forces of freedom and international communism."[6]

Nixon began a dialogue with King in Accra, which would resume months after their return home. King, who had voted for the Republican ticket in 1956, listened carefully to Nixon's overtures concerning civil rights. He joined the vice president in promoting the modest Civil Rights Act passed by Congress in the late summer of 1957. Though duly appreciative of Nixon's commitment to civil rights, which was stronger than President Eisenhower's, King may have harbored some reservations. "Nixon has a genius for convincing one that he is sincere," he observed with remarkable prescience. "[I]f Richard Nixon is not sincere, he is the most dangerous man in America."[7]

Subversion, Liberties, and Security in the 1950s

Attempts to lessen civil liberties marked Richard Nixon's career at beginning and end. The Mundt-Nixon bill of 1948 compromised civil liberty in the name of security. The legislation, named for Nixon and fellow Republican Karl E. Mundt of South Dakota, required the registration of the Communist Party (CP) and front organizations. It did not outlaw the CP, but made it a crime to advocate the creation of a dictatorship and specifically named the CP as the agent of that enterprise. The bill passed the House of Representatives by a wide margin, yet failed in the Senate because of its assault on civil liberties. As a member of the House Committee on Un-American Activities, commonly known as HUAC, Nixon brought credibility to Congress's most notorious committee.[8] In the presidential campaign of 1948, his seat on HUAC provided him a platform to suggest that Republican candidate Thomas Dewey propose suspending the Fifth Amendment in cases involving

---

[5] Penny M. Von Eschen, *Race against Empire: Black Americans and Anticolonialism, 1937–1957* (Ithaca: Cornell University Press, 1997), 181–3.

[6] *New York Times*, April 7, 1957.

[7] Quoted in Taylor Branch, *Parting the Waters: America in the King Years, 1954–63* (New York: Simon & Schuster, 1988), 219.

[8] Stephen E. Ambrose, *Nixon: The Education of a Politician, 1913–1952* (New York: Simon & Schuster, 1987), 141–52.

national security. Playing on the growing fear of subversion that the Cold War had generated, Nixon believed that such a restriction "would certainly meet with popular approval at this time."[9]

Mundt-Nixon evolved into the Internal Security Act of 1950, a law requiring "subversive" groups to register with the government, which could then deny passports to members of those groups. A Subversive Activities Control Board was established to oversee the registration of groups, and concentration camps were created, presumably to house left-wing dissidents. Congress easily overrode Truman's veto. Before the veto, J. Edgar Hoover urged Truman to "protect the country against treason, espionage and sabotage" by ordering the Justice Department to "apprehend all individuals potentially dangerous to the internal security."[10]

Disagreement over the degree to which the government should suppress the free speech of communists reflected matters of nuance and politics, while not seriously questioning the need to suppress. The Loyalty Review Board, established by an executive order in 1947, inexorably moved toward placing the burden of proving one's loyalty on the accused, not the accusers.[11] In effect, the Department of Justice had decided that security imperatives were sufficient to trump individual rights. Eleven communists went on trial in 1949 and were convicted of a conspiracy to advocate revolution by violence. In his dissent in *Dennis v. United States*, 341 U.S. 494 (1951), Supreme Court Justice Hugo L. Black expressed the hope that the Court would in the future "restore the First Amendment liberties to the high preferred place where they belong in a free society."[12]

Joseph McCarthy may have been the most visible enemy of basic civil liberties, although the Truman administration and Richard Nixon did more to institutionalize the primacy of security concerns over core values. McCarthy faded from the national scene in 1954; the siege mentality that was by then part of a globalist foreign policy remained intact. Intellectuals who might have been expected to defend historic rights and liberties did so, but selectively. Liberals were especially keen to identify themselves as anticommunists. Leading liberals, such as Eleanor Roosevelt, Sidney Hook, and Arthur M. Schlesinger Jr., helped found the Congress for Cultural Freedom (CCF) at a meeting held in Berlin in 1950. An offshoot of the CCF, the American Committee for Cultural Freedom (ACCF) began operations one year later. The ACCF, briefly made up of both liberals and conservatives, rejected the

---

[9] Morris, *Richard Milhous Nixon*, 376–8; quoted words, 441.

[10] U.S. Department of State, *Papers Relating to the Foreign Relations of the United States, 1950–1955: The Intelligence Community, 1950–1955* (Washington, D.C.: Government Printing Office, 2007), 19.

[11] Stanley I. Cutler, *The American Inquisition: Justice and Injustice in the Cold War* (New York: Hill and Wang, 1982), 34–8.

[12] Stephen J. Whitfield, *The Culture of the Cold War*, 2d ed. (Baltimore: Johns Hopkins University Press, 1996), 45–9; quoted words, 49.

idea that communists should enjoy the same basic rights as all Americans. Liberal elitism drove a wedge between left and right in the ACCF by 1957. In criticizing what they decided were the excesses of right-wing anticommunism, liberals hastily claimed as their own "essential features of the rightist worldview," as historian and cultural critic Christopher Lasch points out, and then presented them as the conventional perspective.[13]

A potent drive for conformity suffused the public and private realms in America throughout the 1950s. Noted historian Henry Steele Commager reminded Americans in 1954 that for "our democracy to flourish it must have criticism."[14] Whether in national politics, intellectual life, or private behavior, the bounds of acceptable dissent were manifestly narrower than during the Depression. To be far to the left of the "vital center," in Arthur Schlesinger's artful formulation, itself an attempt to induce conformity, was to put the nation at risk. To be a communist or a "fellow traveler" was to be not only un-American but more precisely anti-American and consequently not entitled to enjoy the cherished rights and liberties of citizenship.

Just as J. Edgar Hoover funneled information, at times of dubious validity, to select members of HUAC to help the committee ferret out suspected subversive activity, he also instructed American women about their own patriotic duties. Hoover's wartime advice surely held true for the Cold War struggle as well: "*There must be no absenteeism among mothers....* Her patriotic duty ... is on the home front." Historian Elaine Tyler May cogently observes, "As the Cold War took hold over the nation's consciousness, domestic containment mushroomed into a full-blown ideology that hovered over the cultural landscape for two decades."[15]

Presiding over the broader national terrain, Dwight David Eisenhower embodied the central features of American globalism. His understanding of the nation's political economy, best characterized as "containment capitalism," was consistent with the organizational developments and multinational goals that arose in the 1930s as business and government joined forces to save capitalism from both its worst excesses and popular disdain. If Eisenhower did not place his trust in popular democracy as a way to chart the nation's future, he did understand that class conflict could impair America's ability to play the dominant role in world affairs. For Eisenhower, economic or political abuses of power could irrevocably damage prospects for world order, itself only conceivable under American leadership. "[T]he

---

[13] Christopher Lasch, *The Agony of the American Left* (New York: Vintage Books, 1969), 63–87; quoted words, 81; Ellen Schrecker, *No Ivory Tower: McCarthyism and the Universities* (New York: Oxford University Press, 1986), 240 ff.

[14] Henry Steele Commager, *Freedom, Loyalty, Dissent* (New York: Oxford University Press, 1954), 153.

[15] Elaine Tyler May, *Homeward Bound: American Families in the Cold War Era*, rev. and updated ed. (New York: Basic Books, 1999), 64, 79 (emphasis in original).

difficulties and uncertainties of disrupted trade, security, and understand-ings," he confided to his diaries, "further the aims of world revolution and the Kremlin's domination of all people." And yet, "masses of people have suffered under the injustices inflicted by people controlling the means of production."[16]

Extreme political partisanship made for bad decision making in Eisen-hower's belief system, which is why he never wholly trusted his vice pres-ident. Yet, the president clearly was a "more complex and devious man than most people realized," Nixon wrote in his pugnacious first memoir, *Six Crises*.[17] Eisenhower's contradictions came to the fore in the Rosenberg and Oppenheimer cases. In the former, despite international pleas, he refused to halt the execution in June 1953 of Julius and Ethel Rosenberg, who had been found guilty of conspiracy to commit espionage in a controversial case involving atomic information. Eisenhower's impassioned denunciation of communism in his diaries on the one hand suggests a disingenuous attempt to curry favor with ultimate readers of his previously private thoughts. To the extent it was a response to the threat of communism at home, it was needless because the CP self-destructed during the president's first term in office.[18] On the other hand, his words reflect a paranoia about security that cannot easily be separated from the worldview that took form as American globalism.

Assessing the impact of this self-created fear, with its origins in the distant past, greatly complicates the writing of the nation's modern history. To what extent were the fears of communism well founded? To what extent were they a subterfuge, invoked to serve dishonorable political purposes? Did using the term "international communism" help the making of policy? Or did it facilitate an evasion of history? In fact, each of the last two questions can be answered affirmatively. In any case, the bounds of legitimate public discourse were narrowed, and the opportunity of numerous Americans to exercise their basic rights was lessened. The challenge to core values in the Eisenhower years was at once profound and disturbing.

Concern about espionage, if not treason, became obsessive in the fifties, most notably in the controversy over J. Robert Oppenheimer. Eisenhower wrote in his diary that "there is no evidence that implies disloyalty on the part of Dr. Oppenheimer. . . . *[T]his does not mean that he might not be a security risk*."[19] The famed physicist, an opponent of the development of

---

[16] Griffith, "Corporate Commonwealth," *passim*; Robert H. Ferrell, ed., *The Eisenhower Diaries* (New York: W.W. Norton & Company, 1981), 223, 230 (quoted words), 242–5 for ruminations on problems inherent in capitalism.

[17] Richard M. Nixon, *Six Crises* (Garden City: Doubleday, 1962), 161.

[18] Joseph R. Starobin, *American Communism in Crisis, 1943–1957* (Cambridge: Harvard University Press, 1972), 221–37.

[19] *Eisenhower Diaries*, 260 (emphasis added).

the H-bomb, which would become central to America's strategic arsenal and thereby serve as an imposing symbol of free world defense and U.S. security, had his security clearance revoked. Oppenheimer fought to save his reputation. Friends appealed to public opinion, prompting the president to comment, "This fellow Oppenheimer is sure acting like a communist."[20] On February 25, 1967, at a celebration of Oppenheimer's life after his death one week earlier, George F. Kennan recounted what his colleague at the Institute for Advanced Study in Princeton, New Jersey, had said in the dark days of 1953 in response to a suggestion that he take up residence outside the United States. "Damn it," Oppenheimer declared, "I happen to love this country."[21]

Oppenheimer's exile from government work was the tip of the iceberg against which basic rights were colliding. Shortly after the denouement of the affair, National Security Adviser Robert Cutler and Vice President Nixon warned that quick action was needed against known subversives. Attorney General Herbert Brownell proposed that evidence obtained by wiretaps in intelligence cases be admissible in court without judicial authorization. Ignoring the objections of Secretary of State John Foster Dulles, Eisenhower sided with Brownell, mocking concerns raised by "the civil liberties people." Brownell persisted in the face of congressional reluctance, also asking for the authority to deport naturalized citizens convicted of subversion. The only recourse would be a single appeal for a writ of habeas corpus. Before the administration's bill came to a vote, Senate Democrats led by Hubert H. Humphrey of Minnesota introduced their own bill, declaring the CP a conspiracy to overthrow the government. Congress would pass a modified bill, the Communist Control Act of 1954, without a provision for wiretapping.

The effort to disrupt the moribund CP and contain domestic subversion received further impetus in 1956 when the FBI initiated a counterintelligence program, or COINTELPRO, that relied on the widespread use of illegal wiretaps. FBI chief Hoover apparently did not inform the White House of the program for two years. Yet, Eisenhower had for all intents and purposes countenanced COINTELPRO, concludes historian Jeff Broadwater. The program "grew from the administration's policies – its crusading anticommunism, its minimal concern for civil liberties, and its decentralized management style – as if it had been expressly approved" by the president.[22] The "hidden-hand presidency," as scholars sometimes term the Eisenhower

---

[20] Quoted in Jeff Broadwater, *Eisenhower and the Anti-Communist Crusade* (Chapel Hill: University of North Carolina Press, 1992), 103.

[21] Quoted in Kai Bird and Martin J. Sherwin, *American Prometheus: The Triumph and Tragedy of J. Robert Oppenheimer* (New York: Alfred A. Knopf, 2005), 5.

[22] Broadwater, *Eisenhower and the Anti-Communist Crusade*, 169–83; quoted words, 169, 180.

style of governance, abided by constitutional scruples more with rhetoric than reality.[23] As had his predecessors since the 1890s, Eisenhower considered security to be indivisible at home and abroad.

Human Rights, Civil Rights, and the Limits of Self-Determination

The founding of the UN in 1945 enabled African Americans to merge their struggle for civil rights with the international campaign for human rights. The National Negro Congress and the NAACP filed petitions with the UN protesting racial oppression in the United States. This action resulted in Red-baiting of blacks for being sympathetic to the Soviet Union and communism, which some indeed were. Fearing a wave of repression, the NAACP, prompted by liberal friends like Eleanor Roosevelt, withdrew its support from the Draft Covenant on Human Rights. Civil rights thereafter became the battle cry of the majority of African Americans, a course of action that ironically helped prolong the age of Jim Crow.[24] The Truman and Eisenhower administrations could thereby separate the handling of the nettlesome civil rights issue at home from policy toward the anticolonial and nonaligned movements abroad. The cautionary formula in *Brown v. Board of Education of Topeka*, 347 U.S. 483 (1954), "with all deliberate speed," established how Washington would respond over time to independence movements in the postcolonial world.

Eisenhower believed that "dependent peoples" could "maintain independence, once attained," only "through cooperation with the free world." This perspective was consistent with his opinion that race relations in America "will be healthy and sound only if it starts locally."[25] Such gradualism had pronounced political consequences. In the short term, it meant that civil rights were fundamentally legal, not social and economic rights. Progress before the law should therefore serve Cold War ends, rather than promote broad social changes.

Just as radical unions and communists had been purged from the labor movement in the first decade after the war, an effort culminating in the unification of the American Federation of Labor and the Congress of Industrial Organizations in 1955,[26] so too were radicals marginalized in the civil rights movement. Cultural containment of this kind was essential for the creation of a broad consensus about security policy. The effort could not be considered a success, though, until the radical overtones of black-Jewish

---

[23] Fred I. Greenstein, *The Hidden-Hand Presidency: Eisenhower as Leader* (New York: Basic Books, 1982).

[24] Carol Anderson, *Eyes Off the Prize: The United Nations and the African American Struggle for Human Rights, 1944–1955* (New York: Cambridge University Press, 2003).

[25] *Eisenhower Diaries*, 223, 246.

[26] Ronald Radosh, *American Labor and United States Foreign Policy: The Cold War in Unions from Gompers to Lovestone* (New York: Random House, 1969), 434–9.

relations were transformed. From early in the century, African Americans and Jews had forged a relatively close, if sometimes uneasy relationship built on the common ground of discrimination in a country dominated by white Anglo-Saxons.[27]

The imperative of anticommunism proved impossible to resist. Both the NAACP and liberal Jewish organizations banished communists from their governing boards. Talk of class conflict virtually disappeared from the vocabulary of the civil rights movement. Du Bois became an embarrassment to nervous liberals, black and white. On occasion, they cooperated with HUAC and the FBI, in effect legitimating tactics later employed against civil rights leaders themselves. To be sure, the NAACP, the American Jewish Congress, and the Anti-Defamation League opposed loyalty tests, the excesses of HUAC, and restrictions on freedom of speech. Nevertheless, they did not seriously challenge one of the premises behind gradualism: national security. Civil rights gains were nominal then, and amicable black-Jewish relations had reached their limit by the late 1950s, as events in the next decade would demonstrate.[28]

Gradualism also became Eisenhower's preferred, though not exclusive, *modus operandi* for foreign policy in a world deemed fraught with danger. Alliance politics, at least in the North Atlantic Treaty Organization, meant consultation in policymaking. The Southeast Asia Treaty Organization, however, provided cover for the White House as the U.S. role in that region expanded after mid-1954. Strategically, the administration crafted in 1953 its New Look policy – reliance on nuclear capability rather than conventional forces to demonstrate its determination to defend vital interests. U.S. officials, whether through alliances or the New Look, sought to avoid disagreements with European friends and confrontations with foes as they followed the logic of globalism.

This is not to argue that Eisenhower did not desire peace. The ex-general knew that preparedness had a price. In stark terms, he told the American Society of Newspaper Editors in April 1953, "Every gun that is made, every warship launched, every rocket fired signifies, in the final sense, a theft from those who hunger and are not fed, those who are cold and are not clothed.... This is not a way of life."[29] Eisenhower was wrong. The great influence of the security ethos in national life, especially through containment capitalism, should not be underestimated even for a president who resisted excessive spending. In any event, Eisenhower and his foreign policy team

[27] This story is best told in Cheryl Lynn Greenberg, *Troubling the Waters: Black-Jewish Relations in the American Century* (Princeton: Princeton University Press, 2006).

[28] Ibid., 169–204.

[29] "The Chance for Peace," April 16, 1953, *Public Papers of the Presidents: Dwight David Eisenhower, 1953: Containing the Public Messages, Speeches, and Statements of the President, January 1 to December 31, 1953* (Washington, DC: Government Printing Office, 1960), 182.

were not prepared to take risks for peace. The political will to do so was beyond their imagination. The president's fiscal caution led him to consider a minimalist defense posture, focusing on air power and defense of the continental United States. Had Senator Robert A. Taft not died at the end of July, he would have been heartened. Such optimism would have been out of place. What about America's European allies? What about the grand strategy of global containment? The New Look and the threat of massive retaliation provided the answer. Although the administration "wanted to explore the parameters of détente [with the Soviets]," writes Melvyn P. Leffler, it nevertheless determined that "the United States needed to prepare to win the Cold War."[30] The New Look was a lost chance for peace and a harbinger of troubled times ahead for core values.

Complementing the conceptual care in the making of policy was the training of foreign forces in some seventy countries and the deployment of U.S. troops to more than thirty nations around the world. Under military assistance programs, between 1946 and 1961 the United States provided $26.5 million worth of arms and equipment to foreign military and police forces.[31] At the same time, Eisenhower had to cope with pressure from members of the Gaither committee on strategic preparedness.[32] By advocating a stronger nuclear arsenal, especially after the launch of the satellite *Sputnik* in October 1957, the committee impelled the United States toward an arms race with the Soviet Union. It also prepared the way for the policy of flexible response adopted by John F. Kennedy in 1961. The alarmist views of the Gaither report, written in part by Paul Nitze, the main author of NSC-68, were based on uncertain intelligence and a dubious methodology. The report concluded, "USSR intentions are expansionist, and . . . her great efforts to build military power go beyond any concepts of Soviet defense."[33] Nitze's belief in Soviet perfidy was an act of faith that sustained him throughout his years in public life, as his involvement with Team B and the Committee on the Present Danger in the 1970s further indicates (see Chapter 6). This assessment forced Eisenhower to increase defense spending during his final years in office, effectively precluding the chances for a policy of strategic restraint.

Caution was often less in evidence in U.S. policy toward those who did not have the economic or military capacity to pose a direct challenge to

---

[30] Melvyn P. Leffler, *For the Soul of Mankind: The United States, the Soviet Union, and the Cold War* (New York: Hill and Wang, 2007), 103–38; quoted words, 133.

[31] Michael T. Klare, *Supplying Repression: U.S. Support for Authoritarian Regimes Abroad* (Washington, DC: Institute for Policy Studies, 1977), 11.

[32] David L. Snead, *The Gaither Committee, Eisenhower, and the Cold War* (Columbus: Ohio State University Press, 1999).

[33] U.S. Congress, Joint Committee on Defense Production, *Deterrence and Survival in the Nuclear Age (The "Gaither Report" of 1957)* (Washington, DC: Government Printing Office, 1976), 1.

American interests. The "dependent peoples" Eisenhower wrote about were not to be trusted in the battle against communism in part because they had not embraced the security ethos as their own. Their striving for self-determination, embodied in the emergence of the nonaligned movement, showed that the lessons of the early Cold War had not been learned. It would fall to the CIA to provide the requisite mentoring. CIA operations in Iran, Guatemala, Southeast Asia, Cuba, and the Congo, among other places, are well known. What is important to understand is the link between the CIA and the construction of historical memory in a world where America's globalist aspirations held center stage. In not coming to terms with its own history and its relation to basic values like self-determination, the Eisenhower administration initiated a process whereby the United States endeavored to induce other peoples to "misremember" their own histories, all in the name of freedom.[34]

Richard M. Bissell Jr., referring to himself as "[Allen] Dulles's apprentice" at the CIA, recognized that President Jacobo Arbenz of Guatemala was "less of a threat than he appeared at the time."[35] The same might be said about Iran's Muhammad Musaddiq, who was ousted from power in 1953 by U.S. and British intelligence after he nationalized the Anglo-Iranian Oil Company.[36] Nor is it mistaken to suggest that Prime Minister Patrice Lumumba of Congo, who apparently was targeted for assassination in 1960, was not "a Castro or worse... bought by the Communists," as Allen Dulles believed.[37] In each of these instances, the U.S. government set out to revise history, minimizing the connections between the pre-1945 past and recent developments that Washington saw through a Cold War lens. This enforced amnesia, induced through covert operations, obliterated the realities of histories that had been lived in dependent or colonial settings. The past truly was of little meaning to national security policymakers if it did not ultimately lead to an anticommunist present. Bissell and other officials did not care about the consequences of their actions. "U.S. interests over the years might have been better served," he wrote, "if Arbenz had remained in power." Yet, in the cause of bringing security to the free world, there could be no second-guessing: "As to the question of overthrowing a foreign sovereign government, I would approve the same action today without hesitation."[38]

[34] Here I am drawing on an argument in Greg Grandin, *The Last Colonial Massacre: Latin America in the Cold War* (Chicago: University of Chicago Press, 2004).
[35] Richard M. Bissell Jr., with Jonathan E. Lewis and Frances T. Pudlo, *Reflections of a Cold Warrior: From Yalta to the Bay of Pigs* (New Haven: Yale University Press, 1996), 82.
[36] Kermit Roosevelt, *Countercoup: The Struggle for Control of Iran* (New York: McGraw-Hill, 1979).
[37] U.S. Department of State, *Papers Relating to the Foreign Relations of the United States, 1958–60*, vol. 14: *Africa* (Washington, DC: Government Printing Office, 1992), 338–9.
[38] Bissell, *Reflections of a Cold Warrior*, 90–1.

The Eisenhower administration and its successors had various means to produce alignment with the United States against communism. Foreign assistance in support of internal security programs became an effective tool. Internal security aid was nothing new. After World War I, the United States had increasingly trained and relied on local forces for operations related to stability.[39] Some clients who seized the reins of power during the 1930s, including Anastasio Somoza in Nicaragua, Fulgencio Batista in Cuba, and Rafael Trujillo in the Dominican Republic, became unsavory dictators. Such was the unfortunate price of combating disorder, as became apparent on numerous occasions after 1945.[40] Having authoritarians as security assets did raise doubts about the exportability of American values, as we see later. It suggested, too, that U.S. officials placed greater "value" on stability than on self-determination.

After World War II, leftist insurgencies and guerrilla activities were seen as threats to the established order and thus to the interests of Western powers, notably in Southeast Asia and, after the Cuban revolution, in Latin America. The response to insurgency in Southeast Asia was twofold: a combination of military moves to contain or eliminate insurgencies and the creation of political space so that less than fully committed insurgents might abandon their cause. Counterinsurgency efforts generally succeeded in Indonesia, Malaya, and the Philippines, but failed badly in Vietnam because the northern Vietnamese led by Ho Chi Minh were able to claim status as defenders of nationalism. Although the opening of political space was likely the most important factor in limiting the effectiveness of insurgent or revolutionary activity, there arose in the Kennedy White House a mystique about counterinsurgency operations, all the more so given the apparent success of Sir Robert G. K. Thompson in Malaya.[41] That mystique guaranteed reliance on internal security tactics to protect the free-world frontier. By 1961, despite relatively low funding, public safety programs along with CIA operations were an essential means of imposing order on local populations and countering suspected subversive activities.[42]

---

[39] Martha K. Huggins, *Political Policing: The United States and Latin America* (Durham Duke University Press, 1998), 25–40; David F. Schmitz, *Thank God They're on Our Side: The United States and Right-Wing Dictatorships, 1921–1965* (Chapel Hill: University of North Carolina Press, 1999); William Kamman, *A Search for Stability: United States Diplomacy toward Nicaragua, 1925–1933* (Notre Dame: Notre Dame University Press, 1968), 101, 172–3, 209.

[40] Schmitz, *Thank God They're on Our Side*; idem, *The United States and Right-Wing Dictatorships, 1965–1989* (New York: Cambridge University Press, 2006).

[41] Jeff Goodwin, *No Other Way Out: States and Revolutionary Movements, 1945–1991* (New York: Cambridge University Press, 2001), Parts 1 and 2; Robert S. McNamara with Brian VanDeMark, *In Retrospect: The Tragedy and Lessons of Vietnam* (New York: Crown, 1995), 45.

[42] Michael McClintock, *Instruments of Statecraft: U.S. Guerrilla Warfare, Counterinsurgency, Counterterrorism, 1940–1990* (New York: Pantheon Books, 1992), 188–9.

For the United States, a significant part of what was at issue in the second half of the 1950s was the meaning of freedom. The logic of American security policy meant that freedom was Washington's to determine. Belief in Soviet dominance of the world beyond the U.S. orbit accorded Moscow an omnipotence it did not possess. This supposition was a curious one because of the hiatus in the Cold War after Stalin's death and the armistice in the Korean War, which likely led to subsequent Soviet overtures for coexistence and disarmament.[43] Many examples exist, but representative of efforts to control the meaning of freedom are the administration's response to the meeting at Bandung of nonaligned states in April 1955, the decision to support the regime of Ngo Dinh Diem in southern Vietnam, and the Eisenhower Doctrine in the Middle East. In addition, the rupture in relations with Cuba emphasized the inability of the United States to accept self-determination on terms other than its own.

Administration officials were not impervious to the multiplicity of voices raised at Bandung demanding freedom from the vestiges of colonialism. C. D. Jackson, who had devised many psychological operations for the White House, warned that "the ghost of colonialism... is in complete control of the thought processes of Asians, Mideasterners, Africans, and Latin Americans." African American Congressman Adam Clayton Powell, who was present at the gathering, told the president, "The timetable for freedom [is] no longer within our control."[44] The conferees were well aware of the general lack of basic freedoms in their homelands. The final communiqué addressed the need to respect fundamental human rights as one of its ten basic principles.[45] However sensitive the administration may have been to the long-term implications of Bandung on matters of race and foreign policy, it was not prepared to evaluate their importance except through a Cold War lens. Even when Egypt's Gamal Abdel Nasser nationalized the Suez Canal in July 1956, forcing the United States to confront the dilemma of neutralism and making it unwise to ignore the question of race in international affairs, the White House could not easily jettison its reflexive disposition to see the specter of communism looming over a troubled world.

In 1955, Ngo Dinh Diem began an anticommunist denunciation campaign in the southern section of Vietnam that, together with battles against the Hoa Hao and Cao Dai religious sects and the Binh Xuyen gangsters, won Washington's backing for his regime. Yet, Eisenhower's emissary, General J. Lawton Collins, found a "lack of decisive leadership [by] Diem," despite

---

[43] Matthew Evangelista, *Unarmed Forces: The Transnational Movement to End the Cold War* (Ithaca: Cornell University Press, 1999), 45–56, 90–120.

[44] Jason Parker, "Cold War II: The Eisenhower Administration, the Bandung Conference, and the Reperiodization of the Postwar Era," *Diplomatic History* 30 (November, 2006): 867–92; quoted words, 885.

[45] Odd Arne Westad, *The Global Cold War: Third World Interventions and the Making of Our Times* (New York: Cambridge University Press, 2005), 102.

Diem's willingness to use force against his opponents. Shortly after the United States signed an agreement to train Vietnamese forces, Collins advocated withdrawal as "the only sound solution." Secretary of State John Foster Dulles demurred, asserting, "We should continue to back Diem but exert more pressure on him to make changes we consider necessary."[46] Dulles was, in effect, declaring that self-determination was not acceptable for Vietnam, in either the North or the South. The North by definition could not be free because of its communist leadership and ties to the Soviets and Chinese; the South could not be trusted to advance U.S. interests in Southeast Asia. When the CIA and Department of State backed Diem's decision not to hold general elections in 1956 as stipulated by the Geneva Accords, the United States began a twenty-year odyssey that would result in its defeat. In the South, an emboldened Diem endeavored to extend his regime's oppressive control over village life.[47] Not only was Vietnam thereby drawn further into the U.S. security orbit but also the effect of involvement there on American core values would soon become apparent.

Freedom that the United States could warmly endorse was scarcely in evidence in the Middle East in the mid- to late 1950s. The Arabs, Eisenhower wrote in his diary, "are daily growing more arrogant and disregarding the interests of Western Europe and of the United States." The president foresaw the possibility of forging a ring of security treaties to protect the states of the region, including Israel, from the Soviets and themselves. Oil, more than Israel, was vitally important to the United States. Yet, America's options were few, and the prospect of an Arab federation under Egyptian leadership made for "a very sorry situation."[48] The escalation of the Suez Canal crisis that began in July 1956 did nothing to improve Eisenhower's outlook, tied as the crisis was to British prestige, the Algerian revolution, and Israel's security concerns. He feared the outcome might be "to Sovietize the region, including Israel."[49] A defector from the KGB later wrote, "[T]here was no realistic prospect of the emergence of a major Marxist-Leninist regime which would act as a role model for the Arab world and spread revolution through the region."[50] Given his assumptions to the contrary, Eisenhower would have found that assessment unimaginable.

Nor did Algeria offer fertile ground for advancing Soviet influence.[51] The *Front de Libération Nationale* (FLN) was asserting its freedom from French

---

[46] *The Pentagon Papers: The Defense Department History of United States Decisionmaking on Vietnam*, Senator Gravel edition, 5 vols. (Boston: Beacon Press, 1971–1972), I: 226, 228.

[47] David W. P. Elliott, The *Vietnamese War: Revolution and Social Change in the Mekong Delta, 1930–1975*, 2 vols. (Armonk: M. E. Sharpe, 2003), I: 164, 177–81, 184–95.

[48] *Eisenhower Diaries*, 318, 320.

[49] Ibid., 331.

[50] Christopher Andrew and Vasili Mitrokhin, *The World Was Going Our Way: The KGB and the Battle for the Third World* (New York: Basic Books, 2005), 141.

[51] Ibid., 431.

domination there. Nonaligned states including Egypt and Yugoslavia rushed to treat the FLN as a de facto government, which raised questions of self-determination and, inevitably, human rights for postcolonial and nonaligned states. Initially, the United States endeavored to chart a middle course on Algeria, all the more so because France contended that it was defending the West with its efforts against the FLN. Dulles, concerned that "communist-inspired" extremists would maneuver to exploit "premature independence," was sensitive to that position and would not endorse rapid decolonization for Algeria until 1957.[52]

In calling for gradual change, U.S. foreign policy did not reflect the realities of the late fifties in the Middle East where more than half of the population in most Arab states was under the age of twenty.[53] To many of those young people and others who shared his pan-Arab philosophy, Egypt's Nasser was a charismatic figure, much more so than King Saud of Saudi Arabia, Washington's closest Arab ally. The anticommunism that lay at the heart of U.S. policy could not mobilize popular support behind the American agenda. Nevertheless, the Eisenhower Doctrine of 1957 was an attempt to incorporate the Middle East within a recognizable security framework. In addition to guaranteeing access to Persian Gulf oil, its objectives were to prevent the aggrandizement of Soviet power in the region and to contain radical Arab nationalism, or Nasserism. A contest with Nasser was a battle for hearts and minds that the United States could not win. Eisenhower's derision of Nasser as "a puppet" of the Soviet Union prevented U.S. officials from considering events in the Middle East in a less confrontational light.[54] Even a modest rapprochement that materialized in late 1958 did not significantly improve Washington's standing with Nasser's followers. A frustrated Eisenhower, continuing to provide sophisticated military equipment to Israel, commented in 1959, "If you go and live with these Arabs, you will find that they simply cannot understand our ideas of freedom or human dignity."[55]

Fidel Castro fared no better in Eisenhower's judgment. The Cuban revolutionary, considered a "little Hitler" by the president, seized the attention

[52] Quoted in Matthew Connelly, *A Diplomatic Revolution: Algeria's Fight for Independence and the Origins of the Post-Cold War Era* (New York: Oxford University Press, 2002), 85.
[53] Material in this paragraph draws on Salim Yacub, *Containing Arab Nationalism: The Eisenhower Doctrine and the Middle East* (Chapel Hill: University of North Carolina Press, 2004) and Nathan J. Citino, *From Arab Nationalism to OPEC: Eisenhower, King Saud, and the Making of U.S.-Saudi Relations* (Bloomington: Indiana University Press, 2002).
[54] U.S. Department of State, *Papers Relating to the Foreign Relations of the United States, 1958–60*, vol. 11: *Lebanon and Jordan* (Washington, DC: Government Printing Office, 1992), 245.
[55] U.S. Department of State, *Papers Relating to the Foreign Relations of the United States, 1958–60*, vol. 12: *Near East Region; Iraq; Iran; Arabian Peninsula* (Washington, DC: Government Printing Office, 1993), 22.

of the National Security Council with increasing frequency in 1959–60.[56] This inapt metaphor not only denied the legitimacy of grievances against the dictator, Fulgencio Batista, long a U.S. ally, but it also suggested that Cuba, like Iran and Guatemala before it, did not understand its vital place in postwar history as accorded by the United States. The subsequent determination that Castro was a Soviet puppet further discredited the struggle against authoritarian oppression that linked the revolution of 1959 to the 1890s and the early 1930s in Cuban history. The United States had come to terms with Bolivia's revolution in 1952 because Bolivia, whose revolution was strongly nationalist but not demonstrably anticapitalist, did not have a fraught historical relationship with the United States, as did Cuba. Any thought at the State Department or the CIA that Cuba's revolution could be similarly accommodated was fanciful.[57] Castro may not have been averse to a *modus vivendi* with Washington, if it was on terms he could accept.[58] However, CIA chief Allen Dulles dismissed the revolution: Cuba's revolutionaries were rather like certain children, who "if... rebuffed... were capable of almost anything."[59]

Three overarching themes from American history pervade U.S.-Cuban relations under Eisenhower and Kennedy: the imperative of expansion in a capitalist political economy, the preemptive use of force under the guise of self-defense, and the presence of a fear akin to paranoia in the assessment of potential threats to the nation. Together, they suggest why acquiescence in movements for self-determination proved to be so difficult for ColdWar leaders. Freedom, they wholeheartedly believed, was not to be entrusted to neophytes in a dangerous world, especially if Washington did not play a decisive role in defining what freedom meant. The perceived disorder in Iran, Guatemala, the Nasser-led United Arab Republic, and the Cuban revolution therefore challenged the foundations of the free world itself. That was unacceptable to the U.S. government. Trepidation in Washington spawned intervention abroad in an effort to control the unpredictability of independence movements.

The 1960s and the Decline of Civic Virtue

John Fitzgerald Kennedy assumed the presidency in 1961, sharing Eisenhower's fear of disorder but not his predilection for the hidden-hand style of governance. What would be the fate of Berlin, Laos, or Cuba? The world

---

[56] *Eisenhower Diaries*, 379.

[57] Samuel Farber, *The Origins of the Cuban Revolution Reconsidered* (Chapel Hill: University of North Carolina Press, 2006), 98–111.

[58] Thomas G. Paterson, *Contesting Castro: The United States and the Triumph of the Cuban Revolution* (New York: Oxford University Press, 1994), 226–42, 245–52.

[59] U.S. Department of State, *Papers Relating to the Foreign Relations of the United States, 1958–60*, vol. 6: *Cuba* (Washington, DC: Government Printing Office, 1991), 398.

Kennedy inherited seemed almost incomprehensible, the result of failing to appreciate how others viewed the world and why they lived their lives as they did. The quest for conformity against communism in the early 1960s construed self-determination as threatening or, at the least, premature and sought to cast dissent at home as illegitimate or naïve at best.

The array of issues that the administration faced seemed daunting. Yet, within months, some problems had become less vexing. The Berlin Wall lessened tensions over the city where the Cold War began. Following that, however, was a transformation in Franco-German relations that signified substantial differences within the Western alliance.[60] In Southeast Asia, the Americans and the Soviets began negotiating the Laotian issue and quickly agreed to maintain the fiction of neutrality there. In addition, China's nuclear program worried both the United States and the Soviet Union, although Kennedy did not take advantage of the Sino-Soviet split to modify the customary rhetoric of anticommunism, in part because of State Department doubts about the rift.[61] It is worth noting that in 1964, before his fall from power, Khrushchev characterized Mao Zedong as "sick, crazy."[62]

Within the United States, young people and radical intellectuals began to reject political conformity. Before the onset of the antiwar movement, Cuba and civil rights show well the gap between growing segments of the population and the government over the proper role for informed citizens. Two intellectuals, already established as critics of the status quo, sociologist C. Wright Mills and historian William Appleman Williams, wrote books providing an alternative way to understand the Cuban revolution. Mills's *Listen, Yankee* (1960) and Williams's *The United States, Cuba and Castro* (1962) were a balm to supporters of the revolution, at a time when some young Americans were neither reluctant to read nor to engage in radical politics.[63] Advocates of responsible citizenship, Mills in *The Power Elite* (1956) and Williams in *The Tragedy of American Diplomacy* (1959 and later editions) were read by and influenced countless students in the 1960s and 1970s.[64] As public intellectuals, they shouldered the legacy of Charles A. Beard, whose books were also widely read in his prime.

---

[60] Tony Judt, *Postwar: A History of Europe since 1945* (New York: Penguin Press, 2005), 249–54, 270ff.

[61] Aleksandr Fursenko and Timothy Naftali, *Khrushchev's Cold War: The Inside Story of an American Adversary* (New York: W. W. Norton & Company, 2006), 323–37, 361–2.

[62] Quoted in Andrew and Mitrokhin, *The World Was Going Our Way*, 260.

[63] Van Gosse, *Where the Boys Are: Cuba, Cold War America and the Making of a New Left* (London: Verso, 1993), 158, 175–83.

[64] Kevin Mattson, *Intellectuals in Action: The Origins of the New Left and Radical Liberalism, 1945–1970* (University Park: Pennsylvania State University Press, 2002), 59, 71–6, 145–6, 152–9. *Tragedy* remains the most influential book about U.S. foreign policy ever written. For Williams, Beard was "the man he obviously admired most." See Paul M. Buhle and Edward Rice-Maximin, *William Appleman Williams: The Tragedy of Empire* (New York: Routledge, 1995), 89.

William McKinley once observed that Cuba and the United States had shared "ties of singular intimacy" for almost a century. Perhaps for that reason, the Bay of Pigs invasion became a catalytic event for dissent against Cold War verities. Those who disdained the sweep of the Cold War and those who came of age, in part, as a result of the impetus toward rigor in higher education, which was a *raison d' être* for the 1958 National Defense Education Act (NDEA), saw the invasion as a betrayal of the values Americans had long cherished. NDEA was meant to manufacture young Cold Warriors; that it did.[65] It also encouraged an independence of thought, leading many college-aged youth to ask why they lived in a world characterized by tension and fear.[66] To dissenters young and old, some of whom came together in 1960 to form the Fair Play for Cuba Committee (FPCC), Cubans had a right to interpret their own past, not as appendages of U.S. security interests, and to defend their nation's sovereignty against its foes.

The Bay of Pigs invasion violated both the ideal of self-determination and the principle of sovereignty. In April 1961, waging Cold War in the hemisphere made a mockery of values for many who participated in radical civic action. At a FPCC protest held in San Francisco, C. Wright Mills, who was too infirm to attend, sent a telegram denouncing the Cold War liberals in the White House who arrogated to themselves the right to determine Cuba's fate. "Schlesinger and company have disgraced us intellectually and morally," Mills wrote. Kennedy adviser Arthur M. Schlesinger Jr. includes the telegram in his history of the administration to demean "impassioned liberals" who opposed the failed operation. His condescension seemed boundless, which was ironic because he would later publish a book entitled *The Imperial Presidency* (1973). Schlesinger did acknowledge, however, that Kennedy made a "misstep" in telling the press that it should "be prepared to censor itself in the interests of national security."[67] Glossing over this suggestion as an indiscretion ignored the intermittently troubled relationship between the security ethos and freedom of the press since the late 1890s. Cold War liberals, it seems, could not abide free speech and freedom of assembly if they became vehicles for popular dissent from U.S. foreign policy.

Condescension, too, often typified responses of conservatives and liberals, black and white, to the increasingly student-dominated civil rights movement. The FBI saw communism at the root of the movement, a charge both laughable and pathetic because students like Diane Nash at Fisk University linked the movement to the struggle against communism, as did their

---

[65] John A. Andrew III, *The Other Side of the Sixties: Young Americans for Freedom and the Rise of Conservative Politics* (New Brunswick: Rutgers University Press, 1997), 26.

[66] Jeremi Suri, *Power and Protest* (Cambridge: Harvard University Press, 2005), 88–94.

[67] Arthur M. Schlesinger Jr., *A Thousand Days: John F. Kennedy in the White House* (Boston, Houghton Mifflin, 1965), 285, 286, 296.

elders in the NAACP.[68] Mainstream politicians, Republican and Democratic, hoped to profit from black political activism. Even before the 1960 election, young African Americans followed the example of their peers who had begun sit-ins in Greensboro, North Carolina, and elsewhere, rather than wait for the electoral process to concoct some watered-down version of freedom. John Lewis, an early leader of the Student Nonviolent Coordinating Committee (SNCC), wrote in his memoir, "There were issues to be forced, and we were going to do what we could to force them."[69]

Civil rights activists suffered so many disappointments in the 1960s that, in their frustration and anger, the movement became for many a battle for liberation and human rights. At the March on Washington in August 1963, on the day W. E. B. Du Bois died in Ghana, Lewis identified the cause of black Americans with that of Africans who were trying to protect their recent independence. Lewis broke with Cold War liberalism in his speech, saying, "The revolution is at hand, and we must free ourselves of the chains of political and economic slavery."[70] For many in SNCC, the followers of Malcolm X in the Nation of Islam, and, later, the Black Panthers, nonviolence became passé and gave way to instances of confrontation with authority. Even Martin Luther King, hounded by the FBI at the order of Attorney General Robert F. Kennedy, transformed his early, more pacifist tactics into an aggressive defense of human rights. The war in Vietnam, in which African Americans were serving and dying in disproportionate numbers, convinced King of the inadequacy of Cold War liberalism as a governing creed. He articulated his reasons most forcefully at Riverside Church in New York City on April 4, 1967, when he argued that it was cruel to draft "young men who had been crippled by our society" to fight for freedoms abroad that they could not fully exercise at home. In his address, King declared that he had begun to "ponder the madness of Vietnam."[71] The white establishment could not understand that the civil rights and black power movements, in one scholar's words, "emerged from the same soil, confronted the same predicaments, and reflected the same quest for African American freedom."[72]

To dissenters from the security orthodoxy that had taken the United States into Vietnam, the political space available for civic virtue was so narrow as

---

[68] Clayborne Carson, *In Struggle: SNCC and the Black Awakening of the 1960s* (Cambridge: Harvard University Press, 1981), 13; John Lewis with Michael D'Orso, *Walking with the Wind: A Memoir of the Movement* (New York: Simon & Schuster, 1998), 98, 270.

[69] Lewis, *Walking with the Wind*, 98.

[70] Ibid., 217.

[71] Martin Luther King, Jr., *I Have a Dream: Writings and Speeches That Changed the World*, ed. James M. Washington (New York: HarperCollins, 1992), 138, 140.

[72] Timothy B. Tyson, *Radio Free Dixie: Robert F. Williams and the Roots of Black Power* (Chapel Hill: University of North Carolina Press, 1999), 3 for the words quoted; Simon Wendt, *The Spirit and the Shotgun: Armed Resistance and the Struggle for Civil Rights* (Gainesville: University Press of Florida, 2007).

to make debate seem useless. That ultimate sense of despair would come – in 1968. Liberalism was on trial by the mid-1960s and faring badly. The organization Students for a Democratic Society (SDS) had distanced itself from Cuba at its founding in 1962, hoping to establish its credentials as a group focusing on domestic issues.[73] By 1965, SDS stood at the forefront of growing opposition to the war in Vietnam. The men and women of SDS, like members of the American Student Union in the 1930s, would soon fall into sectarian wrangling about how best to oppose the war. What they agreed on was the bankruptcy of liberalism; it had destroyed their ideals. Carl Oglesby, president of SDS, denounced Cold War liberals in the manner of Molière in a speech, "How Can We Continue to Sack the Ports of Asia and Still Dream of Jesus?," at a march on Washington in November 1965. Oglesby linked the growing crisis of American cities and militancy of African Americans to disgust with the belief system that took the country to war. He implored humanist liberals, supporters of the 1964 Civil Rights Act and the 1965 Voting Rights Act, to remember their nation's ideals and challenge "corporate liberalism." "Help us build," he said. "Help us shake the future in the name of plain human truth."[74] By 1965, it was too late to resuscitate Roosevelt's humanistic globalism; liberalism's tragedy would not be complete for three more years. Conservative factions were also mobilizing among the Democrats and especially the Republicans, pushing American politics to the right.[75] The prospects for civic virtue and reasoned discourse had not seemed so dim since 1917.

The Chaos of Internal Security Policy

The Cold War made liberalism unsalvageable as a governing philosophy. In the name of modernization – the idea that a capitalist political economy portended peace and prosperity for all – the U.S. government utilized internal security policy to ensure that development would occur in a stable environment. The Alliance for Progress, the vehicle for development in the Western Hemisphere, was compromised from its birth in 1961. Fears that Cuba might spread the contagion of revolution in the Americas led the United States to emphasize order over development,[76] raising serious

---

[73] Gosse, *Where the Boys Are*, 5–6.
[74] Quoted in Walter LaFeber, ed., *America in the Cold War: Twenty-Years of Revolution and Response, 1947–1967* (New York: John Wiley & Sons, 1969), 24.
[75] Mary C. Brennan, *Turning Right in the Sixties: The Conservative Capture of the GOP* (Chapel Hill: University of North Carolina Press, 1995).
[76] National Security File (NSF): Meetings and Memoranda Series (M & M Series), National Security Action Memorandum (NSAM) 10, 6 February 1961, Box 328, John F. Kennedy (JFK) Presidential Library, Boston, Massachusetts; CIA, National Intelligence Estimate (NIE), "The Potential for Revolution in Latin America," NIE 80-90/68, 28 March 1968,

doubts about the ability of an economy premised on containment capitalism to afford security and development. Put more crudely, guns and butter were incompatible.

Internal security policy focused on civic action, one aspect of nation building. U.S. officials wanted the Latin American military to take the lead in civic action not only to bring efficiency to activities such as road building and school construction but also to educate the "primitive" military itself about democracy.[77] Assuming congruity with their own security objectives, Americans provided special training for Latin American armed forces either in the United States or at the School of the Americas in the Panama Canal Zone.[78] Authority to equip security forces resided in the Office of Public Safety (OPS) within the Department of State's Agency for International Development.[79]

U.S. officials seemed hardly to care about the democratic sympathies of their allies. Anticommunist regimes such as the one that ousted Arturo Frondizi in Argentina in March 1962 experienced almost no interruption of aid. Assistant Secretary of State for Inter-American Affairs Edwin M. Martin disingenuously observed that Washington could not dictate who held political office.[80] The United States also supported politicians and military officers in Brazil in their efforts to thwart President João Goulart's independent foreign policy. This activity helped galvanize the antidemocratic forces that overthrew Goulart in April 1964.[81] Shortly after the *golpe*, President Johnson told one of Martin's successors, Thomas Mann, "The Brazil thing went all right."[82] It is worth recalling that in mid-March Mann had said, in what

NSF, NIEs: 80/90 Latin America, Box 8–9, Lyndon B. Johnson (LBJ) Presidential Library, Austin, Texas.

[77] Michael E. Latham, *Modernization as Ideology: American Social Science and "Nation Building" in the Kennedy Era* (Chapel Hill: University of North Carolina Press, 2000). Walt Whitman Rostow, one of the originators of modernization theory, used the word "primitive."

[78] NSF: M & M Series, Staff Memoranda, Memorandum for JFK, 27 January 1961, Box 325, JFK Library; NSF: M & M Series, NSAM 48, 23 April 1961, Box 329, ibid,; NSF: M & M series, NSAM 88, 5 September and 30 September 1961, Box 331, ibid.

[79] NSF: M & M Series, Special Group (CI), 13 August 1962, Box 319, ibid.; NSF: M & M Series, NSAM 177, 1 November 1962, Box 338, ibid.

[80] *Department of State Bulletin*, November 4, 1963, pp. 698–700; Edwin McCammon Martin, *Kennedy and Latin America* (Lanham: University Press of America, 1994), 265–78, 456.

[81] U.S. Department of State, *Papers Relating to the Foreign Relations of the United States, 1961–1963*, vol. 12: *American Republics* (Washington, DC: Government Printing Office, 1996), 475; Stephen G. Rabe, *The Most Dangerous Area in the World: John F. Kennedy Confronts Communist Revolution in Latin America* (Chapel Hill: University of North Carolina Press, 1999), 63, 66–71.

[82] U.S. Department of State, *Papers Relating to the Foreign Relations of the United States, 1964–1968*, vol. 31: *South and Central America; Mexico* (Washington, DC: Government Printing Office, 2005), 45.

became known as the Mann Doctrine, that military and economic aid would depend not on the character of a given regime but on the extent to which U.S. assistance would help it maintain order.[83]

Washington's relative indifference to the fate of constitutional rule also emerges in the case of Guatemala. Documents obtained by the National Security Archive disclose that the Guatemalan military committed to internal security – planning, with U.S. advice, and activating a grisly anti-guerrilla campaign, *Operación Limpieza* (Operation Cleanup), which resulted in a massacre of the Guatemalan Left in March 1966.[84] What did events in Guatemala mean for core values? After the ouster of President Miguel Ydigores Fuentes in March 1963, the United States had sought to make Guatemala a model of counterinsurgency, civic action, and nation building. As the government consolidated its authority by force, the already limited space for political participation narrowed further. U.S. officials on the scene warned about "youthful discontent and frustration with the existing order."[85] The problem was that the existing "order" was devoid of liberty.

In the wake of *Operación Limpieza*, President Julio César Méndez Montenegro "gave the security forces *carte blanche*" to secure the country, concluded a high-ranking Department of State official.[86] The violence of 1966 and after jarred U.S. authorities, but did not result in either suspension of assistance or reconsideration of counterinsurgency planning. Mann's successor and U.S. Coordinator of the Alliance for Progress Covey T. Oliver optimistically assessed the program in fall 1967: "[T]he situation in Guatemala continues to improve." Walt Whitman Rostow, then Johnson's national security adviser, was less sure, noting that "a modest increase in our rural police program is warranted."[87]

Viewed in that light, the anguish of Viron P. Vaky, the deputy chief of mission in Guatemala from July 1964 to August 1967, about the level of state terror there and his government's complicity in it seems almost quaint. Vaky asked, "Have our values been so twisted by our adversary concept of politics in the hemisphere? Is it conceivable that we are so obsessed with insurgency that we are prepared to rationalize murder as an acceptable

---

[83] *New York Times*, March 19, 1964.

[84] Grandin, *The Last Colonial Massacre*, 73–104; National Security Archive Electronic Briefing Book No. 11, Kate Doyle, Project Director, *U.S. Policy in Guatemala, 1966–1996*, http://www.gwu.edu/~nsarchiv/NSAEBB/NSAEBB11/docs/.

[85] U.S. Embassy (Guatemala City) to Department of State DS), 15 January 1964, NSF, Country (CO) File, Latin America, El Salvador–Guatemala, Box 54, LBJ Library; U.S. Embassy (Guatemala City) to DS, 9 March 1964, ibid. (quoted words, p. 8).

[86] Thomas L. Hughes, director of intelligence and research, to Secretary of State Dean Rusk, 23 October 1967, NSF, CO File, Latin America, El Salvador-Guatemala, Box 54, LBJ Library.

[87] For Oliver see *FRUS, 1964–1968*, vol. 31, 152–3; Rostow to LBJ, 6 July 1967, NSF, CO File, Latin America, Box 3, LBJ Library.

counter-insurgency weapon?"[88] In Guatemala, as would soon be true in much of Latin America, there existed little effort or incentive to distinguish between political dissidents and committed revolutionaries. In the wake of the killing of Cuba's Ernesto "Che" Guevara in Bolivia by a U.S.-trained battalion in October 1967, Rostow called counterinsurgency aid "our 'preventive medicine.'"[89] Despite occasional rhetoric to the contrary, the U.S. government at the highest levels did not consider altering its firm belief that all insurgents constituted a threat to national security. This siege mentality had a domestic, albeit less lethal, counterpart.

"The problem of the Negro in American society," Walt Rostow opined in 1968, "is, in many ways, like a foreign aid problem."[90] Yet, aid could generate development only in an orderly setting, according to the tenets of modernization theory. How to create order or stability became linked to issues of political inclusion and therefore to basic rights and liberties. The FBI questioned the loyalty of many persons in the civil rights movement. Hoover consciously distanced himself and the FBI from civil rights activists in the South.[91] Johnson, too, was predisposed to believe that communists were exerting undue influence within the movement.[92] Incredibly, the struggle for civil rights had become a security-related matter in the 1960s. The FBI and local police forces were viewing African American communities in cities outside the South as sites of extensive crime and social disorder. The 1950s had witnessed, as did the 1960s, an exodus of southern blacks to other parts of the country, particularly large urban areas.[93] On these new frontiers, old and young alike wanted to find opportunities for making a better life. African Americans were seeking to claim the American dream as their own and thereby fulfill the charge that Du Bois gave them at the conclusion of the Great War: "Make way for democracy." To a considerable degree, the FBI and the Johnson White House had other ideas.

More than 135 cities with a population of over 30,000 asked the federal government for help in coping with racial disturbances in the mid-1960s. In the process, police officers became highly politicized, acting as witting agents of political repression and giving vent to suppressed rage against

[88] *FRUS, 1964–1968*, vol. 31, 237–41; quoted words, 240.
[89] Memo by Rostow to LBJ, 11 October 1967, NSF, CO File, Latin America, Bolivia, Box 8, LBJ Library.
[90] Walt Whitman Rostow to Joseph A. Califano, Jr., 16 May 1968, NSF, Name File, Box 7, LBJ Library.
[91] William C. Sullivan with Bill Brown, *The Bureau: My Thirty Years in Hoover's FBI* (New York: W. W. Norton & Company, 1979), 125.
[92] Michael R. Beschloss, ed., *Taking Charge: The Johnson White House Tapes, 1963–1964* (New York: Simon & Schuster, 1997), 461–2, 466–7.
[93] Allen J. Matusow, *The Unraveling of America: A History of Liberalism in the 1960s* (New York: Harper & Row, 1984), 61.

rioters.[94] A look at the disturbances, or revolts, in Harlem in July 1964 and Watts in August 1965 reveals important conceptual similarities between government responses to those events and Washington's promotion of internal security in Latin America.[95]

What occurred in Harlem should not have surprised the White House. Although former presidential aide Eric F. Goldman perceptively wrote, "The American Negro strikingly resembled people of the underdeveloped nations who . . . were going through 'a revolution of rising expectations,'"[96] Lyndon Johnson felt a sense of betrayal and deep disappointment in the summer of 1964. At great cost to his party, if not himself, he had pushed the Civil Rights Act through Congress and had begun work on the initial phases of the Great Society; waiting in the wings was a voting rights bill, which Congress would pass on August 4, 1965.[97] Johnson's dismay inexorably gave way to internal security planning. In Baltimore, Secretary of the Army Cyrus Vance spoke with local officials about how to respond to outbreaks of African American violence.[98] Hoover asked for and received Johnson's pledge to allow the U.S. Army to help the FBI train local police for riot control.[99] Also, Senator Thomas Dodd, a Democrat from Connecticut, considered convening his Internal Security Subcommittee because racial disturbances meant for him the fearsome specter of subversion; he called them "the product of deliberate planning by trained agitators, both Communist and Black Nationalists [*sic*]."[100]

The administration hoped it could head off another round of disturbances in 1965. It created special programs for the young and old, unemployed and underemployed, and for aiding local police forces. These programs, a form of domestic civic action, did not have the desired effect. The Watts

[94] Memorandum to Lee C. White, associate special counsel to the president, 4 September 1964, Files of Lee C. White, Office Files, Box 5, LBJ Library; Jerome H. Skolnick, ed., *The Politics of Protest* (New York: Ballantine Books, 1969), chapter 7.

[95] What to call the disturbances matters. The U.S. government dismissed them as riots, perhaps because of the participation of angry young people, thereby minimizing their political context. The disturbances did not rise to the level of rebellion, which implies organized armed resistance. Whereas uprising is a general term, revolt can suggest a rejection of constituted authority.

[96] Eric F. Goldman, *The Tragedy of Lyndon Johnson* (New York: Alfred A. Knopf, 1969), 205.

[97] Joseph A. Califano, Jr., *The Triumph and Tragedy of Lyndon Johnson: The White House Years* (New York: Simon & Schuster, 1991), 59–64.

[98] Mayor Theodore R. McKeldin to LBJ, 14 September 1964, Files of Lee C. White, Box 5, LBJ Library; White to LBJ, 8 September 1964, ibid.

[99] Memorandum by J. Edgar Hoover, 9 September 1964, ibid.; Hoover to Walter W. Jenkins, special assistant to the president, 1 October 1964, White House Central Files (WHCF), Human Rights, Ex HU 4, Box 59, ibid.

[100] Senator Thomas C. Dodd to Senator Hubert H. Humphrey, 4 September 1964, Files of Lee C. White, Box 5, ibid.

section of Los Angeles burst into flames on the night of August 11.[101] One aide claimed that Johnson was stunned by events in Watts, although that is unlikely. Memoranda addressed to the president before the disturbances in the summer of 1964 indicated that the civil rights movement would probably expand in uncertain ways into black communities beyond the South where, in the words of Attorney General Robert F. Kennedy, "Negro political leaders [do not] carry much credibility with young Negroes caught in urban slums."[102]

A report on Watts summarized the administration's basic dilemma even as it was promising greater antipoverty assistance to Los Angeles. Johnson's special emissary, former Florida governor LeRoy Collins, concluded that the major issue was "the struggle over who is to represent the poor" in federal programs.[103] His analysis suggested that the disturbances in Harlem and Watts amounted to political revolts against state and federal authority. In contrast, the administration's diagnosis of what was troubling the nation's African American communities, set forth in the so-called Moynihan Report, *The Negro Family: The Case for National Action*, argued that the major problem was an economic one. Johnson liked that idea, making it the basis for a commencement address at Howard University in June 1965.[104]

It was a Moynihan-inspired response that Johnson then turned to in the aftermath of Watts. Much like the anticolonial revolts of the late 1940s and 1950s in Indonesia and Malaya and the insurgency in the Philippines, the summer revolts of 1964 and 1965 were primarily political statements by the dispossessed, demands for local empowerment, and rejections of what approximated neocolonial rule by white America.[105] Great Society nation building did not adequately deal with the vital issue of political space for alienated African American citizens. Instead, the government resorted to a program of economic palliatives, avoiding the matter of real political empowerment.

More than other African Americans, black nationalists, like insurgents abroad, elicited real fear. They forcefully challenged the liberal precepts of the Great Society. As one former SNCC member put it, recalling the failure of

---

[101] Humphrey to LBJ, 10 June 1965, WHCF, Human Rights, Ex HU 2, Box 3, ibid.; Gerald Horne, *Fire This Time: The Watts Uprising and the 1960s* (New York: Da Capo, 1997); Horne also refers to Watts as a revolt.

[102] Doris Kearns, *Lyndon Johnson and the American Dream* (New York: Harper & Row, 1976), 305. Richard Goodwin to LBJ, 4 May 1964, WHCF, Human Rights, Ex HU 2, Box 2, LBJ Library; Kennedy's words are in RFK to LBJ, 5 August 1964, WHCF, Human Rights, Ex HU 2, Box 3, ibid.

[103] LeRoy Collins Report on Los Angeles Mission, [September 1965], WHCF, Human Rights, Box 25, ibid.

[104] Matusow, *Unraveling of America*, 194–6.

[105] The neocolonial metaphor appears in John H. O'Dell, "The July Rebellions and the 'Military State,'" in Thomas Rose, ed., *Violence in America: A Historical and Contemporary Reader* (New York: Vintage Books, 1970), 279–95.

the Democrats to seat the Mississippi Freedom Democratic Party at the 1964 national convention, "People saw very clearly that . . . the interests of black people could only be advanced when there was a base of strength, political strength, from which to advance it." These sentiments were widely shared. The most revolutionary African Americans, those who were advocating complete separation, would pay a heavy price.[106]

How the U.S. government responded to black nationalism is a well-known story, made especially heinous with the December 1969 murder by Chicago police, working with the FBI, of Black Panthers Fred Hampton and Mark Clark.[107] Repression became the order of the day, leading to precisely what government officials feared most – a race-based, politically charged insurgency. The Johnson administration saw it coming, as Vice President Hubert H. Humphrey's June 1965 memorandum on the Task Force on Urban Problems indicated. One of the president's most sympathetic chroniclers, Doris Kearns, concludes that his post-Watts response to America's racial problems amounted to an "abdication of leadership."[108]

Hatred of dissent brought the liberal Johnson and the conservative Hoover close together on the issue of internal security at home. Civil rights leaders, black nationalists, and antiwar activists fantastically merged into a hydra-headed threat to security. To Johnson, these critics, many of whom he believed were inspired by communists, needed to be taught a hard lesson about political realities in a time of war. To Hoover, protestors were not part of the America he was committed to protect. In 1967 and 1968, he authorized the creation of COINTELPRO-Black Nationalist-Hate groups and COINTELRPO-New Left.[109] Johnson's and Hoover's stand for law and order resembled aspects of the brutal national security doctrine that was then taking hold among Latin America's armed forces without objection by the U.S. government.[110]

---

[106] Michael Thelwell, quoted in Cheryl Lynn Greenberg, ed., *A Circle of Trust: Remembering SNCC* (New Brunswick: Rutgers University Press, 1998), 206; Stokely Carmichael and Charles V. Hamilton, *Black Power: The Politics of Liberation in America* (New York: Vintage Books, 1967), 86–97; Elaine Brown, *A Taste of Power: A Black Woman's Story* (New York: Pantheon Books, 1992), chapter 6; William L. Van Deburg, *New Day in Babylon: The Black Power Movement and American Culture, 1965–1975* (Chicago: University of Chicago Press, 1992), chapter 4.

[107] Ward Churchill and Jim Vander Wall, *Agents of Repression: The FBI's Secret Wars against the Black Panther Party and the American Indian Movement* (Boston: South End Press, 1988), esp. 15–99; Kenneth O'Reilly, *"Racial Matters": The FBI's Secret File on Black America, 1960–1972* (New York: Free Press, 1989), 293–324.

[108] Humphrey to LBJ, 10 June 1965, WHCF, Human Rights, Ex HU 2, Box 3, LBJ Library; Kearns, *Lyndon Johnson and the American Dream*, 308.

[109] Athan Theoharis, *Spying on Americans: Political Surveillance from Hoover to the Huston Plan* (Philadelphia: Temple University Press, 1978), 145 ff, 175 ff; O'Reilly, *"Racial Matters,"* 238–62; Richard Gid Powers, *Secrecy and Power: The Life of J. Edgar Hoover* (New York: Free Press, 1987), 434.

[110] Brian Loveman, *For la Patria: Politics and the Armed Forces in Latin America* (Wilmington: Scholarly Resources, 1999), 179–84, 187–8, 236–9.

Real security emanated neither from oppressive tactics, no matter how forcibly applied, nor from political repression. Internal security policy reduced the political space in the United States and elsewhere for people questioning the status quo. It prolonged the misery of war in Southeast Asia, helped set the stage for human rights abuses through "dirty wars" in Latin America, and retarded the effort then to make civil rights in the United States more than nominal political rights. Liberal Democrats and Republicans were almost paralyzed as discord engulfed the nation. In supporting the Gulf of Tonkin Resolution of August 1964, liberals further embraced Cold War globalism.[111] For some years thereafter, as war and race dominated public discourse and divided the nation, these political centrists had neither the moral will nor the votes to make defense of America's historic values a priority. Viron Vaky, it turned out, had not been wrong.

Richard Nixon's America

If Richard Nixon could not halt the tumult that was roiling American society as he took office in 1969, he could use the power at his disposal to control its effects. How he chose to do so further rent the fabric of basic vales. It is useful to look at "the unraveling of America," to borrow historian Allen J. Matusow's apt term, to understand the background for Nixon's actions.[112] Several examples suffice to indicate what became of civic virtue after Johnson's decision for war on July 1965. In early 1966, Democrat Senator J. William Fulbright, chair of the Senate Foreign Relations Committee, convened a hearing about U.S. involvement in Vietnam. The "Vietnam Hearings" touched a nerve in the general populace; more than 20,000 Americans responded with communications to the committee. Testimony by General James M. Gavin and George F. Kennan addressed the limits of globalism. Gavin worried that additional commitments in Vietnam would gravely harm "the true meaning of global strategy in world affairs today," which entailed among other things maintaining "a dynamic and viable prospering [export] economy."[113] Kennan averred that the United States was in Vietnam for reasons of prestige, which had led officials to forget their foremost obligation – to preserve freedom at home. What had gone wrong? American leaders, he said, were "affected by some sort of illusions about invincibility on our part.... [T]here are limits to what our duties and our capabilities are."[114] The eminent political scientist Hans Morgenthau, as if to atone for his uncritical support around 1950 of global containment,

---

[111] Robert David Johnson, *Congress and the Cold War* (New York: Cambridge University Press, 2006), 111–16.

[112] Memo by Rostow to LBJ, 11 October 1967, n. 89.

[113] *The Vietnam Hearings*, with an introduction by J. William Fulbright (New York: Vintage Books, 1996), 66, 64. Generally see Robert Buzzanco, *Masters of War: Military Dissent and Politics in the Vietnam Era* (New York: Cambridge University Press, 1996).

[114] *Vietnam Hearings*, 117–8.

joined those advocating limits to the U.S. role in Indochina. "The integrity of the American territory and institutions – those are the interests of America," he wrote in 1967. "The war in Vietnam is the President's; it means nothing to America."[115]

Autumn 1967 was something of a Rubicon for the antiwar movement, which took a more confrontational stance toward the Johnson administration with the October March on the Pentagon. Politically active, mostly white young men and women, many of whom identified with the New Left despite its inveterate misogyny,[116] shared the profound disenchantment of black nationalists with American liberalism. Indeed, the rise of the black power movement and its expressions of nationalism sundered historic, if uneasy, ties between blacks and Jews. Jews saw liberalism as key to fuller acceptance in American society, whereas radical blacks increasingly viewed integration as a path to cultural extinction.[117]

To a wide, vocal spectrum of dissidents, Lyndon Johnson was the enemy, not Ho Chi Minh, Mao Zedong, or Fidel Castro. Morgenthau denounced the president for trying to corrupt, discredit, or silence dissent. Lamenting the excesses of the New Left and the advocates of black power and regretting the choice of many hippies to live outside the political and social order, he nevertheless was moved to observe, "Theirs is a politics of despair." Responsibility for creating discord in America lay with the holders of state power. Moreover, "the trend toward violent repression [of dissent].... coincides with President Johnson's consensus philosophy."[118] Consensus had to be obtained, whatever the cost. Kennan, in stark contrast, feared the effects of youthful and black dissent on core American values as he understood them.[119]

Nixon spent the fall of 1967 preparing to run for the presidency. He ostensibly agreed with Eisenhower's dislike of "the hippie generation."[120] Confrontation with antiwar activists, black radicals, women liberationists, and civil libertarians would come later. Shrewdly, he articulated a tactical retreat from globalism in his essay, "Asia after Vietnam," which appeared in the October issue of *Foreign Affairs*.[121] Not typically remembered for his attention to the daily workings of the nation's economy, Nixon did know, however, that as Vietnam sapped the economy of its strength and credibility,

---

[115] Hans J. Morgenthau, *Truth and Power: Essays of a Decade, 1960–70* (New York: Praeger Publishers, 1970), 34.

[116] Sara Evans, *Personal Politics: The Roots of Women's Liberation in the Civil Rights Movement and the New Left* (New York: Vintage Books, 1980).

[117] Greenberg, *Troubling the Waters*, 217–23, 252–4.

[118] Morgenthau, *Truth and Power*, 36, 38.

[119] George F. Kennan, *Democracy and the Student Left* (Boston: Little, Brown, 1968).

[120] Richard Nixon, *RN: The Memoirs of Richard Nixon* (New York: Grosset & Dunlop, 1978), 290.

[121] Richard M. Nixon, "Asia after Vietnam," *Foreign Affairs* 46 (October 1967): 113–25.

the likelihood of the United States remaining the world's foremost power had to diminish. Economic well-being meant military superiority; hence, America had to cut its losses in Vietnam. With this crucial realization, which formed the core of the Nixon Doctrine, he and Henry Kissinger, his national security adviser, would seek to transform the grand strategy of global containment into a leaner phenomenon, hereinafter termed strategic globalism.

Primacy in world affairs still depended on the supremacy of the dollar, which was essential to the political support of allies, hegemony over client states, and credibility with adversaries. Not until 1971 would Nixon begin to grapple with the literal costs of a globalist foreign policy.[122] When he did, his dollar diplomacy was crudely handled, greatly angering the Japanese. Yet, that development was a small price to pay for the Smithsonian accord of December 1971 that kept the dollar stronger than warranted. The political economy of strategic globalism for the time being had withstood the damage incurred as a result of war in Vietnam. Thus, Sino-American rapprochement and the strategic arms, or SALT, and Anti-Ballistic Missile, or ABM, agreements of May 1972 with Moscow went forward. The Nixon Doctrine would limit America's conventional military role in Asia and, in all probability, elsewhere. As we see in the next chapter, it also would bolster strategic globalism through arms sales and transfers to repressive regimes like Iran, Saudi Arabia, and Pakistan.[123]

The unraveling of America and, ultimately, his presidency made Nixon the central figure of his time. The traumatic events of the late 1960s and their impact on the nation and democracy briefly left him reflective. In response to the 1967 riots in Detroit, Nixon told a private gathering, "This was more than just another Negro riot. The looters were white as well as black. We are reaping the whirlwind for a decade of growing disrespect for law, decency and principle in America."[124] Kissinger likewise felt the "whirlwind" of angry protests, observing, "The comity by which a democratic society must live had broken down."[125] Unfortunately, it was not in them to examine the root causes of the conditions they abhorred.

Respect for law was difficult to find among those disillusioned by the disregard of civic virtue under Cold War liberalism. In 1968, the Tet offensive, the assassinations of Martin Luther King Jr. and Robert Kennedy, the

---

[122] Nixon's adoption of an expedient Keynesian approach in monetary matters was intended to guarantee his reelection in 1972; Allen J. Matusow, *Nixon's Economy: Booms, Busts, Dollars, and Votes* (Lawrence: University Press of Kansas, 1998).

[123] William Bundy, *A Tangled Web: The Making of Foreign Policy in the Nixon Presidency* (New York: Hill and Wang, 1998), 68, 136; Lewis Sorley, *Arms Transfers under Nixon: A Policy Analysis* (Lexington: University Press of Kentucky, 1983); Klare, *Supplying Repression, passim.*

[124] Address by Richard M. Nixon to the Bohemian Club, San Francisco [Bohemian Grove], July 29, 1967; copy at http://www.state.gov/r/pa/ho/frus/nixon/i/20700.htm.

[125] Henry Kissinger, *White House Years* (Boston: Little, Brown, 1979), 226.

"Battle of Chicago" at the Democratic National Convention, and Richard Nixon's election deepened feelings of dispossession in the nation's ghettos and on numerous college campuses. One federal judge, Charles E. Wyzanski Jr., of Massachusetts, who had issued several rulings related to the draft, tried to find vestiges of civic virtue in civil disobedience. Wyzanski feared that violent protest might lead to tyranny, not freedom. At the same time, he wrote in *The Atlantic,* "There are situations when it seems plainly moral for a man to disobey an evil law promulgated by a government which is entirely lacking in ethical character."[126] Wyzanski was making a case for civic virtue in even the worst of times; if officialdom was corrupt, citizens had to take it on themselves to save the republic.

The government's evident racism, as seen in President Johnson's solid support for the provocative activities of the FBI, especially its counterintelligence program, led black radicals to describe their efforts at community organization "as part of a global assault on empire."[127] In the wake of King's assassination, the death of more than forty African Americans and the arrest of perhaps 20,000 others brought home the struggle for freedom against state power. Leftists at the heart of the student movement, from Columbia University to the University of Wisconsin to the University of California, Berkeley, also declared their allegiance to liberation movements around the world.[128] In so doing, they sought to signify political solidarity with black activists, a connection that had been severely tested when organizations like SNCC, for example, threw whites off their governing boards and also refused them membership.

At less politicized institutions in 1968, Ohio State University, for instance, students – unaware of the creation of the American Student Union and student protests there in the 1930s – sought to promote civic virtue on a local level by forming a diverse coalition across racial and gender lines to support an African American studies program. Students raised questions of free speech and assembly and participated in teach-ins about Vietnam and U.S. foreign policy. The university's board of trustees crushed the student effort with well-timed phone calls, intimating that leaders would never graduate if they persisted in their activities. The head of the Black Student Union, John

---

[126] Charles E. Wyzanski Jr., "On Civil Disobedience," *The Atlantic*, February 1968, pp. 58–60; quoted words, 59. This same issue of *The Atlantic* reprinted Leo Tolstoy's 1899 letter, "Advice to a Draftee," in which Tolstoy wrote that "all just people . . . must refuse to become soldiers."

[127] Robin D. G. Kelley, *Freedom Dreams: The Black Radical Imagination* (Boston: Beacon Press, 2002), 63.

[128] The literature on the student movement is vast and contentious; generally see Kenneth J. Heineman, *Put Your Bodies upon the Wheels: Student Revolt in the 1960s* (Chicago: Ivan R. Dee, 2001); W. J. Rorabaugh, *Berkeley at War: The 1960s* (New York: Oxford University Press, 1989). Also important are films, including *The War at Home, Berkeley in the Sixties,* and *The Weather Underground.*

Evans, was suspended from the university. In the racially tinged climate of Ohio, he was the most vulnerable of the coalition's leaders. Two years later, after Nixon's incursion into Cambodia on April 30, anger turned into confrontation when James Rhodes, the governor of Ohio, sent the National Guard and local authorities onto the campus following actions of *agent provocateurs* who were operating out of his office. One law enforcement official remarked that he preferred duty in the black neighborhoods of Columbus, where he did not have to be as careful about using his weapons.[129] Then on May 4, 1970, the Ohio National Guard opened fire on students at Kent State University, killing four. Many white citizens were truly shocked, whereas black radicals were not surprised by the use of live ammunition against young "bums," as Nixon called student protestors.[130] His vitriol was not unique. Governor Ronald Reagan had responded in 1969 to events at the University of California, Berkeley, saying, "If it takes a bloodbath" to stop riots on campus, then "let's get it over with."[131]

Conclusion

Preemptive force had returned to the heartland where it had been used more than two centuries earlier as Americans ventured across the Allegheny mountains into the old Northwest where the French and British were vying for control. The refusal of the White House to denounce the killings at Kent State sanctioned a toxic form of the culture wars that would affect political discourse in the United States for years to come. Like his predecessor, Nixon fought back against angry citizens who despaired of having their voices heard on matters of grave national importance. More than Johnson, he readily drew on an array of responses to discredit protestors. To be sure, the protests of disgruntled citizens often tested the bounds of legality and occasionally became violent. The government still could have used its immense resources to protect the basic right of citizens to dissent; in the main, it chose to do otherwise.[132]

An explanation for this extensive abuse of power – exemplified by the Huston Plan for surveillance of dissidents, by the use of the Internal Revenue Service against political enemies, by support for police attacks against the

---

[129] The information in this paragraph is based on the experiences of the author who was a student at Ohio State University. At the graduation ceremony in June 1968, the trustee reading a citation for an honorary degree being awarded to historian Henry Steele Commager stumbled over and then failed to read the word "radical" in the citation.

[130] *New York Times*, May 2, 1970.

[131] Quoted in Lou Cannon, *President Reagan: The Role of a Lifetime* (New York: Touchstone, 1992), 708.

[132] Especially see J. Anthony Lukas, *Nightmare: The Underside of the Nixon Years*, with a forward by Joan Hoff (Athens: Ohio University Press, 1999); Jonathan Schell, *The Time of Illusion* (New York: Alfred A. Knopf, 1976).

Black Panthers, by efforts to prevent the publication of the Pentagon Papers and destroy Daniel Ellsberg who released them, by the Watergate scandal, and by White House complicity in the fall of Salvador Allende in Chile on September 11, 1973 – lies in recalling how paranoia became an inseparable part of the security ethos essentially from its inception. The inexorable transition from Wilson's internationalism to Roosevelt's globalism entrenched even greater fear into the policymaking process. By the late 1940s, officials had convinced themselves that the safety of the free world was at stake. A growing export economy could not guarantee security, as it arguably had until the late 1890s. The omnipresence of fear in the Cold War era demanded unstinting vigilance against both foreign and, as more government officials than just J. Edgar Hoover believed, domestic foes. At the same time, it made reliable assessment of threats to the nation by the intelligence community an uncertain exercise. Restoring the credibility of the United States, which had been badly squandered in Vietnam, was therefore essential if strategic globalism was to endure.

Richard Nixon's folly, and most lasting legacy, was his disregard for the basic liberties of American citizens and rejection of the right of self-determination for others. In orchestrating a cover-up of the break-in at Democratic Party offices in the Watergate complex in June 1972 and also ordering a similar operation at the Brookings Institution, Nixon violated his oath of office. "What you truly need," he lectured his aides, "is an Ellsberg, an Ellsberg who's on our side."[133] Nixon apparently appreciated Ellsberg's accomplishment as much as he hated Ellsberg for opposing his foreign policy agenda.

Policies that set the stage for the destruction of Cambodia, which occurred in 1975 after his resignation, and meddling in Chile's internal affairs called the president's integrity into question. Forgotten were his words at the Bohemian Grove in July 1967: "American style democracy is not necessarily the best form of government for people in Asia, Africa and Latin America with entirely different backgrounds."[134] When Nixon briefly worried about the costs of destabilizing Allende's government, Kissinger advised him, "In my judgment the dangers of doing nothing are greater than the risks we run in trying to do something."[135] After the coup, Senator Edward M. Kennedy of Massachusetts called for eliminating aid to the junta led by General Augusto Pinochet: "One cannot adhere to values of individual liberty

---

[133] Stanley I. Kutler, ed., *Abuse of Power: The New Nixon Tapes* (New York: Free Press, 1997), 5.

[134] See Nixon's address at http://www.state.gov/r/pa/ho/frus/nixon/i/20700.htm.

[135] Memorandum for the President from Henry A. Kissinger, November 5, 1970; copy at http://www.gwu.edu/~nsarchiv/NSAEBB/NSAEBB110/chile02.pdf. This document is in the collection of documents related to Chile obtained by the National Security Archive, Peter Kornbluh, Project Director.

and then remain silent while those values are destroyed."[136] The actions of the White House constituted an endorsement of the coup and reverberated not so silently beyond the confines of the Oval Office.

Martin Luther King had been right to wonder about Richard Nixon's sincerity in 1957. To conclude that the president was the most dangerous man in America did not seem hyperbolic in the summer of 1973. Senator Sam J. Ervin's Senate Select Committee on Presidential Campaign Activities had begun the investigation that would result in Nixon's downfall. Meanwhile, Congress was considering war powers legislation to limit presidential authority. Prospects for a rejuvenated civic virtue did not seem out of the question. Members of Congress were preparing to push an agenda of human rights onto a reluctant White House.[137] Even the CIA was subject to rare scrutiny. Nevertheless, Nixon's pursuit of strategic globalism had weakened core values in the name of security. His successors would act in much the same fashion.

[136] Quoted in Johnson, *Congress and the Cold War*, 197.
[137] Kathryn Sikkink, *Mixed Signals: U.S. Human Rights Policy and Latin America* (Ithaca: Cornell University Press, 2004), 48–69.

PART THREE

THE AGE OF STRATEGIC GLOBALISM, 1973–2001

6

Core Values and Strategic Globalism through 1988

[W]e have about 50% of the world's wealth but only 6.3% of its population.... Our real task in the coming period is to devise a pattern of relationships which will permit us to maintain this position of disparity without positive detriment to our national security.

George F. Kennan, 1948

My basic approach is that foreigners are out to screw us. Our job is to screw them first.

John Connally, 1971

I had come to believe firmly that people had the right to choose their own governments.

Donald Fraser, 1973

[Ronald Reagan's] determination to reverse the apparent flow of history underpinned the entirety of his foreign policy.

Robert M. Gates, 1996

Martin Luther King Jr. was dead. Walter Lippmann would die in 1974. Senator J. William Fulbright had grown despondent about the "secrecy and deception" of the executive branch and its assault on the Constitution, so much so that he had refused in 1970 to co-sponsor the McGovern-Hatfield "Amendment to End the War" because it would have continued aid for the regime of Nguyen Van Thieu in South Vietnam. The next year he decided not to join Jacob Javits in initiating what would become the War Powers Act.[1] George F. Kennan was ensconced in semi-seclusion at the Institute for Advanced Study in Princeton, New Jersey. Robert F. Kennedy was dead, although his place in this pantheon among the critics of American power

[1] Randall Bennett Woods, *Fulbright: A Biography* (New York: Cambridge University Press, 1995), 594–7; quoted words, 596.

was not secure at the time of his assassination in June 1968. He would be remembered more for what might have been than for any truth he spoke to the power of the imperial presidency, which he had helped insinuate further into American politics while serving as attorney general. In January 1973, amid great uncertainty about the state of the nation, angry members of Congress were about to consider limiting the power of the president to make war.

Several months earlier, just before Richard Nixon was reelected president, Henry Kissinger announced that peace was at hand. After the massive Christmas bombing offensive, North Vietnam returned to the bargaining table in Paris. By the end of January, the Americans and the Vietnamese had initialed a peace agreement. Even though the war would continue for more than two years, the way seemed clear for the White House to begin to give meaning to the concept of strategic globalism and perhaps restore U.S. credibility and global leadership. No matter what Nixon and Kissinger subsequently did, though, nothing like Franklin D. Roosevelt's humanistic globalism was under consideration. Indeed, the impulse to promote modernization within the developing world was receding in light of the Vietnam debacle.[2] Emerging was a more studied variant of globalism, whose architects could not afford to ignore the limits of American power.

Even before the oil crisis that followed the 1973 October War in the Middle East brought those limits into high relief, the decline of the dollar, resulting from the lengthy war in Vietnam and the dilemma that high gold prices posed for the Bretton Woods system, was underway. Secretary of the Treasury John Connally, a conservative Texas Democrat, emphasized how determined the United States was to repel challenges to its economic primacy when he remarked in 1971 about potential opponents, "My basic approach is that foreigners are out to screw us. Our job is to screw them first."[3] Countering a growing perception of weakness was therefore far more important than coming to terms with its reality, as tinkering with monetary policy and the Smithsonian agreement of December 1971 demonstrated.

The objective of the second Nixon administration was not retreat from hegemony but rather the restoration of America's global stature. Nixon and Kissinger longed for this achievement to be their legacy. They found a receptive, if not uniformly enthusiastic audience among defense intellectuals and policy analysts.[4] Yet, strategic globalism and credibility were at odds with core values from the Nixon through the Reagan presidencies. To

---

[2] Especially see James M. Carter, *Inventing Vietnam: The United States and State Building in Southeast Asia, 1954–1968* (New York: Cambridge University Press, 2008).

[3] Quoted in Allen J. Matusow, *Nixon's Economy: Booms, Busts, Dollars, and Votes* (Lawrence: University Press of Kansas, 1998), 117.

[4] Robert E. Osgood et al., *Retreat from Empire?: The First Nixon Administration* (Baltimore: Johns Hopkins University Press, 1973), 9, 30, 340.

understand why, we must begin with an examination of détente and the political economy of the time.

The Resilience of Détente

U.S. hegemony was probably unattainable without détente. Yet, for important segments of the American public and for Chinese authorities, détente was a policy of "ambiguity," which Kissinger acknowledged. To the White House, it meant a lessening of tensions in bilateral relations with the Soviets. To the Kremlin, détente gave legitimacy to an era of competitive coexistence. Thus, the Soviet Union presumed it could pursue what it saw as its legitimate foreign policy interests, particularly in the Third World, without incurring the wrath of American conservatives. That proved not to be possible. In fact, détente's reliance on containment and coexistence would be met with committed opposition from conservatives, just as the Yalta Conference of 1945 became a vehicle for denouncing Roosevelt's efforts to bargain with Soviet leader Joseph Stalin.

The absence of a mutual code of conduct in their relationship turned détente into a political liability for both Soviet and American officials. The essential purpose of détente, which Kissinger never tired of proclaiming, was "to give the Soviets a stake in cooperation even while . . . mak[ing] expansionism too dangerous."[5] Yet, what he considered to be well-calibrated realism lost its luster over time. Like Henry Kissinger, Zbigniew Brzezinski could hardly contain his delight as Jimmy Carter's national security adviser when he realized how broad his mandate was.[6] Desirous of distancing himself from his better known predecessor, he criticized détente for having "been oversold to the American public." In the contentious political atmosphere of the late 1970s, that was a relatively easy argument to make in the abstract, yet it defied precise explanation and provided little policymaking guidance. Whatever foes thought were détente's shortcomings in theory, it proved to have remarkable staying power in practice, albeit in an altered guise.[7]

Brzezinski's and Carter's dismay at any given Soviet action prior to the invasion of Afghanistan in 1979 did not necessarily mean that Moscow was seeking to aggrandize its power at the expense of U.S. interests. Accordingly, their focus on, in Brzezinski's words, "competition and cooperation . . . designed to promote a more comprehensive and more reciprocal détente" reflects a difference in degree, not kind, about détente.[8] Like

---

[5] Henry Kissinger, *Years of Upheaval* (Boston: Little, Brown, 1982), 245.

[6] Zbigniew Brzezinski, *Power and Principle: Memoirs of the National Security Adviser, 1977–81* (New York: Farrar, Straus and Giroux, 1983), 48.

[7] For an instructive, though more conventional perspective on détente, see Melvyn P. Leffler, *For the Soul of Mankind: The United States, the Soviet Union, and the Cold War* (New York: Hill and Wang, 2007), 234–427.

[8] Brzezinski, *Power and Principle*, 146, 148.

Kissinger and Nixon, the Democrats in power were committed to a strategic vision that furthered arms control and resuscitated American credibility as the twin pillars of their approach to geopolitics. Fundamental differences between the superpowers would emerge, however, as Carter prepared for the 1980 election and responded to pressure from anti-détente conservatives, neoconservatives, and Cold War Democrats by getting tough with the Soviets.[9] As a result, a second arms limitation accord never had a serious chance of ratification in the Senate.

After the return to power of the Republican Party with Ronald Reagan's election as president in 1980, the new secretary of state, Alexander M. Haig Jr., was not about to mount a public defense of détente. The ideological base of Reagan's support inside the Washington beltway had long since distanced itself from what it perceived as the amoral globalism of Nixon and Kissinger. Accordingly, the administration had to pursue a détente-like foreign policy with great circumspection. In so doing, it employed the rhetorical sophistry of John Foster Dulles, who had denounced Harry Truman's containment policy without offering a plausible alternative beyond the false promise of rollback.[10] The American people, having grown weary of the jeremiad quality of Carter's public pronouncements, eagerly embraced the optimistic former actor from California.[11] Importantly, Reagan's electoral victory indicated that a significant percentage of the voting public had internalized the security ethos. A growing suspicion of détente, in fact, derived more from the appearance of appeasement of the Soviet Union before the late 1970s than from the actual structure of foreign policy at that time.

How would the administration finesse the matter of détente? Much like Dulles, the president's major foreign policy advisers engaged in linguistic legerdemain, as did Reagan, while shunning action that suggested a confrontation with the Soviet Union was unavoidable. Remarkably sclerotic language notwithstanding, credibility, containment, and coexistence remained the grounds on which Washington relied for the substance of relations with Moscow. In recounting his brief time as secretary of state, Haig noted, "I was convinced that the Soviet Union did not want war."[12] The one major issue that could not ultimately have been managed was Poland. Had the Soviets crushed the Solidarity trade union movement, which was outlawed

9   Gaddis Smith, *Morality, Reason, and Power: American Diplomacy in the Carter Years* (New York: Hill and Wang, 1986), 208–40.
10 Dulles's vacuity was often on display, never more so than in the tragedy that befell Hungary in October 1956. Charles Gati, *Failed Illusions: Moscow, Washington, Budapest and the 1956 Hungarian Revolt* (Washington, D.C. and Stanford: Woodrow Wilson Center Press and Stanford University Press, 2006), 90–1.
11 John Patrick Diggins, *Ronald Reagan: Fate, Freedom, and the Making of History* (New York: W. W. Norton & Company, 2007).
12 Alexander M. Haig, Jr., *Caveat: Realism, Reagan, and Foreign Policy* (New York: Macmillan, 1984), 95.

in 1982 by the Polish government, it is not certain what the United States would have done. What did occur was that the CIA, on consultation with the Vatican, gave covert assistance to Solidarity while the ban was in place.[13] The Soviet Union could not then afford the economic or political costs of intervention.[14]

Moscow refrained from sending troops into Poland, thereby showing no taste for superpower confrontation. This faithfulness to its understanding of détente – a word for which Haig has little use in his memoirs – helped prevent hardliners in either the United States or the Soviet Union from unalterably sidetracking the process of arms control. Haig contends, as does Secretary of Defense Caspar Weinberger in his own memoirs, that Reagan instinctively believed that the fewer nuclear weapons the Americans and Soviets had in their respective arsenals, the more credible a policy of deterrence would be.[15] It would take several years, however, to find a politically viable way of reaching common ground with the leadership cadre in the Politburo on that issue.

However disdainful Reagan was of détente as "a one-way street that the Soviet Union has used to pursue its own aims," he could not jettison its structure unless he was prepared to abandon the larger objective of strategic globalism as well.[16] Suspicion of Soviet motives did not therefore void the foundational logic of détente as bequeathed by Nixon and Kissinger; rather, it altered the public representation of the limits of détente, thereby making containment, one of its key aspects, seem more robust. This negotiation-from-strength approach, championed in some fashion by all U.S. administrations until the eclipse of the Soviet Union, suggests that détente was not an end in itself, despite claims to the contrary by its most vocal critics. Although the diplomatic utility of détente may have run its course by the time the Soviet Union sent troops into Afghanistan, its underlying structure was indispensable for efforts to revitalize American power and authority.

The Soviets recognized that the security ethos had a powerful influence over the making of U.S. foreign policy. Georgi Arbatov, a critic of key aspects of the Soviet system who in 1968 founded the Institute for the Study of the USA and Canada, became a perceptive observer of the United States. Arbatov, who believed the presence of the Soviet military in Czechoslovakia in 1968 and the invasion of Afghanistan were contrary to Moscow's interests,

[13] Raymond L. Garthoff, *The Great Transition: American-Soviet Relations and the End of the Cold War* (Washington, DC: Brookings Institution, 1994), 31–2.

[14] Vladislav M. Zubok, *A Failed Empire: The Soviet Union in the Cold War from Stalin to Gorbachev* (Chapel Hill: University of North Carolina Press, 2007), 265–70.

[15] Haig, *Caveat*, 218–30; Caspar Weinberger, *Fighting for Peace: Seven Critical Years in the Pentagon* (New York: Warner Books, 1991), 341.

[16] Garthoff, *The Great Transition*, 8–13, posits an understanding of détente largely at variance with the structural one advanced herein; quoted words, 8.

found American hubris a major impediment to improved relations. "The hostility and militarism of American policy," he lamented, "did nothing but create further obstacles on the road to reform [in Russia] and heap more trouble on the heads of the reformers. . . . I have seen how negatively such polices can influence events in the Soviet Union."[17] Long-time ambassador to the United Sates Anatoly Dobrynin captured the essence of détente. He contended in his memoirs that Nixon and Kissinger "were not really thinking in terms of bringing about a major breakthrough in Soviet-American relations, and of ending the Cold War and the arms race. . . . [They] sought to create a more stable and predictable strategic situation."[18]

To understand why détente could not readily be cast off by Nixon's successors, it is necessary to acknowledge how thoroughly security and national identity had become entwined in the worldview of key U.S. policymakers. To paraphrase the journalist Chris Hedges, the Cold War was a force that gave meaning to the United States.[19] The Cold War in its several incarnations was both metaphor and reality. It would have been harder to persuade the public of the need for constant vigilance in defense of a globalist foreign policy than it was to rally them against identifiable enemies like the Soviets and their presumptive surrogates. The *reality* was that the Cold War took place in three distinct temporal settings – the late 1940s, the early 1960s, and the 1980s. At other times, when what is commonly known as the Cold War was not at a point of crisis, the Soviet-American relationship might more profitably be understood as modern great power relations. The Cold War as *metaphor*, most famously represented by NSC-68 and the security policies it engendered, transmogrified the logic of vigilance into a call for constant preparedness against all contingencies. Perceived threats to America's security therefore presumably occurred at Moscow's behest.

Détente should have put an end to this obfuscation. Even without a formal code of conduct, the making of détente demonstrated that both superpowers had learned how better to conduct their relationship after October 1962. Yet, despite public doubts about reasons for the war in Vietnam and its implications for the future of U.S. foreign policy, détente made it easier to conjoin the security ethos with a militarized American identity, as Dobrynin and Arbatov observed in their memoirs. The genius of strategic globalism was that it seemed like a retreat from the universalism of NSC-68, which had taken the United States into Vietnam, whereas Nixon and Kissinger

[17] Georgi Arbatov, *The System: An Insider's Life in Soviet Politics* (New York: Times Books, 1993), 313–14.

[18] Anatoly Dobrynin, *In Confidence: Moscow's Ambassador to America's Six Cold War Presidents (1962–1986)* (New York: Times Books, 1995), 195.

[19] Chris Hedges, *War Is a Force That Gives Us Meaning* (New York: Anchor Books, 2003); and see David Campbell, *Writing Security: United States Foreign Policy and the Politics of Identity* (Minneapolis: University of Minnesota Press, 1992).

had actually fashioned the most sophisticated variant of globalism of any administration from Roosevelt's to the present.

The arms race and the prospect of nuclear proliferation made détente mandatory for the two superpowers and, in practical effect, the People's Republic of China. Not only did the two communist powers concern the Nixon administration; so, too, did U.S. allies in Europe, so much so that the White House in April 1973 announced the "Year of Europe." The purpose of the initiative, as Kissinger described in his speech introducing the project, was to fashion a "new Atlantic Charter" for addressing matters of common defense, trade, and East-West relations. The "ambiguous" result convinced Nixon and Kissinger to move resolutely toward their goal of strategic globalism. Kissinger later admitted, "We were so eager to liberate ourselves from the trauma of Vietnam that we failed to give sufficient weight to the fact that Europe could not possibly share this largely American imperative."[20] Perhaps it was strategic globalism that the allies found objectionable.

U.S. strategy was becoming predicated on the selective use of force by the United States or the resort to violence by America's proxies. What impact would these tactics have on core values? Hedges minces few words. "The employment of organized violence means one must, in fact," he wrote, "abandon fixed and established values."[21] An overview of the American political economy of the time provides one revealing lens for understanding the negative impact of grand strategy on values.

Strategic Globalism and Containment Capitalism

Richard Nixon's tinkering with the dollar in 1971 postponed the reckoning that balance-of-payments deficits and later trade deficits forced on the United States.[22] Dollar devaluation and the subsequent suspension of convertibility of dollars into gold made Americans wistful for the halcyon days of the 1950s when U.S. hegemony was at its height. By 1968, America's allies had tired of holding dollars whose worth was declining; the gold crisis in March alerted officials to the inescapable fact that Great Britain, France, Germany, and Japan, among others, were no longer willing to pay the price – inflation – of global containment.[23] So long as the American economy remained competitive, trade and payment deficits were relatively inconsequential. Yet, the growing economic might of Germany and Japan foreshadowed challenges to

---

[20] Kissinger, *Years of Upheaval*, 128–94; quoted words, 152, 154, 193.

[21] Hedges, *War Is a Force*, 26.

[22] Generally see David P. Calleo, *The Imperious Economy* (Cambridge: Harvard University Press, 1982), 105–29.

[23] Robert M. Collins, "The Economic Crisis of 1968 and the Waning of the 'American Century,'" *American Historical Review* 101 (April 1996): 396–422.

hegemony that over time could call into question U.S. leadership on security matters.

A promise of rapid economic growth had accompanied NSC-68, even though containment capitalism could not guarantee domestic prosperity over the long haul. In fact, it tended to undermine growth. Containment capitalism originated with the Marshall Plan in 1947 and NSC-13/2, which resulted in the "reverse course" in relations with Japan, prefiguring the rise of Japanese economic primacy in postwar Asia.[24] For two decades, containment capitalism depended on the acceptance by America's trading partners of U.S. security priorities. Defense needs, as seen in the strategic build-up of the 1960s and the war in Vietnam, dominated economic planning and policy. By the late 1960s, the Department of Defense may have controlled as much as one-half of the federal budget, with the outlay for waging war in Vietnam exceeding $100 billion. Furthermore, the dollar value of federal expenditures on research and development of sophisticated weaponry gave an indication of just how dependent on containment capitalism the economy had become.[25]

As such, rather less investment capital was available for industrial modernization, which in turn kept elevated the cost of capital goods. Consumption was the prevailing trend of the day for members of the Atlantic community and Japan, which brought about an inflationary cycle. Yet, cracks in the postwar economic consensus had appeared even before the crisis of the late 1960s. American economic hegemony would be challenged by what U.S. officials deemed mercantilist practices and policies. For example, lower cost, foreign-made machine tools began to dominate the American market, and by 1970 foreign steelmakers had significantly cut into the market share of domestic producers.[26] Moreover, competition became fierce not just for oil but for many strategic minerals including zinc, tin, chrome, and copper. In short, the postwar global economic division of labor was eroding.[27] Faced with the real possibility of a prolonged inflationary cycle, America's economic partners reconsidered their allegiance to containment capitalism.

Where American security imperatives might still prevail over national economic interests was among so-called less developed states. Washington therefore endeavored to promote defense-related fiscal policy in the developing world. From Asia to Africa to Latin America, as Pentagon critic Seymour Melman found, U.S. foreign military sales served to limit economic

---

[24] Walter LaFeber, *The Clash: U.S.-Japanese Relations throughout History* (New York: W. W. Norton & Company, 1997), 273–9.

[25] Seymour Melman, *Pentagon Capitalism: The Political Economy of War* (New York: McGraw-Hill, 1970), 162, 165, 170–1.

[26] Ibid., 186–8.

[27] Alfred E. Eckes Jr., *The United States and the Global Struggle for Minerals* (Austin: University of Texas Press, 1979), 237, 248, 265.

development and thereby retard the growth of democracy.[28] Jimmy Carter's defense secretary, Harold Brown, judged the practices "in principle correct" and "difficult to discontinue."[29]

Just as New Era capitalism in the 1920s had considered economic inequality a small price to pay for peace and security, a pernicious modern counterpart emerged when it became impossible to ignore the damage that the conflict in Vietnam was doing to America's political economy. In 1948, George Kennan identified the problem that a globalist foreign policy would inevitably pose for the United States. "[W]e have about 50% of the world's wealth but only 6.3% of its population," he commented. "Our real task in the coming period is to devise a pattern of relationships which will permit us to maintain this position of disparity without positive detriment to our national security."[30] Kennan was right. The nation's security, control of strategic resources, and domestic prosperity could not be disentangled in the age of containment capitalism.

Whether culturally or strategically, the United States was not prepared to come to terms with economic power in the developing world, which former Kennedy adviser General Maxwell Taylor derided as "turbulent and disorderly."[31] The influence of oil-producing states in the world economy is well known, as was the inability of the United States to devise an effective response to the fourfold increase in the price per barrel of oil in the wake of the 1973 October War.[32] Although crucially important for security policy, oil exposed the inherent flaws of containment capitalism. Strong nationalist sentiments among oil-producing states, bolstered by the self-interest of banks and multinational corporations, had the potential to affect U.S. strategy and thus have an impact on the nation's international standing.

The decoupling of American-based corporations from their national moorings was perhaps the logical outcome of a historic trade philosophy based on expansion and the pursuit of profits for their own sake. Long gone were the days when leaders like Herbert Hoover expected businessmen and bankers to advance American interests as a central aspect of their foreign operations. Throughout the early postwar era, corporations and the U.S.

---

[28] Melman, *Pentagon Capitalism*, 199–203; Michael T. Klare, *Supplying Repression: U.S. Support for Authoritarian Regimes Abroad* (Washington, DC: Institute for Policy Studies, 1977), 39–40.

[29] Harold Brown, *Thinking about National Security: Defense and Foreign Policy in a Dangerous World* (Boulder: Westview Press, 1983), 166, 167.

[30] U.S. Department of State, *Papers Relating to the Foreign Relations of the United States, 1948*, vol. 1, pt. 2: *General; the United Nations* (Washington, DC: Government Printing Office, 1976), 524.

[31] Quoted in Greg Grandin, *Empire's Workshop: Latin America, the United States, and the Rise of the New Imperialism* (New York: Metropolitan Books, 2006), 179.

[32] See, for example, Stephen J. Randall, *United States Foreign Oil Policy since World War I: For Profits and Security*, 2d ed. (Montreal and Kingston: McGill-Queen's University Press, 2005), 269–94.

government generally had complementary interests.[33] The new corporatist autarky, commencing in Europe in the 1960s, would change that. The irony is that containment capitalism provided the very stability that made Europe an appealing base from which to engage in banking and business ventures. Starting in the late 1950s, dollars held abroad from Canada to Europe to Japan funded the exponential growth of currency markets and international trade. American banks also enlarged their foreign activities, drawn by the relative freedom from government regulations. Internationally oriented banks realized unprecedented profits from balance-of-payments difficulties, not pausing to consider the security-based reasons behind the monetary troubles.[34] The expansion of foreign direct investment greatly enhanced the power of the modern multinational corporation.[35]

The 1970s furthered this impetus toward banking and corporate independence. Banks provided the means for balance-of-payments financing among industrialized nations and also in the developing world. The limited, national character of banking that had been prevalent in the early 1960s had become a relic of older, cautious business mores. An effort in the mid-1970s to narrow the gap between rich and poor nations, seen in the campaign for a New International Economic Order (NIEO), accomplished little. The Ford administration denounced the NIEO as a threat to free market economics. In the strictest sense, that was true, although its advocates promoted enlightened foreign aid and monetary policies that would have opened markets to products from the world's poorest nations.[36] Until 1981, when a severe global debt crisis led to retrenchment, banking expansion for profit, not political stability or continued growth, remained the dominant order of the day.[37]

The implications for U.S. security policy, and ultimately for strategic globalism, were profound. Kennan's fears had become reality: The American share of the world's output was in decline. Without a crisis to compel a reversion to a Cold War mentality for governments and corporations alike, America's international standing would increasingly be at risk. This dilemma played itself out during the 1970s. Monetary policy under Nixon offered a temporary palliative, whereas the Ford and Carter administrations seemed powerless to respond to a changing global economic and security environment.[38]

[33] Robert Gilpin, *U.S. Power and the Multinational Corporation: The Political Economy of Foreign Direct Investment* (New York: Basic Books, 1975), 141.

[34] Benjamin J. Cohen, *In Whose Interest?: International Banking and American Foreign Policy* (New Haven: Yale University Press, 1986), 18–24.

[35] Gilpin, *U.S. Power and the Multinational Corporation*, 139; Alan Wolfe, *America's Impasse: The Rise and Fall of the Politics of Growth* (Boston: South End Press, 1981), 162.

[36] Calleo, *The Imperious Economy*, 120–2; Wolfe, *America's Impasse*, 194–7.

[37] Cohen, *In Whose Interest?*, 24–6.

[38] Mary Kaldor, *The Disintegrating West* (New York: Hill and Wang, 1978).

Carter particularly got swept up in the dilemmas of containment capitalism. As a member of the Trilateral Commission, several of whose members held key posts in his administration and whose first director was Zbigniew Brzezinski, Carter accepted the dogma linking growth economics and security policy even as stagflation – inflation and high unemployment – worsened at home.[39] Turmoil in the world economy engendered by the 1973 oil crisis moved economic wisdom to the right in the United States throughout the decade. Carter's fiscal and monetary policies – continuing devotion to free trade without corporate accountability – and reliance on military spending to spur economic growth demonstrated the persistent hold of Cold War orthodoxy on America's political economy.[40] An oil-import fee, a modest proposal in 1980 to curb inflation and lower the budget deficit, was stillborn. Carter complained in his diary, *"There is no discipline, and growing fragmentation in Congress."*[41] Implicit in this vignette was the reflexive sense of entitlement to control the world's resources, shared by policymakers and the American public. It made impossible serious consideration of strategic globalism's consequences on core values.

Carter's transformation into an active, if not ardent, Cold Warrior by the end of his presidency reflects the extent to which containment capitalism precluded innovation in foreign policy. Even as the events of the 1970s played out, the security ethos remained strong, though not unassailable. Present was a concerted effort to interpose the issue of human rights into the discourse about foreign and security policies, the importance of which for core values and civic virtue should not be overlooked.

The Politics of Human Rights

The political battles of the 1960s faded with astonishing suddenness in the early 1970s. The searing anger provoked across generations by the war in Vietnam, which convulsed America as nothing had since the Civil War, did not result in a broadly based determination to disengage from foreign affairs. George McGovern's peroration in his address accepting the Democratic presidential nomination in July 1972, in which he exhorted the nation with the call to "come home, America," was the exception to the rule.[42] Furthermore, the social, cultural, and personal freedoms at the core of the

---

[39] Secretary of State Cyrus Vance, Secretary of Defense Harold Brown and Secretary of the Treasury W. Michael Blumenthal, along with Director of the Arms Control and Disarmament Agency Paul C. Warnke, were Trilateral Commission members. Smith, *Morality, Reason, and Power*, 37–8.

[40] Wolfe, *America's Impasse*, 200–9.

[41] Jimmy Carter, *Keeping Faith: Memoirs of a President* (New York: Bantam Books, 1982), 529 (italics in original).

[42] The American Presidency Project, University of California, Santa Barbara, http://www. presidency.ucsb.edu/shownomination.php?convid=16.

women's movement were channeled into an Equal Rights Amendment to the Constitution and then shunted to the margins of legitimacy when that amendment failed ratification by a sufficient number of states.[43] Also, the civil rights movement, black power, and black nationalism lost their previous places in the public limelight with the statutory success of the first, the assassination of Martin Luther King, and the government's repression of and internal divisiveness among black radicals. And, few whites at the time were even aware of the affinity between radical black politics at home and global matters relating to race.

No single social movement showed real sustaining power against the constellation of political, economic, and cultural forces arrayed against them. The war was all but over, or so many hoped, by the end of January 1973. The campaign against the Equal Rights Amendment willfully distorted the objectives of the women's movement. And during the Nixon presidency, it became clear that the gains of the 1960s for African Americans had limits. Sociologist Daniel Patrick Moynihan, nominally a Democrat, advised Nixon that a policy of "benign neglect" was politically feasible on matters of race.[44]

Whatever flaws the Black Panther Party possessed, many members perceived the struggle of the late 1960s and early 1970s as one for self-determination, which to them meant community control.[45] The Panthers were hardly altruistic, yet their breakfast and preschool programs for children, along with legal assistance, medical care, and voter registration efforts, spoke to daily needs of the poor and disenfranchised in America. No matter its source, the prospect of control by communities over their own affairs posed a threat to existing white power structures because it rejected the real or quasi-colonial bases of such relationships.[46] Less directly, by questioning political priorities in the Vietnam era as had no other challenge to the status quo since Upton Sinclair's End Poverty in California program in 1934, the focus on power at the local level raised the issue of basic human rights – that is, human security – within America.

The rhetorical solidarity of the Panthers with "the oppressed people of the world" situates their history in more than the context of COINTELPRO and criminal activity and is also suggestive of the urgency with which the human rights movement had burst on the world. Inspired by the 1948 Universal Declaration of Human Rights, which derived in part from attempts to give concrete meaning to the Wilsonian ideal of self-determination and in part

[43] Ruth Rosen, *The World Split Open: How the Modern Women's Movement Changed America* (New York: Viking, 2000), 332–3.

[44] Joan Hoff, *Nixon Reconsidered* (New York: Basic Books, 1994), 80–3.

[45] Robin D. G. Kelley, *Freedom Dreams: The Black Radical Imagination* (Boston: Beacon Press, 2002), 95.

[46] William L. Van Deburg, *New Day in Babylon: The Black Power Movement and American Culture, 1965–1975* (Chicago: University of Chicago Press, 1992), 159–64. To the Panthers, standardized education in America constituted a form of class warfare.

from the experience of the Holocaust, Amnesty International began operating in 1961. It initially concentrated on prisoners of conscience, torture, and the death penalty. Multilateral recognition of human rights through treaties ran counter to official assumptions about the inviolability of American sovereignty and the sanctity of states' rights, the latter because of powerful white southern opposition to the civil rights movement.[47] Nixon's dogged pursuit of strategic globalism as his grand strategy reinforced America's isolation from an emerging international human rights community. It could not long keep the critics at bay, however.

Sending troops into the Dominican Republic in April 1965 had broached the issue of the uneasy linkage between core values and anticommunism. In its desperation to find communists to blame to justify intervention in a sovereign nation, the Johnson White House enabled skeptics in Congress to raise questions about what U.S. support for authoritarian regimes in Latin America and elsewhere meant for American identity and credibility. The decision in July 1965 to become more deeply involved in Vietnam, the succor extended to the colonels who seized power in Greece in 1967, the reflexive support for the junta in Brazil, and the continuing collaboration in counterinsurgency operations with Guatemala's repressive regime became the focus of human rights advocates who were seeking to influence U.S. foreign policy. Representative Donald Fraser, a Democrat from Minnesota who had traveled to the Dominican Republic after U.S. armed forces landed there, articulated the essential issue: "I had come to believe firmly that people had a right to choose their own government."[48]

It was not merely individual members of Congress who expressed concerns about the persistent abuse of human rights in the name of anticommunism. The Latin American Committee of the National Council of Churches denounced Washington's actions in the Dominican Republic and the support it indicated for authoritarian governments. The appearance of human rights as a major foreign policy issue also coincided with the rise of Liberation Theology in Latin America – a byproduct of the Roman Catholic Church's Second Ecumenical Council, or Vatican II, which lasted from 1962 to 1965. Vatican II legitimated two community-based principles. One declared that the Catholic Church was alive in the world; the other averred that it was composed of a community of equals. The spirit and reality of Liberation Theology thus opposed entrenched oligarchs and radicalized believers and many of their clerics, while decrying U.S. military and economic policies in the region.[49] A sense of freedom from the bonds of the authoritarian

47 Kathryn Sikkink, *Mixed Signals: U.S. Human Rights Policy and Latin America* (Ithaca: Cornell University Press, 2004), 51–2.
48 Quoted in ibid., 55.
49 Ibid., 54; Penny Lernoux, *Cry of the People: United States Involvement in the Rise of Fascism, Torture, and Murder and the Persecution of the Catholic Church in Latin America* (Garden City: Doubleday, 1980), 31–41.

state inevitably resulted in clashes within the Catholic Church between radicals and conservatives and between radical clergy, the base communities
(*comunidades de base*), and state officials. If communism was execrable as
a governing philosophy, which authorities of both liberal and praetorian
states believed, the members of Christian communities working among the
poor were just as quick to identify the failures of capitalism, as represented
by the discredited Alliance for Progress.[50] For its part, the CIA derided
these community relationships between priests and the faithful, characterizing Liberation Theology as "an alliance endorsed by Castro as a prototype
for other Latin American revolutionaries."[51]

Kissinger never wavered from his conviction that having to focus on
human rights in making foreign policy detracted from the real business of
grand strategy. Chile proved to be a major thorn in his side, despite his
having once dismissed it as "a dagger pointed at the heart of Antarctica."[52]
In September 1974, during a round of congressional testimony on military
assistance to the government of General Augusto Pinochet, Kissinger, who
by then was serving as secretary of state, wrote in the margins of a cable
demanding that the U.S. ambassador in Santiago, David Popper, "cut out
the political science lectures" about human rights.[53] Two years later, pressure from Congress to address abuses in Chile forced Kissinger to deliver a
speech on human rights while attending a meeting there of the Organization
of American States. "The condition of human rights," he grumbled, "has
impaired our relationship with Chile and will continue to do so." Privately,
the secretary earlier had told Pinochet, "We are sympathetic with what you
are trying to do here. . . . The speech is not aimed at Chile. . . . My evaluation
is that you are the victim of all left-wing groups around the world."[54]

Kissinger's paranoia reflected both his Hobbesian worldview and the
toxic mix that resulted from the conjuncture of the security ethos and the
precepts of NSC-68.[55] A dispassionate assessment of threats to America's

[50] On the limits of the Alliance for Progress, see Jeffrey Taffet, *Foreign Aid as Foreign Policy* (New York: Routledge, 2007).
[51] Central Intelligence Agency, National Foreign Assessment Center "Consolidation of power by Sandinista National Liberation Front (FSLN) discussed," April 1, 1981, in Declassified Documents Reference System (DDRS) (Farmington Hills: Gael Group, n.d.), 16; DDRS is an electronic resource.
[52] Quoted in Seymour Hersh, *The Price of Power: Kissinger in the Nixon White House* (New York: Summit Books, 1983), 263.
[53] *New York Times*, September 27, 1974.
[54] Quoted in John Dinges, *The Condor Years: How Pinochet and His Allies Brought Terrorism to Three Continents* (New York: New Press, 2004), 162, 159, 160.
[55] Scholars have long endeavored to assess Kissinger's foreign policy record and his place in history. One recent attempt, somewhat similar to the one put forward herein, is Jussi Hanhimäki, *The Flawed Architect: Henry Kissinger and American Foreign Policy* (New York: Oxford University Press, 2004), especially 485–92; Hanhimäki does not, however, trace the historical antecedents in the composition of Kissinger's policies.

national interests was not likely in such a contentious environment, as seen most notably in the CIA's estimate of Soviet spending on strategic capabilities. Raymond Garthoff, who worked for the government in many capacities including that of a CIA analyst, maintained that the "confident estimates of a steady acceleration in Soviet military spending were wrong."[56] Opponents of détente hoped to use the CIA's evaluation to scuttle the policy. Making this matter even more troubling was a Defense Intelligence Agency assessment: "A major tenet of Soviet détente policy is to avoid nuclear war."[57] Spending for strategic modernization or parity was not the same thing as trying to achieve first-strike capability, which critics of détente implied.[58] The fixation on détente, whether for or against, harks back to the presence of fear historically in evidence as the United States approached the outside world.

As national security adviser and secretary of state, Kissinger held congressional critics in low esteem while bowing in the direction of shared decision making under the American system of governance. Throughout his years in power, he strove to protect authoritarian governments that ignored human rights and disregarded the rule of law, believing them useful to U.S. strategic objectives. In that respect he helped pave the way for neoconservative Jeane Kirkpatrick's essay, "Dictatorships and Double Standards," in which she excused the dubious human rights records of right-wing governments in the name of anticommunism and stability.[59] The essay landed Kirkpatrick the position of United Nations ambassador in the Reagan administration.

In the case of Greece, the administration defeated efforts to curb arms shipments. Kissinger saw only strategic issues, telling Nixon, "Dealing in an aggressive manner with the Greek colonels will serve to weaken NATO."[60] Likewise in the case of Brazil, Nixon and Kissinger expressed few qualms about dealing with its military government. On a visit there in 1976, Kissinger was fulsome in praise, saying, "There are no two peoples whose concern for human dignity and the basic values of man is more pronounced in the day-to-day lives of their people than Brazil and the United States."[61] Neither Brazil nor Greece merits much consideration in Kissinger's

56 Raymond L. Garthoff, *Détente and Confrontation: American-Soviet Relations from Nixon to Reagan*, rev. ed. (Washington, DC: Brookings Institution, 1994), 876–7.
57 U.S. Department of Defense, Defense Intelligence Agency, *Détente in Soviet Strategy*, September 2, 1975, Digital National Security Archive, Soviet Estimate Collection, Item SE 00486, p. 2.
58 "What Is the Soviet Union Up to?," in Charles Tyroler, II, ed., *Alerting America: The Papers of the Committee on the Present Danger* (Washington, D.C.: Pergamon-Brassey's, 1984), 10–16.
59 Jean Kirkpatrick, "Dictatorships and Double Standards," *Commentary*, November 1979, pp. 34–45.
60 Henry A. Kissinger memorandum to Richard M. Nixon March 16, 1969, DDRS.
61 Quoted in Lernoux, *Cry of the People*, 170.

multivolume memoirs. Such was not the case in Congress, where his critics were increasingly asking whether aid to military governments in those countries was consistent with American principles.

The focus of Congress became the Agency for International Development's (AID) Office of Public Safety (OPS), which along with the CIA was training, among others, Latin American military and police forces to handle suspected terrorists. As revelations about the activities of OPS came to light, in 1974 Congress abolished AID's Public Safety Program, under which OPS operated. Those activities included torture. OPS, in effect, gave its imprimatur to the National Security Doctrine of the region's military and police forces as they sought to pacify or neutralize segments of their populations desirous of democracy or, in some cases, revolution. South America's authoritarian regimes were scarcely interested in differentiating between the two.[62] Less subject to public scrutiny at the time, the School of the Americas, founded under a different name in 1946, continued educating and training officers from throughout the hemisphere at its headquarters in the Panama Canal Zone, where the course of study complemented OPS programs.[63]

"Dirty war" became the term best describing how armed forces terrorized untold thousands of people. Of special note is Operation Condor, an international assassination program orchestrated by Colonel Manuel Contreras, who headed Chile's Directorate of National Intelligence (DINA). U.S. military personnel likened DINA to Hitler's Gestapo and the Soviet KGB. Contreras traveled to the United States in 1974 and 1975, probably to consult with the CIA about anti-subversive activities that DINA was coordinating. In early 1975 and again in August of that year, Contreras met with General Vernon Walters, the CIA's deputy director of central intelligence. On the one hand, the CIA expressed concern about the human rights situation in Chile; on the other, Walters, according to journalist John Dinges, "was Contreras's go-between with Kissinger" while the Condor system was being set up.[64]

Beyond Latin America, Kissinger, Nixon, and Ford systematically endeavored to keep human rights from influencing the course of U.S. foreign policy. Three examples suffice to tell the tale.[65] In 1969, National Security

[62] Klare, *Supplying Repression*, 7–25.
[63] Lesley Gill, *The School of the Americas: Military Training and Political Violence in the Americas* (Durham: Duke University Press), 2004), 73–82.
[64] Dinges, *The Condor Years*, 68–71, 101–25; quoted words, 104.
[65] Two further examples deserve mention. The strategic logic that Nixon and Kissinger applied to the conduct of war in Indochina contributed to setting in motion events that in turn gave rise to the brutal Khmer Rouge in Cambodia, so much so that Kissinger altered passages in his first memoir, *White House Years*, to counter such allegations contained in William Shawcross's critical account, *Sideshow: Kissinger, Nixon, and the Destruction of Cambodia*; see *New York Times*, October 31, 1979. Moreover, the tilt toward Pakistan at the time of the India–Pakistan war in 1971, undertaken so as not to jeopardize Nixon's overtures to China,

Study Memorandum 39 expressed concern for the plight of whites in South Africa, confronted as they were with mounting opposition to apartheid.[66] Roger Morris, who served on the National Security Council staff under Kissinger, admits that "substantial U.S. material interests in the white-ruled states" dominated administration thinking about Africa. He calls the Nixon-Kissinger approach a "disaster."[67] Indeed, it helped set the stage for subsequent covert involvement in Angola in an attempt to counter Cuban and presumed Soviet influence there, about which more presently.

The United States and Iran callously used and abandoned Iraq's Kurd population. The Shah of Iran, Washington's powerful client in the Persian Gulf, proposed using the Kurds to secure Iran's western border against the regime in Baghdad. The United States saw in that endeavor an opportunity to constrain the spread of Soviet influence in the region. In 1972, the Kurds, seeking independence, believed CIA assurances of support for their struggle. Israel also provided covert aid. During the October War in 1973, Kissinger insisted that the Kurds stand down and curtailed assistance to them. The tap was shut off in March 1975 when Iran and Iraq signed the Algiers Agreement delineating their common border. All parties then stood quietly by as the Iraqi army destroyed Kurdish forces, killing civilians in the process. Kissinger refused to extend humanitarian aid, reportedly saying, "Covert action should not be confused with missionary work."[68]

What happened in 1975 when Indonesia's Mohamed Suharto decided to annex the former Portuguese colony of East Timor provides another example of executive branch disdain for human rights. Mere days before his armed forces began a military invasion of the region, Suharto briefed President Ford and Kissinger in Jakarta about what was soon to transpire. The secretary of state, who of course viewed the issue in East-West terms, counseled Ford not to object. Given the stinging defeat in Vietnam some months earlier, the president told Suharto to do what he needed to, saying, "We will understand." On its own terms, the two did not care about East Timor. At least 50,000 civilians were dead by mid-1977, and as many as 200,000 perished by the end of the conflict in the late 1990s.[69] Despite Jimmy Carter's vaunted commitment to human rights, which lent inestimable support to foes of military regimes in several countries in Latin

---

exacerbated human suffering in East Pakistan, which with India's victory in the war became the independent nation, Bangladesh. See John Lewis Gaddis, *Strategies of Containment: A Critical Appraisal of American National Security Policy during the Cold War*, rev. and expanded ed. (New York: Oxford University Press, 2005), 304.

[66] Kenneth Mokoena, ed., *South Africa and the United States: The Declassified History* (New York: New Press, 1993), 210.

[67] Roger Morris, *Uncertain Greatness: Henry Kissinger and American Foreign Policy* (New York: Harper & Row, 1977), 110, 111.

[68] Ibid., 277–8; Garthoff, *Détente and Confrontation*, 357; quoted words, 522.

[69] Hanhimäki, *The Flawed Architect*, 401–3, 477–8; quoted words 402.

America, his administration, like Ford's, did little to help the people of East Timor. One official curtly explained that self-determination there "would not serve our best interests in light of the importance of our relations with Indonesia."[70]

The best efforts of members of Congress could not force Nixon, Ford, or Carter to put human security at the forefront of foreign policy. The hold of the security ethos on policymakers was too tight. Still, several developments augured well for durability of the issue in future debates over the purpose of U.S. foreign policy. The law creating the Office for Human Rights in the State Department, which soon became a bureau and was later renamed the Bureau for Democracy, Human, Rights, and Labor, mandated the department to prepare annual country reports on the status of human rights around the world. This presumption of entitlement to judge the record of other nations would backfire, though, as a result of troubling revelations about the torture of detainees as part of President George W. Bush's war on terror after March 2003.

Congress also placed language in section 502B of the Foreign Assistance Act forbidding the provision of security assistance to any government found chronically to violate international standards of human rights. The changes were necessary, proponents argued, to defend the integrity of basic American values. Then in 1975, Congress added language, commonly known as the Harkin Amendment after Representative Tom Harkin, Democrat of Iowa, to the Foreign Assistance Act that called for the cessation of most economic aid to nations engaged in gross violations of human rights.[71] Yet, even for Carter, strategic interests trumped human rights considerations in deciding whether to provide military and police assistance to authoritarian regimes. Thus, Military Assistance Programs and International Military Education and Training activities continued largely unimpaired throughout the decade.[72] By the late 1970s, the imperatives of grand strategy made it a fair question to ask whether supplying repression had become something akin to a core value for the executive branch.

Human rights did become a powerful weapon to be wielded in the struggle against communism. Opponents of détente were divided over "Basket III," which emerged out of the Conference on Security and Economic Cooperation in Europe (CSCE). In the main, CSCE was intended to ratify existing boundaries as a prelude to improved relations across the continent. Basket III, which conservatives in the United States had initially dismissed as toothless, called for the free movement of people and ideas, a masterstroke that

---

[70] Quoted in Gaddis Smith, *Morality, Reason, and Power: American Diplomacy in the Carter Years* (New York: Hill and Wang, 1986), 103.

[71] Sikkink, *Mixed Signals*, 69–72.

[72] Klare, *Supplying Repression*, 25–37.

inserted human rights into the heart of European politics. Then serving on Ford's National Security Council, future CIA chief and secretary of defense Robert M. Gates has written that the 1975 Helsinki Declaration, signed by the Soviets, "kindled widespread resistance to communist authority . . . throughout Eastern Europe and even in the Soviet Union."[73] Whether or not a line runs from the Helsinki Declaration to the dissolution of the Soviet Union in 1991 remains less certain than the fact that supporters of strategic globalism were turning human rights to their own ends. It also became a useful device, in Gates's self-congratulatory telling, for launching an "attack [on] the internal legitimacy of the Soviet government."[74] Such triumphalism suggests how human rights served the cause of strategic globalism and the restoration of U.S. credibility after Vietnam.

The Helsinki Declaration, in effect, posited political self-determination as a basic human right; that assumption did not necessarily hold true in practice. The prospect of revolution in El Salvador and Nicaragua in the late 1970s was fundamentally a demand for self-determination against historically repressive and authoritarian regimes. The United States nevertheless sought to moderate the Sandinista revolution in Nicaragua by trying to compel its leaders to accept ousted dictator Anastasio Debayle Somoza's brutal *Guardia Nacional* as its own security force.[75] That gambit met with rejection in Managua and gave rise to an adversarial relationship that resulted in attempts by the Reagan administration to remove the Sandinistas from power.

The Salvadoran situation was more complex. Although revolution was averted, a leftist insurgency posed a challenge to the country's oligarchic politics and U.S. security objectives, which military missions and training at the School of the Americas were sustaining. As elsewhere in the Americas, including Guatemala where bloodletting by government forces was a given in the 1970s,[76] counterinsurgency in El Salvador could not obscure the absence of self-determination and the accompanying abuse of human rights. The Carter administration placed its faith in a cadre of military reformers who took power in October 1979. Pressure from the United States, the oligarchy, and conservative leaders of the armed forces forced the reformers

---

73 Robert M. Gates, *From the Shadows: The Ultimate Insider's Account of Five Presidents and How They Won the Cold War* (New York: Simon & Schuster, 1996), 85–9; quoted words, 87.

74 Ibid., 91.

75 Walter LaFeber, *Inevitable Revolutions: The United States in Central America*, 2d ed., rev. and expanded (New York: W. W. Norton & Company, 1993), 225–37.

76 On the sad state of affairs in Guatemala and America's involvement with them, which helps explain the context in which a massacre took place at Panós in May 1978, see Greg Grandin, *The Last Colonial Massacre: Latin America in the Cold War* (Chicago: University of Chicago Press, 2004), esp. 140–65.

from power, ushering in a decade of terror for which the government in San Salvador held the most responsibility. Even the assassination of Archbishop Oscar Romero in March 1980 had no noticeable effect on U.S. policy. Ambassador Robert White commented, "Washington wants something to the right of Nicaragua." Hoping for land reform and a pliable junta, the United States by 1981 was sending military advisers to train El Salvador's army.[77] Ronald Reagan and the proponents of the National Security Doctrine in the region could hardly have asked for more. Central America had become one of the places where the contradictions between the grand strategy of strategic globalism and human rights would be most apparent and divisive for the American people.

Security Assets and American Values

During the 1970s and 1980s, U.S. officials cultivated "security assets" for help in achieving their goals, especially the containment of communism and the restoration of credibility. This was no easy process. The case of Taiwan is noteworthy in this respect. The Chinese Nationalists were an unwelcome reminder, like the war in Vietnam, that the United States was not entirely the master of its fate. Nixon tried to isolate Taiwan from America's strategic calculus so he could incorporate the People's Republic of China into his grand design. The regime in Taipei would not disappear, however, drawing on its longstanding ties in Washington to keep intact both military sales and vital economic links whether a Republican or Democrat was president.[78] Unlike the Kurds in Iraq, other security assets could not so easily be discarded when they outlived their usefulness.

The sale of arms and provision of security guarantees to friendly or client states; the reliance on covert activities in Angola, Afghanistan, and Nicaragua; and the courting of notorious individuals like Manuel Noriega of Panama and Saddam Hussein of Iraq exemplify how the United States sought to reconstruct international preeminence. A major post-Vietnam model for developing a security asset was the relationship with the "conjugal dictatorship" of Ferdinand and Imelda Marcos in the Philippines.[79] Ferdinand Marcos, who came to power in 1965, declared martial law in September 1972. Even as his efforts emboldened communists and led to further suppression of dissent in the vast island nation, Congress and the executive branch took few steps to hold Marcos to account. As Carter's Secretary of State Cyrus Vance explained, the administration made "vigorous efforts to

---

[77] LaFeber, *Inevitable Revolutions*, 244–55; quoted words, 251.

[78] Nancy Bernkopf Tucker, *Taiwan, Hong Kong, and the United States, 1945–1992* (New York: Twayne Publishers, 1994), 123–63.

[79] Generally see Raymond Bonner, *Waltzing with a Dictator: The Marcoses and the Making of American Policy* (New York: Times Books, 1987).

prevent cuts" in aid, and with obvious success.[80] The economic and military ties with Manila were simply too important to subordinate the relationship to strict human rights concerns. This unexceptional reality informed U.S. policy from Nixon to Carter to Reagan, for whom strategic globalism greatly depended on currying favor with strongmen like Marcos.[81] Other considerations, such as human security, were of lesser importance.

Throughout the 1970s, building client states in the Persian Gulf region became especially important as the United States remained suspicious of Soviet interests there. About the Shah of Iran, Kissinger commented that the United States "owed the Shah a great deal for his unflagging loyalty." As a quid pro quo for the arms deal of May 1972, whereby the administration signed an agreement to sell advanced weaponry to Iran, Washington expected Tehran to support U.S. security objectives by providing military equipment to Pakistan, which Congress was increasingly reluctant to do in the wake of the 1971 India-Pakistan War.[82] At stake in relations between the two countries was the security of Iranian oil and, hence, the stability of the Western alliance. This comparative advantage gave the Shah unbroken access to sophisticated conventional weaponry during the decade until his departure from power in 1978.[83] Not even the appalling excesses of "the dreaded SAVAK," Iran's security force, were sufficient during the Shah's reign to bring Carter's human rights concerns to bear on the U.S.-Iranian relationship. Like that of the Philippines, such was the vital role played by Iran as U.S. officials were in quest of the holy grail of strategic globalism.[84]

Saudi Arabia, not as threatened by communism as the White House believed Iran to be, was scarcely less important to American interests in the Middle East. Kissinger's account of a visit to the kingdom in November 1973 admitted that the control of oil by producer states "made possible a revolution in world economics and an upheaval in the world balance of power." Unable to prevent such dramatic developments, Washington needed to turn them to the service of U.S. interests. Kissinger sought to do that by emphasizing Saudi and U.S. fears about the possible growth of radicalism in the region.[85] The practical effect of these concerns meant that

[80] Secretary of State Cyrus R. Vance to U.S. Embassy, Tokyo, for Assistant Secretary of State for East Asian and Pacific Affairs Richard C. A. Holbrooke, September 20, 1977, Digital National Security Archive, Document PH01019.

[81] Similar considerations determined relations with South Korea; see Smith, *Morality, Reason, and Power,* 54, 86, 103–5; Weinberger, *Fighting for Peace,* 224.

[82] Harold H. Saunders to Henry A. Kissinger, July 24, 1973, DDRS; Kissinger, *Years of Upheaval,* 673.

[83] Mark J. Gasiorowski, *U.S. Foreign Policy and the Shah: Building a Client State in Iran* (Ithaca: Cornell University Press, 1991), 110–13.

[84] The characterization of SAVAK is in Kissinger, *Years of Upheaval,* 671.

[85] Ibid., 663–6; quoted words, 663.

the Saudis would continue to purchase modern weapons in their capacity as guarantors of stability in their part of the Persian Gulf; not even Israeli reservations about the strength of Saudi armed forces could prevent the sales.[86] The inability of Western governments to set the terms of trade for petroleum as in the past truly did amount to "an upheaval" in the balance of power. Undersecretary of State Joseph Sisco acknowledged that Iran and Saudi Arabia had become America's indispensable partners. There was, he told Congress, "no way to separate the military and defense aspects of our policies from the . . . economic and other ties we maintain."[87]

After the 1973 October War, Egypt began to distance itself from its patron in Moscow, formally severing strategic ties in March 1976 and gravitating toward the United States. This process culminated in the Camp David Accords of 1978, one result of which was the birth of an Egyptian-American strategic relationship just as the Shah's place in U.S. planning ended.[88] That development was unforeseeable in the dark days of autumn 1973. Other than the Cuban missile crisis, it is difficult to identify in the post-1945 era a more serious challenge to U.S. strategic planning than that which arose during the October War and its aftermath. Détente was coming under critical scrutiny at home, as symbolized by the Jackson-Vanik Amendment to the 1974 Trade Act linking economic concessions to the Soviet Union with the emigration of Jews to Israel.[89] Also, the aggrandizement of Soviet power in the region seemed evident in Washington.[90] The oil embargo, a clear response to Israel's victory, roiled international relations well into 1974, as Kissinger would later acknowledge.[91] And Israel, despite its intimate relations with the United States, seemed so emboldened in the months after the war as to flaunt its military supremacy over its neighbors, which spelled trouble for U.S. influence in the Arab world.[92]

Events in the Middle East further exacerbated pressures on the dollar, which had been devalued on several occasions since December 1971. Other, less volatile currencies were capturing the fancy of speculators.[93] In the Shah of Iran's shocking words, "The industrial world . . . will have to tighten their (*sic*) belts."[94] Strategic globalism was about to become more expensive.

---

[86] Lewis Sorley, *Arms Transfers under Nixon: A Policy Analysis* (Lexington: University Press, of Kentucky, 1983), 126–33.

[87] *Department of State Bulletin*, July 14, 1975, p. 78.

[88] Michael T. Klare, *American Arms Supermarket* (Austin: University of Texas Press, 1984), 140–4.

[89] Robert David Johnson, *Congress and the Cold War* (New York: Cambridge University Press, 2006), 199.

[90] Victor Israelyan, *Inside the Kremlin during the Yom Kippur War* (University Park: Pennsylvania State University Press, 1995), 213–15.

[91] Kissinger, *Years of Upheaval*, 978.

[92] Ibid., *Years of Upheaval*, 1047.

[93] Cohen, *In Whose Interest*, 29.

[94] *New York Times*, December 24, 1974.

To comprehend how client states brought American values into question, it is necessary to ponder Kissinger's pointed reaction to the fate of the Shah of Iran. He told *Newsweek* magazine in December 1978 that "the human rights campaign, as now conducted, is a weapon aimed primarily at allies and tends to undermine their domestic structures."[95] Human rights, to which Kissinger had nominally paid attention, gave practical expression to the concept of liberty – America's finest ideal. Thus, his utter dread at how self-determination in the form of human rights might impair America's role in the world was disquieting.

A selective look at covert activities in the 1970s helps establish that point. As we have seen, Nixon, Kissinger, and their successors were unwilling to allow political developments to run their course in Latin America. As Nixon informed one of his advisers, Donald Rumsfeld, "Latin America doesn't matter."[96] Yet, it certainly did matter so long as Salvador Allende held power in Chile. The problem was not that Chile would become another Cuba; rather, it was that other Chiles might come into being through the electoral process. Nixon also cautioned about entanglements in Africa. Despite their disdain for the two regions, U.S. officials feared the real or imagined power of the Left in both locales. As such, the resort to covert operations during and after Nixon's tenure as president came about mainly as a result of reflexive, unreasoned responses to situations that posed little or no threat to U.S. security.

Angola provides a familiar and instructive case study. After the leftist military coup of April 1974 against the Portuguese government of Marcello Caetano, the CIA in 1975–6 acted to assist Jonas Savimbi's UNITA (National Union for the Total Independence of Angola) movement, thereby blocking the leftist MPLA (Popular Movement for the Liberation of Angola) from seizing power. On their own terms, events in Angola emphasize how the logic of strategic globalism had the capacity to corrupt American values, most notably that of self-determination. In the process, the pernicious effect of the security ethos on values again became apparent.

After Allende's suicide and the evident restraint of Cuban foreign policy in the Americas, the result of increased Soviet economic assistance,[97] Kissinger undertook to improve relations with Havana by supporting in July 1975 the lifting of sanctions on Cuba imposed in 1964 by the Organization of American States.[98] Throughout the U.S. government, the prevailing assumption judged Cuba to be so beholden to the Soviets that Cuban support for the

[95] *Newsweek*, December 11, 1978, p. 56.
[96] Quoted in James Mann, *Rise of the Vulcans: The History of Bush's War Cabinet* (New York: Viking, 2004), 16.
[97] Jonathan Haslam, *The Nixon Administration and the Death of Allende's Chile* (London: Verso, 2005), 222; Piero Gleijeses, *Conflicting Missions: Havana, Washington, and Africa, 1959–1976* (Chapel Hill: University of North Carolina Press, 2002), 225–6.
[98] Gleijeses, *Conflicting Missions*, 225.

MPLA in Angola, when it came to light, must have occurred at Moscow's behest. The *démarche* with Cuba ended during Carter's presidency; pressure from Congress and within his administration about Cuba's presence in Africa compelled Carter to reverse course.[99]

In fact, Yugoslavia had done more than Cuba to assist the MPLA in early 1975 as civil war erupted among the rebel factions UNITA, the MPLA, and the FNLA (National Liberation Front of Angola). The CIA and Kissinger backed the FNLA while recognizing that UNITA was essential to thwarting the MPLA. Savimbi, who had fought with pre-coup Portugal against the MPLA, seemed an appealing client, despite the relative paucity of his forces. He also was willing to work with South Africa, as was the FNLA's Holden Roberto. Thus in July, when the MPLA under the leadership of Agostinho Neto won a battle for Luanda, the capital city, the dye was cast. The CIA would align with any coalition opposing the MPLA, even one including South African forces.[100] The belief that covert activity was called for (because after Vietnam Congress would not fund a military enterprise in Africa) necessitated, in the revealing words of CIA officer John Stockwell, "creating a stable climate to allow genuine self-determination."[101] By the time the Ford administration acted against the MPLA, direct Cuban involvement in Africa in support of radical and revolutionary forces was in the offing and Stockwell's counsel was ignored.[102]

In Stockwell's telling, Kissinger's $14 million "no-win" endeavor was designed "to challenge the Soviets," who presumably were seeking to establish a foothold in Africa. U.S. officials denied that Cuba could be acting independently of the Soviet Union; it had to be a stalking horse for Moscow.[103] In that sense, as historian Piero Gleijeses explains, "Angola was but a pawn in the game."[104] Yet, Soviet military assistance to Neto and the MPLA, which had been withdrawn in 1974, was resumed only after the inception of Cuban assistance.[105] In the anti-MPLA coalition were the United States, Zaire, South Africa, France, Great Britain, and, acting largely on its own, China. As Kissinger feared, covert activity, including the raising of a mercenary force, could not long be kept secret.

The American press had briefly done its part in late 1974 to keep involvement in Angola out of the public eye, again bringing to light the chronically

---

[99] Susan Eva Eckstein, *Back from the Future: Cuba under Castro* (Princeton: Princeton University Press, 1994), 199–200.

[100] Gleijeses, *Conflicting Missions*, 242–54, 280–93.

[101] John Stockwell, *In Search of Enemies: A CIA Story* (New York: W. W. Norton & Company, 1978), 47.

[102] Gleijeses, *Conflicting Missions*, 254–7.

[103] Stockwell, *In Search of Enemies*, 43.

[104] Gleijeses, *Conflicting Missions*, 360.

[105] Eckstein, *Back from the Future*, 182–3.

uneasy relationship between security and freedom of the press. Yet, in that same period, Senator Dick Clark sponsored an amendment to a foreign aid bill prohibiting funds for covert activities in Angola. The 1976 amendment became law as the MPLA was prevailing over U.S. clients with Cuban assistance. On taking office, Ronald Reagan lobbied to overturn the Clark Amendment, finally securing congressional repeal in 1986 after which aid was resumed to Jonas Savimbi and UNITA.[106]

Like others, the Carter administration was not at all loath to sell arms or provide covert assistance to client states and insurgents, especially as relations with the Soviet Union worsened during 1979 and into 1980.[107] The most important presidential finding concerned Afghanistan. Urged on by rebels opposing the pro-Soviet government in Kabul and by Pakistan's Mohammad Zia-ul-Haq, the CIA in July began covertly supplying the Mujahedin "freedom fighters," as Zbigniew Brzezinski characterized them, with lethal aid. The decision to involve the CIA in Afghanistan preceded Soviet intervention by about six months.[108] Most remarkable about this episode is how little the United States strayed from the structure of Nixonian détente. Harsh rhetoric, sanctions including a boycott of the Moscow Olympics in 1980, the Carter Doctrine regarding vital Western interests in the Persian Gulf, and increases in defense spending aside, Brzezinski knew there was too much at stake to provoke a confrontation by sending misleading signals to Moscow.[109] Détente remained intact; it was less certain then how covert involvement in Afghanistan would affect core values. That picture would become clearer over the next decade and beyond, as the United States sought hegemony in a world in which nonstate actors were increasingly important.

Ronald Reagan and the Illusion of Exceptionalism

It is fashionable to praise Ronald Reagan for refurbishing America's international standing. His election isolated those who interpreted defeat in Vietnam as repudiation of the imperial presidency[110] and provided a guide for subsequent foreign policy, or so the conventional interpretation maintains. The CIA's Robert M. Gates wrote, "[Ronald Reagan's] determination to reverse the apparent flow of history underpinned the entirety of his foreign policy."[111] Cold War historian John Lewis Gaddis also championed the idea of a renascent United States under Reagan, observing, "Reagan's

[106] Gleijeses, *Conflicting Missions*, 132, 362–4; Johnson, *Congress and the Cold War*, 221–4, 283–4.

[107] On arms sales, see Brzezinski, *Power and Principle*, 144–5.

[108] Ibid., 428; Gates, *From the Shadows*, 142–9.

[109] Brzezinski, *Power and Principle*, 430, 434.

[110] Arthur M. Schlesinger Jr., *The Imperial Presidency* (Boston: Houghton Mifflin, 1973).

[111] Gates, *From the Shadows*, 194.

decisive victory was a mandate...to reassert American strength."[112] As much as any president since Woodrow Wilson, Reagan articulated the democratic aspirations of many people around the world, dreams he would support with American power.[113] Yet, assent for self-determination typically meant that nouveau democrats needed to have Washington's imprimatur.

However uplifting many American citizens found Reagan's rhetoric to be, there were limits to what his administration could accomplish. The American dollar no longer enjoyed the same power it had long possessed to dominate currency markets and serve as an engine of commerce and economic growth. Even the incredible might of the United States could not guarantee a return to hegemony. As never before, friends and allies were dubious about the beneficence of American exceptionalism.

The term "imperial presidency" is misleading in that it minimizes the support of Congress, defense intellectuals, and to an extent the American people themselves for a grand strategy commensurate with the security ethos. Congress in the 1980s was composed not of neo-isolationists but of new internationalists, as one scholar notes, who desired a moral form, as it were, of strategic globalism.[114] At issue in two major inquiries in the 1970s into abuses of executive power, the Church and Pike investigations, was not whether the United States would play a leading global role, but rather what kind of role was possible after Vietnam.[115] Specifically, the Pike Committee compiled evidence indicating that the activities of the intelligence community were incongruent with the nation's basic values. Yet, by the early 1980s, the U.S. Congress, as a result of concern about Soviet intentions and Republican capture of the Senate, had largely abandoned its reservations about the use of American might and was therefore prepared to go along with a Cold War, Reagan-style.[116]

Applauding this turn to the right were groups like the Committee on the Present Danger, formed in November 1976 following the work of the conservative members of "Team B" of the President's Foreign Intelligence Advisory Board, which had severely criticized the CIA's National Intelligence Estimates of Soviet military strength. Team B judged CIA estimates to be disturbingly low; it also reached unverifiable conclusions about Soviet intentions. Never an exact science, threat perception reflected self-induced fears as much as reliable knowledge about Soviet strategic objectives.[117]

[112] Gaddis, *Strategies of Containment*, 349.

[113] Tony Smith, *America's Mission: The United States and the Worldwide Struggle for Democracy in the Twentieth Century* (Princeton: Princeton University Press, 1994), 265–9.

[114] Johnson, *Congress and the Cold War*.

[115] Kathryn S. Olmsted, *Challenging the Secret Government: The Post-Watergate Investigations of the CIA and FBI* (Chapel Hill: University of North Carolina Press, 1996).

[116] Ibid., 111–43; Johnson, *Congress and the Cold War*, 239–55.

[117] Tim Weiner, *Legacy of Ashes: The History of the CIA* (New York: Doubleday, 2007), 351–3.

Instrumental in fostering the efforts of Team B was George H. W. Bush, who became CIA director late in 1975.[118]

If election results are a guide, numerous Americans wearied of revelations about executive abuses of power, accepting the need for some dubious steps to be undertaken in the defense of freedom. Some critics of the excesses of power lost seats in the Senate and the House by the 1980 election, indicating that the voting public partly identified with the security ethos. Yet, the proponents of executive accountability on intelligence matters did not entirely fail; in 1978, Congress passed the Foreign Intelligence Surveillance Act (FISA), which required a court order before domestic wiretapping could begin.[119] FISA's relationship to constitutional protections under the Fourth Amendment would become politically contentious after the attack by al-Qaeda on the United States in September 2001.

Reclaiming American exceptionalism under Reagan also had an economic aspect. Reagan was fortunate that stagflation eased shortly after he took office. Yet, the Reagan recovery must be attributed in great measure to a revival of containment capitalism. Economic policy derived more from a spend-and-borrow concept, which Richard Nixon, who understood that the illusion of economic strength could destroy strategic globalism, had tried to avoid. Eroding the material base of domestic prosperity ultimately had to redound to the detriment of American values, which had historically been linked to a strong economy. Reagan inherited an $80 billion deficit from Carter; by the time he left office, his administration was averaging a deficit of more than $180 billion per year and the national debt had more than doubled from just over $900 billion to nearly $2.5 trillion.[120]

Increases in military spending without commensurate revenues could not reverse nearly two decades of industrial decline and the loss of a competitive economic edge. The Carter administration had begun a new round of increases that Reagan more than doubled during his two terms in office. Even though Congress balked at funding costly items like the MX missile, the B-1B bomber, and the M1 tank, the defense outlay for fiscal years 1982 through 1987 amounted to $1.5 trillion.[121]

---

[118] Tyroler, ed., *Alerting America*, xv; Anne Hessing Cahn, *Killing Détente: The Right Attacks the CIA* (University Park: Pennsylvania State University Press, 1998), 100–40; John Prados, *The Soviet Estimate: U.S. Intelligence Analysis and Soviet Strategic Forces* (Princeton: Princeton University Press, 1986), 247–57.

[119] Olmstead, *Challenging the Secret Government*, 177; Loch K. Johnson, *A Season of Inquiry: The Senate Intelligence Investigation* (Lexington: University Press of Kentucky, 1985), 252–6.

[120] Benjamin M. Friedman, *Day of Reckoning: The Consequences of American Economic Policy under Reagan and After* (New York: Random House, 1988), 19. In 1986 Congress lowered the top marginal tax rate from 50 to 28 percent.

[121] Ibid., 273–8.

Someone had to pay for the profligate spending and borrowing of the United States as it became a debtor nation. Germany and Japan, however, were no longer willing to absorb the high cost of security that Washington was exporting; by the mid-1980s they were among the world's largest net creditors. The burden fell heavily on Latin America. Washington's imposition in 1971 of a 10 percent surcharge on imports reduced the profit margins for hemispheric trade. The result was the "lost decade," highlighted in August 1982 by Mexico's near default on its financial obligations. Not until 1991 did many Latin America countries begin to emerge from under a cloud of crushing debt.

Economic growth had determined political legitimacy since 1960 partly because of the convergence of the Alliance for Progress and Latin America's National Security Doctrine. After the oil crisis of 1973, access to capital became more costly; at the same time, competition among international banks made abundant capital available to borrowers whose capacity to repay was uncertain. Latin American expert and economic analyst Riordan Roett blames the economic policies of the Reagan administration for creating the preconditions of the 1980s chaos.[122] The ratio of debt service to export earnings by 1981 had risen considerably above what were considered safe levels in Brazil, Chile, Mexico, and Argentina. As interest rates increased under the influence of Reagan administration monetary policy, making debt servicing more expensive, a crisis was sure to follow.[123]

The crisis was political as well as economic. American economic policy was designed to facilitate a refurbished and costly defense policy. U.S. authorities claimed success in promoting democracy in the Western Hemisphere; at the end of the decade when a resurgence of democracy appeared irreversible, Assistant Secretary of State for Inter-American Affairs Elliott Abrams proclaimed, "We...gave it our full support. *Democracy became the organizing principle of our policy.*"[124] Nevertheless, the return of civilian rule in Central America – in the militarized nations of El Salvador, Guatemala, and Honduras – neither enhanced the cause of participatory democracy nor altered the economic and social context in which democracy could prosper. U.S. intervention in Nicaragua and Grenada meant death and radical political change. Also, the return or strengthening of democratic rule in South America was accompanied more by rhetorical support than by economic aid from the United States.[125]

---

[122] Riordan Roett, "The Debt Crisis and Economic Development," in John D. Martz., ed., *United States Policy in Latin America: A Decade of Crisis and Challenge* (Lincoln: University of Nebraska Press, 1995), 249–53.

[123] Ibid., 242–3.

[124] "The Reagan Legacy in Latin America: Active Support for Democracy," January 12, 1989, Current Policy No. 1144, Bureau of Public Affairs U.S. Department of State (emphasis in original).

[125] Thomas Carothers, *In the Name of Democracy: U.S. Policy toward Latin America in the Reagan Years* (Berkeley: University of California Press, 1991).

If the United States was going to return to a position of international leadership, then the contest with the Soviet Union for influence in areas of mutual interest would be a critical measure of success or failure. Three cases, the specific details of which are well known, stand out: American support for autonomy in Eastern Europe, intervention in Nicaragua, and covert assistance to the Mujahedin in Afghanistan. The contest took place, needless to say, in the context of contentious Soviet-American relations.

The Soviet Union, the Democracy Project, and U.S. Hegemony

Richard Nixon envisaged détente as a means of restoring U.S. global hegemony. In fact, détente placed limits on American ambitions, which the White House knew but could not change. Memoirs of Regan administration officials and public statements from the president on down are replete with the impassioned language of rollback, denouncing détente as a bankrupt policy. Secretary of State George P. Shultz told the Senate Foreign Relations Committee in June 1983, two months after the idea of the Strategic Defense Initiative (SDI), or "Star Wars," had been introduced, that "now our goal must be to advance our own objectives, where possible foreclosing and when necessary actively countering Soviet challenges wherever they threaten our interests."[126] Rollback, however, revealed the pervasiveness of obduracy on the U.S. side of the superpower relationship. The Soviets were not immune from similar stubbornness, as Georgi Arbatov lamented in his memoirs, "We became participants in the dismantling of . . . détente."[127] In his testimony, Schultz distanced himself from "containment and détente" as if they were somehow antithetical to freedom itself.[128] Rollback, as seen in the Reagan Doctrine, which interpreted regional conflicts as East-West clashes, would be given its fullest voice in a speech by the president to the Heritage Foundation in October.[129]

Ultimately, the threat of rollback could not restore the dominance that the United States had enjoyed early in 1950 when NSC-68 was being prepared. Nor does evoking rollback make Reagan one of America's "sharpest grand strategists ever," as Gaddis has claimed.[130] Why not? There was no alternative to détente without raising the possibility of a return to the terrifying days of October 1962. That lesson had to be relearned in November 1983 after Soviet officials perceived a simulated U.S. and NATO military exercise, Abel Archer 83, recalled Minister of Defense Dmitry F. Ustinov, as "difficult to

---

[126] George P. Shultz, *Turmoil and Triumph: My Years as Secretary of State* (New York: Charles Scribner's Sons, 1993), 277.

[127] Arbatov, *The System*, 203.

[128] Shultz did call for "direct dialogue and negotiation" as the sole reliable road to peace; Shultz, *Turmoil and Triumph*, 277.

[129] Garthoff, *The Great Transition*, 127.

[130] John Lewis Gaddis, *The Cold War: A New History* (New York: Penguin Press, 2005), 217.

distinguish . . . from the real deployment of armed forces for aggression."[131] American authorities would later acknowledge that the exercise had indeed alarmed the Soviets.

With the rise of Mikhail Gorbachev to power in 1985, rollback lost its salience as a key foreign policy stratagem. Gorbachev's adoption of reforms in order to preserve communism in the Soviet Union arose from internal considerations, encouraged by a transnational coterie of scientists. In fact, there is scant evidence that SDI accelerated the cause of reform.[132] Gorbachev's actions, however, did lessen superpower tensions. The Soviet military did not desire war, as U.S. officials acknowledged. The self-generated fears that pervaded decision making in the White House prolonged the stand-off marking Reagan's first five years in office. George Kennan, who well understood the role of fear in the making of foreign policy, commented that the Soviet Union was not the major issue in the early eighties; rather, "we were anxious to prove [something] to ourselves, about ourselves."[133] The president wanted to validate American exceptionalism by insisting that the United States had the authority "to encourage openness and democracy in the Soviet Union," as then-Ambassador Jack F. Matlock Jr. put it.[134]

Faith in exceptionalism ostensibly gave the United States license to try to remake the world in the name of democracy. That effort would not bear fruit in the Soviet Union. After Gorbachev's resignation as president in December 1991 and the subsequent dissolution of the Supreme Soviet,[135] regimes in Russia headed by the alcoholic Boris Yeltsin and the ex-KGB spymaster Vladimir Putin had only the barest semblance of democracy about them.

To be sure, the United States had promoted democracy there in furtherance of strategic globalism.[136] As such, Schultz's instruction of Nikolai Ryzhkov, head of the Council of Ministers, at a meeting in Moscow in April 1987 becomes explicable. The Soviets, Schultz counseled, "need an internal market and a convertible currency in order to take part in multilateral, currency-based exchange." He repeated the same advice to Gorbachev who seemed "intrigued."[137] Schultz quotes Gorbachev as saying to President-elect Bush on November 12, 1988: "The idea of democratization of the

---

[131] Quoted in Garthoff, *The Great Transition*, 140.

[132] Evangelista, *Unarmed Forces*, 240–45. One looks in vain in Gaddis's *Strategies of Containment* and *The Cold War* for mention of the work of Evangelista.

[133] George F. Kennan, *The Nuclear Delusion: Soviet-American Relations in the Atomic Age* (New York: Pantheon Books, 1983), 230.

[134] Jack F. Matlock Jr., *Reagan and Gorbachev: How the Cold War Ended* (New York: Random House, 2004), xiv, 319–20.

[135] Garthoff, *The Great Transition*, 473–87.

[136] This mission to reform Russia was a lengthy one in relations between the two nations; see David S. Foglesong, *The American Mission and the "Evil Empire": The Crusade for a "Free Russia" since 1881* (New York: Cambridge University Press, 2007).

[137] Schultz, *Turmoil and Triumph*, 889–93; quoted words, 889.

entire world order has turned into a mighty sociopolitical force."[138] And so it had, although its impact was not necessarily salutary.

Beyond the Soviet Union, the Reagan administration promoted democracy as the key to order and stability, ultimately at some cost to core values. For example, public and clandestine support, with help from the Catholic Church, for the Solidarity trade union movement in Poland in the 1980s,[139] although defensible on human rights grounds, narrowed the separation between church and state in American politics. It encouraged political activism among fundamentalists, who were perhaps the president's most avid supporters. Since the 1980s, fundamentalist politics, at the very least, have had a chilling effect on individual freedoms, especially freedom of speech and freedom of the press. The ideal of fairness in print and electronic media was shrewdly appropriated by right-wing zealots and employed as a weapon to inhibit investigative journalism. Yet, nothing suffered as markedly as the nation's system of public education. The teaching of American history became politically contentious, and scientific inquiry itself came under attack from right-wing activists and fundamentalist Christians.[140]

Reagan came into office assuming that America's power matched its interests. Maintaining security ties with Saudi Arabia, standing by Israel, and securing access to oil in the Persian Gulf were vital to the success of the democracy project. Whatever the objective, the lubricant was oil. In a primer for the president, Robert W. Tucker urged going beyond what he condemned as the passivity of the Carter Doctrine to create a tripwire situation in which preemptive force would be used, if necessary, to control the oil supply. Tucker had suggested several years earlier that the United States might have to seize Gulf oil supplies to maintain its global standing.[141] Oil was a major concern, too, as the United States became involved in the Iran-Iraq War that began in 1980. Putting aside its differences with Iraq, the White House courted Saddam Hussein as a security asset despite his use of chemical weapons, sending Donald Rumsfeld to Baghdad in late 1983 to offer assistance. Revolutionary Iran simply had to be contained. Three years later, though, as part of the Iran-Contra affair, Iran received secret U.S. aid in order to prevent the aggrandizement of Iraqi power in the region.[142]

[138] Quoted in ibid., 1106.
[139] Judt, *Postwar*, 585–89, 605.
[140] Thomas Frank, *What's the Matter with Kansas?: How Conservatives Won the Heart of America* (New York: Metropolitan Books, 2004); Chris Hedges, *American Fascists: The Christian Right and the War on America* (New York: Doubleday, 2007); and, generally, Susan Jacoby, *The Age of American Unreason* (New York: Pantheon Books, 2008).
[141] Robert W. Tucker, "American Power and the Persian Gulf," *Commentary*, November 1980, 25–41.
[142] Mann, *Rise of the Vulcans*, 123–6; Dilip Hiro, *The Longest War: The Iran-Iraq Military Conflict* (New York: Routledge, 1991), 213–21.

Support of the anti-Soviet Mujahedin in Afghanistan commencing in 1979 may be one of the three greatest foreign policy blunders in American history.[143] The Carter administration had begun providing lethal aid to the Mujahedin, which the CIA under Reagan expanded as a critical part of its general anti-Soviet efforts and the U.S. drive for predominant influence across the Middle East into Southwest Asia. The unanticipated consequences of this projection of power, including the creation of the Taliban in Afghanistan and the emergence of Osama bin Laden and the transnational jihad of al-Qaeda, made a mockery of Reagan's democracy project. Islamic jihadists, often referred to as freedom fighters, found nothing about the United States worth emulating.[144]

Accompanying the CIA's association with the Mujahedin was the restoration of Pakistani credibility after the execution of former president Zulfikar Ali Bhutto, whom the dictator Zia ul-Haq had overthrown; Pakistan's intelligence agency, the Directorate of Inter-Services Intelligence (ISI), proved indispensable to U.S. goals in Afghanistan. Also, among the Mujahedin leaders who received arms from the CIA were opium traffickers, Gulbuddin Hekmatyar being the most notorious. By early 1989 when Soviet forces abandoned their disastrous enterprise, substantial regions of the country were in thrall to a thriving heroin trade.[145] To secure U.S. interests after the Soviet departure, the CIA maintained ties to favored groups as Afghanistan descended into civil war. Democracy was nowhere in evidence, it is safe to say, as the first Bush administration began pursuing its own version of strategic globalism in Southwest Asia.

In the villages of Panzós in Guatemala in May 1978 and El Mozote in El Salvador in December 1981, untold numbers of people, mostly poor, died in the name of national security.[146] The brutal massacres in these remote locales illustrate the conundrums of U.S. foreign policy in the post-Vietnam era. Counterinsurgency, a tactic once deemed crucial to victory in the Cold War, came under attack. Perhaps as nowhere else, security imperatives and human rights were at odds in Central America. Carter had restricted ties with the Guatemalan government, yet weapons provided by Israel and Taiwan aided a scorched earth campaign, as did secret CIA assistance. Reagan,

---

[143] The present study suggests that going to war with Spain in 1898 was the first of three momentous blunders, the second being the overthrow of Muhammad Musaddiq in Iran in 1953.

[144] Fawaz A. Gerges, *The Far Enemy: Why Jihad Went Global* (New York: Cambridge University Press, 2005), especially 65.

[145] The story of U.S. involvement in Afghanistan is best told in Steve Coll, *Ghost Wars: The Secret History of the CIA, Afghanistan, and bin Laden, from the Soviet Invasion to September 10, 2001* (New York: Penguin Press, 2004); and Tim Weiner, *Blank Check: The Pentagon's Black Budget* (New York: Warner Books, 1990), 143–71.

[146] Grandin, *Last Colonial Massacre*; Mark Danner, *The Massacre at El Mozote: A Parable of the Cold War* (New York: Vintage Books, 1994).

who in 1982 said that born-again Christian General Efraín Rios Montt was "totally dedicated to democracy," outmaneuvered opposition in Congress and restored some economic aid. An additional 100,000 Guatemalans, many of Mayan descent, would die before the civil war ended in 1996.[147] In El Salvador, the U.S.-trained Alcatl Battalion had been responsible for the brutal killings at El Mozote, yet American involvement there would soon deepen. The insurgency against authoritarian rule made El Salvador a critical front in the struggle for Central America. Through the mid-1980s, rebels of the FMLN (Farabundo Martí National Liberation Front) more than once seemed on the verge of success in their efforts to bring down the government. The CIA-assisted victory of José Napoleón Duarte in the 1984 presidential campaign began to marginalize the extreme right and its death squads while clearing the way for greater U.S. involvement in Salvadoran affairs.[148]

The fate of strategic globalism depended as much on reasserting hegemony in Central America as on removing Soviet influence from Eastern Europe and Afghanistan. An advisory group to the Republican Party, the Committee on Santa Fe, warned in 1980 that World War III had begun in the Americas. President Reagan averred in April 1983, "The national security of all the Americas is at stake in Central America." Congress was an impediment to the restoration of U.S. credibility, or so he implied, because some in Congress and the public pointed to the abuse of human rights in opposing administration policy in the region.[149] Reagan never succeeded in getting a free hand to pursue his twin objectives of ridding Central America of suspected communist influence and establishing market-based democracies, the ill-fated Caribbean Basin Initiative notwithstanding.[150]

In Nicaragua, where it was not difficult to connect the Sandinistas and Cuba, if not the Soviet Union, a threat to regional security seemed plausible given Reagan's logic. The National Bipartisan Commission on Central America, or the Kissinger Commission, which began its work in 1983, concluded in its 1984 report that Nicaragua's role as a "base for Soviet and Cuban efforts to penetrate" the region, "with El Salvador the target of first opportunity, gives the conflict there a major strategic dimension.... This is a challenge to which the United States must respond."[151] Central America, in sum, had become an integral part of the struggle against communism and for democracy then being waged by the United States.

[147] Quoted in Walter LaFeber, *Inevitable Revolutions: The United States in Central America*, 2d ed., rev. and expanded (New York: W. W. Norton & Company, 1993), 322; Grandin, *Last Colonial Massacre*, 3.

[148] Cynthia Arnson, *Crossroads: Congress, the President, and Central America, 1976–1993*, 2d ed. (University Park: Pennsylvania State University Press, 1993), 157–63.

[149] Quoted in ibid., 128.

[150] LaFeber, *Inevitable Revolutions*, 284–9.

[151] *The Report of the President's National Bipartisan Commission on Central America*, foreword by Henry Kissinger (New York: Macmillan, 1984), 151.

In December 1982, the House of Representatives explicitly prohibited the use of funds to overthrow the Sandinistas or induce conflict between Nicaragua and Honduras. Yet, Contra forces were not then prohibited from conducting insurgent operations intended to destabilize the government in Managua. How such activities differed from an attempt to overthrow the Sandinistas was unclear. One year later, the House approved additional funding, with the proviso that the CIA could not assist the Contras by drawing on its own contingency funds or shifting money from existing accounts. The turn toward what came to be called the "Enterprise" was about to be taken; the administration began its quest for sources of funds and military supplies that were beyond congressional scrutiny or control. Ironically, by fall 1986, just as the Iran-Contra scandal was about to break, not only had the House agreed to the transmission of overt nonlethal aid but it had also voted to permit the CIA to oversee distribution of $100 million in military assistance.[152]

Why did the administration ignore the limits Congress placed on it and endeavor to overthrow the Sandinistas by whatever means were available? Why did it persist in circumventing Congress, even as that body was responding more favorably to White House wishes? Those involved with the Enterprise believed that Reagan's popularity rendered them impervious to accountability to Congress, should the need to deceive arise. Indeed, lying to Congress became a badge of honor held by Elliott Abrams and Oliver North, among others. They were, at least in the short term, above the law. Criticism of support for conservative and right-wing governments in El Salvador and Guatemala by liberal advocates of human rights, individuals crudely dismissed by Assistant Secretary of State Abrams as the "creeps on the left," was consistently ignored. The group CISPES (Committee in Solidarity with the People of El Salvador) became the object of an FBI investigation and harassment that was eerily reminiscent of COINTELPRO, for which the director later apologized.[153]

Challenges from within the foreign policy bureaucracy or from the public at large to Reagan's Central American policy lend themselves to comparison with earlier times in the nation's history when the ideals of republican virtue and, later, civic virtue were major aspects of deliberations about power and authority. Since 1945, such weighty discussions had transpired in the public realm about Senator Joseph R. McCarthy, the war in Vietnam, and the Watergate scandal. Until Congress in general acquiesced to Reagan's view of the Contras in 1985 and 1986, it was to an extent performing a similar service to the nation. Former State Department official Frank McNeill, who served as ambassador to Costa Rica under Carter and Reagan, denounced the latter's policy as an "occasion for subverting our

[152] Arnson, *Crossroads*, 111–12, 143–6, 180–3, 215–17.
[153] Abrams is quoted in Sikkink, *Mixed Signals*, 158; LaFeber, *Inevitable Revolutions*, 295–6.

political system." He characterized McCarthyism, Watergate, and Iran-Contra as frontal "assaults on due process, individual liberties, and the rule of law," each marked by profound political paranoia that grievously injured rather than protected the nation's security.[154]

Conclusion

Core values did not fare will in the 1970s and 1980s. The trampling of individual liberties under Nixon was systematic, whereas under Reagan, it remained selective. Both administrations impugned the loyalty of their political opponents. If the national media clamored after Nixon with a vengeance, and that is partly accurate, print and electronic journalists were too easily seduced by Reagan's congenial persona. The exposure of institutional abuses of power by the executive branch was like a shooting star, brilliant at inception but a light that faded all too quickly. The memory of Vietnam did prevent U.S. forces from intervening directly in El Salvador's civil conflict, but it did not slow the reliance on proxy war as a tool of American foreign policy there or elsewhere in the hemisphere, in Southwest Asia, or in central Africa. At length, as the Nixon Doctrine morphed into an unending quest for strategic globalism, the very idea of sovereignty was subordinated to Washington's security interests.

More important, the concept of self-determination, which harked back to the time of Woodrow Wilson, and its associated ideal of human rights depended on the largesse of one president after another as in turn they sought to revitalize American credibility. Even a well-intentioned liberal like Jimmy Carter could not free himself from the lure of hegemony. Fixation on the restoration of American authority to its earlier heights ignored the new realities of the post-1973 era. The United States could no longer buy its way to power; the dollar was no longer strong enough to compel deference to its still elevated status among all currencies. Moreover, the postwar conceit that free people everywhere desired to emulate the United States seemed ill founded, an ever widening gap between European and American understanding of their respective vital interests being the most obvious example. For those in U.S. policymaking circles willing to look with open eyes, the rejection by others of the example of American exceptionalism was not uncommon in the years spanning the Nixon and Reagan presidencies.

This appraisal of strategic globalism as grand strategy does not imply that U.S. officials were prisoners of the security ethos. It did, however, give them an available perspective about how the United States should go into the world, one they instinctively called on as they made policy. In addition, it limited, as it long had, the parameters of acceptable discourse about how

---

[154] Frank McNeill, *War and Peace in Central America: Reality and Illusion* (New York: Charles Scribner's Sons, 1988), 206, 207–8.

to keep the nation and its people safe from perceived threats. There were, of course, other ways of seeing. Dependence on the oil and strategic minerals of others and the rise of human rights to the level of global concern could have occasioned reconsideration if not a comprehensive revision of the security ethos. That did not happen. It remained closely linked to an ideology that was driven by the lure of economic hegemony, a readiness to use force to head off potential problems, and the evocation of often irrational fears about the intentions of other great and lesser powers.

That way of seeing the world and America's place in it would not change with the end of the Reagan presidency. Neither George Herbert Walker Bush, nor Bill Clinton, nor George W. Bush would alter that fundamental perspective.

7

The False Promise of a New World Order

What is at stake...is a big idea: a new world order, where diverse nations are drawn together in common cause to achieve the universal aspirations of mankind – peace and security, freedom, and the rule of law.
George H. W. Bush, 1991

Like George Bush, I was of a generation that embraced wholeheartedly the concept of a Pax Americana.
James A. Baker III, 1995

When the Reagan phase of the Cold War ended with a weakened Soviet Union, the discourse about security among policymakers and defense intellectuals, inside the Washington Beltway and at think tanks and universities around the nation, sounded decidedly triumphalist.[1] Protective as ever of his and Nixon's policies and mindful of their legacy, Henry Kissinger continued to chide the critics of détente, in effect refusing to admit that the very word had become anathema for political reasons. Meanwhile, the imperative to contain potential adversaries remained at the very heart of strategic thinking in America. In that respect, containment in some form might survive as a useful tactic even after the Soviet empire finally collapsed.

The Carter and Reagan administrations had accepted the contradictory premises underlying strategic globalism: The application of American power was limited, yet the responsibility to act as the guarantor of order was global in scope.[2] Kissinger grudgingly celebrated Reagan's achievements vis-à-vis

[1] Leo P. Ribuffo, "Moral Judgments and the Cold War: Reflections on Reinhold Niebuhr, William Appleman Williams, and John Lewis Gaddis," in Ellen Schrecker, ed., *Cold War Triumphalism: The Misuse of History after the Fall of Communism* (New York: New Press, 2004), 27–70; Bruce Cumings, "Time of Illusion: Post-Cold War Visions of the World," in ibid., 71–99.

[2] Henry Kissinger, *Diplomacy* (New York: Simon & Schuster, 1994), 766–73, notes the existence of tactical differences in U.S. foreign policy between the 1970s and 1980s; this avowed advocate of the primacy of great powers in world affairs gently critiques Ronald Reagan, who "took Wilsonianism to its ultimate conclusion" (p. 773).

the Soviets, finding in the Californian's actual policies, as distinct from the bellicose rhetoric he had initially employed, vital continuities from his own years in power. As it had been since 1973, the dilemma confronting U.S. officials was that of squaring restrictions on the use of the military with inherently expansive international objectives.

From Nixon through Reagan, containment, détente, and the grand strategy of strategic globalism provided the impetus for the projection of power. By the late 1980s, these post-1945 manifestations of the security ethos were exerting such influence over Washington's global interactions that the unintended consequences of U.S. policies, what the CIA termed "blowback," should have been foreseen. One critic of détente who was a member of the Committee on the Present Danger in the mid-1970s, political scientist Chalmers Johnson, later became a fierce opponent of strategic globalism. He argued that many emergent challenges to the United States after Reagan were self-created, a function of the abuse of history. "It is typical of an imperial people to have a short memory for its less pleasant imperial acts," he wrote, "but for those on the receiving end, memory can be long indeed.... Even an empire cannot control the long-term effects of its policies."[3] In the post-Reagan era, blowback led to attacks on core values in the following ways: arrogant defiance of the separation of powers by the executive branch, the equating of freedom of speech in the form of dissent with a lack of patriotism, and a reflexive tendency toward self-censorship by the American press in times of conflict. Abroad, U.S. willingness to embrace self-determination remained highly situational. The persistence of these developments was not foreseeable in 1989, however. A majority of the American people and their elected representatives, as they transcended an amiable president's excesses, were only putting off having to deal with the consequences of his actions. This reaction was nothing new. Louis Hartz had warned against such "national blindness" in 1955, observing that "America must look to its contact with other nations to provide... that grain of relative insight that its own history has denied it."[4] The ongoing hold of the security ethos on foreign policy made Hartz's charge impossible to fulfill.

The Illusion of American Preeminence

Ronald Reagan bequeathed to George H. W. Bush a remarkable legacy. It was not just that the United States had regained global preeminence, which was partly true. By the late 1980s, the United States, like Rome in its

---

[3] Chalmers Johnson, *Blowback: The Costs and Consequences of American Empire* (New York: Metropolitan Books, 2000), 11–12, 13.

[4] Louis Hartz, *The Liberal Tradition in America* (New York: Harcourt, Brace & World, 1955), 287.

day, stood alone as an imposing military power. American exceptionalism was secure, so the triumphalists longed to believe. Yet, Reagan's primary legacy was one of illusion. In the telling of his most ardent supporters, then and later, people the world around placed great faith in American ideals, particularly democracy. Thus, it was that Afghanistan was perhaps on the verge of freedom, Chinese patriots defended universal values at Tiananmen Square in June 1989, and the Berlin Wall came crashing down in November of that year. The illusion Reagan conveyed was that strategic globalism was succeeding as grand strategy. Accordingly, the Bush White House acted as though the United States had regained the credibility and therefore the preeminent position it ostensibly held some three decades earlier when John F. Kennedy had succeeded Dwight D. Eisenhower as president.

In the years since Kennedy was at the helm in the White House, the United States had matured as a world power, or so Bush and his top advisers wanted American citizens and people elsewhere to conclude. Bush and National Security Adviser Brent Scowcroft saw theirs as "a new and different administration" that would not make mistakes like Iran-Contra.[5] Yet, the continuing failure to break American dependence on Persian Gulf oil was a far more serious blunder. That dependence, which had grown since the 1973 October War, did serve administration interests in the view of Bush and Scowcroft: "Access to the Gulf, . . . with its vast oil resources, was of intrinsically critical economic and security importance to the United States."[6] Neither credibility nor preeminence was imaginable without oil. For many Americans who in their own ways shared the security ethos, the same could be said about freedom.

Keeping the price of oil at an acceptable level linked the fate of strategic planning to the state of relations with Saudi Arabia. The Saudis were prepared to strengthen their ties with Washington in the wake of the Iran-Iraq War, which had bolstered Saddam Hussein's drive for power in the region. On the eve of Iraq's invasion of Kuwait in August 1990, Secretary of Defense Dick Cheney expressed concern about the safety of Saudi oil. To protect it, an extended U.S. military presence in Saudi Arabia was necessary, particularly if Bush's variant of strategic globalism was to have any meaning.[7] As Rachel Bronson, then director of Middle East Studies at the Council on Foreign Relations, aptly put it, the U.S.-Saudi relationship had become "thicker than oil."[8] Soon that would cause a problem in the kingdom. After victory over the Soviets and their allies in Afghanistan, Muslim jihadists including

[5] George Bush and Brent Scowcroft, *A World Transformed* (New York: Alfred A. Knopf, 1998), 37.

[6] Ibid., 305.

[7] Ibid., 316–17, 323, 327–8.

[8] Rachel Bronson, *Thicker than Oil: America's Uneasy Partnership with Saudi Arabia* (New York: Oxford University Press, 2006), 188–90.

Osama bin Laden began to denounce the Wahhabi monarchy for its moral laxity and betrayal of Islam.[9]

So in thrall to Persian Gulf oil as a symbol of power and authority was the United States that, in mid-2007, as the civil wars brought about by the occupation of Iraq raged on, the *New York Times* reported that the chief U.S. military commander for the Middle East, Admiral William J. Fallon, demanded the Iraqi parliament conclude work on an oil law. Not only would the law provide for the distribution of oil revenues among Shi'ites, Sunnis, and Kurds[10] but it also presumably would make that precious resource more predictably available for Western nations. Safeguarding Iraqi oil for the many ends it served was a major reason for the prospect of an indefinite deployment of U.S. forces in that country.[11]

It was, of course, not knowable in 1990 that, little more than a decade later, the United States would be engaged in a second war in the Persian Gulf region and beyond. Despite the problems that Saddam Hussein was causing for the Bush administration's pursuit of regional stability, about which more later, it was possible for leaders who had lived their lives in the vortex of Soviet-American tensions to imagine that a new strategic order was at hand. Their Eurocentric focus made them nearly giddy as the two Germanys became one, as communism rapidly receded in Eastern Europe, and as the Conference on Security and Cooperation in Europe (CSCE) proclaimed "democracy and human rights to be the way of the future," as William G. Hyland, the editor of *Foreign Affairs*, wrote about the Charter of Paris. This momentous achievement received the imprimatur of President Bush and Soviet General Secretary Mikhail Gorbachev at the CSCE meeting in November.[12]

New thinking about order and strategy soon took place within the administration and in the "security community" in the wake of these events. As the term "new world order" came into vogue, the likes of Henry Kissinger and Zbigniew Brzezinski weighed in concerning security policy. Their minimal differences reflected matters of emphasis about how America's constrained power could best serve the cause of strategic globalism and in no way questioned the legitimacy of America's geopolitical goals. That exercise would be left to the likes of ex-Nixon aide and conservative commentator Patrick Buchanan[13] and to critics like Chalmers Johnson and Noam Chomsky,

---

[9] Ibid., 193–200.

[10] *New York Times*, June 12, 2007. It is remarkable that a civilian official did not deliver Washington's demand to Iraqi officials. Also noteworthy was the presence of *New York Times* reporter Michael R. Gordon at the meeting.

[11] On the protracted presence of U.S. troops in Iraq, see *Washington Post*, June 1, 2007 and June 10, 2007.

[12] William G. Hyland, *Clinton's World: Remaking American Foreign Policy* (Westport: Praeger, 1999), 2.

[13] Ibid., 3–4, 8–10.

whose views rarely found their way into the mainstream press. Kissinger, dismissive of nomenclature whose provenance he could not claim, found Bush's new world order a muddled, neo-Wilsonian phenomenon; he worried that Bush was acting "as if it were just around the corner."[14] Brzezinski would later write that this order was "premised on a false hope" of a workable system, one that the "percolating global turmoil" would not permit.[15] Hyland, for his part, judged the "concept of a new world order . . . [to be] quite vague."[16]

No critic could gainsay Woodrow Wilson's influence on subsequent foreign policy and thinking about security. As was his wont, Kissinger praised Wilsonianism for engendering "[s]ome of the finest acts of twentieth-century diplomacy" and derided its "uncritical espousal of ethnic self-determination" and its "dream of universal collective security."[17] At the same time, he recognized the enduring appeal of the nation's belief in its exceptional nature. For the German-born Kissinger, this faith – the historical core of America's national identity – would mean serious problems for policymakers as the Cold War receded into history and memory.[18]

Kissinger was correct, but not for the reasons he advanced. The issue was not the inability of Wilsonian idealism to protect American values and interests in a hostile world. Rather, it was the logic of the security ethos that for nearly a century had turned the exceptionalist credo from an ideal, which others might emulate, into a tocsin, a call to arms as it were, compelling the export of market capitalism and growth of democracy in the name of security. Kissinger failed to appreciate the complex nature of Wilson's legacy. To be sure, Wilsonianism had an idealistic sheen; it also proffered a vision of political economy and a willingness to employ force that had made possible NSC-68 and strategic globalism. Wilsonianism and the various foreign policies it spawned were quintessentially American: They comprised an end-of-history project.[19] If such a conceit was alien to Kissinger's reading of history, it was warmly welcomed and popularized by other intellectuals in the defense-cum-security community, none more so than Francis Fukuyama, who in 1989 published his provocative essay, "The End of History?"[20]

---

[14] Kissinger, *Diplomacy*, 806.

[15] Zbigniew Brzezinski, *The Choice: Global Domination or Global Leadership* (New York: Basic Books, 2004), 137.

[16] Hyland, *Clinton's World*, 7.

[17] Kissinger, *Diplomacy*, 808, 809.

[18] See, for example, Jeremi Suri, *Henry Kissinger and the American Century* (Cambridge: Harvard University Press, 2007).

[19] Andrew J. Bacevich, *The New American Militarism: How Americans Are Seduced by War*, paper ed. (New York: Oxford University Press, 2006).

[20] For a critique of Fukuyama, see Bruce Cumings, "Time of Illusion," 77–89, in which Cumings argues that Fukuyama's was "a deeply conservative argument in favor of the status quo" (p. 85).

Fukuyama, then deputy director of the policy planning staff in the Department of State, concluded that the twentieth century was ending with the "triumph of the West" in "an unabashed victory of economic and political liberalism."[21] If he was correct, then the anxieties of a young Walter Lippmann, who feared that hallowed American traditions could not survive amid the complexities of modern life, could be put to rest.[22] Thus, the door was seemingly open for Bush's new world order, which he formally introduced in his 1991 State of the Union Address one month before Operation Desert Storm began. In his speech, Bush told Congress and the American people, "[W]e stand at a defining hour.... What is at stake ... is a big idea: a new world order, where diverse nations are drawn together in common cause to achieve the universal aspirations of mankind – peace and security, freedom, and the rule of law."[23]

Bush's imagined order was scarcely novel. Fundamentally, it entailed maintaining cordial relations with the Russians under Gorbachev and his unpredictable successor, Boris Yeltsin. Russia's stockpile of some 30,000 nuclear warheads made good relations mandatory. Though initially skeptical of Gorbachev's authenticity as a reformer, Bush realized that America's credibility as the sole superpower depended to a considerable extent on Russian responses to U.S. globalism.[24] Because of a keen need to fashion a broad-based coalition to oppose Iraqi power in the Persian Gulf and the Arab world, the United Nations became indispensable for the creation of a new world order.[25] The United States would not dare go it alone against Saddam Hussein unless it was prepared to incur the wrath of other states, which it clearly was not. In UN debates on Resolution 678 imposing a deadline for the withdrawal of Iraqi forces from Kuwait, Secretary of State James A. Baker III said, "[W]e now have the chance to build the world envisioned by the founders of the United Nations, ... [to achieve] peace and justice across the globe."[26] Baker observes in his memoirs that both he and Bush admired the philosophy behind Franklin Roosevelt's foreign policies: "Like George Bush, I was of a generation that embraced wholeheartedly the concept of a Pax Americana."[27] Bush and Baker were not supporters, however, of the political parity that multilateralism implies, although deference to that concept proved highly useful in forging a coalition against Saddam Hussein.

[21] Francis Fukuyama, "The End of History?," *The National Interest*, no. 16 (Summer 1989): 3–18; quoted words, 3.
[22] See Chapter 3.
[23] For Bush's address, see: http://www.presidency.ucsb.edu/ws/index.php?pid=19253.
[24] Bush and Scowcroft, *A World Transformed*, 164.
[25] Ibid., 486; James A. Baker III with Thomas M. DeFrank, *The Politics of Diplomacy: Revolution, War and Peace, 1989–1992* (New York: G. P. Putnam's Sons, 1995), 10.
[26] Baker, *The Politics of Diplomacy*, 320–8; quoted words, 326.
[27] Ibid., 276; Bush and Scowcroft, *A World Transformed*, 341.

Baker did not contemplate a return to Roosevelt's humanistic globalism, yet he perceived in the dramatic events of 1989–90 a unique opportunity to chart a multilateral course in world affairs. The problem was that, in an increasingly diverse, contentious world, the likelihood of sustaining a multilateral order was small indeed. Yet, Bush and Baker had to try. Not only was Bush inclined to follow Roosevelt's lead in a conceptual sense but he also readily accepted the accretion of power in the office of the president.

The world that Bush's national security team encountered was greatly at variance with what had existed before 1989; it was highly fragmented along political, ethnic, and religious lines. Even as the administration sought to make sense of what was happening in Eastern Europe and the Soviet Union, it dealt with other issues in ways that impaired the credibility of America's commitment to democracy, showed a disregard for collateral damage – the death of innocent civilians – as its security assets became expendable, and deepened involvement in the Persian Gulf and Southwest Asia to the point of helping spark the Islamic backlash that began in earnest in the mid-1990s. The promise of a new world order during the first Bush presidency did not affect such problematic outcomes. Several examples – drug control policy, the ouster from power of Manuel Noriega and Saddam Hussein, and lingering American involvement in Afghanistan – make the point.

Drug Control and Democracy in Latin America

The American public had long seen drug production and trafficking as grave threats to national well-being.[28] By the mid-1980s, the extent of drug consumption had risen to alarming levels, as had fears about violence linked to the drug trade. President Reagan issued National Security Decision Directive No. 221 in April 1986, declaring drugs a matter of national security. This action, which the House Select Committee on Narcotics Abuse and Control had clamored for since its inception a decade earlier, did not lead to a real war on drugs. Officials in Caspar Weinberger's Department of Defense knew that a drug war could not be won in any meaningful way, so they refused to commit more than modest resources to the effort. In fact, if a war on drugs was not going to be waged on the home front, then fighting drugs abroad had to be folded into security policy. Because of the importance of the Mujahedin in Afghanistan and the Nicaraguan Contras to greater security interests despite their involvement in drug trafficking, drug control efforts focused on the Andes and Mexico. When Bush's Andean drug strategy was announced in fall 1989, it was apparent that it shared certain

---

[28] Generally see William O. Walker III, *Drug Control in the Americas*, rev. ed. (Albuquerque: University of New Mexico Press, 1989); in addition see idem, "Drug Control and U.S. Hegemony," in John D. Martz, ed., *United States Policy in Latin America: A Decade of Crisis and Challenge* (Lincoln: University of Nebraska Press, 1995), 299–319.

basic assumptions with U.S. counterinsurgency doctrine of earlier years. Radicals, in this case growers and traffickers, had to be contained with force if democracy, development, and free-market economics were going to flourish.[29] Police, the armed forces, and intelligence services would serve as valuable security assets in that endeavor.

Raising the drug issue with Mexico was politically delicate because the Mexican government viewed consumption as the real drug problem. In contrast, the basis of U.S. policy remained, as before, control at the source. Even though Richard Nixon's 1969 affront to Mexican sensibility, Operation Intercept, had quickly become Operation Cooperation, officials in Mexico City saw U.S. policy as a challenge to their nation's sovereignty. The murder of Drug Enforcement Administration (DEA) agent Enrique Camarena Salazar in early 1985 by Mexican drug gangs greatly complicated matters.[30] Congress reacted by imposing on the State Department a requirement to certify whether foreign governments were complying with U.S. policy; Mexico then felt vindicated in its position and was reluctant to work closely with the DEA or other U.S. agencies. Successes in interdicting South American cocaine in Florida's environs, coordinated in the office of Vice President Bush, had led Colombian traffickers to rely on distribution networks through Mexico. One result was a surge in drug-related corruption and violence that worsened over time. By 2008, state integrity seemed greatly dependent on whether Mexico's government could successfully contain drug-related crime and its corrosive effect on the nation. The desertion of perhaps 120,000 soldiers from military service after 1999 made it difficult for President Felipe Calderón to keep the violence in check.[31]

U.S. authorities have historically had little faith in Mexican drug control. In the late 1980s, though, neither nation could afford a serious strain in relations as they worked to restore Mexico to economic health. The ultimate goal in Washington and Mexico City became passage of the North American Free Trade Agreement (NAFTA). Growing dissatisfaction with Mexico on the drug issue produced a national interest certification in 1988 and a Senate vote for censure. Carlos Salinas de Gortari, who became president in 1988, was committed to extensive privatization of his nation's economy; he welcomed the diversion that NAFTA provided from the constant focus on drugs.[32] Salinas did respond, however, to pressures from Washington

[29] William O. Walker III, "The Bush Administration's Andean Drug Strategy in Historical Perspective," in Bruce M. Bagley and William O. Walker III, eds., *Drug Trafficking in the Americas* (New Brunswick: Transaction Publishers, 1994), 9–11.

[30] William O. Walker III, "After Camarena," in Bagley and Walker, eds., *Drug Trafficking in the Americas*, 395–422.

[31] See http://news.bbc.co.uk/go/pr/fr/-/2/hi/americas/6250200.stm.

[32] George W. Grayson, "U.S.-Mexican Relations: The Challenge of NAFTA," in Martz, ed., *United States Policy in Latin America*, 113–43. Congress ratified NAFTA in November 1993.

by militarizing antidrug campaigns to an unprecedented extent, a step that Mexico would not then have taken on its own, despite identifying drugs as a security concern.

By inserting itself into Mexican affairs, the United States became closely tied to a justice system that followed vastly different standards of prosecution and conviction; to police and military forces that operated with relative impunity despite evidence of gross human rights violations; and to a bureaucracy of the ruling Institutional Revolutionary Party, or PRI, whose primary goal was maintaining its hold on power. During the late 1980s and 1990s, the CIA helped form, equip, and train elite antinarcotics military units that operated far beyond the reach of civilian oversight. Despite endemic corruption, Mexico's intelligence service, the *Dirección Federal de Seguridad* (DFS), had long been a reliable security asset, waging a struggle against communists and the Mexican Left. The DFS was disbanded for complicity in the drug trade in the wake of Camarena's murder. A special antinarcotics unit that was created in the attorney general's office in 1992, the *Instituto Nacional para el Combate a las Drogas* (National Institute to Fight Drugs), met a similar fate when its celebrated leader, General Jesús Gutiérrez Rebollo, was found to be in the pay of the Juárez cartel.[33] Yet, these events did not lead to reconsideration of the security relationship with Mexico, let alone to unease about its detrimental impact on support for democracy abroad. Whatever frustration DEA agents in the field felt about the difficulty of obtaining cooperation from Mexico on drugs, they reluctantly learned to put such concerns aside in the name of greater security interests.[34] "The CIA didn't give a damn about anything but Cuba and the Soviets," lamented one agent who understood that his was a lost cause.[35]

Relations with Mexico had long set the tone for drug control in the Americas. That ceased to be the case with the surge of cocaine consumption and trafficking in the 1980s when Bolivia, Peru, and Colombia seized Washington's attention as never before. By the end of Bush's presidency, the United States had created the Office for National Drug Control Policy (ONDCP), named a drug "czar," and was involved through the Andean Drug Strategy with the three nations in ways that tended both to constrain their sovereignty and restrict democratic access for untold thousands of people. The operating assumptions in Washington, which derived from allegiance to the basic principle of control at the source, were that Bolivia and Peru were inept, and Colombia not much better, where drug control was concerned.

---

[33] Laurie Freeman and Jorge Luis Sierra, "Mexico: The Militarization Trap," in Coletta A. Youngers and Eileen Rosin, eds., *Drugs and Democracy in Latin America: The Impact of U.S. Policy* (Boulder: Lynne Rienner, 2005), 263–302.

[34] Walker, "After Camarena," 399–410.

[35] *Washington Post*, July 16, 1990.

Bolivia, having suffered a "cocaine coup" in 1980, was particularly sus-
ceptible to U.S. pressure to militarize its antidrug policy when civilian rule
returned two years later. A chronically weak economy left Bolivia, as in
the 1920s, in a state of dependency on international financial institutions
and on the whims of drug policy officials. President Victor Paz Estenssoro
implemented austerity measures to control hyperinflation and accepted U.S.
assistance to form and train (initially at the School of the Americas) an elite,
mobile rural counternarcotics force, which like Mexico's DFS was suscep-
tible to corruption. In addition, and without the required approval of the
National Congress, he permitted U.S. troops to participate in Operation
Blast Furnace, an anti-coca campaign lasting from July to November 1986.
Subsequent agreements led to the trans-Andean Operation Snowcap and
allowed the U.S. military and the DEA to continue operating in Bolivia.
Indicative of the depth of U.S. influence was Law 1008, making new coca
planting illegal. It also mandated a plan for coca eradication in traditional
growing regions over the next decade. The Bolivian Congress enacted Law
1008 at Washington's insistence in July 1988, thus guaranteeing the restoration of temporarily withheld economic assistance.[36]

Paz's successor, Jaime Paz Zamora, followed suit, signing a secret agreement (Annex III) in May 1990 with the United States that enhanced the
counternarcotics role of the Bolivian military. This agreement put pressure on special antidrug units to produce results. Human rights violations
increased despite the DEA's supervisory role over operations. Controversial,
too, was the presence of Ambassador Robert Gelbard, who had served in
the Peace Corps in Cochabamba in the 1960s. Determined to make Snowcap a success, Gelbard insinuated himself deeply into Bolivian politics. The
more Paz Zamora gave in to U.S. policy, the more coca growers resisted
the imposition of state authority. Strikes in regions like the Chapare became
common. The National Congress ultimately had little choice but to allow
U.S. advisers to train counternarcotics units in country; permission was
granted in April 1991, furthering the Bush administration's $2.2 billion
policy.[37] The drug war in Bolivia, one analyst concluded, was "dominated
by a Cold War strategy."[38] President Gonzalo Sánchez de Lozada, who
replaced Paz Zamora in 1993, surveyed the situation he inherited: "The
dependency is terrible; the International Monetary Fund comes, the United

---

[36] Kathryn Ledebur, "Bolivia: Clear Consequences," in Youngers and Rosin, eds., *Drugs and
Democracy*, 143–53.

[37] Eduardo A. Gamarra, "U.S.-Bolivia Counternarcotics Efforts during the Paz Zamora Administration: 1989–1992," in Bagley and Walker, eds., *Drug Trafficking in the Americas*, 221–
32.

[38] Eduardo A. Gamarra, "The United States and Bolivia: Fighting the Drug War," in Victor
Bulmer-Thomas and James Dunkerley, eds., *The United States and Latin America: The New
Agenda* (London and Cambridge: Institute of Latin American Studies, University of London
and David Rockefeller Center for Latin American Studies, Harvard University, 1999), 199.

States Embassy comes, the World Bank comes, and they all tell us what to do."[39]

Because of its struggle against the Maoist organization *Sendero Luminoso*, or Shining Path, which may have taken 25,000 lives between 1980 and 1992, Peru resisted falling wholly under the sway of U.S. drug policy. This was no small feat because Peru produced 65 percent of the coca leaf grown in the world. The economic crisis of the 1980s had hit Peru especially hard; the gross national product fell 30 percent and triple-digit inflation rose to more than 7,600 percent in 1990. Two-thirds of all Peruvians lived in or near poverty. Alberto Fujimori took office as president in 1990 and immediately applied shock treatment to bring inflation under control. He also resumed payments, which his predecessor Alan García had suspended, on a large foreign debt to international financial institutions, which resulted in the signing of new agreements of more than $2 billion with the International Monetary Fund, the World Bank, and the Inter-American Development Bank.[40]

More than 600,000 farmers grew coca in Bolivia and Peru. In Peru, many lived in the Upper Huallaga Valley, a Shining Path stronghold, where growing coca brought greater income than alternate crops like cacao and corn. Violence became common in the Upper Huallaga, as growers resisted U.S.-funded eradication campaigns and Shining Path taxed the cocaine paste purchased primarily by Colombian traffickers. Operation Snowcap and Bush's Andean Drug Strategy greatly complicated matters for García, who could not cope with the devastating combination of drugs, guerrillas, and economic woes.

On taking office in July 1990, Fujimori relied heavily on the military to cement his hold on power. He also developed an important relationship with Vladimiro Montesinos, a former army captain who had previously provided intelligence information on the military to the CIA. As a lawyer in the 1980s, he defended drug traffickers and military officers accused of human rights abuses. Fujimori made Montesinos his chief security adviser, prompting the DEA to complain bitterly but to no avail because of overriding CIA interests. The relationship between the CIA and Montesinos apparently continued into the late 1990s as Fujimori, following his *autogolpe* of April 5, 1992, which shut down congress and the judiciary and suspended the constitution, transformed democratic Peru into his personal fiefdom.[41]

The Bush administration determined that order took precedence over democracy. It never decertified Peru despite rampant corruption in the Upper

---

[39] Quoted in Ledebur, "Bolivia," 146.

[40] David Scott Palmer, "Peru, Drugs, and Shining Path," in Bagley and Walker, eds., *Drug Trafficking in the Americas*, 179–81.

[41] Isaias Rojas, "Peru: Drug Control Policy, Human Rights, and Democracy," in Youngers and Rosin, eds., *Drugs and Democracy*, 187–94; Catherine M. Conaghan, *Fujimori's Peru: Deception in the Public Sphere* (Pittsburgh: University of Pittsburgh Press, 2005), 224.

Huallaga Valley, where the military had been placed in charge of drug control and likely used U.S. aid to combat Shining Path while offering protection to coca growers and drug traffickers. About U.S. counternarcotics assistance being used against the *senderistas*, one U.S. military official rejoiced, "We're going back to what we know best – how to fight the commies."[42]

Things did not work out that way, however. In Washington, drug control activists and human rights advocates combined to curtail military assistance to Peru, although some antidrug funding continued. The arrest in September 1992 of Shining Path's leader Abimael Guzmán bought time for Fujimori and Montesinos to seize virtual control of the state. A newly elected Constituent Assembly then proceeded to write a constitution in 1993 allowing for presidential succession that enabled Fujimori to seek the presidency in 1995. With Fujimori's reelection, Montesinos continued as his top aide until two months before the president's resignation in disgrace when he was in Japan in 2000.[43] From 1989 through 1992, the Bush administration neither exercised the influence over Peru that it did over Bolivia nor succeeded in using drug control policy to bolster Peruvian democracy. The often tense relations with Peru reveal instead an abiding belief in intelligence assets as vital to U.S. security.

Relations with Colombia over drug control had been contentious for years. As elsewhere, the issues were drug-related corruption and violence and state sovereignty in the face of U.S. pressure for stronger counternarcotics activity. Compounding the situation was the murder at the behest of the Medellín cartel in August 1989 of Liberal presidential candidate Luis Carlos Galán; Medellín's battle with another cocaine cartel headquartered in Cali; the war against the state waged by the leftist *Fuerzas Armadas Revolucionarias de Colombia*, or FARC (Revolutionary Armed Forces of Colombia), and the *Ejército de Liberación Nacional*, or ELN (Army of National Liberation); and various paramilitary groups who opposed the rebels and later coalesced into the *Autodefensas Unidas de Colombia*, or AUC (United Self-Defense Forces of Colombia), which was notorious for violating human rights with impunity. These conditions, one observer commented, made democracy in Colombia "a sham concealing an authoritarian regime"[44]

President Virgilio Barco Vargas and his successor César Gaviria Trujillo, like others before them, were still struggling with the consequences of the years of violence, or *la Violencia*, that had plagued Colombia following the assassination of Liberal Jorge Gaitán in 1948. From the mid-1980s on, at least 5,000 people were dying annually as a result of violence related to the

[42] *Newsweek*, May 21, 1990, p. 37.

[43] Rojas, "Peru," 192–6.

[44] Quoted in William O. Walker III, "The United States, Colombia, and Drug Policy, 1984–2004: A Study of Quiet Anti-Americanism," in Alan McPherson, ed., *Anti-Americanism in Latin America and the Caribbean* (New York: Berghahn Books, 2006), 244.

drug trade. After Galán's murder, Barco declared war against Medellín and turned the military against the cartel, which made the mistake of responding in kind. With the help of U.S. intelligence and advisers, the dismantling of Medellín's operations had begun.[45]

At the same time, Barco and Gaviria, who took office in August 1990, never lost sight of their main objective – restoring the integrity of the Colombian state. Therein lay the heart of the problem for Washington: To follow Colombia's lead on drugs would be to deny the relevance of traditional supply-side drug policy. The Bush administration had envisioned a war on drugs in the Western Hemisphere as a major part of its pursuit of strategic globalism. Seen in that light, the intense pressure on Bolivia and the quixotic accommodation with Fujimori and Montesinos in Peru become explicable, as does the pattern of forbearance toward Mexico. Yet, because Colombia provided 80 percent of the cocaine and 25 percent of the marijuana reaching the United States around 1990, relations with Bogotá over drug control became a test of wills. Even the surrender in June 1991 of Medellín's feared leader, Pablo Escobar, did not ease tensions. Declared ONDCP head Bob Martinez, "I think Colombia will be on trial with Pablo Escobar."[46] Barco, a former ambassador to the United States, had managed to defend Colombian sovereignty without offending Washington. Gaviria proved to be less adept at appeasing the United States, however; following Escobar's escape from prison in July 1992, he incurred the wrath of critics at home and abroad. Preparing to leave office in July 1994, after he grudgingly accepted U.S. help in the tracking and killing of Escobar the previous December, Gaviria denounced the drug war as "a war that is not ours."[47]

The waning of the Cold War theoretically provided an opportunity for the United States to reconsider its foreign policy and strategic priorities. The Andean Drug Strategy could have been an integral part of that process had it been implemented. Meetings in Cartagena, Colombia, and San Antonio, Texas, in 1990 and 1992 showed the limits of new thinking on the part of the United States.[48] At Cartagena, Barco reminded Bush and Baker of the price Colombia was paying in the war on drugs, Paz Zamora reiterated the importance of economic assistance for Bolivia, and Peru's Garcia brought a coca farmer with him to remind the Americans of the human cost of drug control. Washington's admission, a first at a multilateral gathering, that

---

[45] William O. Walker III, "The Limits of Coercive Diplomacy: U.S. Drug Policy and Colombian State Stability, 1978–1997," in H. Richard Friman and Peter Andreas, eds., *The Illicit Global Economy and State Power* (Lanham: Rowman & Littlefield, 1999), 153–7.

[46] *Washington Post*, June 24, 1991.

[47] Mark Bowden, *Killing Pablo: The Hunt for the World's Greatest Outlaw* (New York: Atlantic Monthly Press, 1991); Gaviria quoted in *El Tiempo* (Bogotá), July 12, 1994.

[48] At a meeting concerning U.S.-Colombian relations, held in Washington, D.C., in June 1993, when it was suggested that U.S. drug policy was not working, a mid-level DEA official turned to me and remarked, "At least we still have Bolivia to kick around."

drug consumption rivaled production and trafficking as a serious problem raised hopes in Latin America about a change in U.S. policy. By the time Mexico joined the four countries at the subsequent meeting in San Antonio, it was clear that any change in U.S. policy would be merely tactical.[49]

A foreign assistance program, which might have made drugs less of an obstacle to democratic inclusion in the Andes, was not in evidence. Rather, the Bush administration, despite well-founded concern in Congress about human rights, continued to emphasize force as the main component of drug control policy.[50] As the Washington Office on Latin America documented in 2005, low-intensity conflict, a mainstay of U.S. security policy during the Cold War, had exerted a negative impact on democracy throughout the hemisphere as it became a basic part of drug control. This effect was seen in a weakening of the rule of law, instability in foreign investment and the flight of intellectual capital, the persistence of poverty, environmental damage, and an escalation of violence against women and children.[51] Why did the administration deem force to be the requisite first response? Like his predecessors, Bush tended to relegate human security to a secondary status. His signal contribution was to bring drug policy fully into the realm of national security.

Panama and Iraq as Security Assets

Bush did nothing quite so novel when he jettisoned two intelligence-cum-security assets, Manuel Antonio Noriega and Saddam Hussein. Over-throwing or causing authoritarian rulers to be removed was not new. The assassination of Ngo Dinh Diem in November 1963 was merely an extreme example of what could happen to clients when they lost their usefulness to Washington. Others who fell from grace included Cuba's Fulgencio Batista, the Dominican Republic's Rafael Trujillo, and Nicaragua's Anastasio Somoza. The Noriega and Saddam examples are noteworthy, though, because they occurred as the White House was trying to purge memories of defeat in Vietnam and restore U.S. credibility around the world.

Beginning in the late 1960s after training at the School of the Americas, Noriega had little trouble ingratiating himself with the U.S. government. Panama was the center of intelligence collection in Latin America, and Noriega as the head of G2, the intelligence branch of Panama's National Guard, was the keeper and purveyor of secrets for anyone willing to pay,

---

[49] Walker, "Drug Control and U.S. Hegemony," 314–15.

[50] Americas Watch, *Peru under Fire: Human Rights Since the Return of Democracy* (New Haven: Yale University Press, 1992); idem, *Political Murder and Reform in Colombia: The Violence Continues* (New York: Americas Watch, 1992); Washington Office on Latin America, *Clear and Present Dangers: The U.S. Military and the War on Drugs in the Andes* (Washington, DC: Washington Office on Latin America, 1991).

[51] See Youngers and Rosin, eds., *Drugs and Democracy*.

including Fidel Castro and the drug bosses of Medellín. Noriega's ability to make himself indispensable to men like CIA Director William Casey and Oliver North as a backer of the Nicaraguan Contras before the Iran-Contra scandal broke seemed to assure his political survival.[52] If he really believed that, then he was deluding himself as subsequent events would show.

Both the CIA and the DEA praised Noriega for his value as an intelligence asset while knowing that the general was untrustworthy. In fact, the CIA had wondered in 1972 whether Noriega should be assassinated because of his reputed involvement with drug trafficking.[53] Bush, as CIA director, evidently warned the Panamanian in December 1976 that he and Omar Torrijos Herrera, who had seized power in 1968, needed to conform to U.S. security policy. They complied but only to the extent that Jimmy Carter was able to obtain Senate ratification of the Panama Canal Treaty in February 1978. Three years later, Torrijos died in a plane crash, precluding a possible turn toward democracy in national politics. Noriega soon dominated the political stage as a result of the transformation of the National Guard into the more powerful Panamanian Defense Force (PDF), which he commanded after promoting himself to the rank of general. He was well positioned and, with $185,000 per year being paid into an account at the Bank for Credit and Commerce International, compensated nicely to serve as Washington's staunch anticommunist ally in a vital locale.

Although evidence remains elusive, a Noriega-Bush connection possibly tightened as the Reagan administration sought to avoid scrutiny of its clandestine support for the Contras. CIA Director William Casey short-circuited whatever pressure may have been building for Noriega to move toward free elections by failing to raise the subject in a November 1985 meeting with the general.[54] Until February 1988, when grand juries in Tampa and Miami handed down indictments against him for racketeering, specifically for drug trafficking and money laundering, Noriega continued to operate with relative ease as a double agent and more.[55]

Like others whose activities Washington countenanced in the name of security, Noriega finally overplayed his hand. He essentially dared the

[52] John Dinges, *Our Man in Panama: How General Noriega Used the United States – And Made Millions in Drugs and Arms* (New York: Random House, 1990); Russell Crandall, *Gunboat Democracy: U.S. Interventions in the Dominican Republic, Grenada, and Panama* (Lanham: Rowman & Littlefield, 2006), 171–224.

[53] Dinges, *Our Man in Panama*, 63–4; U.S. Congress, Senate, *Hearings before the Subcommittee on Terrorism, Narcotics and International Communications of the Committee on Foreign Relations*, "Drugs, Law Enforcement and Foreign Policy: Panama," 100 Cong., 1 sess., 8–11 February 1988, Part 2 (Washington, DC: Government Printing Office, 1988), 391–6. Noriega's association with the illegal drug business was probably greatest between 1981 and 1984, though he never entirely severed his ties to it.

[54] Frederick Kempe, "The Noriega Files," *Newsweek*, January 15, 1990, pp. 19–24.

[55] James Chace, "Getting to Sack the General," *New York Review of Books*, April 28, 1988, pp. 49–55.

U.S. government, which had, in the words of one diplomat, "coddled [him] in the interests of Nicaraguan policy," to withdraw its support.[56] And so it did after initial misgivings, prompted by members of Congress who voiced concerns about violations of human rights, by several Department of State officials who took seriously the Reagan administration's avowed promotion of democracy (at least in Panama), and by the thousands of Panamanians who had wearied of Noriega's repressive rule.

Ferdinand Marcos had recently fallen from power in the Philippines, an event that led to the departure of U.S. forces from Clark air base and Subic naval base,[57] and Jean-Claude Duvalier had fled Haiti in the night for the luxury of the French Riviera. Neither event appeared to affect Noriega. Washington soon transferred Panama's assets to the president in exile, Eric Arturo Delvalle, barred American companies from paying taxes in Panama, and ended the quota on Panamanian sugar. The Department of State advocated a quick strike to remove Noriega from power, whereas the Defense Department wanted to give sanctions more time to work. From early 1988 into mid-1989, the PDF harassed U.S. military personnel and citizens, occasionally shooting at them. On taking office, Bush authorized the CIA to try to get rid of Noriega, although events on the scene outran that effort. Meanwhile, the National Endowment for Democracy spent some $10 million to influence the presidential election in May 1989, the result of which Noriega refused to accept, instead naming an associate as the new president.[58]

Bush sent fresh troops to Panama over reservations of the head of the Joint Chiefs of Staff, Admiral William Crowe, who was replaced by the more willing General Colin Powell. Increasing shows of force throughout the remainder of the year put pressure on Noriega to relinquish his hold on power. A coup attempt in October failed because it did not occur, in words attributed to Powell, "on a U.S. timetable."[59] Regime change was in the offing, though. Operation Just Cause began on December 20; the rapid collapse of the PDF and the violent "Dignity Battalions" left the United States unprepared to restore order or put in place a government that it could work with, one that could win the support of the Panamanian people. On January 3, 1990, Noriega surrendered to American forces, after having been subjected to incessant loud music at the Vatican embassy where he had sought political asylum. "The United States," Secretary of State James Baker later wrote, "was simply enforcing the will of the Panamanian people."[60]

---

[56] Frank McNeill, *War and Peace in Central America: Reality and Illusion* (New York: Charles Scribner's Sons, 1988), 237.

[57] Johnson, *The Sorrows of Empire*, 211–13; Mann, *Rise of the Vulcans*, 206–8.

[58] Crandall, *Gunboat Democracy*, 193–6.

[59] Quoted in ibid., 199.

[60] Ibid., 199–207; Baker, *The Politics of Diplomacy*, 193–4.

Two dozen Americans died in Operation Just Cause. The number of Panamanian dead is uncertain, with perhaps 300 civilians, many of whom were blacks and mestizos, and between 50 and 200 military personnel perishing.[61] What was accomplished? A brutal dictator fell from power, and a form of representative government, benefiting from Washington's blessing, took his place. More than that, the military exercise was "manna from heaven," as the journalist Bob Woodward paraphrased Colin Powell.[62] That is, the invasion perpetuated a belief in America's entitlement to intervene in the internal affairs of other states, their sovereignty notwithstanding. Baker rejoiced that Just Cause altered "the mind-set of the American people about the use of force" and clearly "established an emotional predicate" for the subsequent resort to force in Iraq.[63] Strategic globalism as grand strategy was alive and well in the Bush White House. Saddam Hussein was about to experience what that meant.

Saddam had reason to believe that he was Washington's leading man in the Persian Gulf region in 1989. With the rupture in Iraqi-U.S. relations at the time of the Six Day War in 1967, after which the radical Ba'ath Party leaned toward Moscow, Iran's Islamic revolution led by Ayatollah Ruhollah Khomeini in 1979 helped Saddam begin to repair relations with Washington. At home, Saddam, as worried about the situation in Iran as the Carter administration, consolidated his power, becoming president in July 1979. He feared that the Soviet invasion of Afghanistan in December 1979 could prevent him from achieving preeminence in the region. Several months later in April 1980, Zbigniew Brzezinski seemed to offer Saddam a helping hand, noting, "We see no fundamental incompatibility of interests between the United States and Iraq."[64]

When Saddam's forces attacked Iran in September, Carter and Brzezinski were not prepared to provide assistance, though they apparently did not rule out that option.[65] What they did do, consistent with the Carter Doctrine,[66] was send AWACS planes to the Saudis and hope that Iran could be contained. By 1982, Iran was prevailing in the war with Iraq and was on the verge of

---

[61] Inaccurate, initial estimates for Panamanian casualties exceeded 4,000. Physicians for Human Rights, *Operation "Just Cause": The Human Cost of Military Action in Panama* (Boston: Physicians for Human Rights, 1991), 16–26; John Lindsay-Poland, *Emperors in the Jungle: The Hidden History of the U.S. in Panama* (Durham: Duke University Press, 2003), 118–19.

[62] Bob Woodward, *The Commanders* (New York: Simon & Schuster, 1991), 194.

[63] Baker, *The Politics of Diplomacy*, 194.

[64] Quoted in Bruce W. Jentleson, *With Friends like These: Reagan, Bush, and Saddam, 1982–1990* (New York: W. W. Norton & Company, 1994), 34.

[65] Zbigniew Brzezinski, *Power and Principle: Memoirs of the National Security Adviser, 1977–1981* (New York: Farrar, Straus and Giroux, 1983), 506.

[66] Bacevich, *New American Militarism*, 179–83.

disrupting stability in the Persian Gulf and beyond. The threat to Gulf oil reserves and the prospect of widespread Shi'ite-induced terror, which became a reality in Lebanon in October 1983 with the killing of 241 U.S. Marines in their barracks, moved Washington to overlook whatever affinity still existed between Iraq and the Soviet Union.[67] Thus, it was that Donald Rumsfeld traveled to Baghdad as Reagan's emissary in December 1983 to court Saddam Hussein.

Formal relations were restored and the State Department removed Iraq from its list of nations supporting terrorism. The Commodity Credit Corporation made it possible for Iraq to import food; the Export-Import Bank, under pressure from Vice President Bush, extended credits to help with the construction of an oil pipeline; and despite official neutrality on the Iran–Iraq war, the Reagan administration encouraged third-country arms sales to Baghdad. In addition, through a program overseen by Robert M. Gates, CIA deputy director, Washington began sharing intelligence with Saddam's government, a strong indication of how Iraq fit into U.S. strategic planning.[68]

A Soviet-American initiative forced the war to conclude as a stalemate in August 1988. Despite concern since mid-decade over Iraq's use of chemical weapons, cultivating close relations with Saddam continued uninterrupted. The provision of dual-use technology that could be used to enhance Iraq's nuclear and chemical weapons programs is the prime example of this endeavor. Vice President Bush thought it might make Saddam a more tractable ally.[69] It is little wonder that the Iraqi strongman believed he had a free hand to deal with troublesome Shi'ites and Kurds at home. When the fighting with Iran stopped, Saddam again brutally vented his rage on Kurdish villages close to the Turkish border.[70] Some Kurds sided with Iran against Iraq, provoking Saddam to exact revenge. His efforts took an especially murderous turn early in 1988. As details of the new campaign became known, the White House moved to control the damage by watering down an attempt in Congress to impose wide-ranging sanctions. One leading scholar of U.S.-Iraqi relations has traced the commercial and financial concerns that were brought to bear on American policymaking.[71] It is clear that geopolitics and economic considerations had trumped the U.S. commitment to

---

[67] Jentleson, *With Friends like These*, 36–7; National Security Archive, Electronic Briefing Book No. 167, *Saddam's Iron Grip: Intelligence Reports on Saddam Hussein's Reign*, Document 3: "SNIE 34/36.2–82, Implications of Iran's Victory over Iraq, June 8, 1982," http://www.gwu.edu/~nsarchiv/NSAEBB/NSAEBB167/03.pdf, pp. 10–12.

[68] National Security Archive, Electronic Briefing Book No. 82, *Shaking Hands with Saddam Hussein: The U.S. Tilts toward Iraq, 1980–1984*, Documents 22, 26–55, http://www.gwu.edu/~nsarchiv/NSAEBB/NSAEBB82/index.htm#docs.

[69] Jentleson, *With Friends like These*, 59–67.

[70] Joost R. Hiltermann, *A Poisonous Affair: America, Iraq, and the Gassing of Halabja* (New York: Cambridge University Press, 2007).

[71] Jentleson, *With Friends like These*, 80–6.

human security. At least for Iraqi Kurdistan, the democracy project of the Republican White House was a farce.

Bush did not discard the idea of accommodating Saddam until the invasion of Kuwait in August 1990. National Security Directive 26 (NSD 26), which the president signed in October 1989, called for normal relations between the United States and Iraq. Giving lip service to human rights, NSD 26 advocated the "use of economic incentives for Iraq to moderate its behavior and to increase our influence with Iraq."[72] As with Jiang Jieshi, Ngo Dinh Diem, and other authoritarian rulers with whom the United States had dealt since the turn to globalism in the late 1930s, the hope that reform would accompany the generosity bestowed on a security asset like Saddam Hussein was an exercise in self-delusion. Secretary of State Baker argued otherwise, asserting, "We were under no illusions about Saddam's brutality toward his own people or his capacity for escalating tensions with his neighbors."[73] The available record is not that definitive.

Given the desire of the White House to contain both Iranian and Soviet influence in the greater Middle East, the accommodation of Saddam fit comfortably into Bush's strategic calculus. Iraq, presumably chastened by the losses in the war with Iran and in need of foreign exchange and new opportunities for trade, would become a voice of moderation in the Arab world, at least in private. Were that to happen, the chances of promoting an Israeli-Palestinian peace agreement might improve, which would further insinuate U.S. influence into the Middle East. Baker, in an address in May 1989 to the American Israel Public Affairs Committee (AIPAC), had declared that Israel must "lay aside once and for all the unrealistic vision of a greater Israel" and should "reach out to Palestinians as neighbors who deserve political rights."[74] It was also critically important to the Bush administration to protect Saudi oil, the fuel of U.S. strategy in the region.

Accommodation of Saddam became impossible by July 1990, however. Although a member of the Organization of Petroleum Exporting Countries (OPEC), Kuwait was producing more oil than its allotment, thus further imperiling Iraq's economy and putting Saddam's plans to aggrandize his power at risk. Did it matter who pumped Kuwait's oil? Apparently not to Saudi Arabia's King Fahd or the leaders of Egypt and Jordan, who were not alarmed at an Iraqi troop build-up near the Kuwait border.[75] The Bush administration was concerned about access to Saudi oil and, more broadly, about what Saddam's actions meant for U.S. credibility. Hence, the invasion of Kuwait on August 2 was unacceptable. Deputy Secretary of State Lawrence S. Eagleburger called it "the first test of the postwar system" and

[72] See http://www.fas.org/irp/offdocs/nsd/nsd26.pdf.
[73] Baker, *The Politics of Diplomacy*, 264.
[74] *New York Times*, May 23, 1989.
[75] Bronson, *Thicker than Oil*, 192.

asserted that Saudi Arabia and Israel were now in danger.[76] He was hardly alone; after failing to anticipate Iraq's move into Kuwait, the CIA became similarly alarmist. It reported that Saddam would almost certainly attack Saudi Arabia. This assessment was largely speculative, yet it reinforced what the White House already believed. Journalist Tim Weiner found "no hard evidence behind the warnings."[77]

The United States, having received little of value during its association with Saddam Hussein, was prepared not only to abandon the Iraqi leader but also to teach him a lesson. Whether she did so wittingly or not, Ambassador April Glaspie served as a means to those ends. By the time Glaspie met with Saddam on July 25, U.S. ships were speeding their way to the area to make a show of force. Saddam did not believe that the United States would come to the defense of Kuwait. Glaspie, following policy as she understood it, declared that the United States had no "opinion on inter-Arab disputes such as your border dispute with Kuwait." Furthermore, a last-minute message from Bush seemed reassuring. Making the situation more confusing for Baghdad, the U.S. Senate passed a bill calling for economic sanctions, to which the White House strongly objected. After a meeting of OPEC at which oil prices were raised, though less than Saddam desired, the invasion of Kuwait was all but assured.[78] The courting of Saddam Hussein was at an end.

However indicative Saddam's scheming was of his megalomania, he served U.S. strategic interests. Vast oil reserves had given Saudi Arabia a measure of autonomy in foreign policy that discomfited Bush and his security advisers.[79] In apparent contradiction of Riyadh's earlier position, the Saudi ambassador in Washington, Prince Bandar bin Sultan, told Colin Powell that, should Saddam move against Kuwait, "you will have to help us all."[80] Operation Desert Shield and Operation Desert Storm, in which at least 35,000 Iraqis died, were designed to do just that. They deepened U.S. involvement in the Persian Gulf and shifted the balance in the U.S.-Saudi relationship for a time, enabling the administration to establish a greater presence in the kingdom. It did not matter that relatively few foreign personnel remained there after the defeat of Iraq in March 1991. For radical Islamic critics of the house of Saud, many of whom had waged jihad in Afghanistan assisted by the monarchy's largesse, authorities in Riyadh had gone too far in inviting Western infidels into the kingdom. They also believed

---

[76] Quoted in Bush and Scowcroft, *A World Transformed*, 323.

[77] Tim Weiner, *Legacy of Ashes: The History of the CIA* (New York: Doubleday, 2007), 41.

[78] Lawrence Freedman and Efraim Karsh, *The Gulf Conflict, 1990–1991: Diplomacy and War in the New World Order* (Princeton: Princeton University Press, 1993), 50–61; quoted words, 53. For Bush's message to Saddam, see Jentleson, *With Friends like These*, 172.

[79] Bronson, *Thicker than Oil*, 188–92.

[80] Quoted in Woodward, *The Commanders*, 214.

that, in bearing a large percentage of the costs of the war, Saudi Arabia was becoming even more aligned with the West.

From Washington's vantage point, a new world order, one conducive to strategic globalism, seemed at hand. U.S.-dominated multilateralism had succeeded in restoring American hegemony, or so it appeared.[81] To remove Saddam from power would have prolonged the war, however, producing fissures in the coalition supporting it. Bush therefore chose to contain Saddam by applying economic sanctions. He and Scowcroft explained, "We were concerned about the long-term balance of power at the head of the Gulf.... Had we gone the invasion route, the United States could conceivably still be an occupying power in a bitterly hostile land." Thus, Kurds and Shi'ites were left to fend for themselves with no prospect of Western help. To Bush and his closest advisers, self-determination was "admirable... in principle" but not "practical," given the volatility of conditions throughout the Persian Gulf.[82]

Afghanistan and the Limits of American Power

Restraints on the use of American military power, reflected in the decision not to take the war to Baghdad, were partly undone by the globalist ethos that underlay grand strategy. Although the administration severed its ties to dictators like Manuel Noriega and Saddam Hussein, it did not question the nature of American involvement in either Panama or Iraq. It was also intent on enhancing U.S. influence in Southwest Asia. That meant continuing an uneasy relationship with elements of the Mujahedin in Afghanistan and close cooperation with Pakistan's ISI. These activities, difficult to justify as promoting either democracy or self-determination, prolonged a situation highly conducive to blowback, which became a terrible reality on September 11, 2001. As security assets, the Mujahedin could neither be easily managed nor jettisoned even after the Soviets withdrew from Afghanistan in March 1989.

In Afghanistan, broad self-determination was not possible, even though Bush issued a national security finding to promote it, and in Pakistan, democracy remained an elusive promise. Until he died in a plane crash in August 1988, Mohammed Zia ul-Haq ruled as president, at first under martial law and subsequently in a more open system in which the National Assembly was elected. His death meant shared power for the American-educated prime minister, Benazir Bhutto, the Islamic Alliance, and the military whose acceptance of Bhutto placed limits on her authority. So committed were Ronald Reagan and conservatives in Congress to combating the Soviet Union in

---

[81] Freedman and Karsh, *The Gulf Conflict*, 441.
[82] Bush and Scowcroft, *A World Transformed*, 489.

Afghanistan that they denied the reality of Pakistan's determination to possess a nuclear weapon as a counterweight to India. Abdul Qadeer Khan, head of the uranium-enrichment program, consequently had a free hand to make Pakistan a nuclear power. Zia's many friends in Washington also failed to insist on an accounting of human rights violations. Instead, they worked with the Saudis through ISI to provide the Mujahedin with all the matériel necessary to expel the Soviets. By the time Bush took office, ISI was backing Islamic fundamentalists including Gulbuddin Hekmatyar, whose belief in Islamic revolution had drawn him close to bin Laden,[83] rather than Ahmed Shah Masoud, who had won the support of a new U.S. envoy, Peter Tomsen. In his efforts to create a more open political environment, Tomsen quickly ran afoul of ISI and the CIA, which deemed Afghanistan a lost cause and saw the possibility for stability under the aegis of ISI and the Saudis.[84]

The problem was that Mohammad Najibullah, a Soviet client, remained in power, guaranteeing an extent of intrigue that Washington could not match. Bhutto's freedom of action was limited by poor relations with the military and political opponents. As such, she could neither distance herself from the Mujahedin nor rein in ISI, which was active in fomenting anti-Indian tension in Kashmir at the end of 1989 and the start of 1990 as part of an aggressive attempt to demarcate a defensive perimeter for Pakistan. Bhutto would be removed from office just after Iraq invaded Kuwait. In addition, work on Pakistan's nuclear program continued, prompting Bush to send Deputy National Security Adviser Robert Gates to Islamabad to try to forestall a deterioration in relations between the two countries. That proved impossible, and when Bush declined to certify that Pakistan was not seeking a nuclear capability, nearly $600 million in economic and military assistance was frozen.[85] As was their wont, the Saudis played both sides of the street, relying on the United States to keep Saddam in check while working closely with ISI and its clients to get rid of Najibullah and replace him with an Islamic government beholden to Riyadh. The United States, then in the process of reducing covert aid to the Mujahedin, was no longer able to influence a situation it had helped create.[86]

Just before it broke apart, the Soviet Union suspended aid to Najibullah. He had no option but to resign in mid-April 1992. The entity that took power was bitterly split between, among others, Masoud's northern

[83] Barnett R. Rubin, *The Fragmentation of Afghanistan: State Formation and Collapse in the International System*, 2d ed. (New Haven: Yale University Press, 2002), 213–15.

[84] Dennis Kux, *The United States and Pakistan, 1947–2000: Disenchanted Allies* (Washington, DC: Woodrow Wilson Center Press and Johns Hopkins University Press, 2001), 279–97; Steve Coll, *Ghost Wars: The Secret History of the CIA, Afghanistan, and bin Laden from the Soviet Invasion to September 10, 2001* (New York: Penguin Press, 2004), 189–211.

[85] Kux, *The United States and Pakistan*, 306–13.

[86] Coll, *Ghost Wars*, 225–9.

alliance and Hekmatyar's Islamic radicals. Kabul became the site of bloody intra-Islamic conflict from which Iran, Pakistan, and Saudi Arabia hoped to profit. Afghanistan was a state in name only. Before he fell from power, Najibullah warned, "If fundamentalism comes to Afghanistan, war will continue for many years.... Afghanistan will be turned into a center for terrorism." It would also be, he said, home to drug trafficking.[87] These dire predictions came to pass: The Taliban, the progeny of Saudi, Pakistani, and U.S. support for the Mujahedin, would seize power, declaring itself a force for stability and fundamentalist Islamic order.

Conclusion

George Bush's grand design was in disarray and the system it was designed to maintain not at all secure as he prepared to leave office late in 1992. As a critic of the War Powers Act, Bush differed with Congress over whether he needed authorization to go to war in 1991. Last-minute diplomacy with Baghdad became a useful delaying tactic while he built a coalition in Congress for Desert Storm. Public opinion was increasingly siding with the president, so much so that antiwar resolutions in the House and Senate went down to defeat.[88] Victorious, Bush left to Vice President Dan Quayle the linking of war opponents with Saddam while he minimized the dissent of December and January, observing that only a small percentage of it was "reckless."[89] Segments of the media, led by Cable News Network (CNN), which used sophisticated technology to televise the high-tech war, contributed to an overwhelmingly positive public reception of the war. Live pictures and instant analysis by civilian and military experts convinced Americans that military force was making the nation secure. The experience of the Cold War, capped off by an apparent victory over Soviet communism, disposed numerous citizens to accept what Andrew J. Bacevich describes as "the new American militarism." By believing the use of force assured safety, the tension, if not the incompatibility, between security policy and the protection of basic values was not an issue that troubled supporters of the war.

In important ways, the Bush administration had impaired basic values. The effort to create a new world order had not aided the cause of democratic inclusion in the Andes. Intervention in Panama more resembled the entitlement of a hegemon than a commitment to self-determination for Panamanians. Freedom itself at home, linked throughout the Cold War to the imperative of boundless prosperity, was increasingly dependent after Desert Storm on an American presence in greater Persian Gulf where some 23,000

[87] Quoted in ibid., 234; Rubin, *The Fragmentation of Afghanistan*, 271–80.
[88] Freedman and Karsh, *The Gulf Conflict*, 290–4.
[89] Ibid., 469 n. 35. For Bush, see note 23, *supra*.

troops remained.[90] The potential in the not-too-distant future for blowback, there and elsewhere in the Muslim world, and its baleful effect on the nation's core values stand out as George Herbert Walker Bush's principal legacy to his successor. Irrespective of what government officials and citizens believed had brought about the end of the Cold War, a unique opportunity to rethink the tangled relationship among values, security policy, and grand strategy had been lost. Still in thrall to the security ethos, America's evasion of the realities of its own history would continue after Bush left office.

[90] Andrew J. Bacevich, *American Empire: The Realities and Consequences of U.S. Diplomacy* (Cambridge: Harvard University Press, 2002), 127.

8

Globalization and Militarism

To protect our interests and our values, sometimes we have to stand and fight.
Bill Clinton, 1991

Boy, do I ever miss the Cold War!
Anthony Lake, 1993

[W]e stood by as nearly a million Africans were hacked to death with machetes in Rwanda.
General Wesley K. Clark, 2002

[N]o nation has ever developed over the long term under the rules being imposed today on third-world countries by the institutions controlling globalization.
Tina Rosenberg, 2002

Like George H. W. Bush before him, Bill Clinton found the idea of a new world order utterly compelling.[1] And like Bush, Clinton and his foreign policy advisers were convinced that the road to stability and order went through Moscow. After Clinton and the democratically elected Boris Yeltsin met in April 1993, a $1.6 billion aid package was introduced in Congress to promote "democracy, civil liberties, and free markets."[2] Was the historic mission to remake Russia, long a tale of failure, on the verge of success?[3]

Clinton's long-time friend and chief Russian adviser Strobe Talbott saw assistance to Russia as the linchpin of the administration's version of a new world order, as the key to the furtherance of strategic globalism. Supporting

---

[1] Warren Christopher, *In the Stream of History: Shaping Foreign Policy for a New Era* (Stanford: Stanford University Press, 1998), 11.

[2] Ibid., 37; Strobe Talbott, *The Russia Hand: A Memoir of Presidential Diplomacy* (New York: Random House, 2002), 15.

[3] David S. Foglesong, *The American Mission and the "Evil Empire": The Crusade for a "Free Russia" since 1881* (New York: Cambridge University Press, 2007).

Russia "constitutes the greatest single task facing American foreign policy in the years to come."[4] When Yeltsin ordered a shutdown and then a military assault on the Duma in fall 1993, the administration did not object in the hope that a stronger commitment to democracy would follow.[5] The U.S. Congress soon passed a bill extending aid to Yeltsin's government. Concerning democracy's troubles in Russia, Hillary Clinton opined, "Before we give up on Russia, we should look at Taiwan, or South Korea.... Russia's not really doing so badly when you compare it to Asia."[6]

The salient point is not that her historical comparison was inapt; rather, state-to-state and great power diplomacy dominated Clinton's security planning. National Security Adviser Anthony Lake intimated that time was running out on that way of engaging the world. Lake told Talbott in October 1993, "Boy, do I ever miss the Cold War!"[7] Nonetheless, old ways persisted, and Clinton began rethinking his initial hard-line approach toward China. This was not a popular move given memories of the June 1989 Tiananmen massacre and China's record of human rights abuses.

Yet, Clinton shared his predecessor's contempt for congressional intrusion in the making of China policy. Earlier, Bush had vetoed attempts orchestrated by Democrats in Congress to remove China's most-favored-nation (MFN) trading status; Secretary of State Baker had denounced the endeavor as politically "counterproductive," economically "detrimental," and strategically "dangerous."[8]

To avoid public hearings, Clinton extended MFN status by executive agreement in 1993 and decoupled MFN status from China's performance on human rights the following year. Prominent members of the security community, including Henry Kissinger and Cyrus Vance, praised Clinton's decision.[9] The administration could hardly afford a rift with China because of a number of security-related issues in Asia, including the status of Okinawa, the Japanese economy, U.S. relations with South Korea, and the apparent nuclearization of North Korea.[10] Yet, throughout the Clinton

---

[4] Talbott, *The Russia Hand*, 53. George Kennan, almost ninety years of age, warned that Russia was highly unlikely to institute democratic governance in any way that was recognizable in the United States; see George F. Kennan, *At a Century's Ending* (New York: W. W. Norton & Company, 1996), 332–3.

[5] Stephen F. Cohen, *Failed Crusade: America and the Tragedy of Post-Communist Russia*, updated ed. (New York: W. W. Norton & Company, 2001), 16–17, 124–33; Foglesong, *The American Mission and the "Evil Empire,"* 208.

[6] Talbott, *The Russia Hand*, 86–91; quoted words, 104.

[7] Quoted in ibid., 91.

[8] George Bush and Brent Scowcroft, *A World Transformed* (New York: Alfred A. Knopf, 1998), 275–6; James A. Baker III with Thomas M. DeFrank, *The Politics of Diplomacy: Revolution, War and Peace, 1989–1992* (New York: G. P. Putnam's Sons, 1995), 106.

[9] William G. Hyland, *Clinton's World: Remaking American Foreign Policy* (Westport: Praeger, 1999), 111–15.

[10] Chalmers Johnson, *Blowback: The Costs and Consequences of American Empire* (New York: Metropolitan Books, 2000), chapters 2, 4–5, 7, 8.

presidency, relations with Beijing were intermittently turbulent, which prompted doubts about whether the United States could craft a global grand design after George Bush left office. Thus, the U.S.-Chinese relationship was no harbinger of a new world order. By diminishing the role of human rights as its China policy evolved, expediency or perhaps cynicism became the order of the day. The vexatious relationship with China played itself out over time. It would be years before the administration fully realized that Beijing was not going to assist in the construction of a new global order on terms emanating from Washington.

In addition to its focus on policy toward Russia and China, the Clinton administration was tending to the third pillar of its strategy: the world economy. Clinton would not have become president had Bush, who inherited a national debt of $2.5 trillion, cared more about the state of the domestic economy. The distribution of wealth and income was heavily skewed in favor of the nation's wealthiest 20 percent, a condition neither Bush nor Clinton substantially addressed.[11] Clinton was determined to build his political base at home predicated on growing prosperity. He also resolved not to let adverse conditions in the world's economy short-circuit his presidency; the severe downturns in the previously dynamic Asian economies, therefore, were not inherently a bad thing. If the United States could not regain the hegemonic status it held under the Bretton Woods system well into the 1960s, it still did have the power to prevent competitors, whether friend or foe, from achieving a commanding position in the 1990s.

Building free markets and fostering democracy would maintain economic predominance. Lake told a receptive audience at the School of Advanced International Studies of Johns Hopkins University on September 21, 1993: *"The successor to a doctrine of containment must be a strategy of enlargement – enlargement of the world's free community of market democracies."*[12] Could American-style globalization, which Lake was proposing, really succeed? What would it ultimately mean for core values? That is, was an overall strategy of "engagement and enlargement" responsive to the emerging issues policymakers had to confront?[13] Lake was seeking to broaden the security discourse beyond its customary strategic focus so as to incorporate international political economy more centrally into that discussion. Such would be the crux of Clinton's version of strategic globalism.

Sullying the chances for hegemony and exceptionalism was the harsh reality, in the words of Robert Kuttner, who founded the liberal journal *The American Prospect*, that "the global grand strategy of the United States can

---

[11] Michael A. Bernstein, "Cold War Triumphalism and the Deformation of the American Economy," in Ellen Schrecker, ed., *Cold War Triumphalism: The Misuse of History after the Fall of Communism* (New York: New Press, 2004), 128–31.

[12] See http://www.mtholyoke.edu/acad/intrel/lakedoc.html (emphasis in original).

[13] The White House, *A National Security Strategy of Engagement and Enlargement*, February 1996 (http://www.fas.org/spp/military/docops/national/1996stra.htm#IV).

no longer be sustained by the American economy."[14] Like Bush, Clinton knew he could borrow enough dollars from friendly creditor states to cover America's deficit obligations, and the United States retained sufficient influence with institutions such as the World Bank and International Monetary Fund (IMF) to perpetuate a market regimen for less powerful states.[15] A trade liberalization accord reached by the Uruguay Round of the General Agreement on Trade and Tariffs (GATT) in Clinton's first term worsened the terms of trade for some of the world's less developed countries. In addition, IMF interest rate policies greatly exacerbated the recession throughout capitalist Asia in the 1990s; Clinton officials joined the IMF in blocking the creation of an Asian Monetary Fund because of the power that would surely accrue to Japan and, over time, to China as the fund's main suppliers.[16] The anticipated peace dividend after the fall of the Berlin Wall therefore never arrived, whether as a refurbished foreign aid program to enhance America's image abroad[17] or in the form of recognition by the federal government of its responsibility for workers whose labor had made containment capitalism possible.[18] It would be left to GATT's successor, the World Trade Organization (WTO), to make globalization appealing to less well-off people and states.[19] Clinton's administration, however, did not abandon strategic globalism, inchoate though the efforts in pursuit of it seemed at times. Extensive arms sales and the proliferation of U.S. personnel and bases around the world, even in former Soviet Central Asia, testified to the persistent allure of strategic globalism for the White House and Congress.[20]

Not surprisingly, there existed a group of individuals in the security community, identifying themselves closely with what they saw as the legacy of Ronald Reagan, who steadfastly refused to accept the reality of America's decline. As if in league with the imperious notion of Henry R. Luce more than a half-century earlier, they devised the Project for the New American Century (PNAC), whose statement of principles in 1997 advocated large increases in defense spending "to promote the cause of political and economic freedom abroad." "America," the statement further read, "has a vital role in maintaining peace and security in Europe, Asia, and the

---

[14] Robert Kuttner, *The End of Laissez-Faire: National Purpose and the Global Economy after the Cold War* (New York: Alfred A. Knopf, 1991), 8.

[15] Ibid., 112–13, 251–3.

[16] Joseph E. Stiglitz, *Globalization and Its Discontents* (New York: W. W. Norton & Company, 2002), 7, 109–13.

[17] Jeffrey D. Sachs, *The End of Poverty: Economic Possibilities for Our Time* (New York: Penguin Books, 2006), 143.

[18] Nelson Lichtenstein, "Market Triumphalism and the Wishful Liberals," in Schrecker, ed., *Cold War Triumphalism*, 120–5.

[19] Stiglitz, *Globalization and Its Discontents*, 227–8.

[20] Chalmers Johnson, *The Sorrows of Empire: Militarism, Secrecy, and the End of the Republic* (New York: Metropolitan Books, 2004), 63, 132–3, 151–87, 278–81.

Middle East."[21] Among PNAC's founding members were Elliott Abrams, Jeb Bush, Dick Cheney, Francis Fukuyama, Donald Rumsfeld, and Paul Wolfowitz.

In important respects, Team B of the mid-1970s had been resurrected. It would be assisted by the formation of the Congressional Policy Advisory Board, whose foreign policy experts were Cheney, Rumsfeld, and Wolfowitz.[22] Yet, however serious PNAC's members were about strategic globalism, they were no more so than Bill Clinton. What they could do, though, was focus exclusively on that objective in their mission as members of the neoconservative security community. With the election of George W. Bush and the events of September 11, 2001, PNAC became known to the American public for supporting the augmentation of presidential power, a position consistent with the logic of strategic globalism. As we see in the next chapter, there existed a direct link between grand strategy and the damage inflicted on fundamental American values by the younger Bush and his closest aides. This attack, when it came, grievously injured basic rights of the American people and the nation's foundational values.

Hegemony and Globalization

The Gulf War ostensibly justified America's sense of global mission and also legitimated the inexorable, if still imperceptible, growth of a new militarism. The elder Bush had kept his eye on the prize of strategic globalism by sending U.S. military forces, first, to protect the Kurdish people from Saddam in 1991 and then to help relieve famine in Somalia in 1992. Why? Andrew J. Bacevich minces no words: Troops embarked on their missions as "a quasi-imperial police force."[23] In so doing, they provided a shield behind which Clinton and his national security advisers were endeavoring to revitalize American hegemony.[24] The drive to hegemony under Clinton included the traditional democracy project, an economic policy replete with the promise of modernization, and a flexible defense posture with international application whose underlying militarism was predicated on the selective use of power, not a reflexive global deployment of forces.

William Jefferson Clinton won the 1992 election because he focused on domestic issues, most notably the economy. The first "baby boomer" to become president, he was at the same time highly intelligent and supremely

---

[21] See http://www.newamericancentury.org/.

[22] James Mann, *Rise of the Vulcans: The History of Bush's War Cabinet* (New York: Viking, 2004), 234–47.

[23] Andrew J. Bacevich, *American Empire: The Realities and Consequences of U.S. Diplomacy* (Cambridge: Harvard University Press, 2002), 74.

[24] Generally see Michael H. Hunt, *The American Ascendancy: How the United States Gained and Wielded Global Dominance* (Chapel Hill: University of North Carolina Press, 2007), 308–14.

glib; his political skills rivaled Richard Nixon's, but without the self-doubt and the deep loathing of opponents that had destroyed Nixon. He artfully chose his political allies from among the Democratic Party's power brokers, corporate giants, and the poor of all colors and ethnicities who backed him in part because they had nowhere else to turn. Clinton and his domestic policy advisers, including his wife Hillary Rodham Clinton and Vice President Al Gore, loved to tinker with public policy. Politics was their business and avocation, a quasi-parlor game for the liberal intelligentsia whose liberalism, except on racial matters, was not substantially at odds with that of progressive Republicans of the Nixon era, to place them in comparative perspective. The contagious zeal that Clinton brought to the governing process at home did not, however, carry over into the conduct of foreign affairs.[25]

Much is known about the conceptual underpinnings and substance of Clinton's foreign policy, a mixture of hegemony and globalization.[26] His hegemonic inclination was different in detail, not in kind, from the imperial urge of the 1890s. What is not so apparent is how hegemony and globalization affected core values and helped set the stage for George W. Bush's attack on radical Islam and, thus, the Constitution. In short, during his eight years in power, Clinton infrequently had to respond to serious debate by an informed public and its representatives about American foreign policy. He was, in that respect, more successful than the expansionists of 1898.

The return of civic virtue was not wholly out of the question in the 1990s, though. Considerable public discussion took place about a peace dividend in the aftermath of the Cold War and about finally giving human rights a truly prominent place in the making of foreign policy. In a collection of his public addresses, Warren Christopher, Clinton's first secretary of state, recalls his own service to the cause of human rights at home and abroad under presidents Johnson and Carter. Yet, administration paralysis on the abuse of human security in Bosnia, Rwanda, and elsewhere belies his assertion that he and the president brought "human rights back to the center of foreign policy." More telling is his statement that "human rights should complement, not compete with other objectives," of which strategic globalism remained paramount.[27] The Clinton administration blunted these efforts to generate a wide-ranging public debate by subsuming them under

[25] Sidney Blumenthal, *The Clinton Wars* (New York: Farrar, Straus and Giroux, 2003).
[26] See, for example, Hyland, *Clinton's World*; Bacevich, *American Empire*; and David Scott Palmer, *U.S. Relations with Latin America during the Clinton Years: Opportunities Lost or Opportunities Squandered?* (Gainesville: University Press of Florida, 2006).
[27] Christopher, *In the Stream of History*, 62. See also Warren Zimmermann, *Origins of a Catastrophe: Yugoslavia and Its Destroyers – America's Last Ambassador Tells What Happened and Why* (New York: Times Books, 1996); Samantha Power, *"A Problem from Hell": America and the Age of Genocide* (New York: Basic Books, 2002), 247–327 (Bosnia), 329–89 (Rwanda).

the primary goals of hegemony and globalization. Hegemony precluded consideration of a peace dividend, and globalization was trumpeted as a necessary precondition for real human security.[28]

Since the security ethos emerged in the 1890s, the executive branch had become instinctively intolerant of dissent. Louis Hartz, who in the 1950s dissected American liberalism's contradictions with uncommon insight, had bemoaned the "psychic heritage of... liberal absolutism" that led to intolerance.[29] That attitude resulted from the power to restrict access to information about the nation's safety and, as we have seen, often from an exaggerated fear of adversaries. To justify restrictions on freedom of speech, officials sought to manufacture a popular consensus behind foreign and security policy. This endeavor met with considerable success in the early Cold War, lasting until the American people tired of the Vietnam War. Ronald Reagan substantially restored presidential credibility until the Iran-Contra scandal came to light. George H. W. Bush's success in the Gulf War provided Clinton with the rationale for shrinking the contours of public discourse. The stunning breadth of Clinton's agenda offers insight into why he sought to do so. "*We have to be at the center of every vital global network*," he told Congress in his 2000 State of the Union Address.[30] Critics aspiring to anything less ambitious became obstacles to prosperity and security.

It was, of course, difficult to transform what appeared to be a quest for dominance into actual global leadership by the United States. The brutal killing of eighteen soldiers in Somalia in October 1993, for which swift retribution was impossible, provided a grisly reminder of the limits of American power. It also exposed the administration to unwanted public scrutiny. Columnist Anthony Lewis of the *New York Times* described policy as "tentative, fuzzy, unconvincing" and observed, "The world has caught up with Bill Clinton."[31] So had some members of Congress, who seized the opportunity to denounce the humanitarian mission in Somalia and the multilateralism it foretold.[32] Yet, without even the pretense of multilateralism, there was no new world order, no hegemony.

One lesson Clinton learned from this debacle was that consultation with Congress had to be carefully orchestrated to minimize scrutiny of his foreign policy. The new militarism provided the perfect vehicle for that effort. Recognizing that the military brass was well respected in Congress, the president

[28] The projection of American power and arms sales under Clinton made a peace dividend impossible; see Bacevich, *American Empire*, 125–30, 266 n. 35.
[29] Louis Hartz, *The Liberal Tradition in America* (New York: Harcourt, Brace & World, 1955), 285.
[30] *New York Times*, January 28, 2000 (emphasis added).
[31] Ibid., October 11, 1993.
[32] Hyland, *Clinton's World*, 58–9.

abandoned his youthful reservations about the role of the military in American life and advanced the cause of comprehensive preparedness, linking it to global economic health. Clinton's rebirth of containment capitalism paid political dividends. Except to the most hawkish of conservative critics and to inveterate antiwar liberals and leftists, he had established his security bona fides.[33] In fact, by the end of Clinton's tenure in office, the United States was likely spending more on its military than all other nations combined.[34] The American people, Democrats and Republicans alike, and the military, after a brief contretemps over gays in the armed forces, tended to support the president on matters of national security.[35] He had prepared the ground for this consensus as early as December 1991, telling a receptive audience at Georgetown University, "To protect our interests and our values, sometimes we have to stand and fight."[36] The public was willing to accord the military a greater role in foreign policy than the Joint Chiefs of Staff might otherwise have desired. Madeleine Albright would later term this mission "coercive diplomacy," to Colin Powell's consternation. Clinton's manufacturing of consensus testifies to his talent as a politician, if not to his belief in open inquiry about the conduct of foreign policy.[37]

Globalization was so crucial to the realization of Clinton's strategic vision that his administration resorted to heavy-handed tactics to garner support. "We must forge a new economic policy . . . ," he declared in his Georgetown speech, "by launching a new era of global growth. We must tear down the wall in our thinking between domestic and foreign policy."[38] Domestic prosperity depended in considerable measure on opening and keeping open foreign markets; growth and security were all but synonymous. In the Wilsonian tradition, Clinton identified trade and investment as the hallmarks of peace and prosperity. Within his administration, trade protection replaced communism as the great evil. It therefore had to be extirpated, in the words of Samuel R. Berger, Anthony Lake's successor as national security adviser, "for the benefit of the people of the United States and the world."[39] By "the world," Clinton and his advisers evidently meant Europe where American trade and investment grew more dramatically than anywhere else in the mid-1990s. No matter – the "new isolationists," as Gore portrayed them, were

---

[33] Andrew J. Bacevich, *The New American Militarism: How Americans Are Seduced by War*, paper ed. (New York: Oxford University Press, 2006), 117–21.

[34] Ibid., 125–7.

[35] Wesley K. Clark, *Waging Modern War: Bosnia, Kosovo, and the Future of Combat* (New York: Public Affairs, 2002), 26–7; Dana Priest, *The Mission: Waging War and Keeping Peace with America's Military* (New York: W. W. Norton & Company: 2003). 41–51.

[36] For the text of the address, see http://www.ndol.org/print.cfm?contentid=250537.

[37] Priest, *The Mission*, 52–3.

[38] See http://www.ndol.org/print.cfm?contentid=250537.

[39] Quoted in Bacevich, *American Empire*, 102.

trying "to impede President Clinton's ability to defend American values and interests."[40]

This paranoid style of politics harked back to the early Cold War when manufactured fears constrained debate. The gross exaggeration of Gore and others was a way of obscuring the fact that globalization, like economic policy in the 1920s and foreign policy at the end of World War II, was under the control of individuals whose hubris surpassed their expertise. The result was that core values came under renewed duress. Freedom of speech by serious antiglobalization activists, as distinct from the masked anarchists who regularly attempted to disrupt meetings of the World Trade Organization by the end of the decade, posed undesirable challenges to Clinton's worldview.

The White House had no greater help in muting its critics than one of the leading columnists at the *New York Times*, Thomas L Friedman, globalization's most influential cheerleader other than Clinton himself. Friedman's columns and books were not so much evidence of an attack on freedom of the press as they were indications of the power of the printed word to set the boundaries of legitimate discourse. Were it not for the unmatched presence in American journalism of the *New York Times*, to suggest that his idiosyncratic economic musings had a deleterious impact on diversity in the press would be off the mark. Yet, his facile formulation, "Globalization is U.S.," belonged in publications like *Time* magazine that formerly had hawked its founder Henry Luce's American Century project, rather than in the nation's paper of record.[41] By trying to stack the deck in the debate over globalization, Clinton, Gore, Berger, and others went beyond partisan politics in their efforts to set the terms of permissible discourse and thus denigrate their critics.

The administration's aversion to open inquiry while pursuing hegemony and globalization had its counterpart in foreign affairs where the ramifications could literally mean life and death. This consequence was especially evident in Washington's reluctant response to human rights abuses from the Balkans to Africa to East Timor, the effort to coerce the Colombian government into adopting U.S.-style drug control policies, and the quest for access to scarce strategic resources. These examples make a case for the poverty of hegemonic pretension in the aftermath of the Cold War. Hegemony and Clinton's brand of globalization were arguably incompatible with traditional values. If American exceptionalism had not already run its course,

[40] Ibid., 105; quoted words, 114. For Gore's 1995 address to the Kennan Institute and the U.S.-Russia Business Council, see http://clinton6.nara.gov/1995/10/1995–10-19-vp-gore-to-the-kennan-institute-us-russia-council.html.

[41] Thomas L. Friedman, "A Manifesto for the Fast World," *New York Times Magazine*, March 28, 1999.

its essence was being severely distorted and, as such, no longer worthy of emulation.

Human Security

An uneasy relationship between official regard for the safety of individuals and the vital interests of the state was not new. When Woodrow Wilson included the notion of self-determination in his Fourteen Points, he certainly suspected the problems it might cause. Walter Lippmann later wrote that Wilson "did not believe in it" because to do so would "invite sheer anarchy" and thus imperil state stability.[42] Nevertheless, during the several phases of the Cold War, support for self-determination and democracy became useful tactics to be used against regimes opposed by Washington. Only when expedient did they serve as core values in support of grand strategy.

After the demise of the Soviet Union, the sole remaining superpower had no reason not to make human security the standard by which it engaged the world. The issue became whether the United States would really use its power to help those who could not help themselves. The record during the Bush years was not promising. The United States, Samantha Power observes, had never intended to defend human security because neither the political liabilities at home nor potential costs abroad were deemed worth the risk. What Warren Christopher rightly called "a problem from hell," genocide in the Balkans, did not become a policy priority in time to save untold thousands of men, women, and children from horrible suffering and death.[43]

The new militarism under Clinton reflected an ethos of preparedness more than it constituted a manifesto for combat. This attitude derived from the Powell Doctrine. Colin Powell had worried that civilian officials might be too eager to send troops into battle, especially given the success of Operation Desert Storm. The Powell Doctrine insisted that, before U.S. forces went into battle, vital interests had to be at stake, there had to be an exit strategy, and the willingness to use overwhelming force must be present.[44] The Powell Doctrine was a recipe for inaction and disaster where Bosnia was concerned. As Yugoslavia fell apart in 1991, Bosnia's heterogeneity – Orthodox Serb, Roman Catholic, and Muslim – turned the republic into a potential powder keg. Muslims had few friends in the region and would have to rely on Western powers for protection. The United Nations quickly imposed an arms embargo, further imperiling the Muslim population. U.S. recognition of Bosnia's independence did nothing to promote stability or, by the time

---

[42] Walter Lippmann, *U.S. War Aims* (Boston: Little, Brown, 1944), 173. To Wilson, the threat of Bolshevism dwarfed the potential problems attendant to self-determination.

[43] Power, "*A Problem from Hell*," xi–xxi; quoted words, xii.

[44] Bacevich, *The New Militarism*, 51–6.

Clinton became president, avert "ethnic cleansing" by the Serbs, which continued until 1995.[45]

Perhaps 200,000 people died and more than 2,000,000 were displaced. Clinton and his foreign policy advisers did not dare urge America's allies to intervene any more than had Bush, Baker, Scowcroft, and Cheney. Why not? Neither administration could count on their European compatriots to follow Washington's lead. In short, allied solidarity after the Cold War in the form of multilateralism was a fiction. The same could be said about the restoration of U.S. global leadership.[46]

Despite resignations by Foreign Service officers, heated dissent from within the State Department, and shocking accounts of ethnic cleansing reported by Human Rights Watch, the Clinton administration went no further than to admit that what was occurring in Bosnia was "tantamount to genocide."[47] Christopher's words were not a warning, but rather a cynical verbal legerdemain declaring that Bosnia lay beyond the vital interests of the United States. Warren Zimmermann, the last American ambassador to Yugoslavia, who decided to retire from the diplomatic corps in 1994, has written, "We were watching a cultural genocide, an attempt to wipe out an entire culture."[48]

It took the outrage of July 1995 that was Srebrenica, in which some 7,000 Muslims who had sought refuge in a UN safe area were killed, to move the United States and its allies to take concerted action. Neither a no-fly zone meant as a warning to Serbia nor a series of NATO air strikes had prevented genocide in Bosnia. What did turn the tide and led to the Dayton Peace Accords in November were attacks by the Croat army, with implicit approval of the United States, and a concerted air campaign by NATO forces. In part, Clinton was moved by the horror of what was happening in the Balkans; he was also worried about how Bosnia would affect his chances for reelection. His political calculus included the humiliation that occurred in Somalia and the embarrassment that had arisen out of a poorly conceived attempt at nation building in Haiti.[49] Seeking to demonstrate his command of a desperate situation, Clinton dispatched troops to Bosnia under NATO's auspices, insisting that consultation with Congress was not needed for a mission of what was to be limited duration. After his reelection in November 1996, Clinton extended the mission, thereby turning NATO and U.S. forces into something of a local constabulary. When parliamentary elections finally took place in September 1998, Biljiana Plavsic, long a Serb nationalist and

---

[45] Power, "A Problem from Hell," 247–51.
[46] Hyland, *Clinton's World*, 33–9.
[47] Quoted in Power, "*A Problem from Hell*," 298.
[48] Zimmermann, *Origins of a Catastrophe*, 224.
[49] *New York Times*, April 29, 1994; Palmer, *U.S. Relations with Latin America during the Clinton Years*, 35–6, 47–51.

a former associate of Radavan Karadzic who had been indicted for war crimes, gained the active backing of NATO and Washington. Described as a "moderate" by General Wesley K. Clark, who spent much time in Bosnia on assignment from the Pentagon, she lost to extreme nationalists.[50]

The Powell Doctrine cracked at the edges in Bosnia, in part because the Croat army, which engaged in ethnic cleansing of its own against Serbs, was trained by retired U.S. military personnel working for a Department of Defense contractor. In any event, the presence of 20,000 U.S. troops exposed the unreality of an ethos of preparedness when it was faced with the horrors of genocide. Intervention and subsequent partition in Bosnia ultimately did provide a modicum of stability.[51] How difficult stability would be to sustain in the Balkans became apparent when violence erupted in Kosovo in 1998. As a Serbian province heavily dominated by Albanians who hungered for autonomy, Kosovo presented a more complex situation than had Bosnia.[52] U.S. officials had feared since 1992 that conflict there, not Bosnia, would lead to a wider Balkan war perhaps involving Greece, Turkey, and maybe Russia.

To prevent that from happening, Washington initiated a lengthy air war in March 1999 against Serbian forces, who were then trying to expel the Albanian majority from Kosovo. General Clark, supreme allied commander in Europe, oversaw the bombing, the main purpose of which was to compel Serbian strongman Slobodan Milosevic to recognize Albanian autonomy. Clark also set in motion the planning for a ground campaign, which met with opposition in the White House, Congress, and the Department of Defense where there was substantial resistance to involvement in any ground war.[53] Fortunately, NATO's air strikes broke the spirit of Serbian forces so that the ethnic cleansing, which had led to the exile of more than 1.3 million Kosovars from their homes, did not become genocide. It was a close call, though.

At stake in Kosovo was the future of NATO, then waging its first war. The war was clearly more than a humanitarian campaign, despite Clark's best efforts to portray it in those terms. In Washington, it concerned politics and American credibility. A ground campaign likely would have forced Clinton to consult with Congress, something he continued to resist. "I do not intend to put our troops in Kosovo to fight a war," he declared, hoping to

---

[50] Elizabeth Rubin, "The Enemy of Our Enemy," *New York Times Magazine*, September 14, 1997; Hyland, *Clinton's World*, 39–44; Clark, *Waging Modern War*, 84.

[51] Bacevich, *American Empire*, 164–5; for a suggestive comparison of what occurred in Bosnia and proposals for partition in Iraq, see Thom Shanker, "Divided They Stand, but on Graves," *New York Times*, Week in Review, August 19, 2007.

[52] David Fromkin, *Kosovo Crossing: American Ideals Meet Reality on the Balkan Battlefields* (New York: Free Press, 1999).

[53] Clark, *Waging Modern War*, 295; Power, *"A Problem from Hell,"* 448–9.

turn aside congressional scrutiny.[54] Ultimately, Congress had to acquiesce in the placement of some U.S. troops among the NATO peacekeepers sent to Kosovo. In the strictest sense, the Powell Doctrine held in Kosovo. At the same time, the Serbs had exposed the atavistic nature of America's geopolitical calculations. Yet, the multilateralism of the air war was highly important for strategic globalism. That Clark had turned air power to humanitarian ends was incidental; planning for possible ground operations cost him his position.[55] He acknowledged the irony in the success of the air war, a campaign with numerous critics. "Yet coercive diplomacy had worked," Clark wrote. He was right, even though justice for the Kosovars was not the primary objective in going after Milosevic.[56]

A foreign policy expressly devoted to human security was out of the question in the Clinton White House. Fear of powerful state-based adversaries continued to dominate the policy planning process even as officials professed support for democracy, human rights, and universal freedom. A marked decline in children's health and a more than doubling of mortality in children under age five in the most densely populated regions of Saddam Hussein's Iraq, largely the result of U.S.-backed UN sanctions in the 1990s, exposed the sad outcome of foreign policy as usual. As many as 500,000 Iraqi children died.[57] Nowhere was this ugly gulf between traditional international affairs and pressing human needs any more visible than in places like Haiti and Rwanda. State-based security issues had not disappeared, as the near confrontation with North Korea over nuclear power made evident when the Clinton administration seriously considered a preemptive strike. Yet, it was still possible for creative diplomacy to play a positive role in addressing state-to-state crises, the 1994 Agreed Framework with Pyongyang being a prime example.[58] That was not the case, though, in Haiti and, tragically, in Rwanda.

Race relations had long served as a barometer of American exceptionalism.[59] To be exceptional, on its own terms and in the minds of others, America had to be inclusive in domestic politics and in some meaningful way in foreign policy. Notwithstanding the gains in civil rights in the 1960s, a black critique of foreign policy persisted, focusing mainly on the United States and majority rule in Africa. Jimmy Carter's appointment of Andrew

[54] Quoted in Power, "*A Problem from Hell*," 449; Clark, *Waging Modern War*, 299–306.
[55] Clark, *Waging Modern War*, 408–12.
[56] Power, "*A Problem from Hell*," 460–73; Clark, *Waging Modern War*, 418.
[57] UNICEF, August 12, 1999: http://www.unicef.org/newsline/99pr29.htm; see also *The Independent*, May 8, 2007.
[58] Joel S. Wit, Daniel B. Poneman, and Robert L. Gallucci, *Going Critical: The First North Korean Nuclear Crisis* (Washington, DC: Brookings Institution Press, 2004).
[59] On race, power, and identity in the American nation-state, see Melani McAlister, *Epic Encounters: Culture, Media, and U.S. Interests in the Middle East, 1945–2000* (Berkeley: University of California Press, 2001), 123–4.

Young as UN ambassador stood out as a politically adroit symbol of inclusion at a time when the Supreme Court in the 1978 Baake case was limiting the scope of affirmative action. Young advocated majority rule and engagement with Africa through greater trade and investment. In the political space created by President Carter's genuine, though cautious, commitment to human rights, the Congressional Black Caucus (CBC) and TransAfrica, founded in 1971 and 1976, respectively, aligned with the older NAACP to promote attention to Africa's place in world affairs and to reorient U.S. foreign policy. Moderation in the pursuit of economic and social justice became the widely acceptable means of attaining these objectives.[60]

Haiti and especially Rwanda illustrated the cost of moderation and the lack of innovation in security policy. Clinton wanted to return to power in Haiti a charismatic, leftist priest, Jean-Bertrand Aristide, who was elected president in December 1990. Aristide took office but was then ousted in September 1991 by a military junta, a number of whose members had long-standing ties to the CIA. Despite CIA concerns about Aristide's mental stability and commitment to democracy, the White House brokered the Governors Island Accord, permitting the return of the popular Aristide on October 30, 1993. To cries of "Somalia! Somalia!," a mob encouraged by a CIA asset, Emmanuel Constant, blocked the landing on October 11 – only eight days after the carnage in Mogadishu – of a small force of UN peacekeepers and engineers aboard the USS *Harlan County*. This contingent was supposed to be the vanguard of a nation-building project. For months thereafter, Aristide's supporters were terrorized by Constant's FRAPH, or the Revolutionary Front for the Advancement and Progress of Haiti.[61]

The administration's retreat underscored the inability of the Powell Doctrine to respond to assaults on human security. As if conceding the limitations of traditional politics in a rapidly changing world, Clinton lamented, "[W]e ought to change our policy. It hasn't worked."[62] The president was being disingenuous; his Haiti policy differed little from that of his predecessor. Former Secretary of State Baker noted, "Haiti ... was not sufficiently vital ... to require using military force."[63] Clinton's inertia moved the CBC and TransAfrica to propose a humanitarian response that would include the dispatch of troops. So angry was TransAfrica's Randall Robinson at administration policy, its failed embargo of the junta, and the return of Haitians

---

[60] Thomas Borstelmann, *The Cold War and the Color Line: American Race Relations in the Global Arena* (Cambridge: Harvard University Press, 2001), 248–59.

[61] Hyland, *Clinton's World*, 59–62; see also http://www.cja.org/cases/Constant.shtml, the website of the Center for Justice and Accountability, an international human rights organization founded in 1998.

[62] *New York Times*, April 29, 1994.

[63] Baker, *The Politics of Diplomacy*, 602.

seeking asylum that he began a hunger strike hoping to alter a "cruel, grossly discriminatory and profoundly racist" policy.[64]

Working toward a common goal, Robinson, the CBC, and respected members of Congress like Democrat David Obey of Wisconsin kept alive the idea of a nation-building mission. Reluctance arising from a legacy of prior U.S. interventions in Haiti and the frustrations of Somalia, Bosnia, and Rwanda gave way in September 1994 to a peacekeeping force of 20,000 and the return of Aristide to the presidency. That number dwindled to less than 5,000 U.S. troops by spring 1995. Four years later, the American force of regular troops, engineers, doctors, and nurses numbered less than 500, with an equivalent UN contingent of peacekeepers remaining in a country where instability and poverty presented what seemed to be intractable problems.[65]

On the scale of human security, Haiti constituted a success story compared to that of Rwanda. When genocide began there in April 1994, Washington paid scant attention. In defense of the administration, Clinton adviser Sidney Blumenthal claimed that there was no pressure to intervene from either TransAfrica or Capitol Hill. In a strict sense, that may have been true at the outset of the crisis, if only because reliable information was unavailable. As Human Rights Watch gathered evidence of genocide, it became clear that nothing more than lukewarm support existed in Congress or the executive branch for intervention. Journalist Tim Weiner asserts willful blindness, charging that "the White House studiously ignored a CIA study" in January indicating that 500,000 people could perish in a conflict.[66] Wesley Clark ultimately could not hide his anger, saying, "[W]e stood by as nearly a million Africans were hacked to death with machetes in Rwanda." The Congressional Black Caucus expressed the same sentiment in mid-June after the enormity of the slaughter became apparent.[67]

An explanation for why the administration did not intervene in Rwanda must go beyond conventional reasons that stress a lack of awareness or the absence of vital interests. On a trip to Kigali, Rwanda's capital, in March 1998, Clinton excused his woeful inaction: "[We] *did not fully appreciate* the depth and speed with which you were being engulfed by this *unimaginable* terror."[68] That was partly true because the administration equated Rwanda with Somalia, Bosnia, and Haiti and feared that another foreign policy "failure" might both harm its domestic agenda and impair relations with the military. Rather than a large peacekeeping operation, which it opposed and

---

[64] *New York Times*, April 15, 1994.

[65] Ibid.; and see *New York Times*, April 1, 1995 and August 26, 1999.

[66] Blumenthal, *The Clinton Wars*, 632–3; Power, "*A Problem from Hell*," 373–7; Tim Weiner, *Legacy of Ashes: The History of the CIA* (New York: Doubleday, 2007), 445.

[67] Clark, *Waging Modern War*, 415; *New York Times*, June 27, 1994.

[68] Quoted in Blumenthal, *The Clinton Wars*, 633 (emphasis in original).

did not want to fund, the White House grudgingly accepted a small mission headed by Canadian Major General Roméo Dallaire. Unfortunately, it was not enough to protect the minority Tutsi population from systematic killing by Hutu government forces.

The content of a presidential decision directive, PDD-25, makes clear that the administration did not consider Rwanda a priority. PDD-25, prepared under the direction of Richard A. Clarke of the National Security Council, set the terms of support for UN peacekeeping missions. There were sixteen factors that, much like the Powell Doctrine, reduced the likelihood of U.S. troops engaging in combat. As Representative Obey well understood, PDD-25 provided cover for officials who wanted to do nothing and who refrained from helping others intervene.[69] How, for instance, could anyone actually prove that the national interest was involved in Rwanda? Preventing genocide was not inherent in the security mindset. In fact, the administration did what it could to keep from using the "g–word" because doing so would have compelled U.S. action under the 1948 genocide convention. Yet, by mid-June, evidence of genocide was so overwhelming that State Department officials had to admit that "acts of genocide" were occurring. At length, it was Tutsi rebels and not the U.S. government or the international community who ended the carnage. A small U.S. deployment assisted in humanitarian relief efforts with the strict proviso that there would be no expansion of the mission to include peacekeeping.[70] Dallaire, who experienced severe depression after his assignment concluded, had only scorn for "the great humanitarians... [who] wanted no part of anything inside Rwanda that could lead to American casualties."[71]

When violence descended on East Timor in late August and early September 1999 in the wake of an overwhelming vote in favor of independence from Indonesia, the international response proved to be decisive.[72] More than 400,000 people had been forced from their homes and 1,000 had died; it could have been far, far worse. The UN Security Council, with U.S. support, decided to intervene for several reasons: Human rights organizations lobbied incessantly; the horrors of Rwanda and Srebrenica weighed heavily on the collective international conscience; pressure by the International Monetary Fund for reform during Indonesia's financial crisis beginning in

---

[69] Power, "*A Problem from Hell*," 341–2, 358–62.

[70] Ibid., 362–3, 380–2.

[71] Roméo Dallaire, *Shake Hands with the Devil: The Failure of Humanity in Rwanda* (Toronto: Random House Canada, 2003), 490.

[72] Geoffrey Robinson, "If You Leave Us Here, We Will Die," in Nicolaus Mills and Kira Brunner, eds., *The New Killing Fields: Massacre and the Politics of Intervention* (New York: Basic Books, 2002), 159–83; for more on the situation in 1999 in East Timor, see Theodore Friend, *Indonesian Destinies* (Cambridge: Belknap Press of Harvard University Press, 2003), 273–7, 431–59. In July 2008, the government of Indonesia acknowledged that "gross human rights violations" had occurred; Associated Press, July 15, 2008.

1997 worsened the situation[73]; and the ouster of General Suharto in May 1998 had created a window of opportunity for action. Even so, the Clinton administration was initially cautious about calling for intervention. Furthermore, security ties with Indonesia's military had been important to U.S. grand strategy in Southeast Asia since at least the Ford-Kissinger visit of December 1975.

A key issue in Washington was whether self-determination for East Timor would impair the security relationship or limit access to Indonesia's oil reserves. It did not help that two East Timorese were awarded the Nobel Peace Prize in 1996, thus giving greater attention to the independence movement. In February 1999, wrote Geoffrey Robinson, a member of the UN Mission for East Timor, "State Department officials were still searching for alternatives to a direct popular ballot."[74] Faced with the inevitability of a vote, that search was certain to fail. The Pentagon resisted intervention until the very end. Chairman of the Joint Chiefs of Staff Hugh Shelton informed a Senate committee, "I cannot see any national interest there that would be overwhelming, that would call for us to deploy U.S. forces on the ground in that area."[75] The White House also delayed serious consideration of a multinational force until September 10. Senators Tom Harkin of Iowa and Patrick Leahy of Vermont, both Democrats, mounted congressional pressure to cut ties with the Indonesian military pending verifiable reform. The senators were supported by a new ambassador Robert Gelbard, fresh from service in the Balkans after tours of duty in Bolivia and at the State Department as assistant secretary for narcotics matters. Thus, Clinton had no choice but to suspend arms sales and agree to participate in the UN mission.[76] Before his term ended, he resumed military education and training programs for Indonesia's armed forces. The tension between human security and grand strategy continued. After September 11, conventional order was restored as Indonesia quickly became an important front in the war on terror.

Coercing Colombia

The test of wills with Colombia during the Bush presidency did not diminish until well into Bill Clinton's second term in office. As part of the effort to reassert hegemony, the White House and the State Department deemed drug control a matter of vital interest, whereas the Gaviria, Samper, and Pastrana administrations pursued state stability as their most important goal.[77] For the United States, the logic of strategic globalism included drug

---

[73] Stiglitz, *Globalization and Its Discontents*, 89–98.
[74] Robinson, "If You Leave Us Here, We Will Die," 165.
[75] Quoted in Priest, *The Mission*, 234.
[76] Ibid., 232–7; Robinson, "If You Leave Us Here, We Will Die," 177–81.
[77] I have argued that drug policy was part of an effort to restore U.S. hegemony in Latin America in the wake of the turbulence that characterized hemispheric relations south of

policy, which as always emphasized control at the source, as one of a set of symbols of international order and, thus, American leadership. To officials in Bogotá, order as a general condition mattered little so long as state integrity remained at risk. Indeed, in much of Colombia there was little popular faith in democracy or the market to improve the lives of people living at the margins of society. The question arises about what it implied for core values because U.S. policy contributed to the undermining of democracy in Colombia in the 1990s.

Not only had the Bush administration conceptualized the drug issue in traditional security terms but it had also made it more difficult for Bogotá to incorporate drug control into its policy agenda. In precipitating the July 1989 collapse of the International Coffee Agreement, the White House essentially compelled some coffee growers to turn to coca or opium as their only reliable cash crop. Moreover, despite the "Washington consensus" identifying neoliberalism as the economic wave of the future, nothing was done to make Colombia a partner to NAFTA. These developments had a negative impact on bilateral relations, leaving intellectuals and the political elite to wonder whether a Clinton presidency would be beneficial for Colombia.[78]

They did not have long to wait to learn there would be no significant change as the administration crafted its Colombia policy. Furthering democracy and expanding market capacity in the home of the world's cocaine trade would proceed on U.S. terms, as constituent parts of strategic globalism. By the late 1990s, concludes scholar Brian Loveman, "almost the entire policy agenda for Latin America had been 'securitized.'"[79] The Agency for International Development (AID) would have been the lead agency to assist with pressing economic and social needs, thereby supporting greater democratic inclusion in Colombia. One AID report on democracy and governance admitted, "The core of our strategy is... a pragmatic commitment to see freedom take hold where that will help us most. Thus, we must target our efforts to assist states that assist our strategic interest."[80] However explained by administration officials, Bogotá's own priorities were incidental to U.S. security objectives. Thus, it was that drug policy became more coercive and exacerbated Colombia's political impasse.

Canada under Reagan. See William O. Walker III, "Drug Control and U.S. Hegemony," in John D. Martz, ed., *United States Policy in Latin America: A Decade of Crisis and Challenge* (Lincoln: University of Nebraska Press, 1995), 299–319.

[78] See, for example, Juan Gabriel Tokatlian, "Latin American Reaction to U.S. Policies on Drugs and Terrorism," in Lars Schoultz, William C. Smith, and Augusto Varas, eds., *Security, Democracy, and Development in U.S.-Latin American Relations* (Miami: North-South Center Press, University of Miami, 1994), 126–9.

[79] Brian Loveman, "U.S. Security Policies in Latin America and the Andean Region, 1990–2006," in Brian Loveman, ed., *Addicted to Failure: U.S. Security Policy in Latin America and the Andean Region* (Lanham: Rowman & Littlefield Publishers, 2006), 10.

[80] Quoted in ibid., 8.

In the early 1990s, the prospect of a surge in drug trafficking and insurgency was considerably more believable than any prognosis about democracy. Experts pointed to "the absence of land reform or a strategy for rural development that would ensure sustainable livelihoods for Colombia's small farmers" as evidence of how untenable the situation had become. Also, "justice remain[ed] elusive. Impunity [was] nearly absolute, both for common crimes and for violations of human rights." At the heart of the problem were not only elites who were geographically and psychologically remote but also a military that was often in league with murderous paramilitary forces.[81] This is not to say that the elites were unaware of this situation. They were not.[82] The famed writer Gabriel García Márquez decried what he called "the moral catastrophe of the political class."[83] Rather, the critical issue was whether awareness could be transformed into the political will to address social and economic wrongs and thus salvage Colombian democracy. There was much to be done. As the twenty-first century began, the richest 10 percent of the population earned nearly half of all national income, whereas more than 40 percent of Colombians lived in poverty.[84]

The rebel insurgency and the autonomy of paramilitary forces reduced the amount of land over which the government had effective control. The effective decapitation of the Cali and Medellín cocaine cartels early in the Clinton presidency created a space for many new, smaller drug trafficking bodies, or boutique cartels. With their appearance came a shift in U.S. tactics away from interdiction and toward aerial eradication of coca via PDD-14 in late 1993 as Washington redoubled its efforts to bring about control at the source.[85] This change more or less coincided with the defeat of the Maoist Shining Path (*Sendero Luminoso*) guerrillas by the Peruvian government of Alberto Fujimori and the presence of blight in coca fields there.

The violence in Colombia, where some 3,000 people were still killed annually, convinced U.S. officials of the efficacy of eradication through aerial spraying, which Bolivia and Peru had previously rejected as an alternative to manual eradication – in part for cultural and economic reasons, in part as a defense of sovereignty. To persuade presidents Ernesto Samper Pizano

---

[81] Maria Clemencía Ramírez Lemus, Kimberly Stanton, and John Walsh, "Colombia: A Vicious Cycle of Drugs and War," in Coletta A. Youngers and Eileen Rosin, eds., *Drugs and Democracy in Latin America: The Impact of U.S. Policy* (Boulder: Lynne Rienner, 2005), 99–101; quoted words, 100.

[82] William O. Walker III, "The United States, Colombia, and Drug Policy, 1984–2004: A Study of Quiet Anti-Americanism," in Alan McPherson, ed., *Anti-Americanism in Latin America and the Caribbean* (New York: Berghahn Books, 2006), 250–5.

[83] *La Jornada* (Mexico City), February 29, 1996.

[84] Ramírez Lemus, Stanton, and Walsh, "Colombia: A Vicious Cycle of Drugs and War," 100.

[85] Walker, "The United States, Colombia, and Drug Policy, 1984–2004," 246–50; Adam Isacson, "The U.S. Military in the War on Drugs," in Youngers and Rosin, eds., *Drugs and Democracy in Latin America*, 22–7.

(1994–8) and Andrés Pastrana Arango (1998–2002) to accept herbicidal spraying of coca, the White House pledged continued assistance for judicial reform and alternative development programs. The problem, as many saw it in Colombia, was the imbalance in aid dollars, the vast majority of which went for programs that securitized aid. The focus on force nicely paralleled the growth of militarism in U.S. security planning under Clinton. Together, the State and Defense Departments promoted a combat ethos in the making of drug policy toward Colombia and held civilian officials accountable for their response. This approach ultimately helped undermine the growth of civil society and governability in Colombia.

Fumigation meant extensive environmental degradation. The area that was subject to spraying grew from 5,600 hectares in 1996 to more than 125,000 hectares seven years later. Small farmers, many of whom fled their homes, lost their crops, suffered from diseases once unknown to them, and had to face aggressive enforcement by the police and special counternarcotics forces. The upshot was an increase in coca and opium growth in regions not previously known for cultivation.[86] Alternative development projects, never seen by the White House as the major solution to drugs in the Andes, were pushed further aside as the number of Colombians in internal exile rose dramatically.[87]

In addition, the militarization of the drug war resulted in a kind of democratization in rural Colombia. Coca growers in the departments of Guaviare, Putumayo, and Caquetá, among them many recent arrivals, engaged in mass demonstrations against fumigation. Perhaps between 60 and 80 percent of the campesinos in these departments were trying to make a living in the illicit coca business.[88] To join the FARC guerrillas made sound economic sense for some displaced Colombians. Others were less sure, including one women's peace movement, *La Ruta Pacífica de las Mujeres* (The Women's Peaceful Path), which opposed violence of the Left and the Right and objected to U.S.-sponsored spraying. Demonstrators often carried signs reading, "*Votamos Samper, no por la DEA*" (We voted for Samper, not the DEA).[89] Yet, there was little Ernesto Samper could do to alleviate the plight of the poor in light of pressure from the United States on drug policy and the historic inability of the political class to act on their behalf.

Thus, Colombia faced a crisis in governability beginning in the mid-1990s. The actions of the Clinton administration amounted to a denigration of sovereignty. Richard Feinberg, an expert on Latin America in the

---

[86] Isacson, "The U.S. military in the War on Drugs," 27; Ramírez Lemus, Stanton, and Walsh, "Colombia: A Vicious Cycle of Drugs and War," 101.

[87] On Colombian reaction to fumigation, see Juan Tokatlian, *Globalización, Narcotráfico y Violencia: Siete ensayos sobre Colombia* (Bogotá: Grupo Editorial Norma, 2000), 122–30.

[88] *El Tiempo* (Bogotá), August 11, 1996.

[89] Walker, "The United States, Colombia, and Drug Policy, 1984–2004," 253–5.

National Security Council, declared, "Sovereignty... has become a refuge for scoundrels."⁹⁰ Myles Frechette, ambassador to Colombia from 1994 to 1997, acknowledged the extent of the U.S. government's animus against Samper: "Washington hated the idea of Samper [as president.]"⁹¹ Indeed, U.S. officials did all they could to cultivate friendly relations with the head of the National Police, Rosso José Serrano, in an effort to "isolate and debilitate" Samper, as Frechette put it.⁹² The vitriolic anti-Samper crusade, one Colombian scholar concludes, "contributed to the erosion of Colombian democracy."⁹³

Ernesto Samper was a controversial figure in Colombian politics, to say the least. He had previously riled U.S. officials by suggesting that marijuana should be excluded from bilateral drug control efforts and should be legalized. Of greater importance, his presidential campaign accepted money from the Cali cartel through the intercession of Fernando Botero, who subsequently became minister of defense. Outraged U.S. officials refused to certify Colombia as cooperating in the drug war and denied Samper a visa to travel to the United States to speak at the UN. Hoping to pressure the president's foes to drive him from office, an effort that failed when a partisan congressional vote dominated by members of his Liberal Party cleared him in a campaign scandal, Drug Enforcement Administration head Thomas A. Constantine thundered, "The fate of Colombia hangs in the balance."⁹⁴ Indeed it did, but less so because of the drug trade than because of FARC advances during Samper's tenure in office. In April 1998, a State Department evaluation found that Colombia's army had suffered "its most disastrous defeat in 35 years of civil war." Army collusion with paramilitary forces was rampant in parts of the country, and abuses of human rights were jeopardizing bilateral military assistance.⁹⁵

Something of far greater magnitude was going on, however, than the castigation of a reluctant participant in the war on drugs. Colombia was a testing ground for the new militarism that characterized strategic globalism under Clinton. The U.S. military could not fight a drug war in Colombia because it would contravene the Powell Doctrine, nor would Congress approve it.

⁹⁰ *El Tiempo*, July 20, 1996.
⁹¹ Quoted in Russell Crandall, *Driven by Drugs: US Policy toward Colombia* (Boulder: Lynne Rienner, 2002), 101.
⁹² *Washington Post*, June 30, 1996.
⁹³ Diana M. Pardo, "The US Foreign Policy Making Process towards Colombia during the Administration of Ernesto Samper Pizano (1994–1998): The Certification Decisions," (Ph.D. diss., University of Miami, 2003), 2.
⁹⁴ See http://www.usdoj.gov/de/cngrtest/ct96-6-6.htm, DEA Congressional testimony, June 6, 1996.
⁹⁵ See http://www.gwu.edu/~nsarchiv/NSAEBB/NSAEBB69/col61.pdf, U.S. Department of State, Bureau of Intelligence and Research, Intelligence assessment, "Colombia: Momentum against Paramilitaries Lost," April 7, 1998.

The White House did not give up the fight, however, all the more so because 1996 was an election year. Clinton named General Barry R. McCaffrey, a veteran of the Vietnam and Gulf wars, to head the Office of National Drug Control Policy. McCaffrey proved to be a splendid liaison with Colombia's National Police.[96] To oversee the coca fumigation campaign, Washington turned to defense contractors; by 2000, under a new counterdrug program, Plan Colombia, Virginia-based DynCorp was one of several such firms waging a drug war primarily designed by McCaffrey.[97] DynCorp, along with Blackwater USA, was largely immune from State Department oversight; both would later profit handsomely for their role in the occupation of Iraq.[98]

As Samper prepared to leave office in 1998, the United States acknowledged that drug control had fared reasonably well during his tenure.[99] His successor, Andrés Pastrana of the Conservative Party, had to cope not only with a civil war but also with U.S. pressure to wage war on drugs. Pastrana decided to negotiate with the FARC, noting, "The root problem of Colombia's crisis is not violence, or even drugs. It is the poverty [in the nation] that fuels both guerrilla recruitment and the drug trade." By early 1999, his public position was similar to that of the White House, State, and Defense Departments: "The first enemy of peace is narco-trafficking."[100] Accommodating the FARC proved impossible; by the end of the decade, the FARC either controlled or moved freely in as much as 60 percent of the countryside. As governability ebbed and chances for democracy declined in Colombia, Pastrana found himself at the mercy of the United States. He proposed what became Plan Colombia, initially conceived as an attempt at nation building to be funded by Colombia, a group of European nations, and the United States. In practice, it placed a disproportionate emphasis on security.[101]

Making Colombia the third largest recipient of U.S. security assistance after Israel and Egypt, Plan Colombia put on display conceptual deficiencies in post-Cold War foreign policy. Its multilateral design, though unrealized showed that real multilateralism with shared decision making was regarded with suspicion in Washington. In addition, its reliance on preemptive force to control drugs served better the presumption of hegemony than the values U.S. policymakers were hoping to inculcate abroad. Furthermore, the resort

[96] Walker, "The United States, Colombia, and Drug Policy, 1984–2004," 250–1.

[97] Bacevich, *American Empire*, 159–62.

[98] *New York Times*, October 23, 2007.

[99] U.S. General Accounting Office, *Drug Control: U.S. Counternarcotics Efforts in Colombia Face Continuing Challenges*, GAO/NSIAD-98-60 (Washington, DC: General Accounting Office, February 1998).

[100] *Miami Herald*, October 31, 1998; *New York Times*, January 6, 1999.

[101] Ramírez Lemus, Stanton, and Walsh, "Colombia: A Vicious Cycle of Drugs and War," 105–9.

to preemptive force by the National Police, acting in concert with American contract firms, brought fear to campesinos entrapped in the coca economy. It threw some of them into the arms of the FARC and tended to merge counterguerrilla and counterdrug activities, which resulted in innumerable violations of human rights.[102] Congress responded by passing the 1997 Leahy Amendment, renewable on an annual basis, prohibiting U.S. aid for foreign police or military forces credibly believed to have engaged in human rights abuses without accountability.[103]

Neither fate nor the United States was kind to Andrés Pastrana in 2000. A state of profound crisis overwhelmed his already beleaguered presidency. Washington acted as though the $1.6 billion it was spending on Plan Colombia entitled the United States to exert decisive influence over the internal affairs of Colombia. Influential members of the Liberal Party even welcomed an American military presence. Trying to make a plausible defense of state sovereignty, Pastrana asserted that his nation was not being torn apart by civil war. The claim lacked credibility. Peace talks were failing, Serrano planned to leave his post, and the minister of defense was asking for greater U.S. assistance. The Clinton administration concluded that Pastrana was not a fit partner in the drug war nor up to the task of leading his people. With no indication of irony, the State Department's Thomas Pickering dryly observed, "I hope that in twenty-five years Colombia can reach its goal of being a peaceful nation."[104] Meanwhile, the wait for a politician more dynamic and tractable than either Samper or Pastrana would continue. Fortunately, for Washington's purposes in the wake of September 11, 2001, the wait was not long. That individual materialized in the winner of the 2002 presidential election, Álvaro Uribe – "the war president to end all war presidents" as Robin Kirk of Human Rights Watch put it.[105]

The war on drugs was about to become a secondary front in the war on terror. Whether that development would enhance participatory democracy remains to be seen. A study in 2005 by the Washington Office on Latin America, *Drugs and Democracy in Latin America: The Impact of U.S. Policy*, was not encouraging. Nor was the effect of drugs on civil society in Mexico, where conditions had deteriorated to such an extent by late 2008 that comparison with Colombia a decade earlier was not unwarranted. Hoping to counter attacks on the Mexican state, the Bush administration pushed through Congress something akin to a Plan Colombia for Mexico – a

---

[102] Human Rights Watch and the Washington Office on Latin America were perhaps the two major organizations publishing numerous reports from eyewitness accounts that substantiate this point.
[103] Isacson, "The U.S. military in the War on Drugs," 27.
[104] *El Tiempo*, August 11, 2000; Walker, "The United States, Colombia, and Drug Policy, 1984–2004," 257–9.
[105] Robin Kirk, *More Terrible than Death: Massacres, Drugs, and America's War in Colombia* (New York: Public Affairs, 2003), 279.

$400 million aid package.[106] As in Colombia, though, Mexico's problems were far more structural than the U.S. response to them suggested.

Oil and Strategic Globalism

American hegemony and globalization were unimaginable without secure access to strategic resources, the most basic of which was oil. Oil fueled Bill Clinton's view of America's place in the world. If oil was the *sine qua non* of power and credibility, for many Americans, it was also the lifeblood of the values they held most dear. As a result, the underlying premise behind the security ethos – that the more the United States was involved in the world, the safer it surely would be – continued to link ordinary citizens with schemes for global hegemony, even if that goal was not economically sustainable. Thus, it was that the Clinton administration sought to ingratiate itself with new regimes in the Caspian Sea basin of former Soviet Central Asia, a place where democracy was as alien as in post-Cold War Russia.

One-fifth of the world's reserves of oil and one-eighth of known natural gas reserves invariably pulled U.S. security interests eastward, reversing the geographic direction of Frederick Jackson Turner's frontier thesis. Commencing in September 1997 with joint U.S.-Kazak military exercises, the conjunction of security policy and core values in Kazakhstan, Uzbekistan, Azerbaijan, Kyrgyzstan, and Turkmenistan signaled the breadth of Clinton's hegemonic ambitions. The president presented the terms of the discussion. By gaining access to Caspian oil and natural gas, "we ... diversify our energy supply and strengthen our nation's security."[107] This declaration came five years after the oil giant Chevron agreed to develop Kazakhstan's Tenghiz oil field, perhaps the largest untapped field in the world. The United States, ignoring how much its place in the world was tied to a self-defeating energy policy, counted on the voraciousness of oil companies for access to the Caspian region after the Soviet Union fell apart. Clinton's statement, it is worth noting, followed several years of Kazak-American cooperation in dismantling SS-19 ballistic missiles that the Soviets had housed in Kazakhstan.[108]

Security studies scholar Michael T. Klare observes that the affinity for scarce resources on the Caspian frontier "represents little more than a return to the status quo ante – that is, to the strategic environment that prevailed during the first half of the twentieth century."[109] Simply, oil meant power

---

[106] Youngers and Rosin, eds., *Drugs and Democracy in Latin America*; *Washington Post*, October 23, 2007 and July 11, 2008.

[107] Michael T. Klare, *Resource Wars: The New Landscape of Global Conflict* (New York: Owl Books, 2002), 1–5; quoted words, 4.

[108] Ahmed Rashid, *Jihad: The Rise of Militant Islam in Central Asia* (New Haven: Yale University Press, 2002), 59–60.

[109] Klare, *Resource Wars*, 7.

and influence. The United States therefore had to engage Russia in a contest for influence in the Caspian basin, where competition with China also loomed.[110]

However tempting it might be to view this development as "the Great Game for Empire" meets "the frontier thesis," such whimsy would miss the point. The drive for hegemony has always had a price, one that most Americans generally have ignored because of their sense of exceptionalism. Testifying before Congress in 1936 about natural disasters, Secretary of Agriculture Henry A. Wallace put it this way: "[W]e have been thus far in our history a spendthrift people, squandering natural resources. It is time that we develop a sense of thrift in these vital matters, and a sense of shame."[111] The hegemonic urge entailed unfortunate consequences for core values, particularly since the late 1930s when Franklin Roosevelt began to formulate foreign policy with a globalist bent. Clinton, for his part, squandered much of the remaining moral capital in American values by tying security to strategic resources and undemocratic regimes in Central Asia. The quest for strategic resources bespeaks an attitude of entitlement to the subsoil patrimony of other peoples and states, whereas the support for authoriatrian leaders emphasizes how selective was the U.S. commitment to real democratic governance.

In the late 1990s, plans for expanding the resource base of national security policy into the Caspian region challenged Russia's own security interests. Boris Yeltsin told Strobe Talbott, "I don't like it when the U.S. flaunts its superiority. Russia's difficulties are only temporary. . . . Russia will rise again."[112] Clinton, who likened Yeltsin to "an Irish poet," understandably feared what might happen if Russia were "lost": "You just can't underestimate the impact on our own economy and national security and on the global economy if Russia goes south."[113] That Russia even partly held the key to globalization's success was an astonishing admission of the limits of American power, especially in the face of the unilateral nature of the administration's grand strategy.

The mercurial and malleable Yeltsin would soon fade from the scene. Vladimir Putin became prime minister in August 1999 and then acting president at year's end when Yeltsin resigned. Those changes plus disturbances in the North Caucasus, most notably in Chechnya, where the Russian military engaged in human rights abuses, and tensions with Georgia because of the presence there of Chechen refugees underlined the precariousness of U.S. ambitions in Central Asia. Putin's brutal search for order in the Caucasus

---

[110] Ibid., 88–97.
[111] Quoted in Fredrick B. Pike, *The United States and Latin America: Myths and Stereotypes of Civilization and Nature* (Austin: University of Texas Press, 1992), 269.
[112] Talbott, *The Russia Hand*, 193.
[113] Quoted in ibid., 285, 286.

had the potential to jeopardize American access to resources there. His KGB background led Talbott to find him "enigmatic," a man who had "a knack for being in the right place at the right time with the right protectors." Clinton, though, respected Putin's ability to chart the troubled political landscape he inherited, a position shared by George Kennan, who counseled patience in dealing with Putin and post–Soviet Russia.[114]

As American interests developed in the greater Caspian region, the likelihood was that they would come up against radical Islam. The shadow of Osama bin Laden loomed large. In February 1998, he had announced the inauguration of the World Islamic Front for Jihad against the Jews and the Crusaders, linking groups across the Muslim world in the early stages of a war against the United States that he declared in August 1996. Well before the events of September 2001, bin Laden's orbit stretched from Sudan to Saudi Arabia to Afghanistan to Chechnya, where he reportedly was financing rebel Chechen operations against Russia.[115] Given the presumptive importance of those places to American security, a deadly clash with Islam was likely in the offing.

Clinton did not shrink from confronting terrorists. By the time the president called terrorists "the enemy of our generation" in August 1996, Richard Clarke, who later broke with the administration of George W. Bush over the conduct of the war on terror, was in charge of counterterrorist operations in the National Security Council.[116] Bin Laden's activities were of paramount interest to Clarke, whose efforts to neutralize the Saudi national's al-Qaeda network assumed even greater urgency after the bombing of U.S. embassies in Tanzania and Kenya on August 7, 1998. A strike by cruise missiles against an al-Qaeda camp in Afghanistan failed to kill bin Laden, perhaps because of intercession by Pakistani intelligence.[117] Clarke was convinced that had Pakistan "wanted to capture bin Laden or tell us where he was, [it] could have done so with little effort." Indicative of the nascent struggle between radical jihad and strategic globalism, Clinton had ordered the air attack one month prior to a military exercise in Uzbekistan and Kyrgyzstan.[118]

The American presence in Central Asia highlighted the problems of a foreign policy of globalization and militarism. It was unclear early in America's engagement with the new Asian regimes how something as alien as a market economy would take hold. Militarism in the form of training and the emplacement of bases would provide one answer in the same way that

[114] Ibid., 400–01.
[115] Peter L. Bergen, *Holy War, Inc.: Inside the Secret World of Osama bin Laden* (New York: Free Press, 2001), 92–101; Talbott, *The Russia Hand*, 360.
[116] Blumenthal, *The Clinton Wars*, 655–8; quoted words, 656.
[117] ISI's ties with Islamic militants continued to bedevil the United States throughout the war on terror; see *New York Times*, July 30, 2008.
[118] Richard A. Clarke, *Against All Enemies: Inside America's War on Terror* (New York: Free Press, 2004), 181–9; quoted words, 189. And see Klare, *Resource Wars*, 5.

U.S. armed forces had previously assisted American trade and investment in other parts of the world.[119] The presence of a U.S. air base in Uzbekistan became a lightning rod for extremists, particularly Uzbeks and Kazakhs in the Islamic Movement of Uzbekistan, after September 11. Bases there and throughout the region in Afghanistan, Kyrgyzstan, and Pakistan were constructed to protect oil pipelines and solidify a U.S. presence.[120] The effort in the Clinton years to work with the Taliban in Afghanistan had the same goals: Pipeline security was national security. Pakistani journalist Ahmed Rashid called pipelines "the driving force behind Washington's interest in the Taliban."[121] The Taliban, of course, would be subjected to U.S. firepower shortly after the attacks of September 11 on the World Trade Center and the Pentagon.

Conclusion

Bill Clinton would be out of office before it became clear just how problematic was the Washington-Moscow security axis in the Caspian. After meeting with Putin in Slovenia in June 2001, George W. Bush gushed, "I looked the man in the eye.... I was able to get a sense of his soul.... We've got common interests." Putin went so far as to call it "a pragmatic relationship."[122] Sooner rather than later, Russia would balk at acting as America's junior partner in its sphere of influence, the former Soviet republics.[123] Bush and Vice President Dick Cheney worked assiduously to insert American corporations and U.S. influence into the expanding oil regions of sub-Saharan Africa, namely, Nigeria, Gabon, Congo, Angola, Equatorial Guinea, and Sudan. Although the extent of their oil and gas reserves was not unusually large, the introduction of Western money and technology in most of these countries accelerated the "curse of oil" – an explosion of want and corruption amid a proliferation of petrodollars. Worse still for U.S. security objectives, China became America's foremost competitor in Sudan where Beijing backed the Sudanese government in its fight against rebels in Darfur who were sabotaging oil pipelines.[124] The ugly reality of genocide in Darfur

---

[119] This aspect of Clinton's new militarism would be continued under Bush until the United States had more than 700 bases worldwide; Johnson, *The Sorrows of Empire*, 151–61, 167.

[120] Rashid, *Jihad*, 156–80, 190–3.

[121] Ahmed Rashid, *Taliban: Militant Islam, Oil, and Fundamentalism in Central Asia* (New Haven: Yale University Press, 2000), 163.

[122] Quoted in Talbott, *The Russia Hand*, 405–6.

[123] See, for example Dmitri Trenin, "Russia Leaves the West," *Foreign Affairs* 85 (July/August 2006): 87–91; Dmitri K. Simes, "Losing Russia: The Costs of Renewed Confrontation," *Foreign Affairs* 86 (November/December 2007): 36–46.

[124] John Ghazvinian, *Untapped: The Scramble for Africa's Oil* (Orlando: Harcourt: 2007); *Washington Post*, December 23, 2004; Reuters News, October 25, 2007; David Zweig

in western Sudan again revealed the nearly hopeless cause of human security wherever scarce strategic resources and great power ambitions coalesced.

Clinton was not blind to the linkage between the nonrenewable resource that was oil and high energy consumption in the United States. The president and his top advisers accepted warnings about adverse effects on the environment of continuing reliance on fossil fuels by signing the Kyoto Protocol on Climate Change; the U.S. Senate refused to ratify the accord, however.[125] What Clinton proved incapable of undertaking was a rethinking of the security ethos in ways that would significantly alter American energy consumption. By 2001, his belief that the nation must play a hegemonic role in world affairs made attempts at resource conservation all but farcical. The United States and major American oil companies were inextricably involved in some of the most unstable regions of the world, where events beyond their control threatened to embroil the country in an endless series of crises. Pursuit of strategic globalism blinded U.S. officials to the scarcity of other resources, water being the most obvious, and how it could involve the United States in local or regional conflicts perhaps beyond extrication.[126] Tantalum (or coltan), another scarce and indispensable resource, is a hard metal found in the volatile Democratic Republic of Congo, formerly Zaire. Tantalum is essential for manufacturing mobile phones, night vision goggles, fiber optics, and capacitors, all of which helped sustain Clinton's dual objectives of hegemony and globalization.[127] Without tantalum, clandestine military operations would be less likely to succeed and instant communication, the essence of a globalized economy, would be less reliable.

Despite apparent differences between George W. Bush and Al Gore in the 2000 election, where security policy was concerned the difference was one of degree, rather than kind. Just as Clinton had followed the elder Bush in accepting the imperatives of strategic globalism, so too did the younger Bush and the neoconservatives who advised him on security policy believe that America's avowed exceptionalism mandated a global mission in the Wilsonian tradition. Indeed, like many of his predecessors, Clinton had reserved the right to strike preemptively in defense of American values and interests. In that regard, he issued Presidential Decision Directive-39 in June 1995; still classified, it evidently authorizes all necessary action to counter terrorist threats to national security.[128] What was impossible to see in the heat of the contested election and its bitter aftermath was the cost that would soon be exacted on core values. The charter of the Project for the

---

and Bi Jianhai, "China's Global Hunt for Energy," *Foreign Affairs* 85 (September/October 2005): 25–38 .

[125] Dilip Hiro, *Blood of the Earth: The Battle for the World's Vanishing Resources* (New York: Nation Books, 2007), 274–6, 284–6, 293–5.

[126] Klare, *Resource Wars,* especially chapters 6 and 7.

[127] See http://www.worldpolicy.org/projects/arms/news/dollarsandsense.html.

[128] See http://www.fas.org/irp/offdocs/pdd39.htm.

New American Century did not appreciably differ from NSC-68 or from the plethora of Cold War doctrines issued in the names of various presidents. The message was the same: America was under siege and must become more deeply engaged abroad to save the nation. Engaged it was, prompting historian John Lewis Gaddis, a favorite in the Bush White House, to write, "There's not the slightest doubt in my mind that the world was a better place at the end of the twentieth century because the United States rejected its earlier isolationism and assumed global responsibilities during it."[129] He did not add "except under Bill Clinton."

Those responsibilities were, of course, related to the exercise of presidential power. We have seen how reluctant Clinton was to consult with Congress about security issues, showing disdain for the separation of powers and, by implication, critical public discourse. Something more was at work here than is at first apparent. If public discourse – that is, the essence of democracy – had the potential to affect America's new militarism, then economic competition abroad might impair the pace of globalization. Thus, it was that the U.S. government and the International Monetary Fund welcomed the crisis of the "Asian Tigers" in the late 1990s. The crucial role of the state in the booming economies of South Korea, Malaysia, Indonesia, the Philippines, and Thailand had to be reduced. The proximate cause of the crisis, a scarcity of dollars backing Thailand's currency, set off a domino effect. When the dust settled, multinational businesses were finding more opportunities to trade and invest in Asia than had been available for some time. Clinton minimized the severity of the crisis, whereas Thomas Friedman honestly observed that "globalization did us all a favor by melting down [these] economies." Any sense of victory was short-lived; reaction against IMF shock therapy and American triumphalism reared its head at the WTO gathering in Seattle in 1999. Not merely did young protestors take to the streets in anger to condemn globalization; inside the conference, developing countries refused to consider additional concessions on trade until the United States and its industrial allies altered their own longstanding protectionist policies.[130] *New York Times* editorial writer Tina Rosenberg commented, "[N]o nation has ever developed over the long term under the rules being imposed today on third-world countries by the institutions controlling globalization."[131]

Disdain for debate about security policy and near paranoia about challenges to IMF- and American-style globalization revealed the shortcomings

---

[129] John Lewis Gaddis, *Surprise, Security, and the American Experience* (Cambridge: Harvard University Press, 2004), 117.

[130] Naomi Klein, *The Shock Doctrine: The Rise of Disaster Capitalism* (New York: Metropolitan Books, 2007), 263–80; Thomas L. Friedman, *The Lexus and the Olive Tree* (New York: Farrar, Straus and Giroux, 1999), 452.

[131] Tina Rosenberg, "The Free-Trade Fix," *New York Times Magazine*, August 18, 2002.

of strategic globalism. A modern capitalist political economy could not sustain the government's hegemonic pretensions; core values would be much the poorer for them in time of crisis. For instance, religiously motivated non-state actors, "the enemy of our generation," had to be dealt with severely. Clinton turned as early as 1996 to the practice of extraordinary rendition to seize radical Muslims in Africa. Richard Clarke has disclosed, "By the mid-1990s these snatches were becoming routine" by the FBI and CIA. "President Clinton approved every snatch that he was asked to review."[132] The salient issue is the fate of habeas corpus as applied to such adversaries. To suspend it was to weaken the rule of law and inevitably damage the core values that sustained it. Clinton evidently did not order, as did his successor, the National Security Agency (NSA) to spy on the electronic communications of American citizens at home, a violation of the Foreign Intelligence Surveillance Act (FISA) of 1978. He left that task to the FBI, which perhaps acted within FISA's guidelines.[133] Congress increased antiterrorist funds for the FBI in 1996, but balked at granting broader authority to the president for domestic spying. What Clinton did accomplish, though, helped free Bush to regard core values as mere expedients after September 11, 2001.[134]

To be sure, September 11 was as exceptional as Japan's attack on Pearl Harbor in 1941. That Bush appropriated the understanding of that event to imperil rights, liberties, constitutional guarantees, and adherence to international agreements was unique only in its thoroughness. After all, core values had suffered during World War I and after, when innocent Japanese and Japanese Americans were incarcerated in 1942, and during the Nixon era. In the wake of September 11, the damage that had been done to foundational ideals – that is, to the nation's very identity – in the long age of the security ethos rendered them vulnerable to a frontal assault by George W. Bush and his administration.

---

[132] Clarke, *Against All Enemies*, 142–5; quoted words, 143, 145.

[133] On FISA and the NSA, see James Bamford, *Body of Secrets: Anatomy of the Ultra-Secret National Security Agency from the Cold War through the Dawn of a New Century* (New York: Doubleday, 2001), 440–3; James Risen, *State of War: The Secret History of the CIA and the Bush Administration*, paper ed. (New York: Free Press, 2007), 42–3.

[134] *New York Times*, October 1, 2001.

PART FOUR

THE BUSH DOCTRINE

9

The War on Terror and Core Values

I think for us to get American military personnel involved in a civil war inside Iraq would literally be a quagmire.... Once we got to Baghdad, what would we do?... I think it makes no sense at all.

Dick Cheney, 1991

[O]ur nation is best when we project our strength and our purpose with humility.

George W. Bush, 2000

Necessity creates war, not a hovering zeitgeist called "law."

John Yoo

After taking office in January 2001, George W. Bush borrowed from his father and Bill Clinton as he prepared to chart the nation's course in foreign policy. Access to oil reserves in the Persian Gulf and elsewhere was, of course, a crucial policy objective.[1] Cordial, if not close, relations with Russia would determine his success in the diplomatic realm. Hoping for more, Bush identified President Vladimir Putin as an ally on major issues like democratization, economic integration, and missile defense. The last was the core of an initiative that would entail abandoning the 1972 Anti-Ballistic Missile Treaty with the Soviet Union. Bush badly underestimated Putin's desire to restore Russia's global influence, which led to much unease in Moscow about the growing American presence in the greater Caspian region. Nor did he understand that differences of opinion with Russia were, in fact, substantive; as a result, there was great dismay as Putin opposed key

---

[1] Well into Bush's second term as president, the United States was still importing at least two-thirds of its petroleum needs, with Saudi Arabia, Venezuela, and Russia the second, fourth, and eighth largest suppliers, respectively. In November 2007, as oil prices neared $100 per barrel, among the countries poised to profit the most were Iran, Venezuela, and Russia – none of which could be counted on as reliable supporters of U.S. security policy. See *Washington Post*, November 10, 2007.

aspects of U.S. security policy in the former Soviet republics, Europe, and the Middle East, where differences over how to respond to Iran's nuclear program soured U.S.-Russian relations throughout Bush's second term.[2]

From the outset of his presidency, Bush dismissed humanitarian intervention in places like Haiti as outside the vital interests of the United States, forgetting his father's belated efforts to help the Kurds in Iraq, not to mention the ill-fated mission to Somalia. The corollary of such activism – nation building – was judged irresponsible; the U.S. role in the 2004 ouster of President Jean-Bertrand Aristide in Haiti and the subsequent chaos highlighted the cavalier ways in which wealthy nations dealt with the world's most impoverished people, scarcely acknowledging either their security needs or dignity.[3] The situation in Haiti offers one example of how two pillars of Washington's democracy project, human rights and self-determination, were at best selectively incorporated into the making of Bush's foreign policy. The sale of arms, a major aspect of U.S. security policy, compromised the democracy project. In 2006, U.S. arms sales were nearly double that of its nearest competitor, Russia, with the United States the leading supplier in the developing world. Among the major recipients of military hardware were Pakistan and Saudi Arabia, key allies in the war on terror and countries not known for their defense of human rights.[4]

The ideals of human security and self-determination fared badly during the Bush presidency, nowhere more so than in Iraq. It is not the purpose of this book to narrate a history of the war, a task that others have successfully undertaken.[5] Iraq barely existed as a viable state, let alone one on the path to democratic governance by the end of 2006. The *Iraq Study Group Report* – directed by James A. Baker III and former Democratic congressman from Indiana and vice chairman of the 9/11 Commission, Lee H. Hamilton – began with these words: "The situation in Iraq is grave and deteriorating."[6] The report did present several ideas to improve the political and security situation of the national unity government that came into existence in May 2006, while expressing concern about how closely the country's fate seemed tied to oil.[7] By late 2007, though, the war may have been costing American

---

[2] *New York Times*, October 17, 2007.

[3] Joan Hoff, *A Faustian Foreign Policy from Woodrow Wilson to George W. Bush: Dreams of Perfectibility* (New York: Cambridge University Press, 2008), 161–2; Noam Chomsky, Paul Farmer, and Amy Goodman, *Getting Haiti Right This Time: The U.S. and the Coup* (Monroe: Common Courage Press, 2004), especially 11–36.

[4] *New York Times*, October 1, 2007.

[5] See, for example, George Packer, *The Assassins' Gate: America in Iraq* (New York: Farrar, Straus and Giroux, 2005); Thomas E. Ricks, *Fiasco: The American Military Adventure in Iraq* (New York: Penguin Press, 2006); Peter W. Galbraith, *The End of Iraq: How American Incompetence Created a War without End*, paper ed. (New York: Simon & Schuster, 2007).

[6] James A. Baker III and Lee H. Hamilton, co-chairs, *The Iraq Study Group Report* (New York: Vintage Books, 2006), xiii.

[7] Ibid., 24.

taxpayers more than $700 million per day.[8] By the middle of 2008, the U.S. military presence had helped reduce the level of violence, but that was no guarantee of political stability.[9] No amount of money expended truly protected the most vulnerable in Iraq where infant mortality rose from the inflated levels of the 1990s: The 2005 figure was 125 deaths per 1,000 live births.[10] There was in Iraq, the UN Assistance Mission for Iraq found in June 2007, a human crisis: "Daily life for the average Iraqi civilian remains extremely precarious."[11] Women were especially at risk for rape in a land where Sunni, Shi'ites, and Kurds zealously guarded their own or regional interests at one another's and the common expense.

Building on the renascent militarism of the Clinton years, Bush, perhaps with North Korea's nuclear ambitions in mind, was determined to enhance U.S. military capabilities further. He also derailed Clinton's efforts to reach a *modus vivendi* with Pyongyang. Had American politics not been so turbulent after Bush's disputed electoral victory, President Clinton and Kim Jong Il might have exchanged high-level visits.[12] In any event, Bush took office claiming, "I don't want to be the world's policeman." On nominating Colin Powell to be his secretary of state, Bush observed, "[O]ur nation is best when we project our strength and our purpose with humility."[13] If American foreign policy had been in more experienced hands, namely, those of Bush's Democratic opponent Al Gore, it would have looked much the same: Strategic globalism remained the paramount foreign policy goal, until 9/11.

In the presidential campaign, Bush did not emphasize the issue of terror, even though al-Qaeda struck the Navy destroyer USS *Cole* on October 12 in Yemen, killing seventeen Americans. This omission alarmed Richard Clarke, still serving as the expert on antiterror operations on the National Security Council when the new president settled into power. Bush's national security advisor, Condoleezza Rice, decided that Clarke's position would be administratively downgraded despite "the imminent al-Qaeda threat." Rice apparently had never heard of al-Qaeda before Clarke briefed her in January.[14] In fact, Secretary of Defense Donald Rumsfeld's top deputy, Paul Wolfowitz, downplayed the reach of Osama bin Laden's influence or his

---

[8] *Washington Post*, September 22, 2007; the figure included projections for health care for veterans and interest on the debt resulting from the war.

[9] *New York Times*, July 22, 2008.

[10] *The Independent* (U.K.), May 8, 2007.

[11] UN Assistance Mission for Iraq, *Human Rights Report: 1 April–30 June 2007*, 3.

[12] Joel S. Wit, Daniel B. Poneman, and Robert L. Gallucci, *Going Critical: The First North Korean Nuclear Crisis* (Washington, DC: Brookings Institution Press, 2004), 375–7; Madeleine Albright with Bill Woodward, *Madam Secretary: A Memoir* (New York: Miramax Books, 2003), 578–600.

[13] James Mann, *Rise of the Vulcans: The History of Bush's War Cabinet* (New York: Viking, 2004), 256, 264.

[14] Richard A. Clarke, *Against All Enemies: Inside America's War on Terror* (New York: Free Press, 2004), 227–31; quoted words, 231.

organizational skill: "You give bin Laden too much credit. He could not do [all he did] . . . without a state sponsor."[15]

Powell later told a skeptical 9/11 Commission that, early on, "Bush was very concerned about al-Qaeda and the safe haven given them by the Taliban" in Afghanistan. The Commission, however, found no "diplomatic initiatives on al-Qaeda with the Saudi government before 9/11." In fact, officials "did not begin their major counterterrorism policy review until April 2001."[16] The incongruity between Powell's testimony and the Commission's report reflected differences within the administration over the focus of security policy, with Powell attempting to make a case for prescience against terrorist activities by the administration.

If there was any farsightedness, it was better represented by Wolfowitz, who framed security issues in line with his own understanding of strategic globalism. That is, counterterrorism could not stand alone; it had to defer to the grand strategy of securing America's status as an unrivaled unipolar power. That had been his position in 1992 when, as one of then-Secretary of Defense Dick Cheney's assistants, Wolfowitz and his aide I. Lewis Libby prepared the 1992 Defense Planning Guidance. Though the exercise was controversial, as evidenced by negative public reaction following a story in the *New York Times*, Cheney viewed its tough language as essential to post-Cold War security policy, seeing it as "a rationale for our role in the world."[17] The Defense Planning Guidance, which has been likened to NSC-68, prefigured the charter document of the Project for the New American Century (PNAC) by five years.[18] As the new militarism gathered steam under Clinton and Bush,[19] the presumption that the United States should maintain strategic hegemony indefinitely was consistent with the imperatives underlying the security ethos. That the Bush administration might act with humility in world affairs was inconceivable, before or after 9/11.

Political Economy and Grand Strategy

Before examining how core values fared under the Bush administration, it is worth recalling that structural weaknesses in the American economy since the early 1970s had constrained the prospects for strategic globalism. When Bush took office, the national debt stood at just under $6 trillion; the

[15] Ibid., 231–2.

[16] Steven Strasser, ed., *The 9/11 Investigations* (New York: Public Affairs, 2004), 73, 92 (Powell), 454.

[17] Mann, *Rise of the Vulcans*, 208–13; quoted words, 211; *New York Times*, March 8, 1992.

[18] Packer, *The Assassins' Gate*, 12–14.

[19] Mann, *Rise of the Vulcans*, 214–15; Andrew J. Bacevich, *The New American Militarism: How Americans Are Seduced by War*, paper ed. (New York: Oxford University Press, 2006), 89–91, presents a slightly different interpretation, emphasizing the growing potential of neoconservatives in the late 1990s to influence security policy.

projected budget surplus over the next decade was $5 trillion.[20] This amount was squandered long before his reelection in 2004. Entering his final year in power, Bush had increased the national debt to more than $9 trillion.[21] Once they took the reins of government, the PNAC neoconservatives and Bush quickly abandoned the tenets of Republican fiscal orthodoxy, spending lavishly, cutting taxes, and burdening future generations with a mountain of debt. What was most painful for traditional conservatives was the unhappy fact that homeland security and the Iraq war only accounted for about half of the spending that produced Bush's first-term deficit. Economic mismanagement by a Republican-controlled Congress abounded as the White House moved to curry favor with corporate interests.[22] This banquet for the rich also symbolized the inherent deficiencies of globalization as practiced by Washington, its allies, and most multinational businesses throughout the world.

As we saw in the previous chapter, globalization was fundamental to America's identity as the world's hegemon. Critics of both the philosophy underlying globalization and the institutions on which it depended – the World Bank, the International Monetary Fund (IMF), and the World Trade Organization (WTO) – argued that globalization perpetuated historic inequities between the developed world and those nations without political and economic clout.[23] Economist Jeffrey Sachs, known for his work on behalf of the IMF and structural adjustment from Bolivia to Poland, shared the concerns of the antiglobalization movement while decrying its more extreme and violent tactics. Sachs parlayed his reputation as a supporter of the economic establishment to issue a call for what he termed "Enlightened Globalization." Passionately, he contended that "capitalism with a human face" was a real possibility, in large part because of the antiglobalization protests. "Too many protesters," he wrote, "do not even know that Adam Smith shared their moral sentiments and practical calls for social improvement." The solution, if there was one, was to hold multinational corporations to account for their impact on the poorest of the poor. Ending poverty was therefore a question of human rights – that is, of human security – in a dangerous world.[24]

[20] Jeffrey E. Garten, "The Global Economic Challenge," *Foreign Affairs* 84 (January/February 2005), 40.
[21] See http://www.treasurydirect.gov/NP/BPDLogin?application=np for up-to-date debt calculations.
[22] John Micklethwait and Adrian Wooldridge, *The Right Nation: Conservative Power in America* (New York: Penguin Press, 2004), 254–60.
[23] Generally, see Catherine Caufield, *Masters of Illusion: The World Bank and the Poverty of Nations* (London: Pan Books, 1998); Caufield writes, "The [World] Bank does not have a history of taking a strong stand on human rights" (p. 206).
[24] Jeffrey D. Sachs, *The End of Poverty: Economic Possibilities for Our Time* (New York: Penguin Books, 2006), 353–9; quoted words, 357.

Whatever the shortcomings of the IMF and the WTO, Sachs pointed to the United States as the greatest obstacle to overcoming poverty. America must "end its reveries of empire and unilateralism and rejoin the world community in multilateral processes." The costly war in Iraq, in effect funded through budget deficits rather than taxation, precluded enlightened globalization. Sachs, like Joseph Stiglitz and other critics of globalization, could not help but conclude, "The United States simply does not hold a margin of economic advantage sufficient to sustain any real attempt at global empire, however good or bad such an idea might be."[25]

Throughout the war in Iraq, the Bush administration pursued a shifting version of globalization. The rules of the IMF and the regulations of the WTO were for their weak and presumably compliant trading partners, including the European Union, Canada, Japan, India, China, Mexico, and Brazil, to accept. Meanwhile, the United States would continue protecting declining industries like steel and favored segments of American agribusiness, particularly cotton. Cotton, of course, had enjoyed a special protected status for decades. In addition, American law essentially subsidized some major exporting firms to shield them from what the WTO deemed fair competition.[26]

Bowing to pressure from other industrial powers, the United States did give way on steel, but resisted on cotton, a move that was particularly harmful to poor farmers in West Africa and Brazil.[27] During trade negotiations in 2004 at Doha, Qatar, American representatives rejected the claim by nations in the Southern Hemisphere that agribusiness lobbyists and the money they contributed to members of Congress and the White House to finance campaigns were comparable to the governmental corruption that Washington disdained in the developing world.[28] What Alice H. Amsden, a professor of political economy at MIT, described as the "Second American Empire" arose coincident with the election of Ronald Reagan and established two rules for maintaining U.S. hegemony: Demand open markets and insist on economic liberalization by trading partners. This system failed the poorest of Africa's poor. Malawi, for example, was beset by famine until 2005 when President Bingu wa Mutharika decided to practice not what Washington and the World Bank preached, but what the United States practiced: subsidies for farmers. By supporting the price of fertilizer and quality seeds, Malawi's government turned the country into a net exporter of food in the region. Local food prices in Malawi fell and farm income rose. As of late 2007, the United States had not provided financial support for the subsidy program.[29]

---

[25] Ibid., 359.

[26] *New York Times*, September 1, 2004 and January 22, 2005.

[27] Ibid., December 7, 2003 and January 16, 2004.

[28] Alice H. Amsden, *Escape from Empire: The Developing World's Journey through Heaven and Hell* (Cambridge: MIT Press, 2007), 132.

[29] *New York Times*, December 2, 2007.

Thus, Sachs was not wrong to conclude that U.S. interests were impeding the widespread desire in the developing world for self-determination.[30]

Looming large over the attempt to project American power into the twenty-first century via strategic globalism was China. If China was not the military threat some neoconservatives believed it to be,[31] neither was it the accommodating trading partner many in Washington hoped for. The administration had trumpeted Beijing's entry into the WTO, saying that it "will dramatically cut import barriers imposed on American agricultural products. This agreement... expands our access to a market of over one billion people." Secretary of State John Hay could scarcely have expected anything more when he announced the Open Door policy at the outset of the twentieth century. In 2006, on the fifth anniversary of China's membership in the WTO, U.S. Trade Representative Susan C. Schwab was much less euphoric: "China's overall record is decidedly mixed."[32] A trade war, though unlikely, was not out of the question because of Chinese disregard for intellectual property rights and its provision of subsidies for firms exporting everything from plastic to steel. For their part, Chinese trade officials acted as though the United States was in dire need of the Chinese market.[33] And so it seemed to be, a fact of post-9/11 life that was not at all conducive to U.S. hegemony. What, one might ask, would become of U.S. security objectives if they depended on the largesse of America's greatest commercial competitor and, in some ways, its foremost military rival in Asia?

Solidifying its recent status as an economic power, China not only accumulated substantial currency reserves but also purchased long-term U.S. Treasury securities. For the first half of the decade, China pegged the yuan to the dollar, thus keeping the yuan's value artificially low, greatly benefiting Chinese exporters yet putting them on a collision course with American merchants. The American trade deficit with China was more than $160 billion in 2004 and reached at least $230 billion two years later. China's dollar peg ended in July 2005, and the value of the yuan subsequently rose by about 10 percent. That revaluation did not stop China from replacing Canada as America's biggest trade partner for the early months of 2007, at which time China also became the world's second largest commercial exporter after Germany. Meanwhile, China was searching for more lucrative markets, especially in the European Union where a strong euro allowed China to consider diversifying its immense holdings in foreign currency.[34] This move, which President Bush termed "foolhardy," resulted from the overwhelming imbalance in trade with the United States; by late 2007, China held nearly

---

[30] Sachs, *The End of Poverty*, 259.

[31] John Gittings, *The Changing Face of China: From Mao to Market* (New York: Oxford University Press, 2005), 296–7; Mann, *Rise of the Vulcans*, 242–3, 260, 281–3.

[32] See http://www.fas.usda.gov/itp/china/accession.html.

[33] *New York Times*, April 18, 2007.

[34] Ibid.; Associated Press, May 21, 2007.

$1.5 trillion in currency reserves, primarily dollars.[35] The problem for the United States was that it was financing abroad more than 90 percent of its national debt through the sale of Treasury securities.[36] It was unlikely, however, that China would precipitously reduce its dollar or securities holdings; congressional insistence that China slow the rate of growth of its economy or face U.S. retaliation had become a persistent, contentious issue in bilateral relations.[37]

The dollar and thus globalization came under attack from other quarters as the Bush administration began its last eighteen months in power. Close to home, the most ambitious and threatening project was the founding of the Banco del Sur, an alternative regional development bank and the brainchild of Hugo Chávez of Venezuela, with strong support from Néstor Kirchner of Argentina, Evo Morales of Bolivia, and Rafael Correa of Ecuador.[38] In South America, more than a few officials saw the World Bank and the IMF, in Chávez's words, as "tools of American imperialism."[39] The Washington Consensus promoting free trade and private sector development, crafted in the wake of the lost economic decade of the 1980s, seemed a distant memory.[40]

A weak dollar had the potential to undermine strategic globalism. One country that would surely suffer were the dollar to remain weak indefinitely was Saudi Arabia.[41] The kingdom's security was closely linked to U.S grand strategy, which in turn was an illusion without access to oil. The virtual exception of Riyadh from sermons about the duty of Arab nations to democratize civil society testified to Saudi Arabia's almost unparalleled place in U.S. security planning. The Saudis therefore viewed with alarm the price of oil as it neared $100 per barrel late in 2007 and $150 per barrel

---

[35] Agence France-Presse, November 11, 2007.

[36] *New York Times*, February 18, 2006.

[37] See, for example, http://www.bloomberg.com for July 30, 2007 and November 10, 2007. Japanese investors were not reluctant to diversify their foreign holdings in order to reduce risk; see *New York Times*, November 23, 2007.

[38] See http://www.bicusa.org/en/Article.3299.aspx, Bank Information Center, "Banco del Sur: A reflection of declining IFI relevance in Latin America," April 2007; *La Nación* (Buenos Aires), November 11, 2007 and December 4, 2007. For more on leftist and populist politics in Latin America, see Jorge G. Castañeda, "Latin America's Turn to the Left," *Foreign Affairs* 85 (May/June 2006): 28–43.

[39] Quoted in *Washington Post*, May 11, 2007.

[40] On the Washington Consensus, see David Scott Palmer, *U.S. Relations with Latin America during the Clinton Years: Opportunities Lost or Opportunities Squandered?* (Gainesville: University Press of Florida, 2006), 14–18.

[41] When Rachel Bronson, then at the Council on Foreign Relations in New York, wrote in a book published in 2006 that Riyadh's interest in higher oil prices would put strains on the Saudi-American relationship, she did not foresee the dangerous implications of a price spike and the tumbling strength of the dollar. Rachel Bronson, *Thicker than Oil: America's Uneasy Partnership with Saudi Arabia* (New York: Oxford University Press, 2006), 228–30, 250–2.

in mid-2008, promising as they often had before to increase production to keep prices down. The reality, however, was that it was no longer easy to deliver on that promise. Financing the war in Iraq through borrowing had weakened the power of the dollar as the monetary arbiter in world affairs. At a meeting of OPEC in November 2007, Mahmoud Ahmadinejad of Iran denounced the dollar as "a worthless piece of paper."[42] Chávez assented, with a warning, "The dollar is in free fall, *everyone should be worried about it.*"[43] Well into 2008, the dollar barely held its own against other major currencies.

It bears repeating: The United States could no longer afford a hegemonic grand strategy without mortgaging the nation's future. Yet, the quest persisted throughout the Bush presidency in the war on terror, with decidedly negative consequences for core values. The transformation of grand strategy from strategic globalism to preemption under the Bush Doctrine helps explain what happened.

The Bush Doctrine

The attacks of September 11 brought the United States to an exalted place in the post-Cold War era. Misgivings about American power and its exercise were set aside by much of the world. The outpouring of support for the victims, their families, and the nation itself was heartfelt and deeply moving, a testament to the resilience of the human spirit, to the desire for security by peoples everywhere. George W. Bush, after initial near paralysis, rose to unexpected heights as a leader. Many of his critics suspended prior reservations about his ability to govern a diverse, divided nation. Americans longed to find strength in their president and integrity in their government. They were wasting their time.

Within a year, the Bush administration had adopted a response to terrorist attacks that came straight from the fancies of the neoconservatives populating the Project for the New American Century. Particularly Saddam Hussein in Iraq, but tyrants everywhere were put on notice that they too could suffer the wrath of the United States. Saddam and the leaders of Iran and North Korea were singled out as members of an "axis of evil." Unfortunately, the condemnation likely terminated Tehran's willingness to cooperate in stabilizing Afghanistan's chaotic political and security situation.[44] Before that warning went out in Bush's 2002 State of the Union Address, the Northern Alliance, aided by U.S. airpower and Special Forces troops, seized Kabul,

---

[42] Associated Press, November 19, 2007.

[43] *New York Times*, November 21, 2007; emphasis added.

[44] CNN News, "The Situation Room," December 6, 2007 as reported by Frank Sesno in an interview with former state department official James Dobbins; see also *USA Today*, June 9, 2005.

forcing the Taliban and numerous Arab fighters to flee. Osama bin Laden could not be flushed from the rugged mountains of Tora Bora near the Afghanistan-Pakistan border, where he was probably hiding perhaps with the help of Pakistan's ISI.[45] Washington had no interest in holding accountable General Pervez Musharraf, who came to power in a coup in 1999, despite Pakistan's cozy relationship with the Taliban.

As its predecessors had long done, the Bush administration was moving toward engagement abroad as the best way to assure the nation's safety. Grand strategy soon had a sharper focus than in the senior Bush and Clinton administrations. Along with Iraq, Afghanistan and Pakistan became critical indicators of success or failure. Yet, by late in Bush's second term, the Taliban was resurgent in southern Afghanistan, so much so that U.S. officials had to wonder if NATO allies could hold the country together. Chairman of the Joint Chiefs of Staff Admiral Mike Mullen admitted, "In Afghanistan we do what we can. In Iraq we do what we must." In Pakistan, the unpopular Musharraf attempted to hold the United States hostage to his own political ambitions even as Taliban and al-Qaeda forces were turning sections of the border with Afghanistan into an autonomous region.[46] On December 27, 2007, less than two weeks before scheduled parliamentary elections, opposition leader Benazir Bhutto was assassinated.[47] Musharraf's actions thereafter and a growing urban presence of al-Qaeda in Pakistan brought into question ties between the government, the military, and ISI and the United States, placing Washington's democracy project in disarray and leaving the administration with few viable options.[48]

Such dispiriting developments were far in the future as the war on terror got underway. Core values were about to meet their sternest test. If, as the previous chapter contends, Bill Clinton had put American exceptionalism on life support, then George W. Bush pulled the plug.[49] Journalist Ron Suskind wondered, "[C]an America prevail in this struggle while staying true to its defining principles?"[50] As the Bush Doctrine emerged, both endeavors would be fraught with peril.

---

[45] Clarke, *Against All Enemies*, 279–81; Lawrence Wright, *The Looming Tower: Al-Qaeda and the Road to 9/11* (New York: Vintage Books, 2007), 418–21; Seymour M. Hersh, *Chain of Command: The Road from 9/11 to Abu Ghraib*, paper ed. (New York: Harper Perennial, 2005), 128–33.

[46] Reuters News, November 21, 2007 and *Washington Post*, December 21, 2007 for Afghanistan; Mullen quoted by the Associated Press, December 11, 2007; and *New York Times*, November 18, 2007 for Pakistan.

[47] CNN News, December 27, 2007.

[48] *Washington Post*, July 12, 2008; *New York Times*, July 20, 2008.

[49] Andrew J. Bacevich, *The Limits of Power: The End of American Exceptionalism* (New York: Metropolitan Books, 2008).

[50] Ron Suskind, *The One Percent Solution: Deep inside America's Pursuit of Its Enemies since 9/11*, paper ed. (New York: Simon & Schuster, 2007), 339.

Making a list of the core values that were abused in the struggle against terror creates a kind of litany. It includes freedom of speech, due process of law, freedom of the press, the right to privacy, and protection from unreasonable search and seizure. Expanding this list beyond the nation's borders raises questions about U.S. acceptance of sovereignty, the ideal of self-determination, adherence to international law, indefinite detention and habeas corpus, and the resort to torture in the name of security. Binding everything together are foundational beliefs about the limits of executive power and the inviolability of the rule of law. The war on terror, in short, made a mockery for many inside and outside the country of America's commitment to freedom, democracy, and human rights. This was true even though the president told graduates at the U.S. Military Academy in June 2002, "Our nation's cause has always been larger than our nation's defense. We fight, as we always fight, for a just peace – a peace that favors human liberty. . . . We are in a conflict between good and evil, and America will call evil by its name."[51] The clear Wilsonian echoes in Bush's rhetoric were not an accident. Woodrow Wilson surely believed, as John Lewis Gaddis has written, that "the American sphere of responsibility must extend to ensure American security: . . . it would extend everywhere."[52]

The universalism that suffused Bush's address was a reminder of the role of preemptive action throughout American history. Military force was always to be at the ready to protect and therefore spread the nation's inter-ests and ideals. Contextualizing Bush in this manner helps explain why the United States left Saddam Hussein in power in 1991 at the end of the first Gulf conflict – and why George W. Bush made a different decision ten years later. President George H. W. Bush feared that removing Saddam from power would possibly destabilize the broader Middle East, making the United States "an occupying power in a bitterly hostile land."[53] Secretary of Defense Dick Cheney said in April 1991 about seizing Baghdad, "I think for us to get American military personnel involved in a civil war inside Iraq would literally be a quagmire. . . . Once we got to Baghdad, what would we do? . . . I think it makes no sense at all."[54]

What changed after 9/11? Why did Saddam Hussein become the primary target, rather than Osama bin Laden, despite Bush's promise to take bin Laden "dead or alive"? Though still conjectural, threads of an explanation do exist. Like their predecessors, Bush and his advisers thought in terms of

---

[51] See http://www.whitehouse.gov/news/releases/2002/06/20020601-3.html for the text of the address.

[52] John Lewis Gaddis, *Surprise, Security, and the American Experience* (Cambridge: Harvard University Press, 2004), 42.

[53] George Bush and Brent Scowcroft, *A World Transformed* (New York: Alfred A. Knopf, 1998), 489.

[54] Quoted in Christian Alfonsi, *Circle in the Sand: Why We Went Back to Iraq* (New York: Doubleday, 2006), 218.

a state-based world. A paradigm shift in security thinking was out of the question, no matter how forcefully mavericks like Richard Clarke argued for one; it did not matter that Clarke and other intelligence analysts warned the administration some forty times about al-Qaeda before 9/11.[55] It was an article of faith to Bush and his national security advisers that Saddam Hussein of Iraq endangered the key objectives of American grand strategy – hegemony and globalization.[56] In contrast, Osama bin Laden could impair but not mortally wound vital U.S. interests.

Had it been possible to capture or kill bin Laden, the goal would still have been to remove Saddam from power because Saddam Hussein, given Iraqi oil reserves and his regional ambitions, directly threatened U.S. interests, or so the White House believed. By way of contrast, the Clinton administration did not view Saddam Hussein as imminent a threat to interests in the Persian Gulf as did the neoconservatives who implored Clinton to depose Saddam. Without enthusiasm, Clinton signed the Iraq Liberation Act of 1998, which required the government to support anti-Saddam Hussein groups in Iraq while prohibiting the use of U.S. forces. In any event, Clinton felt constrained by the Powell Doctrine, a limitation Bush cleverly circumvented by naming the general to be his secretary of state.[57] Before Bush decided on war, the same neoconservatives who had prodded Clinton were urging him to act. In a January 2002 issue of *The Weekly Standard*, reminiscent of *The New Republic* before Woodrow Wilson took the United States into war in 1918, leading neoconservatives Robert Kagan and William Kristol prophesied, "[T]he contours of the emerging world order ... [e]ither will be a world order conducive to our liberal democratic principles and our safety, or it will be one where brutal, well-armed tyrants are allowed to hold democracy and international security hostage."[58]

Although the neoconservative drumbeat was important in keeping Iraq in the public eye, it does not reveal much about how or when decisions for war were made in the White House. Commencing in January 2001, the National Security Council (NSC) discussed Iraq and what to do about it. U.S. officials increased contact with the Iraqi opposition in exile, as personified by Ahmed Chalabi of the Iraqi National Congress, which tended to provide the information the White House desired; air strikes reminded the Iraqi leadership that there was still a no-fly zone in parts of the country; and Paul Wolfowitz, Clarke wrote, "urged a focus on Iraqi-sponsored terrorism against the U.S. even though there was no such thing."[59]

---

[55] Thomas Powers, "Secret Intelligence and the 'War on Terror,'" *New York Review of Books*, December 16, 2004, p. 50.

[56] For a related interpretation, see Alfonsi, *Circle in the Sand*, 386.

[57] Ibid., 369–70; Bacevich, *New American Militarism*, 87–91.

[58] Robert Kagan and William Kristol, "What To Do about Iraq," *The Weekly Standard*, January 21, 2002, p. 23.

[59] Alfonsi, *Circle in the Sand*, 378–85; Clarke, *Against All Enemies*, 264 (quoted words).

The attacks of 9/11 were not two days old when Bush told Clarke "to go back over everything, everything. See if Saddam did this. See if he's linked in any way. . . ." Within the next week, the president would say, "I believe Iraq was involved." The NSC was instructed to make contingency plans to strike Iraq should evidence warrant military action. In November, Secretary of Defense Donald Rumsfeld received a similar charge.[60] The National Security Agency (NSA) and the CIA were soon exceeding their statutory authority, on the orders of President Bush, by developing programs to spy on people within the United States. As NSA chief Lieutenant General Michael Hayden emphatically put it, "I could *not* not do this."[61]

The Bush Doctrine, asserting the centrality of preemption in military strategy, was almost at hand. In 1953, former Secretary of State Dean Acheson admitted, "Korea came along and saved us."[62] And, just as the invasion of South Korea by North Korean troops helped the Truman administration persuade Congress to approve the level of spending necessary to implement NSC-68,[63] the Bush administration needed incontrovertible evidence that Iraq posed an imminent threat in order to move against Saddam. Weapons of mass destruction (WMDs) thus became the twenty-first century counterpart of the North Korean army. The difference was that the feared WMDs did not exist. That WMDs *should* have existed was an assumption based on faulty logic and wishful thinking, rather than reliable intelligence analysis.[64] Not accepting responsibility for politicizing the CIA, the White House let it bear the burden of public scrutiny and ire. The fault was a shared one; the CIA was complicit in the misuse of intelligence. "It's broken," a former CIA officer told Tim Weiner. "It's so broken that nobody wants to believe it."[65] In a very real sense, the failure of intelligence and leadership on WMDs may stand as the most pernicious legacy of the security ethos, one that nearly sacrificed the nation's core values.

George W. Bush reveled in the belief that the events of 9/11 and after validated a turn toward unilateralism beyond what his father and Clinton had achieved. There is little doubt that he truly was convinced it was his

[60] Clarke, *Against All Enemies*, 32; Packer, *The Assassins' Gate*, 41; Alfonsi, *Circle in the Sand*, 386; Mark Danner, "The Secret Way to War," *New York Review of Books*, June 9, 2005, p. 70.

[61] Tim Weiner, *Legacy of Ashes: The History of the CIA* (New York: Doubleday, 2007), 482–3; quoted words, 483 (emphasis in original); see also Eric Lichtblau, *Bush's Law: The Remaking of American Justice* (New York: Pantheon Books, 2008), 146–62.

[62] Quoted in Walter LaFeber, *America, Russia, and the Cold War, 1945–2006*, 10th ed. (Boston: McGraw-Hill, 2007), 105.

[63] John Lewis Gaddis, *Strategies of Containment: A Critical Appraisal of American National Security Policy during the Cold War*, rev. and expanded ed. (New York: Oxford University Press, 2005), 106.

[64] Generally see Scott McClellan, *What Happened: Inside the Bush White House and Washington's Culture of Deception* (New York: Public Affairs, 2008).

[65] Quoted in Weiner, *Legacy of Ashes*, 500.

duty to restore the international credibility of the United States. Bush firmly believed, too, that he was up to the task as the chosen agent of his God and history. "[H]istory," he remarked in March 2002, "has called us into action and we are not going to miss that opportunity to make the world more peaceful and more free."[66] Bush had found his mission: He would lead the United States away from America's strategic drift since the Cold War. "A writ of infallibility," one observer wrote, " . . . guided the inner life of the White House."[67]

The absence of the Soviet Union scarcely affected the use of pugnacious rhetoric by Bush. The intimations of preemptive action against Iraq, Iran, or North Korea harked back to the French and Indian War in the 1750s, if not even earlier.[68] In March 2002, Bush apparently blustered, "Fuck Saddam. We're taking him out," as if he had already issued the order to attack Iraq.[69] Underlining the president's crudeness and willingness to go it alone if need be in the war on terror was his retort in July 2003, "Bring 'em on,'" when informed that maintaining an imposing U.S. military presence in Iraq after the downfall of Saddam's government would likely unleash a radical Islamic backlash.[70]

Preemption's modern lineage did not start with Bush's West Point address, nor with the PNAC manifesto, nor with the Defense Policy Guidance, and not even with the Team B report of the mid-1970s. It can be found in the hyperbolic language of NSC-68: "The Soviet Union . . . is animated by a new fanatic faith."[71] Like others who linked security to a global presence, the authors of NSC-68 warned about the perils of inaction:

Even if there were no Soviet Union we . . . would face the fact that in a shrinking world the absence of order is becoming less and less tolerable. . . . The risks we face are of a new order of magnitude, commensurate with the total struggle in which we are engaged. . . . The risks crowd in on us . . . so as to *give us no choice, ultimately, between meeting them effectively* or being overcome by them.[72]

Given the undercurrent of fear amid bravado, there is little difference between the tenor of NSC-68 and Bush's succinct, inelegant challenge to America's foes. Preemption in some form was the only reliable road to security.

---

[66] Quoted in Robert Jervis, "Understanding the Bush Doctrine," *Political Science Quarterly* 118 (Fall 2003), 368.

[67] Ron Suskind, "Without a Doubt," *New York Times Magazine*, October 17, 2004.

[68] See chapter 1.

[69] Quoted in Packer, *The Assassins Gate*, 45.

[70] See http://www.cnn.com/2003/ALLPOLITICS/07/02/sprj.nitop.bush/.

[71] U.S. Department of State, *Foreign Relations of the United States, 1950*, vol. I: *National Security Affairs; Foreign Economic Policy* (Washington, DC: Government Printing Office, 1977), 237.

[72] Ibid., 262–3 (emphasis added).

Bush formally introduced preemption to the American public with the release in September 2002 of his National Security Strategy. Calling 9/11 and its aftermath "this moment of opportunity," the president pledged "to extend the benefits of freedom across the globe... [and] actively work to bring the hope of democracy, development, free markets, and free trade to every corner of the world." He promised to respond to threats "before they are fully formed.... In the new world we have entered, the only path to safety is the path of action." In Bush's White House, willingness to resort to preemption was critical: "We cannot let our enemies strike first."[73]

It is not enough to conclude that the neoconservative strategic agenda was finally in its ascendancy: Something more basic was at work. From the early days of containment through the several variants of strategic globalism, U.S. officials sought to shape the reality of the world in which they operated. Ron Suskind expressed surprise when a Bush aide dismissed the work of journalists and scholars, the "reality-based community," who believe their work reflected reality. The aide explained, "We're an empire now, and when we act, we create our own reality."[74] The statement that "history's actors," as the aide termed administration officials, understood the creation of reality to be a fundamental part of their activities should occasion little surprise. Attempting to alter the way friends and foes perceived reality and deny others the right to interpret their own history had long complemented U.S. grand strategy. Perhaps no one put the matter more clearly than Dean Acheson, who once remarked, "We are willing to help those who believe the way we do to continue to live the way they want to live."[75] That convergence of beliefs in the post-1945 era did not happen without conscious effort, and it almost created more than an "empire by invitation,"[76] something many Cold War scholars have celebrated. What they are applauding, it seems, is a moment in time – the late 1940s – when America's allies came as close as they ever would to accepting the security ethos as their own.

The Professoriate and the Bush Doctrine

Coming to terms with the Bush Doctrine seemed relatively straightforward. Prudence dictated that all possible steps be taken so that there would be no recurrence of 9/11 on American soil. Popular anguish at the horror of that day created a space in which Bush's national security strategy received an

---

[73] *New York Times*, September 20, 2002.

[74] Suskind, "Without a Doubt."

[75] Quoted in William Appleman Williams, *The Contours of American History*, paper ed. (Chicago: Quadrangle Books, 1966), 474.

[76] This term is most famously used in Geir Lundestad, "Empire by Invitation? The United States and Western Europe, 1945–1952," *Journal of Peace Research* 23 (September 1986): 263–77.

initially welcome reception. Much the same held true within the intellectual class. Former left-wing critics of American globalism, including Paul Berman and British radical Christopher Hitchens, who severed his ties with the liberal magazine *The Nation,* found common cause with the administration in supporting the effort to bring freedom, democracy, and free-market enterprise to the Middle East – "a chance," as Berman characterized it, "to undo the whole of Muslim totalitarianism." The puzzle for Berman and others was how to accomplish that goal.[77]

If Berman had no sure answer to his dilemma, some leading academics ostensibly did. They welcomed the prospect of a novel grand strategy, one relevant to fighting a war on terror. To be sure, there appeared various impassioned critiques of administration foreign policy and how it raised echoes of the debacle that was Vietnam. Yet, books like *Iraq and the Lessons of Vietnam* were not widely read; the contributors' pleading – a kind of progressive civic virtue – that the nation must learn from its past went largely unheard in public discourse, no matter how many people turned against the Iraq war.[78] Large though the numbers were, it was not at all clear that the public opposed America's post-Cold War militarism. Instruction of the informed public was typically undertaken by centrist-to-conservative scholars. Three stood out: Joseph S. Nye Jr. and Robert Jervis from political science and John Lewis Gaddis from history. If they did not exude the same gravitas as Hans Morgenthau, Reinhold Niebuhr, Walter Lippmann, or George F. Kennan in his post-State Department days, they were nevertheless among the most recognizable scholars of foreign policy in the early twenty-first century.

Each found something to laud in the Bush Doctrine and its presentation of a new grand strategy. Jervis of Columbia University commented that the Bush Doctrine "does have a strong logic in it, especially if deterrence cannot cope with dedicated adversaries, most notably terrorists. When defense is ... inadequate, the United States must use preventive measures.... To make itself secure, [the United States] must impinge on the security of nondemocracies."[79] Yet, Jervis was no unblinking backer of Bush's doctrine; about the 2002 National Security Strategy, he observed, it "is a policy that is likely to bring grief to the world and the United States." That was because "[t]he adoption of a preventive war doctrine ... is not foreign to

[77] Paul Berman, *Terror and Liberalism,* paper ed. (New York: W. W. Norton & Company, 2004), 196–202; quoted words, 199; Packer, *The Assassins' Gate,* 56–8.

[78] See, for example, Lloyd C. Gardner and Marilyn B. Young, eds., *Iraq and the Lessons of Vietnam: Or, How Not to Learn from the Past* (New York: New Press, 2007). At the beginning of 2008, this book remained outside the top 300,000 books purchased on Amazon.com; Andrew Bacevich's *New American Militarism* came in just under 30,000.

[79] Robert Jervis, "The Remaking of a Unipolar World," *The Washington Quarterly* 29 (Summer 2006), 9, 11.

normal state behavior. It appeals to states that have a values position to maintain."[80] And that could be a dangerous thing.

Joseph Nye's qualms about the Bush Doctrine were of a different order. Nye, a professor of government at Harvard University, had served under Carter and Clinton in several capacities. An advocate of using "soft power" in service to security interests, Nye did not discount the importance of a show of strength, concluding, "[T]he Bush administration was correct in its change of focus" away from traditional state-centered security planning toward the novel threat posed by diverse nonstate actors. "This shifting ground is what the new Bush strategy gets right."[81] In addition, "the new unilateralists are right that maintaining U.S. military strength is crucial and that pure multilateralism is impossible."[82] What most bothered Nye was the possible use of force without due regard for either the weakened condition of the American economy or the chaos-inducing role of nonstate actors. Accordingly, "the United States should incline toward multilateralism whenever possible as a way to legitimize its power and to gain broad acceptance of its new strategy."[83] To Nye, a multilateralism evocative of the first Gulf War would make palatable the more objectionable features of American hegemony.

Within weeks of the issuance of Bush's national security strategy, historian John Lewis Gaddis of Yale University became a fervent advocate. Wilson's great endeavor had to be completed: "[T]he world must be made safe for democracy, because otherwise democracy will not be safe in the world."[84] Indeed, Gaddis found much to commend in the universal assumptions underlying the Bush Doctrine: "U.S. hegemony is . . . linked with certain values that all states and cultures – if not all theorists and tyrants – share."[85] Two years later, a more reflective Gaddis addressed what had become a troubled nexus of preemption, hegemony, and consent. The problem was not Bush's strategy per se, but that its proponents did not know "when to begin consolidating the benefits [the strategy has] provided."[86] Building a real coalition was beyond the capacity of the White House.

Bush's dilemma, the result of basing his security strategy on preemption, could be resolved, Gaddis seemed to suggest, if the administration would embrace the idea that the United States stood for an empire of liberty as

[80] Jervis, "Understanding the Bush Doctrine," 366, 376, 383.
[81] Joseph S. Nye, Jr., "U.S. Power and Strategy after Iraq," *Foreign Affairs* 82 (July/August 2003), 62, 63.
[82] Ibid., 65.
[83] Ibid., 67, 69.
[84] John Lewis Gaddis, "A Grand Strategy of Transformation," *Foreign Policy* No. 133 (November/December 2002), 56.
[85] Ibid., 52.
[86] Gaddis, *Surprise, Security*, 93–104; quoted words, 101.

it had in Jefferson's time. Hegemony as the modern counterpart of expansion would "safeguard liberty." Drawing on lessons from the early American republic, Gaddis averred that "liberty ... could only flourish within an empire that provided safety."[87] This prescription for how to apply the national security strategy was at odds with his fear in late 2002: "If we aren't [welcomed in Baghdad], the whole strategy collapses."[88] That American hegemony and safety may not correlate lies at the heart of the present discussion about the professoriate and the Bush Doctrine.

The National Security Strategy assumed that the American political system, and thus its core values, could accommodate so dramatic a change in strategic thinking. Jervis had his doubts: "The U.S. political system was not constructed to support an active foreign policy, much as Bush wishes that it were."[89] Yet, he warned that engagement abroad was critical or "the international environment will become more menacing to America and its values."[90] The irony was that "hegemony ... magnifies the sense of threat" felt by Americans and may in fact be harmful to its interests and values.[91]

Fear, whether from external threats or self-induced as a consequence of political paranoia, traditionally has not been kind to core values. In historical terms, the Bush Doctrine was a product of fears, the result of policymaking under the security ethos. Its intrinsic militarism threatened the stability of the Western-led, post-1945 international community, another scholar argued.[92] Moreover, in rejecting more than fifty years of multilateral interests in favor of unilaterally promulgating ideals like democracy, those ideals came to seem cynical to domestic opponents of the war and to those in the Middle East and elsewhere who were the intended recipients of U.S. largesse.

The fundamental question was not how to transform the Bush Doctrine into something resembling the Powell Doctrine, but whether the pursuit of security objectives under the rubric of either global containment or strategic globalism had really protected core values. The history of the security ethos in the post-1945 era shows grand strategy often to be detrimental to core values. Consensus over grand strategy, whatever its form, limited the prospects for civic virtue. Since the early days of containment, when Walter Lippmann challenged George Kennan's dystopian brainchild, civic discourse had been badly circumscribed. The intellectual class and the mainstream professoriate in general did not fully comprehend the negative impact of the Bush Doctrine on civic virtue. As we see in the conclusion, one academic, Andrew

---

[87] Ibid., 107.
[88] Gaddis, "A Grand Strategy," 55.
[89] Jervis, "Remaking of a Unipolar World," 18.
[90] Jervis, "Understanding the Bush Doctrine," 383.
[91] Jervis, "Remaking of a Unipolar World," 13.
[92] Melvyn P. Leffler, "9/11 and the Past and Future of American Foreign Policy," *International Affairs* 79 (October 2003): 1045–63; idem, "9/11 and American Foreign Policy," *Diplomatic History* 29 (June 2005): 395–413.

J. Bacevich of Boston University, who had fought in Vietnam to defend grand strategy as it were, would have uncommon second thoughts about militarism as he watched the United States become ensnared in the Bush administration's misguided war in Iraq.

The Bush Administration and Core Values

The crushing impact of the war on terror on core values was long in the making. Indeed, beyond the intellectual class, a majority of the members of Congress, the leading print media, and the general public accepted a global grand strategy. Since the late 1890s, the logic of internationalism and globalism had on occasion brought about a suspension or alteration of core values in the form of rights, particularly freedom of speech and the public's access to information, and liberties, such as protection from unreasonable search and seizure. The very idea of a right to privacy also lost some of its certainty in the name of providing security from feared threats like communist subversion. Outside America's borders, self-determination and state sovereignty were far from absolutes in a world perceived as dangerous. The growing association of the United States with authoritarian governments had become an unsavory political reality in the decades after 1900.[93] In the process, human security invariably gave way to national security, as it again did after September 11, 2001.

After 9/11, rights and liberties were constrained, and the rule of law was brought into question by government actions at home and abroad. Before the end of the Bush presidency, legal scholars were examining how and why these things occurred.[94] For present purposes, four related issues – aggrandizement of power by the executive branch, limits on freedom of speech and the press, electronic surveillance and restrictions on privacy, and treatment of detainees – provide useful insight into the interplay among values, the war on terror, and the state of civic virtue.

Further centralization of power in the executive branch over matters of security was an objective of the Project for the New American Century. It is important, though, not to separate PNAC's aspiration from the history of the imperial presidency, a history that was largely coterminous with the evolution of the security ethos. Arthur M. Schlesinger Jr. captured the bond between a dynamic political economy and strong executive power: "The rise of foreign affairs [in the 1890s] coincided with the rise of a national

---

93 See David F. Schmitz, *Thank God They're on Our Side: The United States and Right-Wing Dictatorships, 1921–1965* (Chapel Hill: University of North Carolina Press, 1999).

94 Frederick A. O. Schwarz Jr. and Aziz Z. Huq, *Unchecked and Unbalanced: Presidential Power in a Time of Terror* (New York: New Press, 2007); Robert M. Pallitto and William G. Weaver, *Presidential Secrecy and the Law* (Baltimore: Johns Hopkins University Press, 2007).

economy dominated by interstate business . . . and this brought the President to the front of affairs too."[95]

The adverse reaction in Congress and among the American people in the 1970s to Watergate and Nixon's efforts to use his power with little or no restraint slowed the accretion of power in the office of the president. Extreme public antipathy toward Nixon did halt for the time being CIA and NSA spying on Americans within the United States, a violation of the legal authority of those two agencies. The War Powers Act of 1973, however, did not truly take power away from the president, only requiring him to report to the Congress within a given amount of time *after* committing troops. And few, if any, citizens believed that Congress would bring forces home once they were engaged in combat.[96] Debate concerning executive primacy over foreign affairs returned to the heart of American politics during the Iran-Contra hearings. The minority response to the official report, attributed to Representative Richard Cheney of Wyoming and staff lawyer David Addington, who later served as Vice President Cheney's senior legal adviser, attempted in carefully calibrated, yet uncompromising language to make the case for inherently broader executive authority – the "unitary executive" as it was called by Reagan's Justice Department.[97] The events of 9/11 were therefore fortuitous in clearing the way for what legal scholars term the "monarchical executive" theory of government. Unlike any of his predecessors, Bush embraced the theory that he could disregard for reasons of "national security" or "military necessity" any law with which he disagreed.[98]

Such instrumentalist reasoning implicitly denied a substantive constitutional role for Congress in foreign affairs. The president had no authority to take the nation into war on foreign soil absent the assent of Congress; this division of power, so important to the Framers of the Constitution, had effectively been rendered meaningless, given the nature of conflict since World War II. What a president was empowered to do under the Constitution was safeguard the nation by responding to attacks on it. What had in fact occurred was a momentous expansion of executive power that altered how the U.S. government regarded international law.[99]

[95] Arthur M. Schlesinger Jr., *The Imperial Presidency* (New York: Popular Library, 1974), 90.

[96] Pallitto and Weaver, *Presidential Secrecy and the Law*, 37–8, 218.

[97] Joel Brinkley and Stephen Engelberg, eds., *Report of the Congressional Committees Investigating the Iran-Contra Affair, with the Minority View* (New York: Times Books, 1988), Section II; Schwarz Jr. and Huq, *Unchecked and Unbalanced*, 156; and Jane Mayer, *The Dark Side: The Inside Story of How the War on Terror Turned into a War on American Ideals* (New York: Doubleday, 2008), 50–6, 61.

[98] Schwarz Jr. and Huq, *Unchecked and Unbalanced*, 153.

[99] David Cole, "What Bush Wants to Hear," *New York Review of Books*, November 17, 2005, pp. 8–9.

The Justice Department turned the original intent of the Constitution on its head. Attorney General John Ashcroft, reminiscent of A. Mitchell Palmer in 1919, provided a rationale for vast executive power that was difficult to dispute after 9/11: "We need the tools to prevent terrorism." What he never explained, because he could not, was why the administration had downplayed the threat from al-Qaeda during its first eight months in power.[100] By mid-November, Bush had used his authority to create military tribunals to deal with suspected terrorists and alleged collaborators; yet, the criminal justice system with its rules of evidence and constitutional guarantees would play no role in those proceedings. Bush and Defense Secretary Donald H. Rumsfeld oversaw this novel endeavor from the outset. To abide by the precedents of jurisprudence was, in Bush's words, "not practicable" in such an "extreme emergency." The legal system, the White House reasoned, would soon be clogged with Taliban or al-Qaeda detainees because military operations in Afghanistan were already underway.[101]

Early the following year, the United States opened a facility to hold detainees at Guantánamo Bay on the island of Cuba; by mid-2004, 595 individuals were being housed there without due process of law. The White House and Department of Justice viewed the prisoners as "enemy combatants" who had no legal rights because of their designation as terrorists. A Supreme Court ruling at the end of June held that detainees at Guantánamo could challenge their status in federal courts, thereby compelling the government to announce it would hold hearings for the detainees, devoid though they would be of legal guarantees.[102] The tribunals underlined the government's determination, codified by the Military Commissions Act of 2006, to deny to prisoners protections afforded by the Geneva Conventions and to minimize their right to appeal through the device of habeas corpus.[103] When trials for Guantánamo detainees got under way in July 2008, their legal rights remained cloudy, even though a military judge did rule against the admissibility of evidence obtained by coercion.[104]

Enhanced executive power came about through two laws, the Authorization for the Use of Military Force of September 14, 2001, and the USA PATRIOT Act of October 26, 2001, both of which the executive branch interpreted as legal sanction for its radical revision of presidential power.[105] Adding to these statutes, Bush issued several executive orders based on opinions by members of the Office of Legal Counsel in the Justice Department, notably John Yoo. In Yoo's view, the Constitution placed no strictures on

---

[100] *New York Times*, October 1, 2001; the comparison between Ashcroft and Palmer is in Lichtblau, *Bush's Law*, 50.

[101] *Washington Post*, November 14, 2001.

[102] Ibid., July 8, 2004.

[103] Schwarz Jr. and Huq, *Unchecked and Unbalanced*, 142–3.

[104] *Los Angeles Times*, July 22, 2008.

[105] Pallitto and Weaver, *Presidential Secrecy and the Law*, 121–39.

presidential authority in time of war: "Necessity creates war, not a hover-ing zeitgeist called 'law.'" Yoo believed that the president as commander in chief was not bound by the War Powers Act.[106] Co-author of the infamous "torture memo" of August 2002 with his colleague Jay Bybee, Yoo held that actions considered torture under international conventions could not be prosecuted if the activities in question were ordered by the president.[107] In addition, the Military Commissions Act was sufficiently vague on mat-ters like torture as to empower further the executive branch in the name of fighting terror.[108]

Yoo's perspectives on the law and presidential power provided the White House with a rationale to erase the line between domestic and international operations by the CIA and NSA. Carried to their extreme, such activities could to an extent eliminate congressional authority as a separate func-tion of government, could nearly vanquish due process of law, and also could erode beyond recognition individual rights and liberties under the Constitution.[109] David Addington, a Pentagon legal counsel said, "doesn't believe there should be coequal branches."[110] It is possible to argue that such a thoroughgoing redistribution of power and authority entailed "the end of America," as the contemporary critic Naomi Wolf feared.[111]

In response, some members of Congress sought to curb the excesses of executive power, and even a conservative Supreme Court was reviewing the rights of detainees and thus, by implication, America's relationship to international conventions.[112] On that point, the National Defense Strategy of March 2005 warned of challenges "by those who employ a strategy of the weak, using international fora [and] judicial processes."[113] Debate took place in Congress in 2008 about limiting the sweeping authority given to the executive branch in the wake of 9/11. It did not entail, however, a compre-hensive review of presidential rights and prerogatives. Such a move would, in effect, have called into question the objectives of U.S. grand strategy, and few legislators contemplated doing that.

---

[106] Quoted in David Luban, "The Defense of Torture," *New York Review of Books*, March 15, 2007, p. 38; Joseph Margulies, *Guantánamo and the Abuse of Presidential Power* (New York: Simon & Schuster, 2006), 94.

[107] Margulies, *Guantánamo*, 89–90.

[108] David Cole, "The Man behind the Torture," *New York Review of Books*, December 6, 2007, p. 39; see also *New York Times*, September 17, 2007 for an editorial, "Restoring American Justice."

[109] Schwarz Jr. and Huq, *Unchecked and Unbalanced*, 135–9.

[110] Quoted in Mayer, *The Dark Side*, 64.

[111] Naomi Wolf, *The End of America: Letter of Warning to a Young Patriot* (White River Junction: Chelsea Green Publishing, 2007).

[112] See http://www.msnbc.com, December 6, 2007; and see *Washington Post*, December 3, 2007 for a list of key legal rulings on detainee rights.

[113] U.S. Department of Defense, *The National Defense Strategy of the United States of America*, March 2005, p. 5.

The trust that Americans placed in the three branches of their government to keep the nation from harm proved hard to shake, even as numerous citizens found themselves on a "terrorist watch" list. That number grew from 20 before 9/11 to perhaps several hundred thousand names on the list by late 2007. Earlier, in mid-2006, a Harris Poll revealed that 50 percent of those responding to a question still believed that Saddam Hussein possessed WMDs when the United States invaded Iraq in March 2003. At the time of the invasion, termed Operation Iraqi Freedom by the White House, 45 percent of those polled thought that there existed a link between Saddam and 9/11.[114] Never having been averse to using fear to engender support for the Iraq War, President Bush and Vice President Cheney often alluded to such a link. Condoleezza Rice's famous quote about not "want[ing] the smoking gun to be a mushroom cloud" suggests the extent to which the White House was willing to go in that regard.[115] This combination of deception by the nation's two highest elected officials and their advisers, along with the public's need to trust the government in a time of crisis, facilitated further constraints on basic liberties, rights, and freedoms. What happened to core values was more damaging than ex-White House Press Secretary Scott McClellan was prepared to admit in his 2008 book, *What Happened*.

In waging war on terror, the White House and Justice Department regarded freedom of speech and assembly and the right to privacy as contributing to security problems. The omnipresence in daily life of electronic communications blurred existing lines among speech, assembly, and privacy. One goal of the Patriot Act was to expand surveillance within the United States to trace activity deemed suspicious by the government. Thus, criminal prosecutors and counterintelligence personnel would work in concert, which had not previously occurred because of stipulations in the 1978 Foreign Intelligence Surveillance Act (FISA).[116] For some, the Patriot Act brought to mind the Espionage and Sedition Acts passed by Congress during World War I.[117] The tools it employed were ingenious in that they were meant to curb dissent against the war on terror by limiting the exercise of basic freedoms. For example, the FBI could issue "national security letters" in search of information about suspected terrorist activities. From 2003 to 2005, some 143,000 letters were issued. The Department of Defense issued more than 500 letters after 2001 seeking private bank records. Unlike before 9/11, there did not need to be probable cause to issue these letters, based on information obtained primarily from NSA intercepts, only

---

[114] Agence France Presse, October 24, 2007; *Christian Science Monitor*, March 14, 2003.
[115] *New York Times*, September 9, 2002. Rice first uttered these words on CNN's "Late Edition."
[116] Ibid., August 27, 2002.
[117] See chapter 2.

plausible suspicion.[118] That the NSA and CIA were again operating domestically also indicated the growth of executive power and White House disdain for Congress after 9/11, as we see presently.[119]

Partisan politics can have a chilling effect on freedom of speech and assembly, all the more so when the government's intelligence agencies become involved in monitoring how citizens speak truth to the power of government. Around 1970, the CIA provided local law enforcement in the environs of Washington, D.C., with riot-control equipment and training in counterintelligence to monitor anti-Vietnam demonstrations aimed at the Nixon White House and, in at least one instance, to combat street crime.[120] The vague Patriot Act altered how Americans perceived their individual freedoms. Discovering in the early 1970s that one had made Richard Nixon's "enemies list" was for many a badge of honor; recipients of national security letters almost certainly did not feel the same.

Less invasively, a White House manual prepared in October 2002 sought to keep President Bush from encountering dissent. Two transgressors in West Virginia appeared wearing anti-Bush T-shirts at a rally where Bush was speaking on July 4, 2004. Things escalated when the individuals refused to cover their message; they were briefly jailed. The government subsequently paid $80,000 for violating their First Amendment rights, but offered no apology.[121] This incident might be humorous were it not for the fear that the government was seeking to instill among those citizens who protested against the war on terror.[122] Personal privacy had become anathema to the White House and Justice Department. Some critics gave this development an Orwellian moniker, "big-brother conservatism." That it was and more, striking at the heart of individual freedom. It was not surprising, therefore, in October 2007 that Donald Kerr, the principal deputy director of national intelligence, declared that Americans must alter their understanding of privacy to one commensurate with "appropriate levels of security and public safety."[123]

As the erosion of basic rights and the aggrandizement of executive power became increasingly evident, Congress and the print media became more critical. Senator Patrick J. Leahy of Vermont called the Military Commissions Act "a total rollback of everything this country had stood

[118] Suskind, *The One Percent Doctrine*, 39; *New York Times*, September 16 and October 14, 2007.

[119] The CIA reportedly also issued a small number of national security letters; *New York Times*, January 14, 2007.

[120] *Washington Post*, June 27, 2007.

[121] Ibid., August 22, 2007.

[122] Lichtblau, *Bush's Law*, 113–25.

[123] See http://www.dni.gov/speeches/20071023_speech.pdf for the text of Kerr's speech; Micklethwait and Wooldridge, *The Right Nation*, 260–62.

for."[124] Leahy, head of the Senate Judiciary Committee after the 2006 elections gave Democrats a slim majority in the Senate, had a platform from which he defended constitutional rights and core values against the actions of the White House in a manner reminiscent of J. William Fulbright's critique of Lyndon Johnson and the war in Vietnam. Leahy was not alone, even though challenges to executive abuse of power from the Senate and House of Representatives were often, though not always, based on political affiliation. The president's "enablers," as Princeton economist and *New York Times* columnist and Nobel Prize winner Paul Krugman referred to moderate Republicans, were not only members of the president's party but also Democrats who failed to confront the White House about the consequences of security policy.[125] This inaction indicates the general acceptance of the administration's grand strategy by the legislative branch.

If Leahy regularly questioned the effects of unchecked power on human security and basic rights and values, the same cannot be said, for example, about two leading newspapers, the *New York Times* and the *Washington Post*. Neither was quick to analyze the Patriot Act and its implications. If that lapse can be attributed to the need to protect the nation and the American people right after the surprise of 9/11, that dispensation does not explain why the two papers failed to inquire seriously into the motives or examine the evidence that led the United States to war with Iraq until it became apparent that the war was not being won. Put on the defensive, though desirous of exculpation, the *New York Times* admitted that "we have found a number of instances of coverage that was not as rigorous as it should have been."[126] For its part, the *Washington Post* provided extensive coverage of the Abu Ghraib scandal, replete with grisly photos, after the story broke at the end of April 2004. Freedom of speech and the press, although not absolute, lie at the heart of core values. Not to speak freely or to engage in what amounts to self-censorship, as the nation's two major papers did on the issue of the Iraq War, struck a blow against the integrity of those values.[127]

It was incumbent on the media, with their influence and monetary resources, to challenge this most secretive of administrations. Yet, print and visual media were only as free as their practitioners were bold in the face of overzealous classification of documents and manufactured news. For reasons not directly addressed here, newspapers were read less and less and

---

[124] See http://www.democracynow.org for Leahy's remarks, September 29, 2006, on Democracy Now!, Amy Goodman's radio and television program.

[125] *New York Times*, July 20, 2007; see Hersh, *Chain of Command*, 363 for an example of deference by Democrats to the administration's grand strategy.

[126] *New York Times*, May 26, 2004.

[127] Anthony Lewis, "Privilege and the Press," *New York Review of Books*, July 14, 2005, pp. 4–8.

electronic blogs of diverse political persuasions consumed more and more. The prospect of losing an investigative media, however infrequent its revelations about government misdeeds, was not a development to be welcomed, except perhaps at the White House. Charges of liberal bias in the media, especially the national press, were disingenuous. Corporate America and the mainstream press were tightly entwined. That such charges could be seriously leveled pointed to the narrowing boundaries of legitimate political discourse. These allegations also reflected partisan politics and the centrality of profit making in a country where the gulf separating the wealthy and the powerful from the vast majority of the American people was widening.[128]

In the first 125 years of the nation's existence, republican virtue was largely the concern of prominent white men. That changed in the Progressive era, when other voices found their audience through what this study calls civic virtue. Print media prospered in the form of newspapers, and opinion magazines targeted specialized audiences, often enjoying a wide readership. Those years were far from a democratic utopia, although the mind and reading were valued and sometimes feared in times of national crisis. After 9/11, the interactive relationship between the media and their audience demonstrably changed. Reading was poorly honored in a visual age that questioned the utility of public education, even as politics, profits, and a growing conservative culture affected what the American public read and saw. Reporting became increasingly circumspect in deference to "balance" and in fear of losing access to the powerful. The amusements of the famous held the public's fascination far more than revelations about the horrors of war in Iraq, until the number of American deaths became too high to ignore in 2005. The poor, the weak, and the dead received only passing attention unless their stories could be told tabloid-style. The media could not be counted on "to venture into politically sensitive matters, to report disturbing truths that might unsettle and provoke," lamented critic Michael Massing.[129]

Shocking most American citizens and pulling the collective media away from their reluctance to confront the Bush administration about the expansion of presidential power, the war on terror, and the conduct of the war in Iraq was the Abu Ghraib scandal. As investigate reporter Seymour M. Hersh found, there was virtually no accountability in the executive branch for what happened at Abu Ghraib prison, where prisoners were demeaned and abused in ways that were impermissible under the Geneva Conventions. Hersh worried that he could not provide a satisfactory understanding of Abu Ghraib. He did, however, pose several questions, two of which are

[128] Generally, see Michael Massing, "The End of News?," *New York Review of Books,* December 1, 2005, pp. 23–7.
[129] Michael Massing, "The Press: The Enemy Within," *New York Review of Books*, December 15, 2005, p. 44.

pertinent to that endeavor: "How did eight or nine neoconservatives who believed that a war in Iraq was the answer to international terrorism get their way?" And, he asked, "Is our democracy that fragile?"[130] Two books published in 2008, Eric Lichtblau's *Bush's Law* and Jane Mayer's *The Dark Side*, answer the second question in the affirmative.

Hersh's questions suggest that democracy and neoconservatism are at odds; in the strictest sense, that is true. Yet, as this study contends, for more than one hundred years, democracy has been reshaped in direct response to the imperatives of the security ethos, the *lingua franca* of the policymaking community. Thus, neoconservatives did not hijack American democracy; they carried its historical engagement with the world to its logical conclusion. From William McKinley through Bill Clinton, without exception, American presidents found reason to enhance their authority at the expense of the other branches of government. In that sense, what occurred during George W. Bush's tenure in office was not an aberration. It was extreme in its suddenness and thoroughness because no top official – not Vice President Dick Cheney, not Secretary of Defense Donald Rumsfeld, not Secretary of State Colin Powell, not National Security Adviser Condoleezza Rice, not CIA Director George Tenet, and surely not President Bush – were thinking in 2001 about national security in ways that included groups like al-Qaeda as threats of the first order. U.S. grand strategy since early 1950 – namely, global containment and strategic globalism – was in the main predicated on state-based threats and enhancing American hegemony, strategically and economically.

When on September 11, al-Qaeda shattered the basic assumptions of that carefully constructed approach to the world, the Bush administration was quick to act. Three attorneys general – John Ashcroft, Alberto Gonzalez and Michael Mukasey – agreed that the power of the president was nearly unlimited in wartime, although Ashcroft expressed some misgiving from his hospital bed in March 2004 as NSA spying on citizens became more and more invasive.[131] As attorney general, Gonzalez informed members of the Senate Judiciary Committee, "The Constitution doesn't say every individual in the United States or every citizen is hereby granted or assured the right of habeas [corpus]." "There is," he asserted, "no express right of habeas in the Constitution." Incredulous senators pointed out that Article One, Section 9 of the Constitution permitted suspension only in times of "rebellion or invasion."[132] During his confirmation hearing in November 2007, Mukasey declined to identify "waterboarding" as torture even after it had been described to him in gruesome detail. Mukasey, who in fact deemed

---

[130] Hersh, *Chain of Command*, 362.
[131] On Mukasey, see *Washington Post*, October 18, 2007; on Ashcroft, see *New York Times*, May 16, 2007 and Lichtblau, *Bush's Law*, 178–83.
[132] *San Francisco Chronicle*, January 24, 2007.

the practice "repugnant," was deferring, like his two predecessors, to the idea of a monarchical executive.[133]

By 2008, the durability of American core values seemed in serious doubt. To be sure, federal courts and the Supreme Court might rule that enemy combatants had a right to challenge their status and circumstances; the courts might also curb domestic spying by the CIA, the NSA, and the FBI. Yet, even as the courts considered a myriad of appeals concerning the rights of detainees and the scope of surveillance, Congress was willing to broaden the power of the FISA court; it did so in July 2008, along with granting retroactive immunity from prosecution to telecommunications companies that had cooperated in domestic spying, thus giving the executive branch the right to do what the White House claimed was already within its power.[134] What neither the courts nor the U.S. Congress was willing to do was reconsider how the United States perceived the first grave security threat of the twenty-first century. National Intelligence Director Mitch McConnell on numerous occasions defended "enhanced interrogation techniques" and surveillance programs. Regarding aggressive questioning that might reach the level of torture, which Bush knew about and countenanced even if he did not expressly authorize it, he said, "I would not want a U.S. citizen to go through the process. But it is not torture." Rationalizing enhanced authority to conduct surveillance, he told Leahy and the Judiciary Committee, "The threats we face are real, and they are serious." To which Leahy replied that Congress as an equal branch also had an obligation "*to protect Americans' security and American's rights.*"[135]

Perhaps waterboarding could be halted by legislation. Perhaps a challenge could be raised to curtail the use of presidential signing statements, by which means a president could selectively enforce provisions of a given law.[136] Was it possible to end the practice of extraordinary rendition that delivered persons suspected of terrorist activities to "black sites" in Poland, Jordan, Egypt, or Saudi Arabia to be detained, interrogated, and likely tortured? Some of these facilities were run by the CIA until Bush suspended the program after mid-2006. Even Syria, where Canadian Maher Arar was flown after being seized in New York in October 2002 and tortured before being released a year later, had a role to play in the global war on terror. So, too, did NATO allies, even if they opposed the war in Iraq; some high-value

---

[133] *Christian Science Monitor*, November 8, 2007.

[134] By mid-2007, the FISA had been amended six tines; see *New York Times*, May 2, 2007 for an editorial, "Spying on Americans." See also *Washington Post*, July 10, 2008 and *New York Times*, July 10, 2008.

[135] Associated Press, July 22, 2007 on interrogation; Reuters News, September 26, 2007 for the exchange on surveillance (emphasis added). On Bush and torture, see Mayer, *The Dark Side, passim.*

[136] Pallitto and Weaver, *Presidential Secrecy and the Law*, 202. Bush issued more than 800 signing statements before 2007; his predecessors had issued a total of 600 statements.

detainees arrived in Cuba after being flown through the airspace of NATO allies under an agreement signed in October 2001.[137] One might fairly wonder, as did the *New York Times* in a probing depiction of extralegal practices devised by Bush's Justice Department after 2004, whether monarchical executive power can ever truly be controlled. The impetus in 2008 was clearly on the side of an unchecked presidency.[138]

Core values as the living embodiment of American exceptionalism were left in a malignant condition by the Bush administration. What occurred to them after 9/11 was the responsibility of George W. Bush and the executive branch; yet, Bush and his chief advisers did not act without drawing on the legacies of their predecessors. What the Bush White House inherited came to fruition in the decades after 1890 when the United States fully entered the world determined to change it for the better, yet also fearing that America would somehow be transformed in unacceptable ways. This concern did not prevent Wilson from embarking on an internationalist course, did not motivate Franklin Roosevelt to question the wisdom of humanistic foreign policy as John Quincy Adams had done in 1821, did not encourage Harry Truman or those presidents who came after him to discount the trust they placed in global containment and strategic globalism. And fear of what might happen to America as it pursued hegemony in an unwinnable war on terror did not compel George W. Bush to consider changing course.

By July 4, 2007, the United States was "desperately in need of restoring the rights and freedoms surrendered in a false bid for security that has perversely put the nation at greater risk," editorialized the *Baltimore Sun*. "The damage caused by terrorists on 9/11 begins to pale against the havoc wreaked upon America by America itself."[139] We may presume that Benjamin Franklin, who understood what the quest for security, "safety" he called it, could do to freedom, would have agreed.

Coda

This chapter ends not with a conclusion but a coda, linking contemporaneous events to the discussion of the Bush Doctrine, the accretion of executive power, and core values. Offering a conclusion would be misleading, because it could be taken as being more definitive than suggestive. Such is one pitfall of writing contemporary history.

The derogation of core values during George W. Bush's two terms as president can further be demonstrated by looking at how democracy and

---

[137] Jane Mayer, "The Black Sites," *The New Yorker*, August 13, 2007, on CIA "black site" prisons; *New York Times*, September 20, 2006 on Maher Arar; *The Times* (London), November 25, 2007 on flights through airspace of NATO countries.

[138] *New York Times*, October 4, 2007.

[139] *Baltimore Sun*, July 4, 2007 for the editorial, "Liberties Lost."

self-determination were faring at home as he prepared to leave office. Arguably, the object of grand strategy abroad – in part, the promotion of democracy and economic well-being – should find its domestic counterpart. How can the United States serve as the exemplar of public life for others if it does not incorporate its own citizens into civil society? If opportunity seems curtailed for the many and available to the powerful and wealthy few, what credibility has a government that claims uncommon exceptionalism in human affairs? By the end of 2008, America's bounty had been terribly squandered. Borrowing an image from the Vietnam era, it was hard not to conclude that the city on a hill had been destroyed in order to save it.

This tragic development was manifest in a multiplicity of divisions within society. Americans were torn apart by race, class, and gender. Those whom former Nixon lawyer John W. Dean denominated as "right-wing authoritarians" – individuals prepared to submit willingly to established authority and abandon the imperatives of a private moral code – had a vested interest in fomenting confrontational politics over social and economic issues.[140] In so doing, they and the president's most trusted advisers made deference to Bush's domestic agenda seem like the sole acceptable course of action in a land under siege by terrorists, at least in their telling. Eight years of the politics of fear, both a fear of foreigners and fear of progressives at home, had shown Bush's promises in the 2000 presidential campaign of compassionate conservatism to be, in fact, disingenuous.

The examples are many that offered a dismal prognosis for self-determination; several are surveyed here. As a whole, they indicate that the dominance of national politics by right-wing authoritarians in the executive branch and by an often compliant and like-minded Congress cemented deep fissures in the body politic that would not soon be undone. In late 2007, a deeply unpopular president twice vetoed an imperfect bill that expanded health coverage for many children. A five-year, $35 billion program, the State Children's Health Insurance Program, was denounced as a move in the "wrong direction" for the nation's health care system, a system that left perhaps 10 percent of America's children without any health insurance.[141] In addition, the infant death rate in poor areas and among the nonwhite population approached the highest in the modernized world, as reported by the Centers for Disease Control and Prevention for the year 2004. Some 35 million Americans were going hungry each day in 2006; "food insecurity" was noticeably pronounced in homes headed by single women, according to the Department of Agriculture.[142]

Women were also at risk from those who rejected their right to control their own bodies. The fate of *Roe v. Wade*, 410 U.S. 113 (1973), remained

---

[140] John W. Dean, *Conservatives without Conscience*, paper ed. (New York: Penguin Books, 2007).
[141] *Washington Post*, October 2, 2007; Associated Press, December 12, 2007.
[142] Associated Press, November 11, 2007; Reuters News, November 14, 2007.

uncertain in the face of attacks from anti-abortion crusaders and opportunistic politicians. To assert that "pro-life" Americans cared about the future public life of unwanted fetuses was disingenuous, given the data relating to health care, hunger, and mortality. Moreover, the dilapidated state of public education guaranteed that America's living poor children, and many in the middle class, would not be ready to engage in what this book has called civic virtue when they reached the age to do so. Bush's education program, No Child Left Behind, was as controversial politically as it was misguided educationally.[143]

As the United States waged its post-9/11 war on terror in Iraq and Afghanistan, violence occurred to a startling degree on America's streets and in American homes. The age-old veneration of the Second Amendment assured the omnipresence of violence. An individual with a gun might be able to protect what he or she held most dear; a society with untrammeled access to weapons was in danger of losing all but the most deadly of its core values, the right to bear arms. The statistics were numbing: 90 guns for every 100 citizens, three times as many as in France, Canada, and Germany; 270 million of the world's 875 million known firearms owned by Americans who buy more than half of the guns manufactured each year; and 100,000 cases annually of aggravated assault with a firearm. By mid-August 2007, more than 100,000 people had been murdered, most with guns, in the United States since 9/11, on which date 2,973 people died.[144]

What such data meant for the rule of law, and ultimately for democracy, was not encouraging. Nor was a July 2007 report by the Washington, D.C.-based Justice Policy Institute on gang wars and the failure of legislation and police efforts to address gang-related issues in America's largest cities. Gang membership had declined since the late 1990s, yet public spending on policing and surveillance vastly outpaced expenditures for prevention of gang violence or lessening its effects in Los Angeles, for example. "Los Angeles is losing the war on gangs," the report found. The authors charged that officials in Washington, without reliable data, tended to associate gangs with terrorist activity, drug trafficking, and illegal immigration. Local officials frequently perceived gang members as black or brown, whereas the majority of them were white. Membership in gangs was also transitory for most adolescents; ex-members grew tired of incessant violence in their lives. The report was noteworthy, however, because it highlighted cleavages over social policy that would have to be addressed at some point.[145]

---

[143] These issues are raised directly and indirectly in Chris Hedges, *American Fascists: The Christian Right and the War on America* (New York: Free Press, 2006).

[144] Reuters News, August 28, 2007; Bob Herbert, "100,000 Gone since 2001," *New York Times*, August 14, 2007.

[145] Judith Greene and Kevin Pranis, *Gang Wars: The Failure of Enforcement Tactics and the Need for Effective Public Safety Strategies* (Washington, DC: Justice Policy Institute, 2007), 3. See also Associated Press, July 18, 2007 for comments responding to the report, one of which condemned it as being written by "thug-huggers."

The consequences of a Bush presidency for American citizens and the nation's values also became evident in racial matters. Illegal immigration captured like nothing else the persistence of a culture war over national identity, as evangelical religion and so-called family values faded as galvanizing forces in electoral politics. Concerns about the harm illegal immigrants could do to the economic well-being of citizens were misplaced. Migrants, whether industrious or not, had no capacity to outsource jobs, reduce benefits, or crush labor unions. To be sure, privatization in Mexico, for example, did throw men and women out of work or rendered their work so bereft of income or meaning that going north was a natural human response. Just the same, cheap illegal labor did not cause the structural problems faced by the American workforce.[146] Those problems resulted from the global turn in the economy brought on by neoliberal devotion to the working of the market.

For most Americans, race refers to African Americans and implicitly to the status of racial progress. Hurricane Katrina, which devastated the Gulf Coast in August 2005, especially the city of New Orleans, provided an enduring symbol of the enormous racial divide in the Bush era. Federal promises to rebuild the city proved false, evidence of the cynicism of the White House and the vacuity of compassionate conservatism. More alarming, though, was the perception blacks held of how they were faring in George W. Bush's America. The Pew Research Center found pessimism about racial progress to be at a twenty-year high in 2007. Blacks believed that discrimination still limited income, housing, and educational opportunities, a perspective that whites did not share. To many African Americans, benign neglect continued to define their place in society, so much so that less than half of more than 3,000 people surveyed expected an improvement in their situation in the near future.[147] That the White House responded with alacrity to wildfires in wealthy sections of California in October 2007 appeared to validate growing concerns of African Americans about their strikingly different treatment.[148]

As they had been throughout American history, blacks were aware that equality was elusive, which W. E. B. Du Bois had experienced when he exhorted fellow African Americans to seize the opportunity afforded by participation in the Great War to demand political rights in a democracy. By the summer of 2007, fewer blacks than before were enlisting in the military, knowing that they were likely to serve in Iraq in disproportionate numbers. A CBS News poll indicated that more than 80 percent of blacks responding

---

[146] Informing this paragraph are Joseph E. Stiglitz, *Globalization and Its Discontents* (New York: W. W. Norton & Company, 2002), 86, 121; Thomas F. O'Brien, *Making the Americas: The United States and Latin America from the Age of Revolutions to the Era of Globalization* (Albuquerque: University of New Mexico Press, 2007), 287–90, 293–8, 301–2, 313–16; and generally Klein, *The Shock Doctrine*, 283–322.

[147] MSNBC.com, November 14, 2007.

[148] *New York Times*, October 24, 2007.

to a survey disapproved of the war. Echoing the opposition of Muhammad Ali and Martin Luther King Jr. to the conflict in Vietnam, one young man in the Bronx declared, "I'm not really into going overseas with guns and fighting other people's wars."[149] Many of those, black or white, who did fight in Iraq were broken by the war. Suicide among veterans, most notably those aged 20 through 24, reached epidemic status by 2007, according to a CBS News investigation.[150] The quality of treatment for injured soldiers and veterans was scandalous, as the deplorable conditions at Walter Reed Army Medical Center showed.

The case of the Jena 6 in Louisiana, in which protestors demanded fair legal treatment for black teenagers arrested for assault and battery of a white classmate, did more than awaken memories of civil rights marches in the 1960s. That was the easy referent frequently made by national media. More insightful was the comment of one young white woman, Mairead Burke, who observed that more than civil rights was at stake. The march in Jena, she said, was "a human rights issue." Graduates of Spelman College in Atlanta were also thinking in broader terms, calling attention to the plight of abused women. "You cannot advocate for race alone," explained Fallon Wilson. "But when you add in gender and sexuality, it gets harder."[151] In the parlance of this book, human security was not available to many African Americans to the same extent that it was for wealthy and powerful citizens.

To employ Naomi Klein's formulation, the immense cost of the war on terror, which the Congressional Budget Office put at $2.4 trillion for Iraq and Afghanistan,[152] led to the application of a domestic economic "shock doctrine," nowhere more visibly than in black communities.[153] In mid-2008, innumerable Americans irrespective of race were suffering from the consequences of falling house prices and a mortgage crisis, rising indebtedness and poor credit, a weak dollar, and oil prices that threatened to reach $150 per barrel. For the nearly 100 million people living close to and below the official poverty line, Bush's confidence in the economy was certainly hard to fathom. Analysts who saw "a double shock in housing and in the credit crunch . . . [and] potentially [in] oil" shared that assessment.[154]

Since their nation's founding, American citizens have steadfastly believed that the vitality of basic values depended on individual and collective

---

[149] Ibid., August 22, 2007.

[150] CBS News, November 13, 2007; Associated Press, July 28, 2008. The data did not appear to provide numbers by race.

[151] *New York Times*, September 21, 2007; CNN Special Investigations Unit, "Judgment in Jena," September 20, 2007 for Mairead Burke; *Atlanta Journal-Constitution*, October 30, 2007 for Fallon Wilson.

[152] Reuters News, October 24, 2007.

[153] *New York Times*, November 4, 2007. Mortgage interest rates in black neighborhoods in Detroit were markedly higher than in nearby white neighborhoods.

[154] Ibid., November 14, 2007.

prosperity. George W. Bush's years in power negated that presumptive bond. Grand strategy in the form of the Bush Doctrine further skewed a weak economy in favor of the wealthy, the result of tax cuts and profligate spending on the war in Iraq – a conflict for which no substantive justification existed. When a full history of the first decade of the twenty-first century is written, the social and economic consequences of the war on terror will consist of multiple narrative threads. Among them will likely be the fear that stalked the daily life of many citizens; the widespread doubt that the state was a force for good in the post-Cold War era, an age of terror; and the conviction that history failed to provide adequate guidance about how to deal with the allegedly new world brought on by 9/11.[155]

British historian Tony Judt suggests that "in a world increasingly polarized between insecure individuals and unregulated global forces... [o]ur contemporary cult of untrammeled economic freedom" must give way to state regulation if democracy is to thrive. Judt also contends that persons "in authority have lost control as well, to forces beyond their reach."[156] His latter point is somewhat at odds with the major theme of this book. That officials cannot control all events and the diverse forces affecting them in the milieu in which they operate is a truism. Judt errs, it would seem, where the United States is concerned, in placing faith in the capacity of the state to address in constructive ways the insecurities and fears experienced by citizens. The history of the security ethos and its relationship to core values does not warrant his implicit trust in the beneficence of the American state.

In the early 1890s, Alfred Thayer Mahan and like-minded others including Theodore Roosevelt had surveyed the uncertain socioeconomic landscape of the United States and embraced an active foreign policy, one that married ocean-going commerce and its offspring, prosperity, to the growth of military might in the form of naval power. They created an American empire and brought forth the security ethos that went with it. The association of security and prosperity through a global presence found expression over the next century and beyond in four grand strategies: Wilsonian internationalism, global containment, strategic globalism, and preemption via the Bush Doctrine. America's march to hegemony compromised the nation's core values and thus the prospects for a healthy democracy. It is not knowable one decade into the twenty-first century whether the basic values, the rights, and the liberties sustaining American democracy have been damaged beyond repair. The history of the security ethos suggests that such an outcome could in fact be the case.

---

[155] Informing this paragraph is Tony Judt, "The Wrecking Ball of Innovation," *New York Review of Books*, December 6, 2007, p. 27.
[156] Ibid.

Conclusion

The Security Ethos and Civic Virtue

The supreme interest of the United States is the creation and maintenance of a high standard of life for all its people and ways of industry conducive to the promotion of individual and social virtues within the frame of national security.

Charles A. Beard, 1935

Yesterday's not dead or gone. We're just meeting it head-on for the first time in a hundred years.

William Appleman Williams, 1969

Keeping the authoritarian influence of conservatism in check . . . is vital to maintaining our republican form of government.

John W. Dean, 2007

Many Americans, particularly those who find the security ethos congenial, whether they do so consciously or not, like their history seamless, celebratory, and exceptional.[1] They revise their own nation's history while denying others the right to fashion stories of their past absent America's influence. To the extent that America set out almost from its inception in the seventeenth century to improve humanity's lot either by example or active involvement, it arrogated to itself the right to act as the arbiter of what constitutes legitimate

---

[1] The literature about why the writing of history in the United States evokes such passion is vast. See, for example, Frances FitzGerald, *America Revised: History Schoolbooks in the Twentieth Century* (Boston: Little, Brown, 1979); Edward T. Linenthal and Tom Englehardt, eds., *History Wars: The* Enola Gay *and Other Battles for the American Past* (New York: Metropolitan Books, 1996); and Emily S. Rosenberg, *A Date Which Will Live: Pearl Harbor in American Memory* (Durham: Duke University Press, 2003). Useful, too, are portions of Thomas Bender, ed., *Rethinking American History in a Global Age* (Berkeley: University of California Press, 2002) and Thomas Frank, *What's the Matter with Kansas?: How Conservatives Won the Heart of America* (New York: Metropolitan Books, 2004).

history.[2] This sweeping sense of entitlement to determine how others know their own past is pertinent to a critical assessment of the authoritarianism that underlies the security ethos.

Perhaps the most enduring theme in American history is the never-ending battle between conflict and consensus as useful metaphors for comprehending the past. Efforts made to transcend this dichotomy, especially through what is called the cultural turn in scholarship, have not created a new paradigm. Rather, practitioners of the cultural turn have tended to obscure the reality that the single most important issue in American history is the state of the republic at any given moment. To pretend otherwise is to engage in a kind of sophistry by those who seemingly have abandoned their responsibility as intellectuals to speak truth to power.[3] So many people's lives are at stake as the United States engages the world. All historical roads, if they do not lead to Rome (and the imperial allusion is intentional), should in some fashion pass through Philadelphia in 1787. Without the republic as its fulcrum, the American nation's history is left rudderless.

This assertion is not to propose that America's is a static history – quite the contrary. It took great energy for the Founders, many of whom like Gouverneur Morris of Pennsylvania had a "thorough distrust of democratic institutions," to create a government that favored the powerful and the propertied while offering the prospect of prosperity and safety for the general populace.[4] The pursuit of republican virtue – the effort to preserve the integrity of the republic – from 1787 through the mid-1910s was one of the noblest enterprises in our history. It was also terribly flawed because of its many exclusionary assumptions and practices. A unique combination of immigration, war, and intellectual fermentation coalesced around 1917, the year Roger Baldwin took over the National Civil Liberties Bureau, the forerunner of the American Civil Liberties Union, and democratized political discourse as never before.

Thus, it was that civic virtue came to replace republican virtue as the ideal best representing how citizens should strive to make their homeland

---

[2] H. W. Brands, *What America Owes the World: The Struggle for the Soul of Foreign Policy* (New York: Cambridge University Press, 1998), vii; see also Tony Smith, *America's Mission: The United States and the Worldwide Struggle for Democracy in the Twentieth Century* (Princeton: Princeton University Press, 1994).

[3] Informing my critique is Thomas A. Schwartz, "Explaining the Cultural Turn – Or Detour," *Diplomatic History* 31 (January 2007): 143–47. For those who wonder if I am betraying my own scholarly trajectory, I would respond that there is a crucial difference between writing about the relationship between culture and power, which I have done in my work on drug policy, and embracing the cultural turn and critical theory. A worthy, if ultimately unpersuasive, effort to occupy the terrain between more conventional history and the cultural turn is Walter Hixson, *The Myth of American Diplomacy: National Identity and U.S. Foreign Policy* (New Haven: Yale University Press, 2008).

[4] Charles A. Beard, *An Economic Interpretation of the Constitution of the United States* (New York: Macmillan, 1913), 208.

more inclusive and to exercise their basic rights. At the same time, however, the Wilsonian impulse to better humanity's lot guaranteed a future for the nascent security ethos. It was to be a future in which the values that motivated many Americans to strive to make democracy as vital as possible for all citizens would lose their place in the conduct of public affairs, particularly as those values posed a challenge to the direction of security policy.

Right-Wing Authoritarians

With the election of George W. Bush in 2000 and the tragedy of September 11, 2001, the past, except for Wilson's desire to export democracy, had little of relevance to offer to the present, or so the neoconservatives at the helm of government wanted the American people to believe. The world began anew in 2001, just as it had in 1945. And, as a result of more than a century of living under the sway of the security ethos, many did so conclude. Not just neoconservatives wanted to condemn the past to history's dustbin; neoliberals of the 1990s, in thrall to globalization and the daily process of policymaking, also had scant use for an inconvenient history that called into question their *raison d'être.*

Of what good, ultimately, were the many officials who enhanced the power of the executive branch and nearly turned the Constitution and the Bill of Rights into artifacts only to be commemorated on ceremonial occasions? If the Constitution and Bill of Rights ceased being living documents, then the rights and liberties for which they stood would atrophy and lose their meaning. By 2008, such was increasingly the effect of the security ethos and the grand strategies to which it had given rise.

The fault for this situation was primarily, though not solely, that of the nation's elected leaders and their advisers. Citizens who blindly followed the government's lead, especially in times of crisis short of invasion, also bear some of the responsibility for what has befallen core values. It is important here to state clearly that Nazi Germany posed a clear and present danger to the vital interests of the United States and that Franklin Roosevelt's efforts saved the nation from disaster. That said, Americans in the main possess a conservatism that is uncomfortable with radical change and is not quick to question authority, which is typically seen as the fount of personal safety and of national security. This predisposition largely derives from an expansionist political economy that was rarely challenged after 1815, from a longstanding habit of rejuvenating national identity through the resort to force, and from an abiding fear that exceptionalism and prosperity cannot endure. This latent authoritarian tendency in American conservatism, not foreign adversaries, is what has most sullied the American experiment in governance. John W. Dean attempted to address this situation when he observed, "Keeping the authoritarian influence of conservatism in check . . . is vital to maintaining our republican form of government."[5] His counsel did not go far enough.

Republicanism and conservatism, if not wholly interchangeable, have been nearly synonymous throughout the nation's history. That is why the advent of civic virtue in the 1910s was a momentous development; it offered an alternative to the conservative temper that had historically dominated political discourse. It also compelled those whom Dean would expel from the conservative tent, authoritarians masquerading as conservatives, to explain why equality would be invidious in the conduct of public affairs. Nevertheless, democratic victory never came, the achievements of the New Deal and the Great Society notwithstanding. If hope endures at the end of the Bush presidency, it is a faint hope; the weight of the security ethos on democracy has become ever more crushing since the Truman administration adopted its grand strategy of global containment. Truman the Democrat, prompted by Secretary of State Dean Acheson, exaggerated the dangers facing the nation. Former Secretary of State Madeleine Albright contends that Acheson "later admitted to stretching the truth in the early days of the Cold War to alert the public to the Soviet threat"[6] – that is, to "the Soviet threat" as Truman, Acheson, and others in the administration perceived it. As we have seen, threat assessment in the late 1940s was emotionally charged and conducted in a policymaking environment over which the security ethos exerted baneful influence.

Can anything be done to improve if not reverse the woeful status of core values? The prospect for significant change is not encouraging. If there is a chance to regenerate the republic and to restore its ideals, it lies in a call to arms by those willing to engage in civic virtue. The assumption here is that true conservatives and independent progressives possess a common affection for traditional rights and liberties. If these affinities can outweigh their differences, then those who find in the Constitution, the Bill of Rights, and the rule of law the crux of the nation's identity will be able to fight a good fight. They may not prevail against the despotism of authoritarians in the governing class and the security ethos in which they take refuge. Yet, not to struggle is to surrender to contemporary vexations and to accept as well the irrelevance of history. Citizens who believe that history still has meaning in the twenty-first century owe themselves and their nation's past that effort, no matter the outcome.

Those in the governing class and among their supporters who oppose regeneration would not admit that such a result is their intent – quite the reverse. Yet, the consequences of the foreign policies they espouse have

---

[5] John W. Dean, *Conservatives without Conscience*, paper ed. (New York: Penguin Books, 2007), 74.

[6] Madeleine Albright with Bill Woodward, *Madam Secretary: A Memoir* (New York: Miramax Books, 2003), 659.

been the erosion of core values and, under George W. Bush, the denial of executive accountability under the law. Defenders of this revolution – calling it a counterrevolution may be more historically precise – are many, including prominent figures in the intellectual class and within the professoriate.

Other scholars have ably recounted the origins of the Cold War and the rise of neoconservatism.[7] What is now important is to identify the various characteristics of authoritarianism in America. John W. Dean, in an insightful book, *Conservatives without Conscience*, delineated a number of typologies applicable to the present evaluation. He borrowed extensively from the work of social psychologist Bob Altemeyer, the majority of whose scholarship examines the protean nature of social and political authoritarianism in America. To his surprise, Dean discovered that all of the authoritarians he identified were "hard-right conservatives" who took their behavior to "unprecedented" levels.[8] Among authoritarians as a class, there exist followers or right-wing authoritarians; leaders or social dominators; and also a limited number of individuals or double high authoritarians, who combine the worst traits of the others.

For present purposes, the most salient characteristics of authoritarians are those often shared by followers and leaders. Authoritarians play on the fears of others and are fearful themselves, although they typically disguise these fears with aggressive behavior. Self-righteous to a fault, they show little genuine compassion for the suffering of others. When they err in making or supporting ill-considered public policy, they are unreflective about the consequences of their actions. The aura of unrepentance that authoritarian leaders exude conveys the toughness the arch-neoconservative Norman Podhoretz deemed essential in the battle against "Islamofascism."[9] Put to the test, authoritarians are wary of individual rights because they tend to equate freedom with license. Thus, they view equality as a crutch for the weak who fail to understand that a tough-minded hierarchical regime affords them security in a dangerous world. Finally, authoritarians reject the idea that the president is bound by law in the role of commander in chief. For them, adherence to the Constitution and deference to separation of powers are behaviors that are expedient and situationally dependent.

Dean asserted that Vice President Dick Cheney and his top national security aide, I. Lewis Libby, qualified as social dominators, with Libby "an

---

[7] Melvyn P. Leffler, *A Preponderance of Power: National Security, the Truman Administration, and the Cold War* (Stanford: Stanford University Press, 1993); Michael J. Hogan, *A Cross of Iron: Harry S. Truman and the Origins of the National Security State, 1935–1954* (New York: Cambridge University Press, 1998); James Mann, *Rise of the Vulcans: The History of Bush's War Cabinet* (New York: Viking, 2004); and Dean, *Conservatives without Conscience*, especially chapters 3 and 4.

[8] Dean, *Conservatives without Conscience*, 52, 66.

[9] Norman Podhoretz, *World War IV: The Long Struggle against Islamofascism* (New York: Doubleday, 2007).

exemplary authoritarian." Cheney's chief trademark was "bad judgment," a trait hardly atypical for a self-isolated authoritarian. In characterizing President George W. Bush, Dean minces no words: "It is abundantly clear that he is a mental lightweight with a strong right-wing authoritarian personality, with some social dominance tendencies as well."[10] If Dean's assessment is accurate, it explains why the intelligence community gave the executive branch the data it expected, however inconclusive, to make a case for Saddam Hussein as a "gathering threat." As was true at other times in its checkered past, the Central Intelligence Agency was determined to please the White House, denials to the contrary by Director George J. Tenet notwithstanding. Behind this compromise of its obligation to the American people, wrote Thomas Powers, long a CIA observer and critic, lay "painful truths about the character and motives of the President and the men and women around him."[11] As if further evidence were needed, the *New York Times* reported in December 2007 that the former chairmen of the 9/11 Commission, Lee H. Hamilton and Thomas H. Kean, concluded that the CIA had acted to impede the Commission's inquiry.[12] Making things worse, the markers of authoritarianism would seem to encompass the actions of at least the first two of Bush's attorneys general, John Ashcroft and Alberto Gonzalez, and also lawyers in the Office of Legal Counsel, most notoriously John Yoo.[13] David Addington, Cheney's legal counsel, would also have a prominent place on any such list.

Given the propensity within the Bush administration to act aggressively and with conviction that had no place for reflection, which explains in part the nominal influence of Colin Powell as secretary of state in Bush's first term, their adoption of a grand strategy characterized by preemption was unsurprising. It was a strategy that was relatively easy to articulate and defend by like-minded members and sympathizers in the intellectual class. Their writings possess a sense of urgency about the need for a proactive foreign policy to anticipate and confront the dangers facing the country. William Kristol and Robert Kagan of *The Weekly Standard* warned in 1996, "In foreign policy, conservatives are adrift." The Lippmannesque tone should not be overlooked. The "appropriate goal" of the United States was to preserve its "benevolent global hegemony" with a policy of "military supremacy and moral confidence." Calling for a conservative brand of civic virtue as though it were again the 1910s, Kristol and Kagan insisted that it was the duty of

---

[10] Dean, *Conservatives without Conscience*, 78–9, 157–61, 168–9.

[11] George Tenet with Bill Harlow, *At the Center of the Storm: My Years at the CIA* (New York: HarperCollins, 2007); Thomas Powers, "What Tenet Knew," *New York Review of Books*, July 19, 2007, p. 70.

[12] *New York Times*, December 22, 2007, and January 2, 2008 for a Kean-Hamilton op-ed.

[13] See, for example, Mark Danner, "We Are All Torturers Now," *New York Times*, January 6, 2005.

citizens to support America's international mission. Should they do less, "Americans will fail in their responsibility to lead the world."[14]

The battle was thus joined. The contours of permissible discourse narrowed the issue to how the United States should pursue a strategy of strategic globalism. Whether that was an "appropriate goal" could not be asked; it was a given. Kagan buttressed his argument shortly after 9/11 in a brief book, *Of Paradise and Power*, in which he wrote, "The end of the Cold War was taken by Americans as an opportunity not to retract but to expand their reach . . . to stake out interests in parts of the world, like Central Asia, that most Americans never knew existed before. . . . The 'lesson of Munich' came to dominate strategic thought, and . . . today it remains the dominant paradigm."[15]

Q. E. D. Well, not exactly. One admitted neoconservative, Francis Fukuyama, broke with the Bush administration in the months prior to the invasion of Iraq, claiming that neoconservativism had "evolved into something I can no longer support." What he proposed instead was the adoption of a new foreign policy: "realistic Wilsonianism" or "hard-headed liberal internationalism."[16] Under whichever guise, at length this foreign policy comprises an end-of-history project requiring American engagement abroad and thus perpetuation of the security ethos. The role of citizens apparently is to validate, not dissent from this mission. Dissent, as in the 1960s, revealed the true "weakness of contemporary liberal democracy." Without irony, Fukuyama also wrote, "Good governance is ultimately not possible without democracy and public participation; the quality of a bureaucracy that is insulated from public scrutiny and oversight deteriorates over time."[17] Fukuyama was referring only to authoritarian governments that were the object of nation-building by the United States.

Yet, if what was presumably good for others was not valued at home, then what was the point of hegemony? Fukuyama, it seems, took as his point of departure the idea of Fareed Zakaria, editor of *Newsweek International*, that limiting political participation better creates order than a more unfettered democracy, which will inevitably "discredit democracy itself."[18] Zakaria, welcoming constraints on the very electoral majorities that support the growth of executive authority, applauded the distinctiveness of the

---

[14] William Kristol and Robert Kagan, "Toward a Neo-Reaganite Foreign Policy," *Foreign Affairs* 75 (July/August 1996): 18–32.

[15] Robert Kagan, *Of Paradise and Power: America and Europe in the New World Order* (New York: Vintage Books, 2004), 86, 91.

[16] Francis Fukuyama, *America at the Crossroads: Democracy, Power, and the Neoconservative Legacy*, paper ed. (New Haven: Yale University Press, 2007), xxxi for the words quoted.

[17] Ibid., 24, 141.

[18] Fareed Zakaria, *The Future of Freedom: Illiberal Democracy at Home and Abroad* (New York: W. W. Norton & Company, 2003), 255.

American system, not for how democratic it is "but rather how undemocratic it is."[19] This is no heuristic matter because unchecked presidential power, despite occasional demurrals by Congress, does not revert to a separation-of-powers condition once a crisis has passed. Zakaria brought his argument to a close with a clever turn of phrase: "As we enter the twenty-first century, our task is to make democracy safe for the world."[20] Just like right-wing authoritarians, neoconservatives, realists, and Fukuyama's renovated Wilsonians, Zakaria implicitly posited that the core of American identity, its rights and liberties, will survive intact no matter the duress they undergo, no matter the abuse of those principles by authorities in the name of security.

That gamble is fraught with immense peril, as several astute commentators long ago demonstrated. Intermediate measures are not a sufficient remedy for the ills induced by more than a century of empire and hegemony, benevolent or not. In proposing some variant of hegemony plus multilateralism, they therefore ignore the underlying cause of the crisis of American identity: the erosion of core values. Stephen M. Walt of Harvard University's John F. Kennedy School of Government, for example, suggests that the United States must lead by example if it is to retain its global primacy. His is a worthy suggestion, claiming it will protect "America's core values of liberty and opportunity."[21] That is precisely what the proponents of global containment and strategic globalism set out to do; as we have seen, those strategies inexorably morphed into the Bush Doctrine.

Progenitors of Progressive Civic Virtue

Representative of the advocates of civic virtue for a goal other than hegemony were W. E. B. Du Bois, Randolph Bourne, the American Student Union before its break-up, C. Wright Mills, and Rev. Martin Luther King Jr. Omitted from this list are Senator Robert A. Taft and George F. Kennan, who could be included because of their aversion to unbridled internationalism. The conservative Taft, known as "Mr. Republican," had a podium that he could employ at will, even as his warnings about the overextension of American power were eclipsed by Truman's national security policy. Kennan's absence is explained by the insurmountable difficulty he had in

---

[19] Ibid., 22.

[20] Ibid., 256.

[21] Stephen M. Walt, *Taming American Power: The Global Response to U.S. Primacy* (New York: W. W. Norton & Company, 2005), 246 for the words quoted. Despite its defense of American primacy, Kagan's *Of Paradise and Power* presents a variation of Walt's major theme. Of a vastly different order, a prescriptive one that takes as given a form of global governance without addressing matters like the security ethos and grand strategy, is Anne-Marie Slaughter, *A New World Order* (Princeton: Princeton University Press, 2004); Slaughter was then dean of the Woodrow Wilson School of Public and International Affairs at Princeton University.

countenancing participatory democracy, either in the United States or
abroad. Those listed did not enjoy similar proximity to power as did Taft
and Kennan, despite their reservations about America's globalist course.

Charles A. Beard and William Appleman Williams stand out, through
their many publications, as active practitioners of progressive civic virtue
who feared that messianic internationalism – and there has been no other
kind for the United States, however portrayed – had the propensity to compromise if not fatally impair core values. Scholars and public intellectuals,
they authored two of the three most influential books yet written about
American history: Beard's *An Economic Interpretation of the Constitution
of the United States* and Williams's *The Tragedy of American Diplomacy.*[22]
Other scholars have examined Beard's and Williams's careers. Beard lost
his impressive readership after severely criticizing how Roosevelt took the
country into war in 1941; Williams, tired of the destructiveness of the Vietnam War and the increasing anti-intellectualism of war protestors, departed
the University of Wisconsin in 1968 for the refuge of Oregon.[23] The present
concern is the extent to which their thinking about power and how it affected
ideals and values might help revive the practice of civic virtue.

A few years before World War II began, Beard described the obligation
he believed the government owed its citizens: "The supreme interest of the
United States is the creation and maintenance of a high standard of life for
all its people and ways of industry conducive to the promotion of individual
and social virtues *within the frame of national security.*"[24] Beard took it
on himself in the 1930s to warn about the perils of returning to Wilsonian
internationalism. Believing that the United States had acted as a world power
since its founding, he knew the task of getting his fellow citizens to face the
consequences of their own history would be difficult because their material
interests were involved. Sounding like Dean Acheson before Congress in
1944, but with a purpose exactly the opposite, Beard wrote, "American
industry, under the regime of technology, is producing more commodities
than the American people can use or consume, and the 'surplus' must be
exported."[25] Beard, from Indiana, knew that the economic problems of
his day were not unique. Rather, they were extreme manifestations of the
long-term interrelationship of economy and identity – the curious idea in
so bountiful a country that "the *only* escape from the dilemma in which
capitalism is floundering lies in seeking and finding new markets."

[22] Arguably, the third book in this triumvirate is Richard Hofstadter, *The Age of Reform:
From Bryan to F.D.R.* (New York: Alfred A. Knopf, 1955).
[23] For a useful overview, see Andrew J. Bacevich, *American Empire: The Realities and Consequences of U.S. Diplomacy* (Cambridge: Harvard University Press, 2002), especially 11–31;
see also Brands, *What America Owes the World*, 109–43, 238–62, and *passim*.
[24] Charles A. Beard with G. H. E. Smith, *The Open Door at Home: A Trial Philosophy of
National Interest* (New York: Macmillan, 1935), 210 (emphasis in original).
[25] Ibid., 37.

The determination to find in the world a solution to domestic problems simply had to be reversed. To do otherwise, to continue on a course that bolstered the security ethos as a guarantor of prosperity, meant entanglement abroad without end. Thus, the "borders of [public] discussion," Beard wrote in 1935, "must be widened ... to include the totality of culture and world history."[26] The alternative, he counseled, would likely involve the country in war at the behest of a powerful executive "unhampered by popular objections and legislative control."[27] For Beard, that meant despotism, not freedom or security.

If Beard was a political loner who left the Republican Party in 1900 over the issue of imperialism, William Appleman Williams was a radical iconoclast from Iowa who mentored many historians in the "Wisconsin school" of American diplomatic history.[28] Williams taught at several schools, including Ohio State University, before arriving in Madison, where he earned his PhD, in 1957. From the outset of his career, Williams drew from Beard's intellectual well, agreeing with the older man about the foundational linkages between domestic and foreign policy and the centrality of political economy to the American experience.[29] Williams wrote with admiration, "Beard lived by the creed of grappling directly, honestly, and democratically, with any problem be it economic, social, or moral. And he fought hypocrisy and political chicanery with all the militance he could muster, a worthy example for American radicals."[30] Williams demanded this commitment to civic virtue from not only himself but also those who learned from him.

Williams's concept of Open Door imperialism to explain how the United States engaged the world, most famously presented in *The Tragedy of American Diplomacy*, was a major contribution to scholarship. More than that, it was an idea that thousands of students encountered. Radical students in the 1960s seized on Williams's ideas just as earlier generations had greeted Beard's books. Ever the public intellectual, the result of military service after graduation from the U.S. Naval Academy and his commitments to racial equality and social justice, Williams's essays appeared in influential print media, including *Commentary*, *The Nation*, and the *New York Review of Books*. Like Beard, a self-styled student of history who embraced learning as a lifelong endeavor,[31] Williams insisted that Americans must learn from

[26] Ibid., 120 (emphasis in original), 127.
[27] Charles A. Beard, *President Roosevelt and the Coming of the War, 1941: A Study in Appearances and Realities* (New Haven: Yale University Press, 1948), 590.
[28] Brands, *What America Owes the World*, 113, 241, 252.
[29] Paul M. Buhle and Edward Rice-Maximin, *William Appleman Williams* (New York: Routledge, 1995), *passim*.
[30] William Appleman Williams, "Charles Austin Beard: The Intellectual as Tory-Radical," in Henry W. Berger, ed., *A William Appleman Williams Reader: Selections from His Major Historical Writings* (Chicago: Ivan R. Dee, 1992), 115.
[31] Ibid., 111.

their past. Endeavoring to put the turbulence of the 1960s into context, he explained, "Yesterday's not dead or gone. We're just meeting it head-on for the first time in a hundred years."[32]

Williams intuitively understood the historical attraction of the marketplace for the American people and described in his writing its symbiotic relationship with the security ethos. "Expanding the marketplace enlarged the area of freedom," he wrote. "Expanding the area of freedom enlarged the marketplace." To guarantee security, "one needs first a continent, then a hemisphere, next the world."[33] But Williams knew, as had Beard, that the world was not America's to remake, a difficult truth for descendants of the Puritans to accept. Hence, the need for radical civic virtue, or so Williams averred in the hope that it would move Americans in the direction of true community – democratic socialism in his judgment.[34] If the specific prescription was unrealistic, then reclaiming America's past as something other than a prelude to empire and hegemony was essential. That goal was too much to achieve in the maelstrom of the 1960s. Disillusioned as the nation unraveled, Williams quit Madison for more peaceful terrain. Yet, he left a legacy that honored civic engagement as a citizen's highest calling. Americans must somehow learn from his and Beard's examples if they are to rescue what remains of their rights, liberties, and ideals from authoritarians in the executive branch and those in the public and private spheres who enable them, whether in corporate boardrooms or the nation's universities.

The Balance Sheet

Who stood for progressive civic virtue at the beginning of 2008? Two of its best-known practitioners, controversial in conventional academic circles and the mainstream media, were Howard Zinn and Noam Chomsky. Their books sold well in the United States. Zinn's *A People's History of the United States: 1492 to Present* (2005) ranked just outside the top 300 best-selling books on Amazon.com. Two of Chomsky's books, *Hegemony or Survival* (2004) and *Failed States* (2006), ranked around 4,400 and 8,800, respectively. By way of contrast, John Lewis Gaddis's *The Cold War: A New History* (2005) came in just above 9,000.[35] One of the most interesting

---

[32] William Appleman Williams, *The Roots of the Modern American Empire: A Study of the Growth and Shaping of Social Consciousness in a Marketplace Society* (New York: Random House, 1969), ix.

[33] William Appleman Williams, *America Confronts a Revolutionary World: 1776–1976* (New York: William Morrow and Company, 1976), 43, 42 for the words quoted.

[34] William Appleman Williams, *The Contours of American History*, paper ed. (Chicago: Quadrangle Books, 1966), 488.

[35] Howard Zinn, *A People's History of the United States: 1492 to Present* (New York: Harper Perennial, 2005); Noam Chomsky, *Hegemony or Survival: America's Quest for Global Dominance* (New York: Owl Books, 2004); idem, *Failed States: The Abuse of Power and*

indicators of the vitality of an anti-hegemonic civic virtue was the remarkable fund-raising success of libertarian-cum-Republican Ron Paul of Texas in his bid for the Republican Party's presidential nod; his Internet appeal, particularly among young voters, astonished traditional politicians and conventional pundits in print and broadcast media. On several occasions, Paul set a record for the amount of money raised in a day, even though he had no chance to be his party's nominee.[36]

That men dominate the arena of public discourse in the United States is surely no surprise. That two women – one Canadian, one American – were far outselling their male competitors at the start of 2008 was remarkable. Naomi Klein's *The Shock Doctrine: The Rise of Disaster Capitalism* (2007), placed about sixtieth on Amazon, selling slightly less well than the memoir of former Federal Reserve Board Chairman Alan Greenspan, *The Age of Turbulence: Adventures in a New World* (2007), which was in twenty-third place. Naomi Wolf's extended essay, *The End of America: Letter of Warning to a Young Patriot* (2007), ranked just outside Amazon's top 100 best sellers. Unabashedly calling her book "a citizen's call to action," Wolf sounded the tocsin of civic virtue: "So it turns out we really are at war.... It is a war to save our democracy."[37] Wolf saw incipient fascism in the extralegal machinations of the Bush administration. It is worth noting that John Dean's mentor for his analytical framework in *Conservatives without Conscience*, Bob Altemeyer, believed there could be fascist leaders in a democracy, likening the traits of double high authoritarians to those of Adolf Hitler. Dean concluded, however, that the United States was not yet on the road to fascism. Nevertheless, "it would not take much more misguided authoritarian leadership, or thoughtless following of such leaders, to find ourselves there."[38]

For every Zinn and Chomsky, for every Klein and Wolf, progressives who oppose the perpetuation of the security ethos and what it has done to America, there are the likes of Kagan, Fukuyama, and Zakaria who, despite their differences, celebrate the pursuit of hegemony. These neoconservatives, these realistic Wilsonians, these liberals, however one characterizes them, operate in public spaces where their self-styled gravitas provides support for those elected officials and their advisers who have brought core values to their current state. There is no better example of this toxic relationship than Michael Ignatieff, formerly Carr Professor of Human Rights Practice

the *Assault on Democracy* (New York: Owl Books, 2006); John Lewis Gaddis, *The Cold War: A New History* (New York: Penguin Press, 2005).

[36] *New York Times*, December 18, 2007.

[37] Naomi Klein, *The Shock Doctrine: The Rise of Disaster Capitalism* (New York: Metropolitan Books, 2007); Alan Greenspan, *The Age of Turbulence: Adventures in a New World* (New York: Penguin Press, 2007); Naomi Wolf, *The End of America: Letter of Warning to a Young Patriot* (White River Junction: Chelsea Green Publishing, 2007), 153.

[38] Dean, *Conservatives without Conscience*, 47, 61; quoted words, 180.

in the John F. Kennedy School of Government at Harvard University. Two months before the United States launched Operation Iraqi Freedom in March 2003 he wrote, "Those who want America to remain a republic rather than become an empire imagine rightly, but they have not factored in what tyranny or chaos can do to vital American interests." With those words, a champion of human rights abandoned his principles for recognition in the halls of power.[39] Less than four years later, having returned to his native Canada to run for political office in the Liberal Party, Ignatieff issued a half-hearted *mea culpa* for his intellectual indiscretion. In that essay, he also assessed the actions of President Bush: "It was not merely that the president did not take care to understand Iraq. He also did not take care to understand himself."[40] It is worth observing that John W. Dean, who figured prominently in the Watergate scandal during the Nixon presidency, did not have to take the same tortuous journey after 9/11 to reach a similar conclusion.

The problem is that Ignatieff is not alone. He and like-minded others refuse, in effect, to heed the warnings of Benjamin Franklin and John Quincy Adams concerning the fragility of freedom and the peril of losing the nation's soul in foreign entanglement. Such has been the tyranny of the security ethos over elected officials, those who advise them, and many within the nation's intellectual class. Whatever becomes of the war on terror after Bush leaves office in January 2009, there is little chance that hegemony will fall into disrepute. Six months before his election as president, Barack Obama told David Brooks of the *New York Times*, "I have enormous sympathy for the foreign policy of George H. W. Bush."[41] For citizens who believe that maintaining the status quo will further distance America from its foundational principles, can they turn their understanding into effective action to alter this state of affairs?

The odds are not good because the problem is a systemic one that will not give way even to the best intentions. Obama's determination to increase U.S. involvement in Afghanistan indicates the persistence of the security ethos, even in a time of great economic strife. It is far from certain, however, that the government can simultaneously pursue this form of strategic globalism and also rebuild the American economy. Nevertheless, civic virtue remains alive and little victories may be possible, staving off ultimate defeat for an indeterminate period of time. For people not despondent to the point of inertia, there existed several guides for action as the country awaited the Obama presidency. Writing at the dawn of the Reagan era, William Appleman Williams dared to ask Americans what kind of empire they desired. What would be its optimum size? What were the means of controlling it

[39] Michael Ignatieff, "The Burden," *New York Times Magazine*, January 5, 2003.
[40] Michael Ignatieff, "Getting Iraq Wrong," *New York Times Magazine*, August 5, 2007.
[41] *New York Times*, May 16, 2008.

so that it could "produce welfare and democracy for the largest number of the imperial population"? It is impossible to know if Williams penned those words in irony or in resignation to the realities of grand strategy. He nevertheless also asked his fellow citizens to imagine finally saying "no" to empire. That response, he declared, "is now *our* responsibility. It has to do with how we live and how we die. We as a culture have run out of imperial games to play."[42] The relevance of Williams's charge to the conduct of civic virtue in the twenty-first century cannot be overstated.

Like Williams, Joan Hoff insisted that American citizens ask more of themselves and their government. Hoff, a public intellectual, historian, feminist, legal scholar, and former head of the Organization of American Historians, urged Americans to demand "ethical and efficient conduct" in governance. A goal in itself, that outcome would also "explain to average Americans past unethical behavior on the part of the United States." Employing a historical reference that most Americans would recognize, Hoff continued, "[T]he Puritans traditionally prided themselves on being ethical and practical before their 'errand into the wilderness' turned into a justification for economic expansionism." "Clearly, it is time," she wrote, "for both moderate Democrats and Republicans to claim that ethical behavior . . . is truly patriotic and need not be above the law, as moralistic and incompetent behavior often are." The false luxury Americans had enjoyed in denying their nation's past excesses was over because "the myth of exceptionalism is no longer serving the best interests of the United States" and prevents the nation from adopting "a truly global cooperative foreign policy."[43] It is worth wondering whether regenerating the ideal of exceptionalism, not as myth but as a living part of the national past, might not help rescue core values from their current malaise. That they have been distorted and used as tools of empire and hegemony since the nation's founding should not consign them to that role in perpetuity.

Another scholar, Andrew J. Bacevich of Boston University, had much to suggest regarding the future of American foreign policy and, by implication, the exercise of civic virtue it would take if past practices were to be transformed. A Vietnam veteran and thus a latecomer to academic life, he was widely known especially to readers of conservative and neoconservative periodicals as a prolific commentator on contemporary politics and strategy. That audience turned its back on Bacevich after he began criticizing Bush's war on terror.

---

[42] William Appleman Williams, *Empire as a Way of Life: An Essay on the Causes and Character of America's Present Predicament along with a Few Thoughts about an Alternative*, with an introduction by Andrew Bacevich (Brooklyn: Ig Publishing, 2007), 198–9 (emphasis in original); this book was first published by Oxford University Press in 1980.

[43] Joan Hoff, *A Faustian Foreign Policy from Woodrow Wilson to George W. Bush: Dreams of Perfectibility* (New York: Cambridge University Press, 2008), 199, 200, 201.

In late 2007, he declared that the democratic revolution the United States had promised to bring to the Middle East had "demonstrably failed." In Iraq and Afghanistan, the war on terror had become wholly counterproductive to America's vital interests. Even so, during the 2008 presidential campaign, both major party candidates called for a greater U.S. military presence in Afghanistan; so much for learning from history.[44] What, though, might an ethical and efficient government do? And what should citizens demand of their representatives? Bacevich called for the husbanding of American power. "U.S. military strength is finite." "Promise only the achievable," he urged officials. Policymakers and the intellectual class should realize that America "possesses neither the capacity nor the wisdom required to liberate the world's 1.4 billion Muslims." A return to some form of containment was advisable if the United States was ever going to "insulate itself against Islamic radicalism." In the mode of Williams, in whose counsel Bacevich found much to admire, he concluded, "Exemplify the ideals we profess. Rather than telling others how to live, Americans should devote themselves to repairing their own institutions."[45]

Neither Hoff nor Bacevich explicitly articulated what American foreign policy would resemble were the nation to endorse a policy of humility, as Bush suggested in 2000.[46] Perhaps that is an impossible task after more than two centuries of expansionism, hegemony, and the security ethos. Could citizens and the government even recognize humility? Perhaps the answer truly does lie in participating in a global cooperative foreign policy. Perhaps a change more structural, something more than a turn toward multilateralism, would signal the presence of humility as a defining characteristic of U.S. policy. It is worth pondering whether the post- Cold War ethos of militarism, which Bacevich has cogently described,[47] could actually be reversed. Is it thinkable that humility might be more in evidence, and the world's poor the better for it, were the International Monetary Fund and the World Bank located outside the United States? Perhaps Washington might consider increasing its development funding in direct proportion to the amount of savings realized by reducing the nation's costly global military presence. To those skeptics who reflexively would dismiss such ideas, it is now their burden to demonstrate how the values Americans most cherish and the rights of citizens would be any worse off than they currently are under proposals such as these. The history of the security ethos and the likelihood of its

---

44 See Ahmed Rashid, *Descent into Chaos: The United States and the Failure of Nation Building in Pakistan, Afghanistan, and Central Asia* (New York: Viking, 2008).

45 *Los Angeles Times*, November 6, 2007.

46 Bacevich did warn about the folly in the attitude of near-omniscience long prevalent in the making of foreign policy; Andrew J. Bacevich, *The Limits of Power: The End of American Exceptionalism* (New York: Metropolitan Books, 2008), 170–82.

47 Andrew J. Bacevich, *The New American Militarism: How Americans Are Seduced by War*, paper ed. (New York: Oxford University Press, 2006).

continuation do not instill confidence that American identity will long be recognizable if the country fails to abandon its historical and present course.

Hope for the future is in short supply. In reaching this conclusion, I am forced to concur with Andrew Bacevich. He and his wife lost a child in the Iraq War; their son was killed in May 2007. Bacevich subsequently wrote a heartrending op-ed for the *Washington Post*. Evocative of Mark Twain's *The War Prayer*, yet vastly more powerful for its ineffable sadness, the essay rejected the possibility of national redemption through what I have called civic virtue, finding it "an illusion" to presume that such "efforts might produce a political climate conducive to change." The inescapable reason is "money," in academic circles more decorously portrayed as the workings of the marketplace. The marketplace is not ephemeral or situational. It is the check Bacevich received from the U.S. government for the "value" of his son's life, just as thousands of other parents have been similarly thanked because of an unnecessary war in the Middle East. "[Money]," Bacevich observed, "confines the debate over U.S. policy to well-hewn channels. It preserves intact the clichés of 1933–45 about isolationism, appeasement and the nation's call to 'global leadership.'. . . This is not some great conspiracy. It's the way our system works."[48] If Andrew Bacevich failed his son, as he wrote at the end of his essay, then that failure was long in coming and is one shared across generations too numerous to count. More than most Americans, both in and out of public life, he realized what had been lost.

---

[48] Andrew J. Bacevich, "I Lost My Son to a War I Oppose. We Were Both Doing Our Duty," *Washington Post*, March 27, 2007.

Select Bibliography

U.S. Government Documents

American State Papers 04. Foreign Relations, vol. 4, 15th Cong., 2d sess. Publication No. 311.

Brinkley, Joel, and Stephen Engelberg, eds. *Report of the Congressional Committees Investigating the Iran-Contra Affair, with the Minority View*. New York: Times Books, 1988.

Department of State Bulletin.

Guinta, Mary A., ed. *The Emerging Nation: A Documentary History of the Foreign Relations of the United States under the Articles of Confederation, 1780–1789*, vol. 1: *Recognition of Independence, 1780–1784*. Washington, DC: National Historical Publications and Records Commission, 1996.

The Pentagon Papers: The Defense Department History of United States Decision-making on Vietnam. Senator Gravel edition, 5 vols. Boston: Beacon Press, 1971–2.

Public Papers of the Presidents. Dwight David Eisenhower, 1953: Containing the Public Messages, Speeches, and Statements of the President, January 1 to December 31, 1953. Washington, DC: Government Printing Office, 1960.

Records of the Department of State (RG 59), National Archives, Suitland, Maryland Francis White Papers, Latin America File General Records of the Department of State, Decimal File.

The Report of the President's National Bipartisan Commission on Central America, foreword by Henry Kissinger. New York: Macmillan, 1984.

Richardson, James, ed. *A Compilation of the Messages and Papers of the Presidents, 1789–1897*. Washington, DC: Government Printing Office, 1899.

U.S. Congress, Joint Committee on Defense Production. *Deterrence and Survival in the Nuclear Age (The "Gaither Report" of 1957)*. Washington, DC: Government Printing Office, 1976.

U.S. Congress, Senate. *Hearings before the Subcommittee on Terrorism, Narcotics and International Communications of the Committee on Foreign Relations*, "Drugs, Law Enforcement and Foreign Policy: Panama." 100 Cong., 1 sess., 8–11 February 1988, Part 2. Washington, DC: Government Printing Office, 1988.

U.S. Department of State. *Papers Relating to the Foreign Relations of the United States, 1895.* Washington, DC: Government Printing Office, 1896.

———. *Papers Relating to the Foreign Relations of the United States, 1912.* Washington, DC: Government Printing Office, 1919.

———. *Papers Relating to the Foreign Relations of the United States, 1928.* Washington, DC: Government Printing Office, 1942.

———. *Foreign Relations of the United States, 1935,* vol. 3: *The Far East.* Washington, DC: Government Printing Office, 1953.

———. *Foreign Relations of the United States: The Conferences at Cairo and Tehran, 1943.* Washington, DC: Government Printing Office, 1961.

———. *Papers Relating to the Foreign Relations of the United States, 1948,* vol. 1, pt. 2: *General; the United Nations.* Washington, DC: Government Printing Office, 1976.

———. *Foreign Relations of the United States, 1950,* vol. 1: *National Security Affairs; Foreign Economic Policy.* Washington, DC: Government Printing Office, 1977.

———. *Papers Relating to the Foreign Relations of the United States, 1950–1955: The Intelligence Community, 1950–1955.* Washington, DC: Government Printing Office, 2007.

———. *Papers Relating to the Foreign Relations of the United States, 1958–60,* vol. 6: *Cuba.* Washington, DC: Government Printing Office, 1991.

———. *Papers Relating to the Foreign Relations of the United States, 1958–60,* vol. 11: *Lebanon and Jordan.* Washington, DC: Government Printing Office, 1992.

———. *Papers Relating to the Foreign Relations of the United States, 1958–60,* vol. 12: *Near East Region; Iraq; Iran; Arabian Peninsula.* Washington, DC: Government Printing Office, 1993.

———. *Papers Relating to the Foreign Relations of the United States, 1958–60,* vol. 14: *Africa.* Washington, DC: Government Printing Office, 1992.

———. *Papers Relating to the Foreign Relations of the United States, 1961–1963,* vol. 12: *American Republics.* Washington, DC: Government Printing Office, 1996.

———. *Papers Relating to the Foreign Relations of the United States, 1964–1968,* vol. 31: *South and Central America; Mexico.* Washington, DC: Government Printing Office, 2005.

U.S. General Accounting Office. *Drug Control: U.S. Counternarcotics Efforts in Colombia Face Continuing Challenges.* GAO/NSIAD-98-60.Washington, DC: General Accounting Office, February 1998.

The Vietnam Hearings, with an introduction by J. William Fulbright. New York: Vintage Books, 1996.

The White House. *A National Security Strategy of Engagement and Enlargement* (February 1996).

Library of Congress, Manuscript Division, Washington, DC

William S. Culbertson Papers
Nelson T. Johnson Papers: General Correspondence
Philander C. Knox Papers

Herbert Hoover Presidential Library, West Branch, Iowa

Commerce Papers: Public Statements File
Presidential Papers: Foreign Affairs File

John F. Kennedy Presidential Library, Boston, Massachusetts

National Security File: Meeting and Memoranda Series

Lyndon Baines Johnson Presidential Library, Austin, Texas

National Security File: Country File, Name File, National Intelligence Estimates
Lee C. White Files: Office Files
White House Central Files: Human Rights

United Nations

UN Assistance Mission for Iraq. *Human Rights Report: 1 April–30 June 2007.*

Electronic Records

Addresses

Clinton, Bill. "A New Covenant for American Security," December 12, 1991 (http://www.ndol.org/print.cfm?contentid=250537).
Gore, Albert. "Remarks at the Kennan Institute and U.S.-Russia Business Council," October 19, 1995 (http://clinton6.nara.gov/1995/10/1995-10-19-vp-gore-to-the-kennan-institute-us-russia-council.html).
Kerr, Donald. "Address to United States Geospatial Foundation," October 23, 2007 (http://www.dni.gov/speeches/20071023_speech.pdf).
Lake, Anthony. "From Containment to Enlargement," September 21, 1993 (http://www.mtholyoke.edu/acad/intrel/lakedoc.html).
Nixon, Richard M. "Address to the Bohemian Club, San Francisco [Bohemian Grove]," July 29, 1967 (http://www.state.gov/r/pa/ho/frus/nixon/i/20700.htm).

U.S. Government Documents

Declassified Documents Reference System (http://www.gale.cengage.com/pdf/facts/ddrs.pdf).
National Security Archive (http://www.gwu.edu/~nsarchiv/):
Electronic Briefing Book No. 11. *U.S. Policy in Guatemala, 1966–1996.*
Electronic Briefing Book No. 69. *War in Colombia.*
Electronic Briefing Book No. 82. *Shaking Hands with Saddam Hussein: The U.S. Tilts toward Iraq, 1980–1984.*
Electronic Briefing Book No. 110. *The Pinochet File.*
Electronic Briefing Book No. 167. *Saddam's Iron Grip: Intelligence Reports on Saddam Hussein's Reign.*
Digital National Security Archive (http://nsarchive.chadwyck.com).
U.S. Department of Agriculture. Foreign Agricultural Service. "China WTO Accession" (http://www.fas.usda.gov/itp/china/accession.html).

U.S. Department of Defense. *The National Defense Strategy of the United States of America*, March 2005 (http://www.defenselink.mil/news/Mar2005/d20050318ndsi .pdf).

U.S. Department of State. Bureau of Intelligence and Research, Intelligence Assessment. "Colombia: Momentum against Paramilitaries Lost," April 7, 1998 (http:// www.gwu.edu/~nsarchiv/NSAEBB/NSAEBB69/col61.pdf).

U.S. Department of the Treasury. "The Debt to the Penny and Who Holds It" (http://www.treasurydirect.gov/NP/BPDLogin?application=np).

U.S. Drug Enforcement Agency. "Testimony of Thomas A. Constantine," June 6, 1996 (http://www.cja.org/cases/Constant.shtml).

The White House. Presidential Decision Directive–39. "U.S. Policy on Counterterrorism," June 21, 1995 (http://www.fas.org/irp/offdocs/pdd39.htm).

————. President George W. Bush. "Graduation Speech at West Point," June 1, 2002 (http://www.whitehouse.gov/news/releases/2002/06/20020601-3.html).

United Nations

United Nations Children's Fund. "Iraq Survey," August 12, 1999 (http://www. unicef.org/newsline/99pr29.htm).

Miscellaneous

The American Presidency Project (http://www.presidency.ucsb.edu/).

Bank Information Center. "Banco del Sur," May 1, 2007 (http://www.bicusa.org/ en/Article.3299.aspx).

Center for Justice and Accountability. Haiti: Emmanuel "Toto" Constant (http:// www.cja.org/cases/Constant.shtml).

Democracy Now! "Remarks of Senator Patrick Leahy," September 29, 2006 (http:// www.democracynow.org).

Federation of American Scientists. National Security Directive 26. "U.S. Policy toward Persian Gulf," October 2, 1989 (http://www.fas.org/irp/offdocs/nsd/nsd26 .pdf).

Published Memoirs, Papers, Writing, and Other Records

Adams, Charles Francis, ed. *Memoirs of John Quincy Adams Comprising Portions of His Diary from 1795 to 1848*. Philadelphia: J. B. Lippincott & Company, 1875.

Albright, Madeleine, with Bill Woodward. *Madam Secretary: A Memoir*. New York: Miramax Books, 2003.

Andrew, Christopher, and Vasili Mitrokhin. *The Sword and the Shield: The Mitrokhin Archive and the Secret History of the KGB*. New York: Basic Books, 1999.

Andrew, Christopher, and Vasili Mitrokhin. *The World Was Going Our Way: The KGB and the Battle for the Third World*. New York: Basic Books, 2005.

Arbatov, Georgi. *The System: An Insider's Life in Soviet Politics*. New York: Times Books, 1993.

Bissell Jr., Richard M., with Jonathan E. Lewis and Frances T. Pudlo. *Reflections of a Cold Warrior: From Yalta to the Bay of Pigs*. New Haven: Yale University Press, 1996.

Baker III, James A., with Thomas M. DeFrank. *The Politics of Diplomacy: Revolution, War and Peace, 1989–1992.* New York: G. P. Putnam's Sons, 1995.

Baker III, James A., and Lee H. Hamilton, co-chairs. *The Iraq Study Group Report.* New York: Vintage Books, 2006.

Baruch, Bernard M. *My Own Story: The Public Years.* New York: Holt, Rinehart, and Winston, 1960.

Benjamin Franklin's Autobiography. Introduction by Dixon Wecter and Larzer Ziff, ed., *Selected Writings.* New York: Holt, Rinehart and Winston, 1959.

Beschloss, Michael R. ed. *Taking Charge: The Johnson White House Tapes, 1963–1964.* New York: Simon & Schuster, 1997.

Blum, John Morton, ed. *The Price of Vision: The Diary of Henry A. Wallace, 1942–1946.* Boston: Houghton Mifflin, 1973.

Board of Missions of the Methodist Episcopal Church. *Annual Report . . . for the Year 1920.* New York: Board of Foreign Missions, 1921.

Brown, Elaine. *A Taste of Power: A Black Woman's Story.* New York: Pantheon Books, 1992.

Brown, Harold. *Thinking about National Security: Defense and Foreign Policy in a Dangerous World.* Boulder: Westview Press, 1983.

Brzezinski, Zbigniew. *Power and Principle: Memoirs of the National Security Adviser, 1977–81.* New York: Farrar, Straus and Giroux, 1983.

Bush, George, and Brent Scowcroft. *A World Transformed.* New York: Alfred A. Knopf, 1998.

Cappon, Lester J., ed. *The Adams-Jefferson Letters: The Complete Correspondence between Thomas Jefferson and Abigail and John Adams.* Chapel Hill: University of North Carolina Press, 1959.

Carter, Jimmy. *Keeping Faith: Memoirs of a President.* New York: Bantam Books, 1982.

Christopher, Warren. *In the Stream of History: Shaping Foreign Policy for a New Era.* Stanford: Stanford University Press, 1998.

Clarke, Richard A. *Against All Enemies: Inside America's War on Terror.* New York: Free Press, 2004.

Dallaire, Roméo. *Shake Hands with the Devil: The Failure of Humanity in Rwanda.* Toronto: Random House Canada, 2003.

Depew, Chauncey M., ed. *The Library of Oratory, Ancient and Modern.* London: Globe Publishing Co., 1902.

Dobrynin, Anatoly. *In Confidence: Moscow's Ambassador to America's Six Cold War Presidents (1962–1986).* New York: Times Books, 1995.

Ferrell, Robert H., ed. *The Eisenhower Diaries.* New York: W.W. Norton & Company, 1981.

The Federalist Papers. With an introduction by Clinton Rossiter. New York: Mentor Books, 1961.

Ford, Worthington Chauncey, ed. *Writings of John Quincy Adams,* vol. VII: *1820–1823.* New York: Macmillan, 1917.

Gates, Robert M. *From the Shadows: The Ultimate Insider's Account of Five Presidents and How They Won the Cold War.* New York: Simon & Schuster, 1996.

Greenberg, Cheryl Lynn, ed. *A Circle of Trust: Remembering SNCC.* New Brunswick: Rutgers University Press, 1998.

Greenspan, Alan. *The Age of Turbulence: Adventures in a New World.* New York: Penguin Press, 2007.

Grew, Joseph C. *Ten Years in Japan.* New York: Simon & Schuster, 1944.

Haig Jr., Alexander M. *Caveat: Realism, Reagan, and Foreign Policy.* New York: Macmillan, 1984.

Hoover, Herbert. *The Memoirs of Herbert Hoover,* vol. I: *Years of Adventure, 1874–1920.* New York: Macmillan, 1951.

Israelyan, Victor. *Inside the Kremlin during the Yom Kippur War.* University Park: Pennsylvania State University Press, 1995.

Keller, Albert Galloway, and Maurice R. Davie, eds. *Essays of William Graham Sumner,* vol. 2. Hamden: Archon Books, 1969.

Kennan, George F. *At a Century's Ending.* New York: W. W. Norton & Company, 1996.

Kimball, Warren F., ed. *Roosevelt and Churchill: Their Complete Correspondence,* vol. III: *Alliance Declining.* Princeton: Princeton University Press, 1984.

King Jr., Martin Luther. *I Have a Dream: Writings and Speeches That Changed the World,* ed. Washington, James M. New York: HarperCollins, 1992.

Kissinger, Henry. *White House Years.* Boston: Little, Brown, 1979.

Kissinger, Henry. *Years of Upheaval.* Boston: Little, Brown, 1982.

Kutler, Stanley I., ed. *Abuse of Power: The New Nixon Tapes.* New York: Free Press, 1997.

Labaree, Leonard W., et al., eds. *Papers of Benjamin Franklin,* vol. III: *January 1, 1745 through June 30, 1750.* New Haven: Yale University Press, 1961.

Labaree, Leonard W., et al., eds. *Papers of Benjamin Franklin,* vol. VI: *April 1, 1755 through September 30, 1756.* New Haven: Yale University Press, 1963.

LaFeber, Walter, ed. *John Quincy Adams and American Continental Empire: Letters, Papers, and Speeches.* Chicago: Quadrangle Books, 1965.

———. *America in the Cold War: Twenty-Years of Revolution and Response, 1947–1967.* New York: John Wiley & Sons, 1969.

Lewis, John, with Michael D'Orso. *Walking with the Wind: A Memoir of the Movement.* New York: Simon & Schuster, 1998.

Link, Arthur S., et al., eds. *The Papers of Woodrow Wilson,* vol. 28: *1913.* Princeton: Princeton University Press, 1978.

———. *The Papers of Woodrow Wilson,* vol. 34: *July 21–September 30, 1915.* Princeton: Princeton University Press, 1980.

———. *Papers of Woodrow Wilson,* vol. 55: *February 8–March 16, 1919.* Princeton: Princeton University Press, 1986.

———. *The Papers of Woodrow Wilson,* vol. 56: *March 17–April 4, 1919.* Princeton: Princeton University Press, 1987.

———. *The Papers of Woodrow Wilson,* vol. 58: *April 23–May 9, 1919.* Princeton: Princeton University Press, 1988.

———. *The Papers of Woodrow Wilson,* vol. 66: *August 2–December 23, 1920.* Princeton: Princeton University Press, 1992.

———. *The Papers of Woodrow Wilson,* vol. 67: *December 24, 1920–April 7, 1922.* Princeton: Princeton University Press, 1992.

Lipscomb, Andrew A., ed. *Writings of Thomas Jefferson,* vol. XII. Washington, DC: Thomas Jefferson Memorial Association, 1903.

Matlock Jr., Jack F. *Reagan and Gorbachev: How the Cold War Ended*. New York: Random House, 2004.

May, Henry. *Coming to Terms: A Study in Memory and History*. Berkeley: University of California Press, 1987.

McClellan, Scott. *What Happened: Inside the Bush White House and Washington's Culture of Deception*. New York: Public Affairs, 2008.

McNamara, Robert S., with Brian VanDeMark. *In Retrospect: The Tragedy and Lessons of Vietnam*. New York: Crown, 1995.

McNeill, Frank. *War and Peace in Central America: Reality and Illusion*. New York: Charles Scribner's Sons, 1988.

Meyer, Cord. *Facing Reality: From World Federalism to the CIA*. New York: Harper & Row, 1980.

Mokoena, Kenneth, ed. *South Africa and the United States: The Declassified History*. New York: New Press, 1993.

Morison, Elting E., et al., eds. *The Letters of Theodore Roosevelt*, vol. I: *The Years of Preparation, 1868–1898*. Cambridge: Harvard University Press, 1951.

———. *War and Peace in Central America: Reality and Illusion*. New York: Charles Scribner's Sons, 1988.

———. *The Letters of Theodore Roosevelt*, vol. III: *The Square Deal, 1901–1903*. Cambridge: Harvard University Press, 1951.

Nevins, Allan, ed. *The Diary of John Quincy Adams, 1794–1845: American Diplomacy, and Political, Social, and Intellectual Life, from Washington to Polk*, reprint ed. New York: Frederick Ungar Publishing, 1969.

Nixon, Edgar B., ed. *Franklin D. Roosevelt and Foreign Affairs*, vol. I: *January 1933–February 1934*. Cambridge: Belknap Press of Harvard University Press, 1969.

Nixon, Richard M. *Six Crises*. Garden City: Doubleday, 1962.

———. *RN: The Memoirs of Richard Nixon*. New York: Grosset & Dunlop, 1978.

Roosevelt, Kermit. *Countercoup: The Struggle for Control of Iran*. New York: McGraw-Hill, 1979.

Roosevelt, Theodore. *The Strenuous Life: Essays and Addresses*. London: Thomas Nelson & Sons, n.d. [1902?].

———. *An Autobiography*. New York: Macmillan, 1913.

Schlesinger Jr., Arthur M. *A Life in the Twentieth Century: Innocent Beginnings, 1917–1950*. Boston: Houghton Mifflin, 2000.

Shultz, George P. *Turmoil and Triumph: My Years as Secretary of State*. New York: Charles Scribner's Sons, 1993.

Sparks, Jared, ed. *The Writings of George Washington*, vol. II. Boston: Little, Brown and Company, 1855.

Stimson, Henry L., with McGeorge Bundy. *On Active Service in Peace and War*. New York: Harper & Row, 1947.

Stockwell, John. *In Search of Enemies: A CIA Story*. New York: W. W. Norton & Company, 1978.

Strasser, Steven, ed. *The 9/11 Investigations*. New York: Public Affairs, 2004.

Sullivan, William C., with Bill Brown. *The Bureau: My Thirty Years in Hoover's FBI*. New York: W. W. Norton & Company, 1979.

Tenet, George, with Bill Harlow. *At the Center of the Storm: My Years at the CIA.* New York: HarperCollins, 2007.

Tyroler, II, Charles, ed. *Alerting America: The Papers of the Committee on the Present Danger.* Washington, DC: Pergamon-Brassey's, 1984.

Weinberger, Caspar. *Fighting for Peace: Seven Critical Years in the Pentagon.* New York: Warner Books, 1991.

Wilson, Clyde N., and Shirley Bright Cook, eds. *The Papers of John C. Calhoun,* vol. XXVII: *1849–1850 with Supplement.* Charleston: University of South Carolina Press, 2003.

Zimmermann, Warren. *Origins of a Catastrophe: Yugoslavia and Its Destroyers – America's Last Ambassador Tells What Happened and Why.* New York: Times Books, 1996.

Newspapers and News Services

Agence France–Presse
Associated Press
Atlanta Journal-Constitution
BBC News (http://news.bbc.co.uk)
Bloomberg.com (http://www.bloomberg.com)
CBS News
Christian Science Monitor
CNN News (http://www.cnn.com)
The Independent (UK)
La Jornada (Mexico City)
Los Angeles Times
Miami Herald
La Nación (Buenos Aires)
MSNBC (http://www.msnbc.com)
New York Times
Newsweek
San Francisco Chronicle
El Tiempo (Bogotá)
The Times (London)
Washington Post
Reuters News
USA Today
CNN Special Investigations Unit. "Judgment in Jena" (September 20, 2007).

Books and Articles

The books and articles listed are those most pertinent to the themes of this book; all other materials consulted are contained in the notes for individual chapters.

Adas, Michael. *Dominance by Design: Technological Imperatives and America's Civilizing Mission.* Cambridge: Belknap Press of Harvard University Press, 2006.

Anderson, Carol. *Eyes off the Prize: The United Nations and the African American Struggle for Human Rights, 1944–1955.* New York: Cambridge University Press, 2003.

Arnson, Cynthia. *Crossroads: Congress, the President, and Central America, 1976–1993*, 2d ed. University Park: Pennsylvania State University Press, 1993.

Bacevich, Andrew J. *American Empire: The Realities and Consequences of U.S. Diplomacy*. Cambridge: Harvard University Press, 2002.

———. *The New American Militarism: How Americans Are Seduced by War*, paper ed. New York: Oxford University Press, 2006.

———. "I Lost My Son to a War I Oppose. We Were Both Doing Our Duty." *Washington Post* (March 27, 2007).

Beard, Charles A. *An Economic Interpretation of the Constitution of the United States*. New York: Macmillan, 1913.

———. *The Open Door at Home: A Trial Philosophy of National Interest*. New York: Macmillan, 1935.

———. *American Foreign Policy in the Making, 1932–1940: A Study in Responsibilities*. New Haven: Yale University Press, 1946.

———. *President Roosevelt and the Coming of the War, 1941: A Study in Appearances and Realities*. New Haven: Yale University Press, 1948.

———. with G. H. E. Smith. *The Open Door at Home: A Trial Philosophy of National Interest*. New York: Macmillan, 1935.

———. with G. H. E. Smith. *The Idea of National Interest: An Analytical Study in American Foreign Policy*, ed. by Alfred Vagts and William Beard. Chicago: Quadrangle Books, 1966.

Beisner, Robert L. *Twelve against Empire: The Anti-Imperialists, 1898–1900*. New York: McGraw-Hill, 1968.

Berman, Paul. *Terror and Liberalism*, paper ed. New York: W. W. Norton & Company, 2004.

Botts, Joshua. " 'Nothing to Seek and . . . Nothing to Defend': George F. Kennan's Core Values and American Foreign Policy, 1938–1993." *Diplomatic History* 30 (November 2006): 839–66.

Bourne, Randolph S. *War and the Intellectuals: Collected Essays, 1915–1919*, ed. with an introduction by Carl Resek. New York: Harper & Row, 1964.

Bouton, Terry. *Taming Democracy" "The People," the Founders, and the Troubled Ending of the American Revolution*. New York: Oxford University Press, 2007.

Broadwater, Jeff. *Eisenhower and the Anti-Communist Crusade*. Chapel Hill: University of North Carolina Press, 1992.

Bronson, Rachel. *Thicker than Oil: America's Uneasy Partnership with Saudi Arabia*. New York: Oxford University Press, 2006.

Cahn, Anne Hessing. *Killing Détente: The Right Attacks the CIA*. University Park: Pennsylvania State University Press, 1998.

Carothers, Thomas. *In the Name of Democracy: U.S. Policy toward Latin America in the Reagan Years*. Berkeley: University of California Press, 1991.

Clark, Wesley K. *Waging Modern War: Bosnia, Kosovo, and the Future of Combat*. New York: Public Affairs, 2002.

Cohen, Robert. *When the Old Left Was Young: Student Radicals and America's First Mass Student Movement, 1929–1941*. New York: Oxford University Press, 1993.

Cohen, Warren I. *The American Revisionists: The Lessons of Intervention in World War I*. Chicago: University of Chicago Press, 1967.

Coll, Steve. *Ghost Wars: The Secret History of the CIA, Afghanistan, and bin Laden, from the Soviet Invasion to September 10, 2001*. New York: Penguin Press, 2004.

Cole, David. "The Man behind the Torture." *New York Review of Books* (December 6, 2007).

Collins, Robert M. "The Economic Crisis of 1968 and the Waning of the 'American Century.'" *American Historical Review* 101 (April 1996): 396–422.

Costigliola, Frank. "'Unceasing Pressure for Penetration': Gender, Pathology, and Emotion in George Kennan's Formation of the Cold War." *Journal of American History*, 83 (March 1997): 1309–39.

Craig, Campbell. *Glimmer of a New Leviathan: Total War in the Realism of Niebuhr, Morgenthau, and Waltz*. New York: Columbia University Press, 2003.

Croly, Herbert. *The Promise of American Life*. New York: Dutton, 1909.

Dean, John W. *Conservatives without Conscience*, paper ed. New York: Penguin Books, 2007.

Dinges, John. *The Condor Years: How Pinochet and His Allies Brought Terrorism to Three Continents*. New York: New Press, 2004.

Drake, Paul W. *The Money Doctor in the Andes: The Kemmerer Missions, 1923–1933*. Durham: Duke University Press, 1989.

Egnal, Marc. *A Mighty Empire: The Origins of the American Revolution*. Ithaca: Cornell University Press, 1988.

Evangelista, Matthew. *Unarmed Forces: The Transnational Movement to End the Cold War*. Ithaca: Cornell University Press, 1999.

Ferguson, Thomas. "From Normalcy to New Deal: Industrial Structure, Party Competition, and American Public Policy in the Great Depression." *International Organization* 38 (Winter 1984): 41–94.

Foglesong, David S. *The American Mission and the "Evil Empire": The Crusade for a "Free Russia" since 1881*. New York: Cambridge University Press, 2007.

Frank, Thomas. *What's the Matter with Kansas?: How Conservatives Won the Heart of America*. New York: Metropolitan Books, 2004.

Friedman, Thomas L. "A Manifesto for the Fast World." *New York Times Magazine* (March 28, 1999).

Fukuyama, Francis. "The End of History?" *The National Interest*, no. 16 (Summer 1989).

Gaddis, John Lewis. "A Grand Strategy of Transformation." *Foreign Policy* No. 133 (November/December 2002).

――――. *Surprise, Security, and the American Experience*. Cambridge: Harvard University Press, 2004.

――――. *The Cold War: A New History*. New York: Penguin Press, 2005.

Garthoff, Raymond L. *Détente and Confrontation: American-Soviet Relations from Nixon to Reagan*, rev. ed. Washington, DC: Brookings Institution, 1994.

Gerges, Fawaz A. *The Far Enemy: Why Jihad went Global*. New York: Cambridge University Press, 2005.

Gilman, Charlotte Perkins. *Women and Economics: A Study of the Economic Relation between Men and Women as a Factor in Social Evolution*, ed. with an introduction by Carl N. Degler. New York: Harper & Row, 1966.

Gleijeses, Piero. *Conflicting Missions: Havana, Washington, and Africa, 1959–1976*. Chapel Hill: University of North Carolina Press, 2002.

Goodwin, Jeff. *No Other Way Out: States and Revolutionary Movements, 1945–1991*. New York: Cambridge University Press, 2001.

Grandin, Greg. *The Last Colonial Massacre: Latin America in the Cold War*. Chicago: University of Chicago Press, 2004.

Greenberg, Cheryl Lynn. *Troubling the Waters: Black-Jewish Relations in the American Century*. Princeton: Princeton University Press, 2006.

Greene, Jack P. *The Intellectual Construction of America: Exceptionalism and Identity from 1492 to 1800*. Chapel Hill: University of North Carolina Press, 1993.

Hartz, Louis. *The Liberal Tradition in America*. New York: Harcourt, Brace & World, 1955.

Haslam, Jonathan. *The Nixon Administration and the Death of Allende's Chile*. London: Verso, 2005.

Healy, David. *Drive to Hegemony: The United States in the Caribbean 1898–1917*. Madison: University of Wisconsin Press, 1988.

———. *James G. Blaine and Latin America*. Columbia: University of Missouri Press, 2001.

Hedges, Chris. *War Is a Force That Gives Us Meaning*. New York: Anchor Books, 2003.

Herbert, Bob. "100,000 Gone since 2001." *New York Times* (August 14, 2007).

Hersh, Seymour. *The Price of Power: Kissinger in the Nixon White House*. New York: Summit Books, 1983.

Hiro, Dilip. *Blood of the Earth: The Battle for the World's Vanishing Resources*. New York: Nation Books, 2007.

Hoff, Joan. *A Faustian Foreign Policy from Woodrow Wilson to George W. Bush: Dreams of Perfectibility*. New York: Cambridge University Press, 2008.

Hofstadter, Richard. *The Paranoid Style in American Politics and Other Essays*. New York: Vintage Books, 1967.

Hogan, Michael J. *A Cross of Iron: Harry S. Truman and the Origins of the National Security State, 1945–1954*. New York: Cambridge University Press, 1998.

Hunt, Michael H. *The American Ascendancy: How the United States Gained and Wielded Global Dominance*. Chapel Hill: University of North Carolina Press, 2007.

Hyland, William G. *Clinton's World: Remaking American Foreign Policy*. Westport: Praeger, 1999.

Ignatieff, Michael. "The Burden." *New York Times Magazine* (January 5, 2003).

Jacoby, Susan. *The Age of American Unreason*. New York: Pantheon Books, 2008.

Jentleson, Bruce W. *With Friends like These: Reagan, Bush, and Saddam, 1982–1990*. New York: W. W. Norton & Company, 1994.

Jervis, Robert. "Understanding the Bush Doctrine." *Political Science Quarterly* 118 (Fall 2003): 365–88.

Johnson, Chalmers. *Blowback: The Costs and Consequences of American Empire*. New York: Metropolitan Books, 2000.

Judt, Tony. "The Wrecking Ball of Innovation." *New York Review of Books* (December 6, 2007).

Kagan, Robert, and William Kristol. "What to Do about Iraq." *Weekly Standard* (January 21, 2002).

Kazin, Michael. *A Godly Hero: The Life of William Jennings Bryan*. New York: Alfred A. Knopf, 2006.

Klare, Michael T. *Resource Wars: The New Landscape of Global Conflict*. New York: Owl Books, 2002.

Klein, Naomi. *The Shock Doctrine: The Rise of Disaster Capitalism*. New York: Metropolitan Books, 2007.

Kuklick, Bruce. *Blind Oracles: Intellectuals and War from Kennan to Kissinger*. Princeton: Princeton University Press, 2006.

Kuttner, Robert. *The End of Laissez-Faire: National Purpose and the Global Economy after the Cold War*. New York: Alfred A. Knopf, 1991.

LaFeber, Walter. *The American Search for Opportunity, 1865–1913*. New York: Cambridge University Press, 1993.

Lasch, Christopher. *The New Radicalism in America, 1889–1963: The Intellectual as a Social Type*. New York: Vintage Books, 1965.

Leffler, Melvyn P. *For the Soul of Mankind: The United States, the Soviet Union, and the Cold War*. New York: Hill and Wang, 2007.

Lewis, Anthony. "Privilege and the Press." *New York Review of Books* (July 14, 2005).

Lewis, David Levering. *W. E. B. Du Bois: Biography of a Race, 1868–1919*. New York: Henry Holt, 1993.

"Liberties Lost." *Baltimore Sun* editorial (July 4, 2007).

Lichtblau, Eric. *Bush's Law: The Remaking of American Justice*. New York: Pantheon Books, 2008.

Lippmann, Walter. *Drift and Mastery: An Attempt to Diagnose the Current Unrest*, reprint ed. Englewood Cliffs: Prentice Hall, 1961.

Loveman, Brian. *For la Patria: Politics and the Armed Forces in Latin America*. Wilmington: Scholarly Resources, 1999.

Lukas, J. Anthony. *Nightmare: The Underside of the Nixon Years*, with a forward by Joan Hoff. Athens: Ohio University Press, 1999.

MacMillan, Margaret. *Paris 1919: Six Months That Changed the World*. New York: Random House, 2002.

Mahan, A. T. "The United States Looking Outward." *The Atlantic* (December 1890).

———. *The Influence of Seapower upon History, 1660–1783*, American Century Series ed. New York: Hill and Wang, 1957.

Mann, James. *Rise of the Vulcans: The History of Bush's War Cabinet*. New York: Viking, 2004.

Margulies, Joseph. *Guantánamo and the Abuse of Presidential Power*. New York: Simon & Schuster, 2006.

Massing, Michael. "The End of News?" *New York Review of Books* (December 1, 2005).

———. "The Press: The Enemy Within." *New York Review of Books* (December 15, 2005).

Mayer, Jane. *The Dark Side: The Inside Story of How the War on Terror Turned into a War on American Ideals*. New York: Doubleday, 2008.

McCoy, Drew R. *The Elusive Republic: Political Economy in Jeffersonian America*. Chapel Hill: University of North Carolina Press, 1980.

Miscamble, Wilson D. *From Roosevelt to Truman: Potsdam, Hiroshima, and the Cold War*. New York: Cambridge University Press, 2006.

Nye Jr., Joseph S. "U.S. Power and Strategy after Iraq." *Foreign Affairs* 82 (July/August 2003).

Olmsted, Kathryn S. *Challenging the Secret Government: The Post-Watergate Investigations of the CIA and FBI.* Chapel Hill: University of North Carolina Press, 1996.

Pérez Jr., Louis A. *The War of 1898: The United States and Cuba in History and Historiography.* Chapel Hill: University of North Carolina Press, 1998.

Power, Samantha. *"A Problem from Hell": America and the Age of Genocide.* New York: Basic Books, 2002.

Preston Jr., William. *Aliens and Dissenters: Federal Suppression of Radicals, 1903–1933.* Cambridge: Harvard University Press, 1963.

Price, Richard. *Observations on the Importance of the American Revolution, and the Means of Making It a Benefit to the World.* London: Haswell and Russell, 1785.

Rabe, Stephen G. *The Most Dangerous Area in the World: John F. Kennedy Confronts Communist Revolution in Latin America.* Chapel Hill: University of North Carolina Press, 1999.

Radosh, Ronald. *Prophets on the Right: Profiles of Conservative Critics of American Globalism.* New York: Simon & Schuster, 1975.

Ricks, Thomas E. *Fiasco: The American Military Adventure in Iraq.* New York: Penguin Press, 2006.

Risen, James. *State of War: The Secret History of the CIA and the Bush Administration,* paper ed. New York: Free Press, 2007.

Roberts, Geoffrey. *Stalin's Wars: From World War to Cold War, 1939–1953.* New Haven: Yale University Press, 2007.

Rosenberg, Emily S. *Financial Missionaries to the World: The Politics and Culture of Dollar Diplomacy, 1900–1939.* Cambridge: Harvard University Press, 1999.

Rosenberg, Jonathan. *How Far the Promised Land?: World Affairs and the American Civil Rights Movement.* Princeton: Princeton University Press, 2006.

Rosenberg, Tina. "The Free-Trade Fix." *New York Times Magazine* (August 18, 2002).

Rubin, Barnett R. *The Fragmentation of Afghanistan: State Formation and Collapse in the International System,* 2d ed. New Haven: Yale University Press, 2002.

Sachs, Jeffrey D. *The End of Poverty: Economic Possibilities for Our Time.* New York: Penguin Books, 2006.

Salvatore, Nick. *Eugene V. Debs: Citizen and Socialist.* Urbana: University of Illinois Press, 1982.

Schlesinger Jr., Arthur M. *The Imperial Presidency.* Boston: Houghton Mifflin, 1973.

Schmitz, David F. *Thank God They're on Our Side: The United States and Right-Wing Dictatorships, 1921–1965.* Chapel Hill: University of North Carolina Press, 1999.

Schrecker, Ellen, ed. *Cold War Triumphalism: The Misuse of History after the Fall of Communism.* New York: New Press, 2004.

Schwarz Jr., Frederick A. O., and Aziz Z. Huq. *Unchecked and Unbalanced: Presidential Power in a Time of Terror.* New York: New Press, 2007.

Sikkink, Kathryn. *Mixed Signals: U.S. Human Rights Policy and Latin America.* Ithaca: Cornell University Press, 2004.

Suskind, Ron. "Without a Doubt." *New York Times Magazine* (October 17, 2004).

Talbott, Strobe. *The Russia Hand: A Memoir of Presidential Diplomacy.* New York: Random House, 2002.

Taylor, Alan. *American Colonies*. New York: Viking, 2001.

Tucker, Robert W. "American Power and the Persian Gulf." *Commentary* (November 1980).

Turner, Frederick Jackson. "The Problem of the West." *The Atlantic Monthly* (September 1896).

Van Deburg, William L. *New Day in Babylon: The Black Power Movement and American Culture, 1965–1975*. Chicago: University of Chicago Press, 1992.

Walker III, William O. *Opium and Foreign Policy: The Anglo-American Search for Order in Asia, 1912–1954*. Chapel Hill: University of North Carolina Press, 1991.

———. "Crucible for Peace: Herbert Hoover, Modernization, and Economic Growth in Latin America." *Diplomatic History* 30 (January 2006): 83–117.

———. "The United States, Colombia, and Drug Policy, 1984–2004: A Study of Quiet Anti-Americanism." In Alan McPherson, ed., *Anti-Americanism in Latin America and the Caribbean*. New York: Berghahn Books, 2006.

Watts, Sarah. *Rough Rider in the White House: Theodore Roosevelt and the Politics of Desire*. Chicago: University of Chicago Press, 2003.

Weiner, Tim. *Legacy of Ashes: The History of the CIA*. New York: Doubleday, 2007.

White, Richard. *The Middle Ground: Indians, Empires, and Republics in the Great Lakes Region, 1650–1815*. New York: Cambridge University Press, 1991.

Williams, William Appleman. "The Legend of Isolationism in the 1920s." *Science and Society* 18 (Winter 1954): 1–20.

———. *The Contours of American History*, paper ed. Chicago: Quadrangle Books, 1966.

———. *The Tragedy of American Diplomacy*, 2d rev. and enlarged ed. New York: W. W. Norton & Company, 1972.

———. *Empire as a Way of Life: An Essay on the Causes and Character of America's Present Predicament along with a Few Thoughts about an Alternative*, with an introduction by Andrew Bacevich. Brooklyn: Ig Publishing, 2007.

Wills, Garry. *Inventing America: Jefferson's Declaration of Independence*. Garden City: Doubleday, 1978.

Wilson, Joan Hoff. *American Business and Foreign Policy, 1920–1933*. Lexington: University Press of Kentucky, 1971.

Wolf, Naomi. *The End of America: Letter of Warning to a Young Patriot*. White River Junction, VT: Chelsea Green Publishing, 2007.

Wyzanski Jr., Charles E. "On Civil Disobedience." *The Atlantic* (February 1968).

Youngers, Coletta A., and Eileen Rosin, eds. *Drugs and Democracy in Latin America: The Impact of U.S. Policy*. Boulder: Lynne Rienner, 2005.

Zubok, Vladislav M. *A Failed Empire: The Soviet Union in the Cold War from Stalin to Gorbachev*. Chapel Hill: University of North Carolina Press, 2007.

Index